QUARKXPRESS
IN A NUTSHELL

A Desktop Quick Reference

QUARKXPRESS
IN A NUTSHELL

A Desktop Quick Reference

Donnie O'Quinn

O'REILLY™

Cambridge · Köln · Paris · Sebastopol · Tokyo

QuarkXPress in a Nutshell: A Desktop Quick Reference
by Donnie O'Quinn

Published by O'Reilly & Associates, Inc., 101 Morris Street, Sebastopol, CA 95472.

Editors: Tim O'Reilly & Troy Mott

Production Editor: Madeleine Newell

Editorial and Production Services: Nancy Crumpton

Printing History:

June 1998:   First Edition.

This book is printed on acid-free paper with 85% recycled content, 15% post-consumer waste. O'Reilly & Associates is committed to using paper with the highest recycled content available consistent with high quality.

ISBN: 1-56592-399-5

Table of Contents

Part II: Menus

Part III: Palettes

Preface

Computer books traditionally target novice, intermediate, or advanced users. As we collectively gain more and more experience with computers, those distinctions don't always make sense. The *In a Nutshell* series of books targets a new class of user, which we call the "sophisticated user." A sophisticated user may be a novice at using a particular program, but he or she has experience with other programs and is a quick study. Or the sophisticated user may be very experienced with a program but still needs to look up details.

Because they target sophisticated users, the *In a Nutshell* books are oriented towards reference use, although they may include elements of a fast-paced tutorial or overview to get a new user quickly up to the point where the reference material makes sense.

Topics like UNIX or Java lend themselves readily to the *In a Nutshell* reference format, because they include a lot of hard-to-remember syntax. GUI-based programs like XPress may at first seem less appropriate for this format. We've all seen application books that walk through the GUI, repeating only the facts that are already obvious from the GUI itself.

In *QuarkXPress in a Nutshell*, we've avoided this problem by going deep. When we talk about a menu or a dialog box, we tell you the things that are not obvious, providing the deep knowledge that typically comes only with years of experience.

Overview

QuarkXPress has long been the dominant page layout program of the publishing industry. The long awaited upgrade to Version 4.0 features significant new tools, including Bézier drawing tools, long document support, indexing, character-based style sheets, and advanced hyphenation and justification. Now, more than ever, designers and production specialists alike will find QuarkXPress at the heart of the creative process, as suitable for one-color newsletters as it is for complex multi-color projects.

When the abundant features of QuarkXPress are combined with the complex requirements of the print publishing industry, it's easy to see that users must remember many details in order to utilize the software successfully. Unlike most QuarkXPress books—which try to teach XPress—*QuarkXPress in a Nutshell* is a detailed reference that will enable XPress 4.0 users to make informed choices and navigate the many available techniques, reducing the risk of incorrect document-construction decisions.

A growing number of users with many years of experience under their belts neither need nor desire a lot of hand holding—they just want the facts. This book, like other *In a Nutshell* books, raises the no-nonsense approach to an art form. It contains details that even an expert is going to look for again and again, as well as critical background information that assists the new but fundamentally sophisticated user.

Each tool and command in XPress receives the following treatment:

- **Specific Function.** A summary of each item's purpose and function, as well as its context in a production environment.

- **Common Uses.** A list of the most frequent applications of each item. Every use is fully described, and nearly 200 selected uses appear as step-by-step techniques in Appendix A, *Common Techniques*.

- **Common Errors.** A list of complex but avoidable misuses of the software. Since many aspects of XPress are so nonintuitive, this section explains the most common mistakes—and offers real-world solutions.

- **Special Notes.** A list of tips, warnings, notes, and shortcuts. No single part of XPress works in a vacuum, and this section fleshes out the relationship one item has with any other.

- **The Dialog.** Definitions and recommended settings for each option in every dialog. Because the real power of XPress rests in its on-screen controls, a user must understand the cause-and-effect relationship of every setting.

Like many professionals, we use XPress for a living. When the clock is ticking, we know you don't have the time to pore through unnecessary text for the information you seek. We've presented the facts—and only the facts—so you can get in, get out, and get back to work.

Cross References

The contents of this book follow the exact structure of the XPress tools, menu commands, and palettes.

We've taken great pains to include as many cross-references as possible—each item contains a "See Also" section, which lists the tools, commands, and palettes most commonly encountered when using a specific part of XPress.

We mention tools and palettes by their full names, which dovetail with the appropriate chapter title. A menu command might be buried two or three levels deep, so we include its location in the program as part of its title.

For example, when we discuss indexing a long document, we mention the importance of creating a Book using XPress' new Book Palette. This command is found under the File Menu, under the New submenu. We refer to it as "the File: New: **Book** command." If you desire more information, turn to the Table of Contents and follow the hierarchy—find *The File Menu* chapter, find the "New" section, and get the page number for "Book." Or simply use the headers listed at the top of each page as a guide.

Macintosh and Windows Commands

Whenever we mention a keyboard technique, we've included key commands for Mac and Windows users. Mac keys appear in parentheses, Windows keys appear in brackets.

For example:

- Hold down the (Option) [**Alt**] key, and press the arrow keys to nudge an item in .1 pt. increments.

- (Option-Command-Shift) [**Alt-Control-Shift**]-click to select items on underlying layers.

The Techniques Appendix

We've constructed a comprehensive list of nearly 200 step-by-step XPress techniques. These range from simple text formatting, to trapping, to page impositions and preparations for printing.

All techniques are listed in the Common Uses sections of the main text. Easy to find and easy to follow, they appear in Appendix A in the same order as in the chapters. This list further illustrates the most demanding and production-enhancing uses of XPress.

Contents

This book is divided into three sections: tools, menu commands, and palettes. In turn, each section is split into chapters that pertain to one specific category of items. Some chapters are more information-intensive than others—some are sixty pages long, while others are three or four.

Part I, Tools

The first section covers the contents of the XPress Toolbar.

Chapter 1, *Page Tools*
    Covers the Item, Content, Rotation, and Zoom Tools.

Chapter 2, *Box Tools*
    Covers the Text Box and Picture Box Tools, as well as their Bézier-based counterparts.

Chapter 3, *Line Tools*
Covers the Standard Line, Orthogonal Line, Bézier Line, Freehand Line, and Text Path Tools.

Chapter 4, *Linking Tools*
Covers the Linking and Unlinking Tools.

Part II, Menus

The second section covers the XPress menus, from left to right.

Chapter 5, *The File Menu*
Covers all items under the File Menu, in descending order.

Chapter 6, *The Edit Menu*
Covers all items under the Edit Menu, in descending order.

Chapter 7, *The Style Menu (Text)*
Covers all items available under the Style Menu when editing text, in descending order.

Chapter 8, *The Style Menu (Picture)*
Covers all items available under the Style Menu when editing an imported image, in descending order.

Chapter 9, *The Style Menu (Line)*
Covers all items available under the Style Menu when editing lines and paths, in descending order.

Chapter 10, *The Item Menu*
Covers all items under the Item Menu, in descending order.

Chapter 11, *The Page Menu*
Covers all items under the Page Menu, in descending order.

Chapter 12, *The View Menu*
Covers all items under the View Menu, in descending order.

Chapter 13, *The Utilities Menu*
Covers all items under the Utilities Menu, in descending order.

Part III, Palettes

The third section covers the XPress palettes, in the order they appear under the View Menu.

Chapter 14, *The Measurements Palette*
Covers the many fields of the Measurements Palette.

Chapter 15, *The Document Layout Palette*
Covers the use of the Document Layout Palette and its palette controls.

Chapter 16, *The Style Sheets Palette*
Covers the use of the Style Sheets Palette and its palette controls.

Chapter 17, *The Colors Palette*
Covers the use of the Colors Palette and its palette controls.

Chapter 18, *The Trap Information Palette*
   Covers the use of the Trap Information Palette and its palette controls.

Chapter 19, *The Lists Palette*
   Covers the use of the Lists Palette and its palette controls.

Chapter 20, *The Index Palette*
   Covers the use of the Index Palette and its palette controls.

Part IV, Appendixes

This book contains two appendixes, which further expand the information covered in the main text.

Appendix A, *Common Techniques*
   Provides nearly 200 step-by-step techniques referenced by the Common Uses sections of the main text.

Appendix B, *XPress Shortcuts*
   Provides over 300 XPress keyboard shortcuts.

How to Contact Us

We have tested and verified all the information in this book to the best of our ability, but you may find that features have changed (or even that we have made mistakes!). Please let us know about any errors you find, as well as your suggestions for future editions, by writing to:

O'Reilly & Associates, Inc.
101 Morris Street
Sebastopol, CA 95472
1-800-998-9938 (in the U.S. or Canada)
1-707-829-0515 (international/local)
1-707-829-0104 (FAX)

You can also send messages electronically. To be put on our mailing list or to request a catalog, send email to:

   nuts@oreilly.com

To ask technical questions or comment on the book, send email to:

   bookquestions@oreilly.com

You can also contact the authors by sending email to:

   Donnie O'Quinn at *donnie@maine.rr.com*

Acknowledgments

Many thanks to the multitude of people who helped me complete this book:

David Rogelberg, the boogie-woogie bugle boy of StudioB. Tim O'Reilly, editor of the Nutshell series, who gave me the initial thumbs-up. Troy Mott, the Superman, whose insight, skill, and mercy often meant the difference between finishing the book and taking a hostage. Katie Gardner, for surviving the sudden deluge of chapters. Tim Plumer, Steve Kurth, and Kathleen Wilson, who offered invaluable technical advice. Christine Morgan, for the use of her most excellent photographs. Belinda Ray, the best pinch-hitting typist money can buy. Rob Romano, for processing all those graphics.

Also, thanks to the production staff of O'Reilly & Associates. Madeleine Newell was the project manager and production editor. Nancy Crumpton copy-edited the book and wrote the index. Edie Freedman designed the front cover, Nancy Priest designed the inside layout, and Kathleen Wilson designed the back cover and did the layout on both covers. Nicole Arigo, Sheryl Avruch, and Marleis Roberts performed quality control checks.

On a personal note, I thank Christine Morgan (a true friend and—fortunately for me—a true gourmet), Tim Plumer, Steve Kurth (for stepping up to the plate in, like, the nineteenth inning—I owe you both a good Scotch), Brian Gill (*Ich bin hier, und er ist mein Sofa*), and Don and Lois O'Quinn (such talented parents should consider going pro).

PART I

Tools

This section covers the contents of the XPress Toolbar. The order of chapters follows the appearance of the tools from top to bottom. The Toolbar is actually a palette, much like the Colors Palette or Style Sheets Palette, and appears as an option under the View Menu. Press the F8 key to show and hide the Toolbar.

Expanding the Toolbar

The Toolbar contains four pop-up menus—one each for the text box tools, picture box tools, line tools, and text path tools. If desired, you can add tools from these submenus to the actual palette, allowing you to access them more quickly. Hold down the (Control) [**Control**] key while choosing a tool from its pop-up. It appears below the pop-up in the Toolbar. (Control) [**Control**] click a tool to move it back to its pop-up.

Scrolling Through the Tools

To activate the next tool down in the Toolbar, press (Command) [**Control**]-Tab. To activate the next tool up, press (Command-Shift) [**Control-Shift**]-Tab.

To toggle between the Item and Content Tools, press Shift-F8.

PART I

People

CHAPTER 1

Page Tools

Item Selection Overview

Before a page element can be moved, colored, adjusted, resized, rotated, or otherwise affected, it must first be *selected*. This way, XPress is aware of the specific item or items you wish to affect. Unless a single item is selected, the following *item-specific* commands are not available:

- **The File Menu.** Get Picture, Get Text, and Save Text.
- **The Edit Menu.** Cut, Copy, Paste, Clear, Subscribe To, and Subscriber Options.
- **The Style Menus.** All commands.
- **The Item Menu.** All commands.
- **The Utilities Menu.** Check Spelling and Suggested Hyphenation.
- **The Measurements Palette.** All options.
- **The Style Sheets Palette.** All options.
- **The Colors Palette.** All options.
- **The Trap Information Palette.** All options.
- **The Lists Palette.** All options.
- **The Index Palette.** All options.

All remaining commands and palettes are *document-specific* and don't require any selections.

Selecting and Deselecting

Use the Item Tool or Content Tool to select page elements:

- **Selecting a single item**. To select a single item, click it once. To deselect it, click an empty part of the page, click-select a different item, or press the Tab key.

- **Selecting multiple items**. There are two ways to select more than one item:
  - Hold down the Shift key while clicking the desired items.
  - Create a *selection marquee* by clicking and dragging from an empty part of the page. A dotted-line box is drawn—items surrounded or touched by the marquee when you release the mouse button are selected.

- **Deselecting multiple items**. Press the Tab key to deselect all selected items. To deselect specific items when more than one are selected, do one of the following:
  - Hold down the Shift key, and click the desired items.
  - Hold down the Shift key, and drag a selection marquee. Any selected items surrounded or touched by the marquee when you release the mouse button are deselected. However, any unselected items included in the marquee are selected.

Selection Restrictions

After making a selection, the available commands and functions depend on the following:

- **Whether a text box, picture box, line, or text path is selected**. For example, there are three sets of Style Menu commands—one for text, one for graphics, and one for lines.

- **Whether a single item or multiple items are selected**. For example, when different item types are selected, you can't access all the Item: **Modify** options.

- **Whether the Item Tool or Content Tool is active**. For example, you can't edit text when the Item Tool is active; you can't reposition a text box when the Content Tool is active.

For specific selection or editing restrictions, refer to the appropriate tool or command in this book.

Multipage Selections

Regardless of the active tool, you can't select multiple items on different pages. To apply the same command to such items, you must make edits page by page.

Selecting Layered Items

When multiple items are stacked on top of each other, you can't select an underlying item by simply clicking. Instead, hold down the (Option-Command-Shift) [**Alt-Control-Shift**] keys and click repeatedly over the desired item. Each click selects the next item down from the front layer.

When you select an underlying box, you can freely edit its contents—however, portions may be obscured by the items positioned above it. If necessary, choose Item: **Bring to Front**, make your desired edits, and use Item: **Send Backward** to replace the item in its original position. (See "Item: Bring to Front/Send to Back" in Chapter 10, *The Item Menu*, for more information.)

After selecting an underlying item, you can't reposition it. Once you click the item again, you select the topmost item instead. To move an underlying item, you must keep the mouse button depressed as soon as the item selects. This way, you can drag as necessary. (You don't have to keep the (Option-Command-Shift) [**Alt-Control-Shift**] keys pressed as you drag the item.)

Toggling Between Selection Tools

As you construct your document pages, you'll toggle between the Item and Content Tools more than any others. Use the following shortcuts:

- To select the Content Tool while the Item Tool is active, press (Command) [**Control**]-Tab (or press Shift-F8).

- To select the Item Tool while the Content Tool is active, press (Command-Shift) [**Control-Shift**]-Tab (or press Shift-F8).

Selecting Pages

No selection tools are required to select entire document pages. Instead, use the following options:

- Click a master page or document page icon in the Document Layout Palette.

- Choose View: **Thumbnails** and click the desired page.

Both options allow you to reposition pages—including the items they contain—within a document.

If your intent is to select all the items on a page (not the page itself), choose Edit: **Select All**.

Item Tool

Use the Item Tool to select text boxes, picture boxes, lines, and paths. It's important to note that XPress makes a big distinction between an *item* and its *contents*. When the Item Tool is active, you can manually affect the following information:

- Text boxes (but not the text contained within)
- Picture boxes (but not the imported image contained within)
- Lines and Bézier paths
- Text paths (but not the text that flows across them)
- Multiple-selected boxes, lines, and paths
- Groups (but not the individual items within a group)

To edit the contents of a box, text path, or group, you must use the Content Tool.

Common Uses

- **Repositioning items.** To move a selection, drag it with the Item Tool:
  - When you drag immediately after pressing the mouse button, the item reverts to an outline. When multiple items are selected, a rectangular bounding box surrounding the items appears.
  - If you wait a second or two after pressing the mouse button, the selected items flash, and the cursor changes to a series of outward-pointing arrows. At this point, the selected items redraw on-screen as you move them, allowing for more precise and intuitive positioning.

- **Constraining while repositioning.** To constrain the movement to 90° angles, hold down the Shift key immediately *after* you click and drag. If you press Shift *before* moving, the item you click is simply deselected.

- **Resizing boxes.** To resize a text or picture box, drag one of the box handles. Only the box is scaled—in a picture box, the image retains its original position; in a text box, the text reflows to accommodate the new shape. (For information on scaling contents as you manually resize, see "Text Box Overview" and "Picture Box Overview" in Chapter 2, *Box Tools*.)

- **Copying and pasting items.** You can only Edit: **Copy** and **Paste** boxes when the Item Tool is active.

- **Lengthening or shortening lines.** To resize a line, click and drag one of its endpoints. (For information on constraining lines as you resize, see "Line Tool Overview" in Chapter 3, *Line Tools*.)

- **Repositioning a path.** To reposition a Bézier path by clicking and dragging, you must first select the path and uncheck Item: Edit: **Shape**. Otherwise, dragging with the Item Tool reshapes the path instead. To reposition a path without turning off its editing mode, hold down the (Command) [**Control**] key and drag it.

- **Editing Bézier curves.** When a Bézier path is in editing mode, you can use the Item Tool to select and move individual points, manipulate curve handles, and drag segments. Note that you can only delete points when the Item Tool is active. (For more information on editing Bézier curves, see "Bézier Line Tool" in Chapter 3.)

- **Accessing the Item: Modify dialog.** To quickly access the Item: **Modify** command, double-click an item with the Item Tool. The available options depend on the currently selected item. (See "Item: Modify" in Chapter 10 for more information.)

Special Notes

- When any other tool (except the Zoom Tool) is active, you can temporarily access the Item Tool by holding down the (Command) [**Control**] key.

- To reposition selected items with precision, use the following techniques:
  - **Nudge in 1 pt. increments.** Press the arrow keys.
  - **Nudge in .1 pt. increments.** Hold down the (Option) [**Alt**] key while pressing the arrow keys.
  - Enter specific ruler coordinates in the X and Y fields of the Measurements Palette. (See Chapter 14, *The Measurements Palette*, for more information.)

- In earlier versions of XPress, you couldn't import graphics into a picture box while the Item Tool was active. Versions 4.0 and up have removed this restriction. However, when importing text into a text box, you must still select the Content Tool.

- When a single item is selected, it remains selected when you choose any other tool. When multiple items are selected, choosing any tool other than the Item, Content, or Rotation Tool automatically deselects the current selection.

- When the Item Tool is active, pressing the (Delete) [**Backspace**] key removes all selected items, contents and all.

See Also

Content Tool
Rotation Tool
Zoom Tool
Box Tools: **Text Box Overview**
Box Tools: **Picture Box Overview**
Line Tools: **Line Tool Overview**
Line Tools: **Bézier Line Tool**
Edit: **Copy** and **Paste**
Item: **Modify**
Item: **Group**
Item: Edit: **Shape**

Content Tool

Use the Content Tool to select text boxes, picture boxes, lines, and paths. It's important to note that XPress makes a big distinction between an *item* and its *contents*. When the Content Tool is active, you can manually affect the following information:

- **Text within a box.** Here, you can import, enter, and format text, but you can't reposition the box itself.

- **Graphics within a box.** Here, you can import, reposition, recolor, and scale a graphic, but you can't reposition the box itself.

- **Lines and Bézier paths.** Here, you can reshape and recolor lines, but you can't reposition them.

- **Text paths.** Here, you can edit the text that flows along a path, as well as the path itself.

- **Items within a group.** Here, you can edit the contents of a single box or text path in a group.

To edit the position or orientation of a box, you must use the Item Tool.

Common Uses

- **Editing text.** After selecting a text box with the Content Tool, click within the text to insert the flashing cursor. From there, you can manually enter new text, delete existing text, or import a new text file. If desired, use the following techniques to position the cursor:

  - **Move to previous character.** Press the Left arrow key.

  - **Move to next character.** Press the Right arrow key.

  - **Move to previous line.** Press the Up arrow key.

  - **Move to next line.** Press the Down arrow key.

  - **Move to previous word.** Press (Command) [**Control**]-Left arrow.

  - **Move to next word.** Press (Command) [**Control**]-Right arrow.

  - **Move to top of current paragraph.** Press (Command) [**Control**]-Up arrow.

  - **Move to top of next paragraph.** Press (Command) [**Control**]-Down arrow.

  - **Move to beginning of line.** Press (Option-Command) [**Alt-Control**]-Left arrow.

  - **Move to end of line.** Press (Option-Command) [**Alt-Control**]-Right arrow.

  - **Move to beginning of story.** Press (Option-Command) [**Alt-Control**]-Up arrow.

  - **Move to end of story.** Press (Option-Command) [**Alt-Control**]-Down arrow.

- **Selecting text.** Use the following techniques to highlight a range of text in a text box:

  - **Highlight manual range.** Click-drag across text.

  - **Highlight automatic range.** Insert the flashing cursor at the start of the text you want to select. Shift-click at the end of the range. The text in between highlights.

  - **Highlight single word.** Double-click.

  - **Highlight a single line.** Triple-click.

  - **Highlight a single paragraph.** Quadruple-click.

  - **Highlight an entire story.** Quintuple-click, or choose Edit: **Select All**.

  - **Highlight previous word.** Press (Command-Shift) [**Control-Shift**]-Left arrow.

  - **Highlight next word.** Press (Command-Shift) [**Control-Shift**]-Right arrow.

  - **Highlight to top of current paragraph.** Press (Command-Shift) [**Control-Shift**]-Up arrow.

- Highlight to top of next paragraph. Press (Command-Shift) [**Control-Shift**]-Down arrow.

- Highlight to beginning of line. Press (Option-Command-Shift) [**Alt-Control-Shift**]-Left arrow.

- Highlight to end of line. Press (Option-Command-Shift) [**Alt-Control-Shift**]-Right arrow.

- Highlight to beginning of story. Press (Option-Command-Shift) [**Alt-Control-Shift**]-Up arrow.

- Highlight to end of story. Press (Option-Command-Shift) [**Alt-Control-Shift**]-Down arrow.

- **Copying and pasting text.** After highlighting a range of text, you can choose Edit: **Cut** or **Copy**, reposition the flashing cursor in the same text box or a different one, and choose Edit: **Paste**.

- **Repositioning graphics within a box.** When you click-drag a picture box with the Content Tool, the box doesn't move—rather, you move the graphic within the confines of the box. If a picture box is empty, click-dragging with the Content Tool has no effect.

- **Copying and pasting graphics.** When a picture box is selected with the Content Tool, choosing Edit: **Cut** or **Copy** only affects the contents of the box. The only way you can paste the graphic is to select another picture box and make sure the Content Tool is still active before choosing Edit: **Paste**.

- **Resizing boxes.** To resize a text or picture box, drag one of the box handles. Only the box is scaled—in a picture box, the image retains its original position; in a text box, the text reflows to accommodate the new shape. (For information on scaling contents as you manually resize, see "Text Box Overview" and "Picture Box Overview" in Chapter 2.)

- **Lengthening or shortening lines.** To resize a line, click and drag one of its endpoints. (For information on constraining lines as you resize, see "Line Tool Overview" in Chapter 3.)

- **Editing Bézier curves.** When a Bézier path is in editing mode, you can use the Content Tool to select and move individual points, manipulate curve handles, and drag segments. Note that you can't delete points when the Content Tool is active. (For more information on editing Bézier curves, see "Bézier Line Tool" in Chapter 3.)

Special Notes

- You can't Edit: **Copy** and **Paste** a line or path while the Content Tool is active.

- When you highlight a word by double-clicking it, XPress does not include the space following the word. This way, you can enter a new spelling without having to insert a new space. If you cut or delete a word, however, the space following it is removed.

- To reposition a graphic within a picture box with precision, use the following techniques:

    - **Nudge in 1 pt. increments.** Press the arrow keys.

    - **Nudge in .1 pt. increments.** Hold down the (Option) [**Alt**] key while pressing the arrow keys.

    - Enter specific ruler coordinates in the X+ and Y+ fields of the Measurements Palette. (See Chapter 14 for more information.)

See Also

Page Tools: **Item Tool**
Box Tools: **Text Box Overview**
Box Tools: **Picture Box Overview**
Line Tools: **Line Tool Overview**
Line Tools: **Bézier Line Tool**
Edit: **Copy** and **Paste**
Edit: **Select All**

Rotation Tool

Use this tool to manually rotate items on a page. Before doing so, you must first determine the *axis*, or the point the selected items will rotate around.

To rotate, position the cursor over the desired axis, and press the mouse button (do not click). For the best results, drag the cursor a couple inches away from the axis, then move the cursor in a clockwise or counterclockwise circle. When the item is properly positioned, release the mouse button.

If the item you wish to rotate is not selected when you choose this tool, you must click-drag directly on the item to simultaneously select and rotate. This method offers limited possibilities—you can only rotate a single item, and the axis can't be located beyond the item bounds. If you make a selection before using the Rotation Tool, the axis can be located anywhere on the page.

Common Uses

Refer to Appendix A, *Common Techniques*, for full descriptions of the following:

- Rotating a single item around a specific point
- Rotating a series of duplicate items around the same point
- Selecting and rotating a series of items in quick succession

Common Errors

- **Failing to click-drag as you attempt to rotate.** XPress' Rotation Tool doesn't work the same as the tool in many other applications. In Illustrator, for example, you must click twice to manually rotate an item: once to set the axis, and once to grab the item you wish to rotate. In XPress, you set the axis at the same time you rotate. If you simply click, the command is canceled.

- **Failing to drag the cursor away from the axis before rotating.** The farther away from the axis you drag the cursor, the more leverage you have while rotating. If you attempt to rotate when the cursor is very close to the axis, you have little control over the position of the item.

Special Notes

- Hold down the Shift key as you rotate to constrain the angles to 45° increments.

- To rotate an item using a precise value, enter a value in the Angle field of the Measurements Palette. If you're rotating a line, the Angle field is not available if Endpoints is set in the Mode pop-up.

- Lines created with the Orthogonal Line Tool are restricted to 90° angles. If you rotate one with this tool, the line is still restricted to right angles, relative to its current angle.

See Also

Appendix A (**Rotation Tool**)
The Measurements Palette

Zoom Tool

Use the Zoom Tools to increase or decrease the magnification percentage of the document window. The current percentage is displayed in the lower left corner of the window. (See "Zoom Field" in Chapter 12, *The View Menu*, for more information.)

This tool defaults to the Zoom In Tool, which increases the magnification. Here, the cursor appears as a magnifying glass with a plus sign. There are two ways to zoom in:

- **Click the document.** When you do, the zoom percentage increases by the value entered in the Increment field, in the Edit: Preferences: Document: **Tool** panel. By default, this value is 25%. Therefore, when you click, the percentage changes from 100% to 125%, to 150%, to 175%, and so forth.

- **Drag a zoom box.** When you do, the contents of the box fill the window, regardless of the exact percentage. This allows you to precisely target part of a document for up-close editing.

Hold down the (Option) (**Alt**) key to access the Zoom Out Tool. The cursor changes to display a minus sign. When you click, the zoom percentage is decreased by the default increment value. You cannot drag a zoom box to decrease the magnification.

Special Notes

- You can temporarily access the Zoom Tools while using any other tool:

  - To zoom in, hold down the (Control) [**Control-Spacebar**] keys, and either click or drag a zoom box.

– To zoom out, hold down the (Control-Option) [**Alt-Control-Spacebar**] keys, and click.

• Rather than use a wide variety of zoom options, many users use a simpler approach: to zoom in on part of a document, use the shortcut previously described. To zoom back out, choose (Command) [**Control**]-1 to set the view to 100%, or (Command) [**Control**]-zero to set the view to Fit In Window.

See Also

Edit: Preferences: Document: **Tool**

CHAPTER 2

Box Tools

Text Box Overview

Any text entered or imported into a document must be placed in a text box. There are two types of text box:

- **Fixed-Shape**. The first four tools are fixed-shape boxes. When you click and drag, a preview outline extends outward from your starting point. Release the mouse button to convert the preview to an actual text box.

- **Variable-Shape**. The last two tools use Bézier curves to create a wide variety of customized box shapes.

When you select an empty text box, the flashing text insertion cursor appears in the upper left of the box. The following information applies to all text boxes, regardless of their shape.

Editing a Text Box

To manually reposition a text box, drag it with the Item Tool. To edit its contents, select it with the Content Tool. (See "Item Tool" and "Content Tool" in Chapter 1, *Page Tools*, for more information.)

Applying Accurate Text Box Dimensions

There's no way to automatically generate a text box at a specific value—each one must be initially drawn with one of the text box tools. Instead of relying completely on your eye when drawing, positioning, or resizing a box, you can use the Measurements Palette to enter the precise width, height, and page location. (See Chapter 14, *The Measurements Palette*, for more information.)

Preformatting a Text Box

If desired, you can apply character and paragraph formatting to a text box before it contains text. After drawing the box, select it with the Content Tool to insert the flashing cursor. Then apply a style sheet, or choose the desired settings from the Style Menu. When you manually enter text in the box, the text is already formatted.

Note that this formatting does not necessarily affect imported or copy/pasted text.

Drawing Text Boxes in Quick Succession

After you finish drawing a single text box, the Tool Palette reverts back to the Item or Content Tool (depending on which one was last active). When you (Option) [Alt]-click the desired text box tool, it remains selected as you draw as many boxes as you need. Manually choose the next tool when finished.

Creating Columns

There are three ways to create multiple text columns:

- **Subdivide a single box.** You can add up to 30 internal columns to a single text box, using the Columns field in the Item: Modify: **Text** panel, or the Cols field in the Measurements Palette. Use this method when you need columns with identical dimensions placed side by side.

- **Link separate boxes.** Here, you use the Linking Tool to create a text chain. Use this method when creating a staggered-column layout, or when you need multiple columns of different heights or widths.

- **Subdivide the automatic text box.** When creating a new document with an automatic text box, the box is subdivided by the value entered in the Columns field of the File: New: **Document** dialog.

Converting Text Boxes

To convert a text box to a different box type, select it, and choose Item: Content: **Picture** or **None**. Any text in the box is deleted. To convert a picture box or empty box to a text box, select it, and choose Item: Content: **Text**.

Changing Text Box Shapes

If you want to change the current shape of a text box, there's no need to create a new one. Instead, select it, and choose an Item: **Shape** option. If the box already contains text, it's not deleted. If you convert a text box to a line option, the result is a text path. If the box is part of a text chain, the links are not affected.

To convert a fixed-shape text box to editable Bézier curves, choose Item: Shape: **Bézier Box**. The original shape doesn't change, but you can further edit the individual points and segments.

Resizing Text Boxes

Use the following techniques to manually resize a text box:

- Drag one of the box handles with the Item or Content Tool to change the box dimensions with no constraints. The text reflows to accommodate the new shape.

- Shift-drag a handle to snap the box to perfect proportions (square or circle). The text reflows to accommodate the new shape.

- (Option-Shift) [**Alt-Shift**]-drag a handle to retain the box's original proportions when scaling. The text reflows to accommodate the new shape.

- (Command) [**Control**]-drag a handle to resize the box with no constraints. The text is scaled relative to the new box dimensions.

- (Command-Shift) [**Control-Shift**]-drag a handle to snap the box to perfect proportions, as well as scale the text relative to the new box dimensions.

- (Option-Command-Shift) [**Alt-Control-Shift**]-drag a handle to retain the box's original proportions, as well as scale the text relative to the new box dimensions.

Orienting Text Within a Box

Text box attributes, such as text angle, text skew, columns, vertical justification, and the position of the first baseline, are controlled by the options in the Item: Modify: **Text** panel.

Adjusting Text to Fit a Box

After text has been formatted with the desired character and paragraph attributes, it often requires additional "massaging" to fit precisely in its box. Usually, one or two lines have overflowed the box (although occasionally, the text simply doesn't reach the bottom of the box). Try the following techniques:

- **Edit the copy.** This is the simplest solution. If possible, add or remove enough text to fill the box as desired. This way, you don't have to change any text formatting. If the text cannot be altered, try the next option.

- **Adjust the tracking.** Here, you reduce or expand the spaces between letters and words. For the best results, apply a value between –3 units (to reduce the space) and 3 units (to expand the space). Highlight as much text as possible before adjusting the tracking this way. For example, instead of retracking a single line, select the entire paragraph. This results in a smoother transition between a story's tracked and untracked text. (See "Style: Track" in Chapter 7, *The Style Menu (Text)*, for more information.)

- **Adjust the leading.** Here, you increase or decrease the line spacing. For the best results, apply changes between .25 pt. and .5 pt.—any more, and the effect becomes visible, especially on small-sized body copy. (See "Style: Leading" in Chapter 7 for more information.)

- **Adjust the point size.** Here, you increase or decrease the size of the text characters. For the best results, apply a change between .25 pt. and .75 pt.—any

Box Tools

more, and the text will appear visibly different from other occurrences throughout the document. (See "Style: Size" in Chapter 7 for more information.)

- **Adjust the horizontal scale.** Here, you compress or expand the text characters. For the best results, apply a change between 96% and 104%—any more, and the character shapes become visibly altered. (See "Style: Horizontal/Vertical Scale" in Chapter 7 for more information.)

- **Adjust the column width.** By widening or narrowing column width, you change the amount of available space in the text box.

Often, more than one of the techniques must be used on the same body of text. Whenever possible, make such changes on the style sheet level, which ensures that text throughout the document is consistently formatted. If this isn't possible, print test pages after making the adjustments, to make sure that the altered text doesn't look awkward.

Setting Text Box Preferences

Set the default Item: **Modify** settings for each text box in the Edit: Preferences: Document: **Tool** panel.

Inserting Special Characters

Refer to "Text Box Tool" in Appendix A, *Common Techniques*, for charts listing the keystrokes required to insert special characters in a text box:

Handling Text

The text box tools are only used to create the actual text boxes—beyond that, they have nothing to do with the text they ultimately contain. Details on handling and formatting text are covered throughout this book:

- **Inserting the flashing cursor.** See "Content Tool" in Chapter 1 for more information.

- **Highlighting text.** See "Content Tool" in Chapter 1 for more information.

- **Importing text.** See "File: Get Text" in Chapter 5, *The File Menu*, for more information.

- **Exporting text.** See "File: Save Text" in Chapter 5 for more information.

- **Finding and replacing text.** See "Edit: Find/Change" in Chapter 6, *The Edit Menu*, for more information.

- **Formatting text.** See Chapter 7 for more information.

- **Defining style sheets.** See "Edit: Style Sheets" in Chapter 6 for more information.

- **Applying style** sheets. See Chapter 16, *The Style Sheets Palette*, for more information.

- **Replacing fonts.** See "Utilities: Usage" in Chapter 13, *The Utilities Menu*, for more information.

- **Spellchecking**. See "Utilities: Check Spelling" in Chapter 13 for more information.

- **Coloring text**. See Chapter 17, *The Colors Palette*, for more information.

- **Trapping text**. See Chapter 18, *The Trap Information Palette*, for more information.

- **Anchoring boxes and lines in a text box**. See "Edit: Paste" in Chapter 6 for more information.

- **Converting text to a box**. See "Style: Text to Box" in Chapter 7 for more information.

See Also

Appendix A (**Text Box Tool**)
Page Tools: **Content Tool**
Page Tools: **Linking Tools**
File: **Get Text**
File: **Save Text**
Edit: **Paste**
Edit: **Find/Change**
Edit: **Style Sheets**
The Style Menu
Item: Modify: **Text**
Item: **Shape**
Item: **Content**
Utilities: **Check Spelling**
Utilities: **Usage**
The Style Sheets Palette
The Colors Palette
The Trap Information Palette

Rectangular Text Box Tool

Use this tool to create a rectangular text box. This is the most commonly used box type, as it results in the square-edged columns preferred by the vast majority of publications.

Hold down the Shift key while dragging to create a perfectly square box.

Rounded Corner Text Box Tool

Use this tool to create a text box with rounded corners. These boxes are actually rectangular, but XPress automatically applies a corner radius of .25 inches (you can check this in the Item: Modify: **Box** panel). If desired, you can increase the radius up to 2 inches or convert the box to a rectangle by setting a radius of 0.

Box Tools

Beveled Corner Text Box Tool

Use this tool to create a text box with beveled corners. The point at which the bevel begins is established by the Corner Radius value in the Item: Modify: **Box** panel. For example, this value defaults to .25 inches—therefore, each beveled corner starts a quarter inch from each corner box handle.

Concave Corner Text Box Tool

Use this tool to create a text box with inverted rounded corners. The depth of each corner is determined by the Corner Radius.

Elliptical Text Box Tool

Use this tool to create an elliptical text box. Hold down the Shift key while dragging to create a perfectly circular box.

To make a body of text conform to the shape of a round text box, highlight the text, and choose Style (Text): Alignment: **Justified**.

Bézier Text Box Tool

Here, you create a text box by clicking or click-dragging a series of points with XPress' version of a pen tool.

To create a box consisting of straight segments, simply click (without dragging) to add the points—the first click places a single point; each successive click places a new point that connects to the previous one with a straight segment. Click the first point to close the shape, converting it to a text box. If you select any other tool before clicking the first point, a straight segment connects the first and last points, automatically closing the shape.

To create a box consisting of straight and curved segments, you must understand how XPress handles Bézier curves. (See "Bézier Line Tool" in Chapter 3, *Line Tools*, for more information.)

Special Notes

To constrain a new segment to 45˚ angles, hold down the Shift key as you click to place a point.

Freehand Bézier Text Box Tool

Here, you draw the shape of a text box completely by hand. As you draw, a thin preview of your shape appears on-screen. When you complete the shape by releasing the mouse button, XPress converts the preview to a series of points and curved segments.

When drawing a shape, it's recommended that you end on the same point you initially clicked. Otherwise, a straight segment is added to the shape, joining the first and last points.

You can't draw incredibly extravagant shapes with this tool:

- The bulk of your shape must be drawn in one pass—as soon as you release the mouse button, the shape closes to create the text box. Therefore, accuracy depends quite a bit on your hand-eye coordination.

- The more finely detailed a box is, the less likely it is that text will flow through all parts of it.

To further edit the shape of the box, you must understand how XPress handles Bézier curves. (See "Bézier Line Tool" in Chapter 3 for more information.)

Box Tools

Picture Box Overview

Any graphic imported into a document must be placed in a picture box. There are two types of picture box:

- **Fixed-Shape.** The first four tools are fixed-shape boxes. When you click and drag, a preview outline extends outward from your starting point. Release the mouse button to convert the preview to an actual picture box.

- **Variable-Shape.** The last two tools use Bézier curves to create a wide variety of customized box shapes.

When you first import a graphic, it appears flush to the upper left of the box. The following information applies to all picture boxes, regardless of their shape.

Editing a Picture Box

To manually reposition a picture box, drag it with the Item Tool. To edit its contents, select it with the Content Tool. (See "Item Tool" and "Content Tool" in Chapter 1 for more information.)

Applying Accurate Picture Box Dimensions

There's no way to automatically generate a picture box at a specific value—each one must be initially drawn with one of the picture box tools. Instead of relying completely on your eye when drawing, positioning, or resizing a box, you can use the Measurements Palette to enter the precise width, height, and page location. (See Chapter 14 for more information.)

Drawing Picture Boxes in Quick Succession

After you finish drawing a single picture box, the Tool Palette reverts back to the Item or Content Tool (depending on which one was last active). When you (Option) [Alt]-click the desired picture box tool, it remains selected as you draw as many boxes as you need. Manually choose the next tool when finished.

Converting Picture Boxes

To convert a picture box to a different box type, select it, and choose Item: Content: **Text** or **None**. Any graphic in the box is deleted. To convert a text box or empty box to a picture box, select it, and choose Item: Content: **Picture**.

Changing Picture Box Shapes

If you want to change the current shape of a picture box, there's no need to create a new one. Instead, select it, and choose an Item: **Shape** option. If the box already contains a graphic, it's not deleted unless you choose one of the line options.

To convert a fixed-shape picture box to editable Bézier curves, choose Item: Shape: **Bézier Box**. The original shape doesn't change, but you can further edit the individual points and segments.

Resizing Picture Boxes

Use the following techniques to manually resize a picture box:

- Drag one of the box handles with the Item or Content Tool to change the box dimensions with no constraints. The contents are not affected.

- Shift-drag a handle to snap the box to perfect proportions (square or circle). The contents are not affected.

- (Option-Shift) [**Alt-Shift**]-drag a handle to retain the box's original proportions when scaling. The contents are not affected.

- (Command) [**Control**]-drag a handle to resize the box with no constraints. The contents are scaled relative to the new box dimensions.

- (Command-Shift) [**Control-Shift**]-drag a handle to snap the box to perfect proportions, as well as scale the contents relative to the new box dimensions.

- (Option-Command-Shift) [**Alt-Control-Shift**]-drag a handle to retain the box's original proportions, as well as scale the contents relative to the new box dimensions.

Cropping a Graphic

An imported graphic is cropped when it extends beyond the boundary of a picture box. After resizing the box as necessary, drag the image with the Content Tool to reposition it within the box. Keep the following guidelines in mind:

- Portions of the image hidden by the picture box must still be processed during output, even if no printed information results. If you find yourself cropping large portions of a pixel-based image, consider opening the image in Photoshop, cropping it there, and reimporting it in XPress.

- When your intent is to use smaller portions of a large image throughout a document—for example, if you're dividing a picture of a group of people into individual head shots—*do not* keep importing the larger image and cropping as needed. For the best results, open the image in Photoshop, divide the image into the necessary smaller images, and import each one. The file will output more quickly, and XPress won't get bogged down as you work on the document.

Scaling the Contents of a Picture Box

Use the following commands to scale a graphic without changing the size of a picture box:

- To increase the horizontal and vertical scale in 5% increments, press (Option-Command-Shift) [**Alt-Control-Shift**]-period.

- To decrease the horizontal and vertical scale in 5% increments, press (Option-Command-Shift) [**Alt-Control-Shift**]-comma.

- To scale a graphic to precisely fit the current box dimensions, press (Option-Command-Shift) [**Alt-Control-Shift**]-F. The image is scaled unevenly, if necessary.

- To center a graphic in a text box, press (Command-Shift) [**Control-Shift**]-M.

Orienting a Graphic Within a Box

Picture attributes such as offset, angle, and skew are controlled by the options in the Item: Modify: **Picture** panel.

Merging Multiple Boxes

To create new shapes by combining multiple picture boxes, use the Item: **Merge** commands.

Setting Picture Box Preferences

Set the default Item: **Modify** settings for each picture box in the Edit: Preferences: Document: **Tool** panel.

Handling Graphics

The picture box tools are only used to create the actual picture boxes—beyond that, they have nothing to do with the graphics they ultimately contain. Details on handling graphics are covered throughout this book:

- **Importing a graphic.** See "File: Get Picture" in Chapter 5 for more information.

- **Manipulating the color content of a graphic.** See "Style: Contrast" in Chapter 8, *The Style Menu (Picture)*, for more information.

- **Applying a custom screen value to a halftone.** See "Style: Halftone" in Chapter 8 for more information.

- **Applying a color to a graphic.** See Chapter 17 for more information.

- **Trapping a graphic.** See Chapter 18 for more information.

- **Framing a picture box.** See "Item: Frame" in Chapter 10, *The Item Menu*, for more information.

- **Reviewing graphic links.** See "Utilities: Usage" in Chapter 13 for more information.

- **Anchoring a picture box in a text box.** See "Edit: Paste" in Chapter 6 for more information.

- **Converting text to a picture box.** See "Style: Text to Box" in Chapter 7 for more information.

See Also

Page Tools: **Item Tool**
Page Tools: **Content Tool**
File: **Get Picture**
Edit: **Paste**
Edit: Preferences: Document: **Tool**
Style (Text): **Text to Box**
Style (Picture): **Halftone**
Style (Picture): **Contrast**
Item: Modify: **Picture**
Item: **Frame**
Item: **Merge**
Item: **Shape**
Item: **Content**
Utilities: **Usage**
The Trap Information Palette
The Colors Palette

Rectangular Picture Box Tool

Use this tool to create a rectangular picture box. This is the most commonly used box type, as it results in the square-edged boundary used by the majority of publications. Hold down the Shift key while dragging to create a perfectly square box.

Rounded Corner Picture Box Tool

Use this tool to create a picture box with rounded corners. These boxes are actually rectangular, but XPress automatically applies a corner radius of .25 inches (you can check this in the Item: Modify: **Box** panel). If desired, you can increase the radius up to 2 inches or convert the box to a rectangle by setting a radius of 0.

Beveled Corner Picture Box Tool

Use this tool to create a picture box with beveled corners. The point at which the bevel begins is established by the Corner Radius value in the Item: Modify: **Box** panel. For example, this value defaults to .25 inches—therefore, each beveled corner starts a quarter inch from each corner box handle.

Concave Corner Picture Box Tool

Use this tool to create a picture box with inverted rounded corners. The depth of each corner is determined by the Corner Radius.

Elliptical Picture Box Tool

Use this tool to create an elliptical picture box. Hold down the Shift key while dragging to create a perfectly circular box.

Bézier Picture Box Tool

Here, you create a picture box by clicking or click-dragging a series of points with XPress' version of a pen tool.

To create a box consisting of straight segments, simply click (without dragging) to add the points—the first click places a single point; each successive click places a new point that connects to the previous one with a straight segment. Click the first point to close the shape, converting it to a picture box. If you select any other tool before clicking the first point, a straight segment connects the first and last points, automatically closing the shape.

To create a box consisting of straight and curved segments, you must understand how XPress handles Bézier curves. (See "Bézier Line Tool" in Chapter 3 for more information.)

Common Uses

Refer to Appendix A for a full description of creating a single picture box from multiple Bézier shapes.

Special Notes

To constrain a new segment to 45° angles, hold down the Shift key as you click to place a point.

Freehand Bézier Picture Box Tool

Here, you draw the shape of a picture box completely by hand. As you draw, a thin preview of your shape appears on-screen. When you complete the shape by releasing the mouse button, XPress converts the preview to a series of points and curved segments.

When drawing a shape, it's recommended that you end on the same point you initially clicked. Otherwise, a straight segment is added to the shape, joining the first and last points.

You can't draw incredibly extravagant shapes with this tool. The bulk of your shape must be drawn in one pass—as soon as you release the mouse button, the shape closes to create the picture box. Therefore, accuracy depends quite a bit on your hand-eye coordination.

To further edit the shape of the box, you must understand how XPress handles Bézier curves. (See "Bézier Line Tool" in Chapter 3 for more information.)

CHAPTER 3

Line Tools

Line Tool Overview

Before you can incorporate lines into your document layout, you must first create them using one of the four line tools. There are two types of line:

- **Straight**. Use the first two line tools to draw perfectly straight lines by clicking and dragging to the desired length. (Note that the Bézier Line Tool can also draw straight lines if you click a series of points without revealing the curve handles.)

- **Curved**. Use the two Bézier line tools to create curved lines.

The following information applies to all lines, regardless of their shape.

Moving a Line

To manually reposition a straight line, drag it with the Item Tool. To reposition a curved line, (Command) [**Control**]-drag it, or turn off the Item: Edit: **Shape** option and drag it with the Item Tool.

Applying Accurate Line Dimensions

There's no way to automatically generate a line at a specific length—it must be initially drawn with one of the line tools. Instead of relying completely on your eye when drawing, positioning, or resizing a line, you can use the Measurements Palette to enter the precise length, angle, and page location. (See Chapter 14, *The Measurements Palette*, for more information.)

Specifying Line Width

To establish the thickness of a line, choose an option from the Style (Line): **Width** submenu, or enter a value in the Width field of the Measurements Palette. (See "Style: Width" in Chapter 9, *The Style Menu (Line)*, for more information.)

Resizing a Line

To manually resize a straight line, drag one of its endpoints with the Item or Content Tool:

- When resizing a standard line, you can also rotate the line to any angle as you resize. To constrain the line to 45° angles (starting from its original angle), hold down the Shift key as you resize. To completely constrain to the current angle, hold down the (Option-Shift) [**Alt-Shift**] keys as you resize.

- When resizing an orthogonal line, the current angle is automatically constrained to 90° angles. To completely constrain the current angle, hold down the (Option-Shift) [**Alt-Shift**] keys as you resize.

To extend a Bézier line, do one of the following:

- Drag one of the endpoints with the Item or Content Tool. If the line is curved, this will alter the first or last segment of the path. If necessary, adjust the curve handles.

- Draw another Bézier line, starting from an endpoint of the original line you want to extend. When the second shape is drawn, select the overlapping endpoints, and convert the two separate lines into one by choosing Item: Merge: **Join Endpoints**.

To scale a Bézier line, turn off the Item: Edit: **Shape** option, and do one of the following:

- To scale with no constraints, drag one of the bounding box handles.

- To scale proportionately, hold down the Shift key as you drag.

Drawing Lines in Quick Succession

After you finish drawing a single line, the Tool Palette reverts back to the Item or Content Tool (depending on which one was last active). When you (Option) [**Alt**]-click the desired line tool, it remains selected as you draw as many lines as you need. Manually choose the next tool when finished.

When creating a series of equal-length parallel lines—as in form or graph, for example—draw the first line, and use Item: **Step and Repeat** to automatically duplicate and position the lines as needed.

Adding Arrowheads

To add an arrowhead to an existing line, select it, and choose an option from the Style (Line): **Arrowheads** submenu. The same options appear in the far-right popup of the Measurements Palette.

Converting Lines

Use the following techniques to convert a line to another line type or a box:

- To convert a straight line to a Bézier line, select it, and choose Item: Shape: **Bézier Line**. You can then drag curve handles from the endpoints.

- To convert a line into a Bézier box, select it, and choose Item: Shape: **Bézier Box**. The new box traces the exact shape of the line.

- To convert a line into a fixed-shape box, select it, and choose a box type from the Item: **Shape** submenu. The new box matches the width and height of the line's endpoints.

Applying Dashes and Stripes

To apply an existing dash or stripe style to a line, choose an option from the Style: **Line Style** submenu. The same options appear in the second pop-up from the right in the Measurements Palette.

To apply a gap color to a dash or stripe, use the Gap controls found in the Item: Modify: **Line** panel.

To apply a custom dash or stripe, you must first create it using Edit: **Dashes & Stripes**. After doing so, it's available in the Line Style submenu and Measurements Palette pop-up. (See "Edit: Dashes & Stripes" in Chapter 6, *The Edit Menu*, for more information.)

Setting Line Tool Preferences

Set the default settings for each line tool in the Edit: Preferences: Document: **Tool** panel.

Merging Lines with Boxes

You can add or remove line shapes from a box using the Item: **Merge** options. When a line shape is added to a box, the new portion of the box traces the current width of the line. When a line shape is removed from a box, the new empty space also traces the current width of the line. (See "Item: Merge" in Chapter 10, *The Item Menu*, for more information.)

Handling Lines

The line tools are only used to create lines—beyond that, they have nothing to do with their size, color, or relationship to other items. Details on handling lines are covered throughout this book:

- **Coloring lines.** See Chapter 17, *The Colors Palette*, for more information.

- **Trapping lines.** See Chapter 18, *The Trap Information Palette*, for more information.

- **Grouping lines.** See "Item: Group" in Chapter 10 for more information.

- **Anchoring lines in a text box.** See "Edit: Paste" in Chapter 6 for more information.

- **Adding a rule above or below a paragraph.** See "Style: Rules" in Chapter 7, *The Style Menu (Text)*, for more information.

See Also

Page Tools: **Item Tool**
Page Tools: **Content Tool**
Edit: **Paste**
Edit: Preferences: Document: **Tool**
Edit: **Dashes & Stripes**
Style (Text): **Rules**
Style (Line): **Line Style**
Style (Line): **Width**
Style (Line): **Arrowheads**
Item: Modify: **Line**
Item: **Step and Repeat**
Item: **Group**
Item: **Merge**
Item: Edit: **Shape**
The Measurements Palette
The Colors Palette
The Trap Information Palette

Line Tool

Click and drag with this tool to create a standard straight line. Each line consists of two endpoints: the point where you first press the mouse button, and the point where you release the mouse button after dragging. Constrain the new line to 45° angles by holding down the Shift key as you drag.

As you drag with this tool, you determine the line's *angle* as well as its length. If the line must be positioned at an exact angle, don't bother trying to eyeball it as you create it. Instead, set the appropriate value in the Angle field of the Measurements Palette after drawing the line.

Orthogonal Line Tool

Click and drag with this tool to create a perfectly vertical or horizontal line. Each line consists of two endpoints: the point where you first press the mouse button, and the point where you release the mouse button after dragging.

You can't set an angle other than 0° or 90° by manually dragging the line. To numerically rotate an orthogonal line, enter a value in the Angle field of the Measurements Palette (after doing so, the line is still constrained to right angles). To be able to rotate an orthogonal line by dragging, you must convert it to a standard line by selecting it and choosing Item: Shape: **Line**.

Bézier Curves Overview

XPress now offers a series of Bézier tools, which allow you to manually create and edit object-oriented paths. These are based on *Bézier curves*, similar to those employed by vector-based programs like Adobe Illustrator or Macromedia FreeHand.

Paths offer an impressive array of editing capabilities—especially for a page layout program. If you're used to the more powerful toolsets found in Illustrator, Free-Hand, and Photoshop, you may find XPress' curves rather counterintuitive. However, these tools allow you to accomplish the following techniques directly in XPress, without resorting to outside software:

- **Generate a clipping path.** See "Item: Clipping" in Chapter 10 for more information.

- **Convert text to outlines.** See "Style: Text to Box" in Chapter 7 for more information.

- **Create customized box shapes.** See "Bézier Text Box Tool" and the "Bézier Picture Box Tool" in Chapter 2, *Box Tools*, for more information.

- **Finely customize a text runaround curve.** See "Item: Runaround" in Chapter 10 for more information.

- **Apply text to a curve.** See the various text path tools covered in this chapter for more information.

- **Merge multiple items into a single shape.** See "Item: Merge" in Chapter 10 for more information.

If you're more comfortable using outside software to create some of these effects, by all means continue to do so.

Path Components

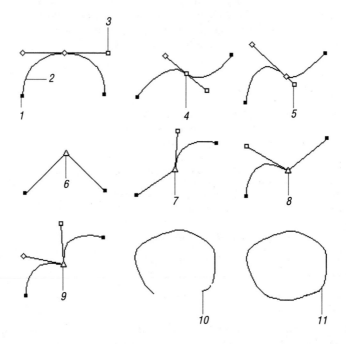

1. **Point**

   Click once with one of the pen-based Bézier tools to place a single point. Paths are created one point at a time—they're the hot spots, acting like the dots in a connect-the-dot puzzle.

2. **Segment**

   As you place points, a line connects the new point with the previous point. These segments ultimately form the shape of the path.

3. **Curve Handles**

   Each point contains two curve handles. When you simply click to place a point, both handles are hidden. If you drag the cursor before releasing the mouse button, you extend the handles. Manipulate them as you drag (or later with the Item or Content Tool) to curve the segments connected to the point. It's not necessary to reveal the handles, but without them, you can only create straight lines.

4. **Symmetrical Point**

   This point (viewed on-screen as a square) displays two locked and parallel handles. As you lengthen and rotate one handle, the opposite one mirrors its position. When you initially click-drag a point, it's automatically a symmetrical point—as soon as you release the mouse button, it converts to a smooth point.

5. **Smooth Point**

   This point (viewed on-screen as a diamond) allows you to lengthen each handle independently. However, when you rotate one of the handles, they remain locked and parallel.

6. **Corner Point**

   This point (viewed on-screen as a triangle) displays no handles, resulting in straight segments. Place corner points by simply clicking with one of the pen-based tools. Also, when you break the parallel link between two curve handles, the point converts to a corner point.

7. **Single-Curve Point** (straight segment into curved)

   This point displays one handle, resulting in a straight segment meeting a curved segment. After click-dragging to place a symmetrical point, hold down the (Option-Command) [**Alt-Control**] keys, and click the handle that affects the most recent segment. That handle is hidden, and the remaining one affects the next segment, which appears when you place the next point.

8. **Single-Curve Point** (curved segment into straight)

   This point displays one handle, resulting in a curved segment meeting a straight segment. After click-dragging to place a symmetrical point, hold down the (Option-Command) [**Alt-Control**] keys, and click the handle that will affect the next segment. That handle is hidden, resulting in no curve being applied to the next segment.

9. **Double-Curve Point**

   This point displays two unlocked handles, allowing you to separately adjust the two segments on either side of the point. To convert a smooth or symmetrical point to a double-curve point, (Control) [**Control-Shift**]-drag one of the handles. The point automatically converts to a corner point.

10. **Open Path**

    A path with a distinct beginning and end is considered *open*. A simple line— two endpoints connected by a straight segment—is the easiest example. In XPress, all lines created with the Bézier Line Tool or Freehand Line Tool are open shapes that can only be stroked, not filled.

11. **Closed Path**

    A path with no distinct beginning and end is considered *closed*. A circular path—a shape with no beginning or end—is the easiest example. In XPress, any shape created with the Bézier Text Box Tool or Bézier Picture Box Tool, as well as custom boxes generated using Item: **Merge**, are automatically closed.

Selecting Points and Segments

To select an individual point or segment, you must first activate Item: Edit: **Shape**. To select a point, click it once with the Item or Content Tool. To select a segment, click it once to select the points on either side of it.

Converting Points and Segments

Use the following techniques to convert a selected point or segment:

- **Convert a selected point to a corner point.** Press (Option) [**Control**]-F1, or click the appropriate button in the Measurements Palette.

- **Convert a point to a smooth point.** Press (Option) [**Control**]-F2, or click the appropriate button in the Measurements Palette.

- **Convert a point to a symmetrical point.** Press (Option) [**Control**]-F3, or click the appropriate button in the Measurements Palette.

- **Convert a point to a straight segment to a curved.** Press (Option-Shift) [**Control-Shift**]-F1, or click the appropriate button in the Measurements Palette.

- **Convert a curved segment to a straight.** Press (Option-Shift) [**Control-Shift**]-F2, or click the appropriate button in the Measurements Palette.

See "Item: Point/Segment Type" in Chapter 10 for more information.

Editing Points

Use the following techniques when adjusting a point or its handles:

- **Add a new point.** (Option) [**Alt**]-click a segment.

- **Delete an existing point.** (Option) [**Alt**]-click a point.

- **Convert smooth point to corner.** (Control) [**Control-Shift**]-drag a handle.

- **Convert corner point to smooth.** (Control) [**Control-Shift**]-drag a handle.

- **Snap segment to 45° angle.** Shift-drag a point.

- **Snap handles to 45° angles.** Shift-drag a handle.

- **Hide one curve handle.** (Option) [**Alt**]-click a handle.

- **Hide both curve handles.** (Control) [**Control-Shift**]-click a handle.

- **Reveal both curve handles.** (Control) [**Control-Shift**]-drag from a point.

See Also

Page Tools: **Item Tool**
Page Tools: **Content Tool**
Box Tools: **Bézier Text Box Tool**
Box Tools: **Bézier Picture Box Tool**
Line Tools: **Bézier Line Tool**
Line Tools: **Freehand Line Tool**
Line Tools: **Line Text Path Tool**
Style (Text): **Text to Box**
Item: **Runaround**
Item: **Clipping**
Item: **Merge**
Item: Edit: **Shape**
Item: **Point/Segment Type**
The Measurements Palette

Bézier Line Tool

Use the Bézier Line Tool to draw a line based on Bézier curves. Here, you must manually place points by clicking or click-dragging, using the tools described earlier in this chapter in "Bézier Curves Overview."

Common Uses

Refer to Appendix A, *Common Techniques*, for full descriptions of the following:

- Drawing a line consisting of straight segments
- Drawing a basic curved path
- Joining two open paths
- Scaling a path
- Converting an open path to a closed shape
- Converting a closed shape to an open path

See Also

Appendix A (**Bézier Line Tool**)
Line Tools: **Bézier Curves Overview**

Freehand Line Tool

Here, you draw a line completely by hand. As you draw, a thin preview of its shape appears on-screen. When you complete the line by releasing the mouse button, XPress converts the preview to a series of Bézier points and curved segments. You can't draw incredibly extravagant shapes with this tool. The bulk of your shape must be drawn in one pass—as soon as you release the mouse button, the shape converts to a line. Therefore, accuracy depends quite a bit on your hand-eye coordination.

To further edit the shape of the box, you must understand how XPress handles Bézier curves. (See the previous section, "Bézier Line Tool," earlier in this chapter for more information.)

Text Path Overview

A text path is a line that can carry editable text. After drawing a text path, the flashing text-insertion cursor automatically appears at the endpoint you initially clicked to create the line. From there, you can enter the text you wish to flow across the path. If desired, you can even choose File: **Get Text** and import a word processing file.

Line Tools

Editing Text on a Path

To insert the flashing cursor in a text path, click the text path with the Content Tool (clicking the actual characters has no affect). If the text path is already selected, choosing the Content Tool automatically inserts the flashing cursor.

If you enter more text than the path can contain, a text overflow symbol (a small cross-out square) appears at the end of the path. The only way you can reveal the hidden text is by lengthening the path or by linking it to another text path or text box. (See "Linking Text Paths," later in this chapter.)

Moving a Text Path

To manually reposition a straight text path, drag it with the Item Tool. To reposition a curved text path, (Command) [**Control**]-drag it, or turn off the Item: Edit: **Shape** option and drag it with the Item Tool.

Editing a Text Path

To edit the shape of a path, check the Item: Edit: **Shape** option and manipulate the points, segments, and handles. (See "Bézier Curves Overview," earlier in this chapter.)

Orienting Text on a Path

To reorient the position of text across a path, you can apply the Style (Text): **Alignment** options, add indents in the Paragraph Attributes dialog, or add tab spaces using Style (Text): **Tabs**. To change the way that the text adheres to the path itself, set an option in the Item: Modify: **Text Path** panel.

Resizing a Text Path

To uniformly resize a text path, you must first select the path and turn off the Item: Edit: **Shape** option. Then use one of the following techniques (note that none of these affect the width of the text path):

- Drag one of the bounding box handles with the Item or Content Tool to change the path dimensions with no constraints. The text reflows to accommodate the new shape.

- Shift-drag a handle to snap the bounding box to a perfect square. The text reflows to accommodate the new shape.

- (Option-Shift) [**Alt-Shift**]-drag a handle to retain the path's original proportions when scaling. The text reflows to accommodate the new shape.

- (Command) [**Control**]-drag a handle to resize the path with no constraints. The text is scaled relative to the new path dimensions.

- (Command-Shift) [**Control-Shift**]-drag a handle to snap the path to perfect proportions, as well as scale the text relative to the new dimensions.

- (Option-Command-Shift) [**Alt-Control-Shift**]-drag a handle to retain the path's original proportions, as well as scale the text relative to the new dimensions.

Converting Text Paths

Text paths can be converted as follows:

- To convert a line to a text path, choose Item: Content: **Text**.

- To convert a text path to a line, choose Item: Content: **None**.

- To convert a text box to a text path, choose one of the line options from the Item: **Shape** submenu. Any text inside the box automatically flows across the new path.

- To convert a text path to a text box, choose one of the box options from the Item: **Shape** submenu. Any text flowing across the path automatically appears in the new box.

Drawing Text Paths in Quick Succession

After you finish drawing a single text path, the Tool Palette reverts back to the Item or Content Tool (depending on which one was last active). When you (Option) [**Alt**]-click the desired text path tool, it remains selected as you draw as many as you need. Manually choose the next tool when finished.

Coloring a Text Path

By default, a text path has a hairline width, and is colored None. This ensures that the path itself is as unobtrusive as possible. If desired, you can increase the width of the path and color it, just like any other line. To determine how the text is positioned relative to this visible path, use the Text Alignment options in the Item: Modify: **Text Path** panel.

Linking Text Paths

You can use the Linking Tools to create a chain of text paths, just as you can with text boxes. (See Chapter 4, *Linking Tools*, for more information.)

Flipping Text Across a Path

To flip text onto the opposite side of a path, check the Flip Text box in the Item: Modify: **Text Path** panel.

Handling Text on a Path

The text path tools are only used to create the actual text paths—beyond that, they have nothing to do with the text they ultimately contain. Details on handling and formatting text are covered throughout this book:

- **Inserting the flashing cursor.** See "Content Tool" in Chapter 1, *Page Tools*, for more information.

- **Highlighting text.** See "Content Tool" in Chapter 1 for more information.

- **Importing text.** See "File: Get Text" in Chapter 5, *The File Menu*, for more information.

- **Exporting text.** See "File: Save Text" in Chapter 5 for more information.

Line Tools

- **Finding and replacing text.** See "Edit: Find/Change" in Chapter 6 for more information.

- **Formatting text.** See Chapter 7, *The Style Menu (Text)*, for more information.

- **Defining style sheets.** See "Edit: Style Sheets" in Chapter 6 for more information.

- **Applying style sheets.** See Chapter 16, *The Style Sheets Palette*, for more information.

- **Replacing fonts.** See "Utilities: Usage" in Chapter 13, *The Utilities Menu*, for more information.

- **Spellchecking.** See "Utilities: Check Spelling" in Chapter 13 for more information.

- **Coloring text.** See Chapter 17 for more information.

- **Trapping text.** See Chapter 18 for more information.

- **Converting text to a box.** See "Style: Text to Box" in Chapter 7 for more information.

See Also

Page Tools: **Item Tool**
Page Tools: **Content Tool**
Line Tools: **Bézier Curves Overview**
Linking Tools: **Linking Tool**
File: **Get Text**
Edit: **Style Sheets**
Style (Text): **Text to Box**
Item: Modify: **Text Path**
Item: **Shape**
Item: **Content**
Utilities: **Check Spelling**
Utilities: **Usage**
The Style Sheets Palette
The Colors Palette
The Trap Information Palette

Line Text Path Tool

Click and drag with this tool to create a straight text path. Each path consists of two endpoints: the point where you first press the mouse button, and the point where you release the mouse button after dragging. Constrain the new line to 45° angles by holding down the Shift key as you drag.

As you drag with this tool, you determine the line's *angle* as well as its length. If the line must be positioned at an exact angle, don't bother trying to eyeball it as you create it. Instead, set the appropriate value in the Angle field of the Measurements Palette after drawing the line.

Orthogonal Text Path Tool

Click and drag with this tool to create a perfectly vertical or horizontal text path. Each line consists of two endpoints: the point where you first press the mouse button, and the point where you release the mouse button after dragging.

You can't set an angle other than 0˚ or 90˚ by manually dragging the endpoints. To numerically rotate an orthogonal text path, enter a value in the Angle field of the Measurements Palette (after doing so, the line is still constrained to right angles). In order to rotate an orthogonal text path by dragging, you must convert it to a standard text path by selecting it and choosing Item: Shape: **Line**.

Bézier Text Path Tool

Use this tool to draw a text path based on Bézier curves. Here, you must manually place points by clicking or click-dragging, using XPress' Bézier toolset. (See "Bézier Curves Overview," earlier in this chapter, for more information.)

Common Uses

Refer to Appendix A for full descriptions of the following:

*   Applying text to a closed shape
*   Applying text above and below a circular shape

See Also

Appendix A (**Bézier Text Path Tool**)
Line Tools: **Bézier Curves Overview**
Line Tools: **Bézier Line Tool**

Freehand Text Path Tool

Here, you draw a text path completely by hand. As you draw, a thin preview of its shape appears on-screen. When you complete the line by releasing the mouse button, XPress converts the preview to a series of Bézier points and curved segments.

You can't draw incredibly extravagant shapes with this tool:

*   The bulk of your shape must be drawn in one pass—as soon as you release the mouse button, the shape converts to a line. Therefore, accuracy depends quite a bit on your hand-eye coordination.
*   If the path is too finely detailed, text will not properly flow across it.

To further edit the shape of the text path, you must understand how XPress handles Bézier curves. (See "Bézier Curves Overview" earlier in this chapter for more information.)

CHAPTER 4

Linking Tools

A single text box cannot display text that flows beyond its bottom edge. When this occurs, a text overflow symbol (a small cross-out square) appears in the lower-right corner of the box. To flow text through a series of text boxes, you must create a *text chain*, or a series of linked boxes. There are two ways to work with linked text boxes:

- **Use an automatic text box.** Here, a text box is linked to a master page. When text overflows the box, XPress inserts a new page to accommodate the text. There are two ways to create an automatic text box:

    - Check the Automatic Text Box option in the File: New: **Document** dialog when creating a new document. When you do, the default master page— "A-Master A"—contains a single linked box.

    - To manually produce an automatic text box, create a new master page, draw the desired text box, and use the Linking Tool to link the box to the broken-link icon in the upper-left corner of the master page.

- **Create a chain manually.** Here, you use the Linking Tool to connect a series of text boxes. The way you approach this will depend on your needs:

    - You can draw as many boxes as your layout requires, then link a series of empty chains. This way, the text you import or enter will automatically flow as needed.

    - You can create new boxes as you need them, linking them to the end of the current chain.

It's important to note that only automatic text boxes insert new pages. If text overflows a manually linked chain, the text overflow symbol appears in the lower-right corner of the last box in the chain.

Linking Tool

Use the Linking Tool to create a link between two text boxes.

A text chain is best viewed as a real chain: there's a first link, a last link, and the remaining links appear in linear order from the beginning to the end. When creating a text chain, the first box you click with the Linking Tool is the first link—when you import text, it begins flowing from the upper-left corner of this box. As you add links to the chain, you determine the order of boxes that will contain the text.

There are two ways to create a chain:

- **Link boxes one at a time**. Linking is a two-step process. After selecting the Linking Tool, click the last box of the current chain, then click the box you want to add to the chain:

  - To link two separate text boxes, click the first box of the chain (it highlights), then click the last box. An arrow extends from the lower right of the first box to the upper left of the second.

  - To link a box to the end of an existing chain, click the current last box of the chain (it highlights), then click the box you want to add. An arrow extends from the lower right of the last box to the upper left of the new box.

  - To insert a new box in the middle of an existing chain, click the box positioned before the one you want to add (it highlights), then click the new box. An arrow extends from the lower right of the first box you click to the upper left of the new box. Another arrow extends from the lower right of the new box to the upper left of the box following it in the chain.

- **Link several boxes at once**. When you simply select the Linking Tool, it reverts back to the Item or Content Tool after you create a single link. To quickly link a series of existing boxes, (Option) [**Alt**]-click the Linking Tool before using it. This way, the Linking Tool remains active as you click the entire order of the chain. When finished, manually select the next desired tool.

When you initially click a box with the Linking Tool, it remains highlighted until you click another box or choose another tool. This allows you to create links that skip several pages. For example, to link a box on page 2 to a box on page 16, click the page 2 box, navigate to page 16, and click the desired box. As long as the Linking Tool is selected, you can see an arrow extending from the lower right of the page 2 box, over the pages in between, to the upper left of the page 16 box.

If you change your mind after highlighting a box with the Linking Tool, simply select a different tool to cancel the command.

Common Uses

Refer to Appendix A, *Common Techniques*, for full descriptions of the following:

- Creating a text chain on a single page
- Creating a text chain on multiple pages

- Adding a new first box to an existing chain

- Adding a new box to the middle of an existing chain

- Creating an automatic text box on a single-sided master page

- Creating an automatic text box on a facing master page

- Creating an automatic text box consisting of multiple boxes

- Adding a "Continued on" jump line

- Adding a "Continued from" jump line

- Including a text path in a chain

Common Errors

- **Attempting to undo a link.** You cannot choose Edit: **Undo** after creating any part of a text chain. To reverse the effect, you must use the Unlinking Tool to break the unwanted links.

- **Linking side-by-side boxes to create multiple columns.** To create the effect of equal-sized text boxes appearing side by side, don't use the Linking Tool. Instead, draw a single text box, and add a number of internal columns using the Item: Modify: **Text** panel (or the Cols field of the Measurements Palette). This removes the risk of accidentally repositioning one of the boxes, resulting in uneven text baselines.

- **Attempting to create a chain by Item: Merging text boxes.** For example, if you select a series of text boxes and choose Item: Merge: **Union**, text will flow throughout all the boxes. However, you have much less control over the text flow than if the boxes were linked—here, you can't easily reposition each box, and the text flow changes unpredictably as you edit the box shapes.

- **Dragging thumbnails containing linked boxes.** Many users copy pages from one document to another by choosing View: **Thumbnails** and dragging the thumbnails. When copying pages that contain a single linked chain, don't drag them one at a time. If you do, the text boxes on each page are unlinked, and each one contains the entire story that flowed through the chain in the original document. To preserve the chain, select *all* the thumbnails containing the text chain, and drag them to the second document all at once.

- **Attempting to link two boxes that already contain text.** XPress doesn't allow you to link two boxes if they both contain text. To accomplish this, you must acquire an XTension such as *Missing Link*, from Visions Edge. At the very least, you can draw a new text box, add it to the chain, then copy/paste the text from the unlinked box to the newly linked box.

Special Notes

- The arrows that indicate links between boxes are not visible until you click one of the boxes with the Linking Tool. You can click as many linked boxes as you desire, with no adverse affect—the highlight merely shifts from box to box. Just remember that when you click an unlinked box after clicking a linked box, it's included in the chain. To deselect a highlighted box without choosing another tool, hold down the (Command) [**Control**] key, and click an empty space on the page. Release the key, and click a new box.

- When you delete the first box of a text chain, the second box becomes the new first box. When you delete a box from the middle of a chain, the text flows through the remaining boxes. However, if a box in the middle of a chain is grouped with other page elements (using Item: **Group**), deleting the group breaks the chain. All boxes before the deleted item remain linked, but all boxes following it are unlinked.

- Selecting text that flows through a series of boxes can be tricky. If you drag across multiple boxes with the Content Tool, the highlighted range will extend through the different boxes. To select a specific range more easily, insert the flashing cursor at the start of the range, navigate to the appropriate box, then Shift-insert the cursor at the end of the range. The text between the insertion points automatically highlights. To select all the text in a chain, simply choose Edit: **Select All**.

- You can't select multiple boxes in a chain and apply Edit: **Copy** and **Paste**. When you copy/paste a single box in a chain, the new box is unlinked and doesn't contain the entire story. Rather, it contains the text that starts at the upper left of the box through the end of the story. A text overflow symbol appears at the bottom of the box.

See Also

Appendix A (**Linking Tools**)
Page Tools: **Item Tool**
Page Tools: **Content Tool**
Box Tools
Linking Tools: **Unlinking Tool**
Edit: **Select All**
Edit: **Copy** and **Paste**
Item: Modify: **Text**
Item: **Group**
Item: **Merge**
Page: **Page Overview**
View: **Thumbnails**

Unlinking Tool

Use the Unlinking Tool to remove a linked box from a text chain. There are three ways to use this tool:

- **Splitting a text chain.** Select the Unlinking Tool, and click the arrow that connects two linked boxes. You must click either the arrow's head or tail-feather—simply clicking a box with the Unlinking Tool has no effect. The chain is broken at the point you click. Boxes before this point remain linked and contain any text; boxes beyond this point remain, but are unlinked and contain no text.

- **Removing a box from a chain.** Hold down the Shift key, and click the box you wish to remove from the chain. The box remains, but the text flows through the remaining boxes as if the removed box never existed.

- **Removing multiple boxes from a chain.** When you simply select the Unlinking Tool, it reverts back to the Item or Content Tool after you break a link. To quickly unlink a series of existing boxes, (Option) [**Alt**]-click the Unlinking Tool before using it. This way, the Unlinking Tool remains active as you Shift-click the desired series of boxes. When finished, manually select the next desired tool.

Common Errors

- **Attempting to undo a broken link.** You cannot choose Edit: **Undo** after unlinking any part of a text chain. To reverse the effect, you must use the Linking Tool to restore the desired links.

Special Notes

If an end of a linking arrow is obscured by another page element, you will not be able to click it with the Unlinking Tool. Attempting to do so selects the item instead. Work around this problem by Shift-clicking the text box itself to unlink it, or use the Item: **Bring to Front** or **Send to Back** commands to fully reveal the arrow.

See Also

Linking Tools: **Linking Tool**
Item: **Bring to Front**
Item: **Send to Back**

PART II

Menus

This section covers the XPress menus, from left to right.

When you first examine a menu, you see two things: commands and submenus. Each chapter lists these items in descending order of appearance. Each submenu lists its contents in the same order.

To help you navigate through the information in this book, we refer to each of these commands by its location in the menus. For example, the New Library command is referred to as "File: New: **Library**." When another item in the book mentions this command, it allows you to turn to the Table of Contents, quickly find the appropriate page number, and refer to this item for additional information.

CHAPTER 5

The File Menu

File: New: Document
(Command) [Control]-N

Use this command to create a new XPress document. Once you enter the desired page dimensions in the New Document dialog and click OK, a single-page document appears in a new window.

Common Errors

- **Entering incorrect page dimensions.** For example, when creating a 4 × 4-inch advertisement, many users open a letter-sized document and use ruler guides to define the desired work area. Since the page dimensions determine the placement of crop and registration marks, they would be improperly positioned during final output, resulting in potentially unusable films.

- **Failing to double-check the values of the New Document dialog.** The dialog always retains the previously entered values. If you assume they are correct without double-checking, you may have to recreate the document.

- **Confusing page size with paper size.** *Page size* refers to the dimensions of a single XPress page. *Paper size* refers to the size of the paper sheets used to reproduce a document on-press. More than one document page usually appears on such a sheet, which is later trimmed and bound. Unless you have a specific reason for doing otherwise, the width and height of your document should equal the dimensions of a single page.

Special Notes

- Unlike other layout programs (such as PageMaker), you cannot establish a specific number of pages at this stage. Instead, you must enter the desired dimensions, click OK, then use Page: **Insert**. When adding pages, remember that each new document already contains one page.

- When planning your document, use a paper mock-up as you determine the number of pages, distribution of text and graphics, spreads and crossovers, and so forth. Such a device makes it easier to visualize the document and allows you to keep track of details and changes as the project progresses. This mock-up will also provide valuable information to your print shop.

- When choosing this command, you don't have to slide the cursor into the File: **New** submenu—just choose New from the File Menu, and the New Document dialog will appear.

The New Document Dialog

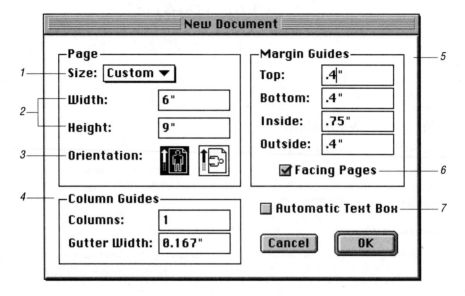

1. **Size**

   Choosing an item from this pop-up automatically inserts one of five standard page dimensions in the Width and Height fields. However, choosing an option does not affect the Orientation setting below. If you desire a size that does not appear here, you must manually enter the Width and Height values. When this happens, the pop-up changes to read "Custom"—you do not need to select this item before entering custom values.

   To change the page dimensions of an existing document, you must use File: **Document Setup**.

   The five available page sizes are listed in the following table (all values are width × height):

	Inches	*Picas*	*Centimeters*
U.S. letter	8.5 × 11	51p × 66p	21.6 × 27.94
U.S. legal	8.5 × 14	51p × 84p	21.6 × 35.56

	Inches	*Picas*	*Centimeters*
A4	11.693 × 8.268	70p1.9 × 49p7.3	21 × 29.7
B5	9.843 × 6.929	41p6.9 × 59p0.7	17.6 × 25
Tabloid	11 × 17	66p × 102p	27.94 × 43.18

2. **Width and Height** (1 to 48 inches)

   To create a page size not listed in the Size pop-up, enter the width and height in these fields. Values can range from 1 to 48 inches. Whenever the Width is less than the Height, the Portrait orientation icon is automatically chosen. When the Width is greater than the Height, Landscape is automatically chosen.

   Other industry standard page sizes include those in the following table (all values are width × height):

	Inches	*Picas*	*Centimeters*
A3	11.93 × 16.535	70p1.9 × 99p2.55	29.7 × 42
A5	5.827 × 8.268	34p11.55 × 49p7.3	14.8 × 21
Compact disk	4.722 × 4.75	28p4 × 28p6	11.99 × 17.06
Magazine (Standard)	8.375 × 10.875	50p3 × 65p3	21.27 × 27.62
Magazine (Narrow)	8.125 × 10.875	48p9 × 65p3	20.64 × 27.62
Magazine (Wide)	9 × 10.875	54p × 65p3	22.86 × 27.62
Magazine (Broad)	10 × 12	60p × 72p	25.4 × 30.48
9" monitor (512 × 342)	7.111 × 4.75	42p8 × 28p6	18.06 × 12.06
13" monitor (640 × 480)	8.889 × 6.667	53p4 × 40p	22.58 × 16.93
17" monitor (832 × 624)	11.556 × 8.667	69p4.03 × 52p0.2	29.35 × 22.01
20" monitor (1024 × 768)	14.222 × 10.667	85p4 × 64p	36.12 × 27.09
Slide/SVGA (800 × 600)	11.111 × 8.333	66p8 × 50p	28.22 × 21.17
NTSC video (648 × 486)	9 × 6.75	54p × 40p6	22.86 × 17.15
PAL video (768 × 576)	10.667 × 8	64p × 48p	27.09 × 20.32

3. **Orientation**

   These icons allow you to choose between vertical (*portrait*) and horizontal (*landscape*) page alignment. Choosing one option over the other swaps the values in the Width and Height fields.

   Note that choosing an option only affects the orientation of the individual XPress pages—it does not affect the orientation setting of the File: **Print**

File Menu

dialog, which defaults to Portrait. Failing to check that value before printing—especially in a document with horizontally oriented pages—could result in clipped printouts.

4. **Column Guides**

This option allows you to divide the active area of a page—the space between the left and right margin guides—into a series of columns. These columns exist only as guides (they are affected by View: **Snap to Guides**) and assist in placing text boxes, rules, and graphics. Unfortunately, you cannot create columns of varied widths with this command—here, you must manually create a page template using ruler guides. (See "View: Show/Hide Rulers" in Chapter 12, *The View Menu.*)

When adding multiple columns to a new document, you actually apply them to the default master page, "A-Master A." To change the number of columns set with the New Document dialog, you must go to that master page and choose Page: **Master Guides**. To create pages with different numbers of columns, you must create additional master pages. (See "Page: Master Pages" in Chapter 11, *The Page Menu.*)

Columns are based on two values:

Columns

This value determines the number of columns appearing on the new page. Note that you don't enter a specific column width—rather, the width of each column equals the distance between the left and right margin, minus the total gutter widths, divided by the Column Guides value.

If you don't want additional columns, don't enter 0. Instead, enter 1—the default value—to create the single column that extends from the left to the right margin guide.

Gutter Width

This value determines the *gutter*, or the space between columns.

5. **Margin Guides**

This option adds nonprinting guidelines around the sides of a page. Margin guides do not affect the contents of a page, nor can they be printed. Once a document exists, you can change them by turning to the appropriate master page and choosing Page: **Master Guides**.

Most often, these guides are used for two things:

– **Defining print boundaries.** Most laser printers can't print beyond a quarter inch or so from the edge of the page. When creating documents for output only on such a device, it's common to mark this boundary with margin guides, ensuring that you don't place text or graphics in a nonprintable area.

– **Defining the "active" area of a page design.** As part of the design process, margins are used to specify the area where the majority of text and graphics will be placed. Typically, information such as headers, footers, and page numbers are placed outside this area.

The orientation of the margins depends on whether or not the Facing Pages option is checked (see the next item, "Facing Pages").

6. **Facing Pages**

This option refers to a printed multipage publication, where the left page always faces the right. When a document is created with this box checked, additional pages are positioned side by side, allowing the designer to work with this relationship in mind. When unchecked, all additional pages are *single-sided*, or not immediately viewable next to another page. (However, you can use the Document Layout Palette to reposition single-sided pages side by side.) Once a document is created, you can turn the Facing Pages option off or on using File: **Document Setup**.

In a single-sided document, the Margin Guides offer settings for left, right, top, and bottom, and the guides are placed identically on each page. In a facing pages document, the left and right settings change to inside and outside. This allows you to spec a measurement that accommodates the binding.

7. **Automatic Text Box**

When this box is checked, a text box is placed on the default master page of the new document. Its dimensions are based on the position of the Margin Guides.

This box is automatically linked—if you import a large text file into the box that appears on the first page, new pages are automatically inserted to accommodate the need for additional pages. The new pages refer to the default master page, so each one contains an automatically linked text box. The boxes behave as if they are linked in sequence, allowing the text to flow from beginning to end. This is especially useful when working on a project such as a book or book chapter, where a large body of imported text must flow through a series of similarly designed pages.

If any text is deleted, however, none of the additional pages are removed. They must be deleted manually using Page: **Delete**. (See "Page: Master Pages" in Chapter 11 for specific automatic text box issues.)

See Also

Box Tools
Linking Tools
File: **Document Setup**
File: **Page Setup**
File: **Print**
Page: **Insert**
Page: **Master Guides**
Page: **Master Pages**
View: **Snap to Guides**
The Document Layout Palette

File Menu

File: New: Library
(Option-Command) [Alt-Control]-N

A library is an auxiliary XPress file used to store and retrieve commonly used page elements. Once you use this command to create a library, it appears on-screen as a floating palette.

To utilize libraries most effectively, you must plan their contents ahead of time. Typically, a library consists of one of the following types of information:

- **Individual graphics.** Here, each library follows a certain theme. Examples include vector-based credit card logos, screenshots of application dialogs, client logos, commonly needed pricing codes, and corporate identity images.

- **Complex page elements.** Here, a single library item contains graphics, text, and/or rules. Examples include graphics with captions, custom headers and footers, publication mastheads, formatted figure callouts, and sidebars.

- **Page layouts.** Here, each item is a standalone page layout, to be dropped into a larger document or quickly accessed at a later date. Examples include ads for a periodical and predesigned page templates.

Once a library has been created and saved, access it by choosing File: **Open** and selecting the appropriate file, similar to opening any other XPress document.

Common Uses

Refer to Appendix A, *Common Techniques*, for full descriptions of the following:
- Adding text to a library
- Adding graphics to a library
- Adding combinations of page elements to a library
- Retrieving items from a library
- Labeling items in a library
- Repositioning items in a library
- Removing items from a library

Common Errors

- **Discarding or misplacing image files.** A library only contains a low-resolution, on-screen version of an added graphic. When you add a library item to a document, you must still maintain the link to the actual image file, just as if you imported it using File: **Get Picture**. Likewise, when you retrieve type from a library, the appropriate font must be available to your system.

- **Discarding or misplacing the library file.** A library is an individual XPress document. When you select this command, you have the option to specifically place the file somewhere on your hard drive. Unless you save them in an easily retrievable location (such as a single folder titled "Libraries"), you cannot access the stored page elements.

Special Notes

- There is no limit to the number of libraries you can have open at one time.

- There is no command to save the contents of a library—it automatically saves when you close the floating palette. If the Auto Library Save box is checked in the Edit: Preferences: Application: **Save** panel, the library is saved every time you add or delete a new item.

- If desired, one or more libraries can be automatically opened when you launch XPress. Simply leave them open when you quit the application. The next time XPress is launched, they appear in exactly the same position.

- Since libraries are nothing more than slightly modified XPress documents, they cannot be opened by earlier versions of the software. For example, you cannot open a library created in XPress 4.0 while using XPress 3.31. Typically, this only poses a problem when multiple users share the same library files. If this occurs, the only solution is to upgrade the older version of the program.

- When labeling a library item, there is virtually no limit to the number of characters you can enter. On one hand, this allows you to be very explicit. On the other, if you use more than 100 to 120 characters, the label pop-up may extend right off the screen when selected.

The Library Palette

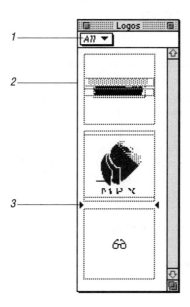

1. Label

Use this pop-up to categorize the items in a library. Two default labels are always available: *All* and *Unlabeled*. When All is set, every thumbnail in the library is visible. When Unlabeled is set, only items not yet labeled appear. The only way to add more selections to this pop-up is to label an item by double-clicking its thumbnail.

2. **Item Thumbnail**

   Every item placed in a library appears as a 1 × 1-inch thumbnail, regardless of the size of the page element. This can be problematic, especially when you add large page layouts or fields of text. If you cannot visually identify an item by its thumbnail, be sure to add a specific label.

3. **Position Indicator**

   These arrows indicate where a thumbnail will be positioned when you release the mouse button. They appear in two situations: when you add an item to a library, and when you reposition an item already in a library.

See Also

Appendix A (File: New: **Library**)
Box Tools
File: **Open**
Edit: Preferences: Application: **Save**

File: New: Book

This command facilitates long-document construction by allowing you to treat a project as smaller component files, such as chapters or sections. Similar to one large document, each file in a book must share the same style sheets, color information, H&Js, lists, and dashes and stripes.

Similar to a library, a book exists as a separate document and appears as a floating palette. By adding documents to a book, you create a link between them, which consists of the following:

- The first added document becomes the *master chapter*. This chapter ultimately forms the basis for all document information such as styles, colors, and H&Js.

- When further documents are added, the page numbering of each one is altered to follow the sequence of all pages in the book, from the first page of the master chapter to the last page of the last file.

- Assuming that the names of the defined styles, colors, H&Js, and so forth are consistent throughout all the book documents, you can *synchronize* the information to the master chapter, or force these items to match the master settings.

This feature is particularly useful for coordinating projects involving multiple writers or designers.

Common Uses

Refer to Appendix A for full descriptions of the following:

- Creating a book of chapters with consecutive page numbering
- Creating a book with sectional page numbering
- Defining a new master chapter
- Editing the style sheets of a book
- Editing the H&Js of a book
- Editing the colors of a book
- Outputting a book

Common Errors

- **Discarding or misplacing the book file or its component documents.** A book file only creates a connection between existing documents. If any of the files are removed from your hard drive, they are listed as "Missing" in the Book Palette and cannot be accessed.

- **Attempting to synchronize irregularly named document information.** For example, if one document in a book contains style sheets titled differently than the others, they cannot be synchronized, nor can they be appended using the Book Palette. To use this command properly, you must use a consistent series of names for this information.

- **Setting the incorrect master chapter.** When defining the master chapter, you must make sure that it contains properly defined style, color, and H&J values. If you add the incorrect document first, you run the risk of applying incorrect values throughout the remaining chapters.

- **Mistakenly adding irregular page sizes to a book.** Although the Book Palette allows you to add chapters with varying page sizes, it is rare that you will actually be required to include such files in a book.

Special Notes

- There is no command to save a book—it automatically saves when you close the floating palette.

- When the appropriate Book Palette does not appear on-screen, you can open, edit, and close the chapters individually. If you edit them while the palette is open, closing the palette automatically closes each document after prompting you to save them.

- If you remove a document from the Book Palette, the document itself is untouched. Likewise, if you delete the book file, the component documents are untouched—only the connection between them is discarded. Any edits, including page numbering and document information, made to the documents while part of a book remain intact.

File Menu

The Book Palette

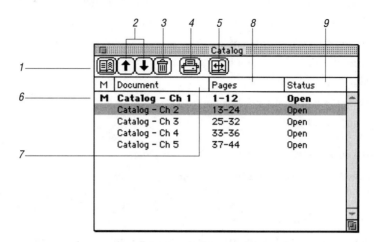

1. **Add Chapter**

   Click this button to add a new document to the book. The first-added document is established as the master chapter. If no existing chapters are selected when you add a new one, it's placed at the bottom of the list. If a chapter is selected, the new one is inserted immediately before it.

2. **Move Up/Move Down**

   After selecting a chapter by clicking it once, use these buttons to reposition it up or down in the Book Palette. (Option) [**Alt**]-dragging a chapter achieves the same effect. When a chapter is moved, its pages are renumbered to follow the new sequence.

   You can only move one chapter at a time—if you select more than one, the up/down buttons are not available.

   If you use these tools to position a chapter all the way at the top of the palette, it does not become the master chapter—that chapter is simply displaced, and its pages renumbered.

3. **Delete Chapters**

   Click this button to remove the selected chapter from a book. You can delete more than one chapter at once.

4. **Print Book**

   Click this button to access the File: **Print** dialog. From there, you can establish your desired print settings and otherwise prepare the book for output. Printing from the Book Palette, however, has certain quirks and limitations:

   – A document does not have to be open in order to print its pages from the Book Palette.

- To output all the pages of the book, click this button with either no chapters selected or all chapters selected.

- To output a specific range of chapters, select them by Shift-clicking their items in the palette before clicking this button.

- You cannot specify a page range that overlaps two chapters. For example, if Chapter 1 contains pages 1–10 and Chapter 2 contains pages 11–20, you cannot output pages 8–15. To print these pages, you must print twice: once to print pages 8–10, again to print pages 11–15.

- You cannot simultaneously output individual pages from two different chapters. For example, if Chapter 1 contains pages 1–10 and Chapter 2 contains pages 11–20, you cannot output pages 10 and 11. To print these pages, you must print twice: once to print page 10, again to print page 11.

5. **Synchronize Chapters**

Click this button to make the style sheet, color, H&J, lists, and dashes and stripes values of all chapters consistent with the master chapter. This technique only applies to definitions that share the same name in every chapter. For example, if one chapter contains an additional style sheet, its values are unaffected when this command is applied.

6. **Master Chapter**

In this column, the master chapter of the book is labeled with a capital "M." The chapter title itself appears in boldface text.

7. **Document**

This column displays the chapter title.

8. **Pages**

This column displays the page range of each chapter, as it fits into the sequence of the book.

9. **Status**

This column displays the current status of a chapter. There are five possibilities:

Available

This option indicates that the chapter is not currently open, but the palette is aware of its location. Double-click the item to open the document.

Open

This option indicates that the chapter is currently open.

Modified

This option indicates that the chapter is not currently open and the palette is aware of its location, but the document has been edited since the last time it was opened using the Book Palette.

Missing

This option indicates that the chapter has been either deleted or placed into a different folder since the last time it was opened using the Book

Palette. If the chapter has only been moved, you can double-click the item to access a navigation window, which allows you to re-establish the link.

Printing
This option indicates that the chapter is currently being output.

See Also

Appendix A (File: New: **Book**)
File: New: **Document**
File: New: **Library**
File: **Open**
File: **Save**
File: **Print**
Edit: **Style Sheets**
Edit: **Colors**
Edit: **H&Js**
Edit: **Dashes & Stripes**
View: **Show Lists**

File: Open
(Command) [Control]-O

Use this command to open an existing XPress document.

Common Uses

Refer to Appendix A for full descriptions of the following:

*   Opening a PageMaker document in XPress

*   Opening an XPress document in PageMaker

*   Opening an XPress document in Illustrator

*   Opening an XPress document in FreeHand

*   Opening an XPress document in Photoshop

Common Errors

*   **Attempting to open a document using an earlier program version.** XPress is not *forward-compatible*, meaning that older versions cannot open documents created in newer versions. If you know that a document created in XPress 4.0 must be opened later on using XPress 3.3, you must choose "3.3" from the Version pop-up in the File: Save As dialog.

*   **Existing files are difficult to find.** In lieu of a sound file management system, documents often wind up in the QuarkXPress application folder or scattered over the Desktop. Whenever possible, keep all files in well-labeled job folders.

*   **Attempting to open a file without the proper XTensions installed.** Often, when a designer has installed a particular XTension, a document created using that

version of XPress cannot be opened on a workstation lacking that XTension. When you attempt to do so, an alert appears, stating the name of the necessary file. To avoid this problem, you must supply (or request) a copy of the XTension when you hand a document over to another user.

Special Notes

- Make an Alias (Macintosh) or Shortcut (Windows) of the XPress 4.0 application icon, and place it on the Desktop. This way, any XPress document—even those from earlier versions—can be dragged onto it, simultaneously launching XPress and opening the file.

- If you open a document that has been locked, an alert appears, stating that you will not be able to save any changes. You can still open and edit the document, but in order to save the changes, you must choose File: **Save As**, and save a new copy.

The Open Dialog

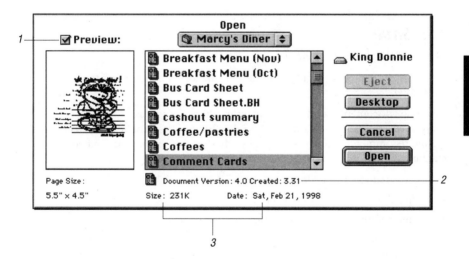

1. **Preview**

   When this box is checked, a thumbnail of the currently selected document appears in the field below. This is only possible if the Include Preview box was checked in the File: Save As dialog when the document was originally saved.

2. **File Type**

   When any XPress file—documents, libraries, or books—is selected in the Open window, this item provides a brief description of its type and XPress version. File types recognized by File: **Open** include documents, libraries, and books.

3. **Size and Date**

When an XPress file is selected in the Open window, these items display its file size and the day of its last modification.

See Also

Appendix A (File: **Open**)
File: **Save**
File: **Save As**
Photoshop in a Nutshell (File: **Opening Vector-Based Images**)

File: Close
(Command) [Control]-W

This command tells XPress to close any active image window. If any changes have been made since the last save, a prompt appears, asking whether to Save, Don't Save, or Cancel.

File: Save
(Command) [Control]-S

This command allows you to write the information in a document to a file on your hard drive.

Save your documents soon and frequently. Although you can tell XPress to periodically save your documents using the Edit: Preferences: Application: Save dialog, I highly recommend that you manually choose this command immediately after reaching certain "milestones" in your work. For example:

- After creating a new document
- After designing your master pages
- After defining style sheets, colors, or custom H&Js
- After executing a particularly complex design or production technique, such as linking a chain of text boxes or rearranging pages in the Document Layout Palette

Common Uses

- **Saving documents.** Once a document has been saved, selecting File: **Save** again updates the current file without bringing up the Save As dialog. This allows you to save your work as you go along, reducing the possibility of time-consuming frustration if your system crashes.
- **Placing files.** When you initially save a document, you have an opportunity to place the file in its proper location on your hard drive or removable media.

Common Errors

- **The keyboard shortcut is chosen by accident.** Several commonly used keyboard shortcuts—most notably (Command) [**Control**]-E for File: **Get Text/Picture** and (Command) [**Control**]-A for Edit: **Select All**—are dangerously close to the shortcut for File: **Save**. Many users have accidentally updated a file when attempting to apply a different command. While this doesn't necessarily harm the document, it prevents you from choosing File: **Revert to Saved** to reverse a series of commands.

- **Files are poorly named.** Several designers I know fall into the habit of creating multiple versions of a document, adding the numbers "2," "3," or "4" after each variation. Then they tag the word "final" at the end of their preferred file. If they make a series of last-minute edits, they wind up with filenames containing "final FINAL," "REAL final," or "USE THIS ONE," which can lead to the wrong document being used—or worse, deleted. Filenames should be as clear and simple as possible. If you save multiple copies of a document, make sure you routinely discard the unnecessary versions.

Special Notes

- There is no File: **Save** dialog. When you save a document for the first time, the Save As dialog appears, as if you chose that command from the File Menu.

- Save commands cannot be reversed by choosing Edit: **Undo**.

- If no changes have been made to a document since the last time it was saved, the command is not available from the File Menu. If you try the keyboard shortcut, an alert sounds.

- Many users prefer File: **Save As** to File: **Save**, even when updating a previously saved document. The Save As dialog always appears, giving you the option of renaming the document or canceling the action. To simply update the image, save it to the same location without changing the name to replace the previous file.

See Also

File: **Save As**
File: **Revert to Saved**
Edit: **Undo**
Edit: Preferences: Application: **Save**

File: Save As
(Option-Command) [Alt-Control]-S

This command allows you to save an additional copy of a document. It's similar to the first time you save a document. From the same dialog, you name the file and place it somewhere on the hard drive. There's an important difference, however:

this time, the original file is left untouched, and a new document containing all the most recent edits is written.

File: **Save As** uses the same dialog that appears when you choose File: **Save** for the first time. XPress automatically inserts the current filename in the "Save current document as" field.

Common Uses

- **Saving a document into an earlier XPress format.** If you know that someone using an earlier version of XPress will be working on an XPress 4.0 document, you must choose "3.3" from the version pop-up in the Save As dialog. Only do this if it is absolutely necessary—saving into an earlier format will eliminate many Version 4.0–specific features, such as character-based styles and XPress clipping paths.

- **Preserving the original document.** Use this command when you need to create different variations of a document for later use. This often occurs for two reasons:

    - When you are updating a periodical publication. This way, you retain the overall design of the document, but you are free to edit the content without altering the previous version.

    - When you are testing a series of radical design changes. By creating an entirely new document, you can apply and save as many edits as you wish without the need to later choose File: **Revert to Saved**.

Common Errors

- **Creating unnecessary multiple copies of a document.** Avoid this for two reasons. First, it leads to confusion about which document to finally use. Second, although XPress files don't tend to be as large as, say, high-resolution Photoshop images, they can still be quite large. Unneeded copies will devour hard drive space.

- **Accidentally overwriting the original document.** If you intend to create a separate file, you must enter a new name. Leaving the name unchanged and saving it to the same location as the original document could overwrite the original with the new copy, just as if you'd chosen File: **Save**.

- **Saving a new copy to the wrong place.** If you assume that XPress automatically places the new copy in the right place, it may wind up in the XPress application folder, on the Desktop, a previous job folder, or any other location on your hard drive.

The Save As Dialog

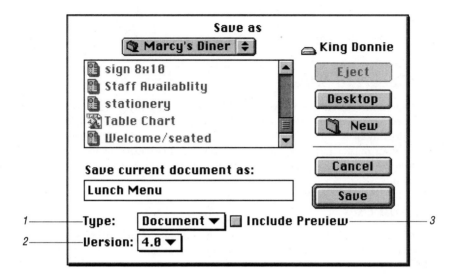

1. Type

Two items appear in this pop-up:

Document

> When this option (the default) is set, the file is saved as a standard, editable XPress document.

Template

> When this option is set, the resulting file cannot be accidentally overwritten. When you open a template, you actually open an unsaved duplicate of the file. Choosing File: **Save** opens the Save As dialog, and the Save Document As field is blank, ready for a new filename. This feature is commonly used to create a series of reusable page designs.

> To save an updated copy of a template, enter the template's filename in the Save As dialog, set the Type pop-up to Template, and overwrite the original file.

2. Version

This pop-up allows you to write a file compatible with earlier versions of XPress. It defaults to 4.0, which results in a file that can only be recognized by XPress 4.0. By selecting 3.3, you create a file that can be recognized by both XPress 3.3 and 4.0, but it may come at a cost—many of XPress 4.0's new features do not translate to Version 3.3.

3. Include Preview

When this box is checked, a thumbnail-sized preview of the document is saved with the file. The File: **Open** dialog refers to this image when you check the Preview box.

See Also

File: **Open**
File: **Save**
File: **Revert to Saved**

File: Revert to Saved

This command tells XPress to reload the most recently saved version of a document, clearing any edits made since then. Successful reverting requires that you save a document at the stage you want to be able to get back to, such as after defining your master pages or before attempting a new design change. At the very least, save a document whenever you make a change you know you want to keep permanently.

Common Uses

Reversing a test series of commands or design changes. Many users save a document before attempting a long series of commands. Since XPress has only one undo level, this allows you to reverse a long chain of edits.

Common Errors

Failing to save a document at the proper time. To successfully use this command, you must be aware of the last time you chose File: **Save**. After reverting, you cannot choose Edit: **Undo**.

Special Notes

* If a document isn't saved at least once, File: **Revert to Saved** is not available.

* Rather than use File: **Save** and **Revert to Saved** to test a series of commands, many users create a quick copy of a document using File: **Save As** and try the commands there. If you are satisfied with the results, keep the current document and discard the previous one.

See Also

File: **Save**
File: **Save As**
Edit: **Undo**

File: Get Text
(Command) [Control]-E

Use this command to import the contents of a separate text file into a box drawn with one of the text box tools. These files are typically generated from two sources:

* **A word processing program.** XPress supports most of the major applications, including Microsoft Word and WordPerfect for both Mac and Windows.

- **Another page layout program.** PageMaker, for example, allows you to export either a range of selected text or an entire story as a wide variety of text files. These files are imported the same as if they were originally created in the appropriate word processing program.

Once the contents of a text file have been imported into a text box, you are free to apply any style sheets or localized formatting, just as if you had keyed the text manually.

Common Uses

- **Importing text into a single, empty text box.** When you use this command to place text in a single box, the new text begins at the upper-left corner. If the size of the box cannot accommodate the amount of text, it extends past the bottom of the box. A small cross-square appears in the lower-right corner, indicating that additional text exists. To view this text, you must increase the size of the box, link the initial box to another text with the Linking Tool, or format the text to a smaller size.

- **Importing text into a text box chain.** When you use this command to place text into a linked chain, it always begins at the start of the chain—or the first box selected with the Linking Tool—regardless of the box currently selected. To place text into a box that appears deep within a chain, you must either unlink the box using the Unlinking Tool or create a new text box before choosing this command.

- **Importing text into a box or chain already containing text.** If text already exists in the currently selected box, the new text will begin wherever the flashing cursor is positioned. If a range of text is highlighted, the new text will replace it.

Common Errors

- **Attempting to import text into the wrong type of box.** If a picture box is selected, this command appears in the File Menu as "Get Picture," and text files are unrecognized. If no box or a blank box is selected, no import command is available.

- **Attempting to import text while the incorrect tool is active.** This command is only available when a text box is selected and the Content Tool is active in the Tool Palette.

- **Attempting to import text from a file not supported by XPress.** XPress can only recognize text files when the appropriate XTensions are loaded. These XTensions act as filters, which convert the contents of the word processing document into information readable by XPress. If your version of XPress lacks the appropriate filter, it will not recognize your text files. For the sake of consistency, many users save their text as Microsoft Word documents, the most universally accepted word processing format, or as ASCII, a rudimentary text-only format recognized by most word processing programs.

- **Mistakenly importing text into an automatic text box.** If you create a file containing an automatic text box, importing text into it may result in additional pages being added to the document. If you do not want additional pages, you must delete or unlink the automatic text box.

Special Notes

- You cannot choose Edit: **Undo** after importing text. To remove a range of unwanted text, choose Edit: **Select All**, and press the (Delete) [**Backspace**] key.

- If XPress does not recognize the files generated by your particular word processing program, you can usually save them into a recognizable format via a pop-up appearing in that program's Save As dialog.

- If you cannot access this command because you have drawn the wrong type of box, you can convert it to a text box by selecting it and choosing Item: Content: **Text**.

- If the text file you import contains fonts not currently available to your system, a dialog appears alerting you to this fact. If you click the Continue button, the text imports as a default font. If you click the List Fonts button, the Missing Fonts for "XXX" dialog appears, listing all the unavailable fonts. Choose a replacement font by highlighting an item, clicking the Replace button, and choosing a font from the subsequent pop-up. If you only want to preview the missing fonts, click OK without making any changes. After the text appears in the document, you can continue to apply any style sheets or formatting.

- XPress cannot recognize files from many applications, including spread sheets, databases, and illustration programs. To import such information, you must first export the file's text into a recognizable format—most of these programs support at least ASCII or Text Only.

The Get Text Dialog

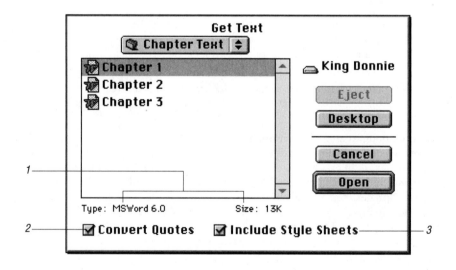

1. **Type and Size**

   These items display the file type and size of the currently selected text file.

---

2. **Convert Quotes**

When this box is checked, XPress automatically converts the following information when importing a text file:

Straight Quotes

Straight single and double quotes, most commonly used as inch and foot symbols, convert to typographer's quotes. If the text file already contains these characters (also known as *smart quotes*), it does not matter if this box is checked.

Double Hyphens

Double hyphens convert to em dashes. This is not necessarily the fix-all it seems. For example, if someone uses hyphens to create a dash as if they were using a typewriter, the dashes have empty spaces on either side. When XPress converts these hyphens to an em dash, a space still exists on either side of it. Since this is an inappropriate use of an em dash, you should use Edit: **Find/Change** to replace all occurrences of "space em dash space" with a simple em dash.

3. **Include Style Sheets**

When this box is checked, XPress imports any style sheets that were defined in the word processing program used to generate the text file.

When you import a text file that contains its own style sheets, some of those styles may be named the same as existing styles in the XPress document. If this occurs, an alert appears, proclaiming "A style sheet named XXX already exists. What do you want to do?" There are two options:

Rename New Style

When you click this button, the style in the text file is imported into the document under a different name (the old one immediately followed by a number). This allows you to use the old style while continuing to edit the document. Any duplicate style sheet imported into XPress using this technique appears as a character style as well as a paragraph style.

Use Existing Style

When you click this button, the formatting of the old style is replaced by the style defined in the XPress document. No additional items appear in the Style Sheets Palette, and no new character styles are created.

If you are importing a document containing a series of multiple styles, you can check the Apply to All Duplicates box to affect all the copies the same as the first one. To cycle through all the duplicates and decide whether to keep or purge them individually, leave this box unchecked.

See Also

Text box tools
File: New
Edit: **Find/Change**
Style Menu (Text)
Item: Content: **Text**
Utilities: **Usage**

File: Get Picture
(Command) [Control]-E

Use this command to import a graphic into a box drawn with one of the picture box tools.

It's important to note you never import the entire contents of a graphic file. Instead, you import a low-resolutionolution preview into the picture box, which you can reposition, scale, rotate, and if desired, tonally adjust. A link is created between the on-screen image and the actual graphic file on your hard drive. If this link is broken—which usually occurs when a graphic has been deleted or was not supplied to a service provider—XPress cannot access the information required to output the image successfully. (See "Utilities: Usage" in Chapter 13, *The Utilities Menu*, for more information on picture linking.)

Common Uses

- **Importing an FPO (For Position Only) graphic.** If your document graphics are going to be conventionally stripped, a common practice is to make a series of low-resolution scans of the original artwork. These are imported into the document only to provide a visual aid while designing and to demonstrate their position to the prepress professional responsible for handling the loose separated films.

- **Importing a DCS preview.** If you are working with five-part DCS files (a variation of a Photoshop EPS file generally used for large full-color graphics), you import a low-resolution preview of the actual image file. When the document is output, the preview will be linked to the remaining high-resolution components.

- **Importing a standard graphics file.** When a graphic file is readily available, you can access it directly with this command. If a graphic is vector-based or Photoshop EPS, a low-resolution preview is built into the file, which is imported into XPress. If it's a pixel-based TIFF, XPress must generate the preview as the image imports. For this reason, TIFFs tend to take a few seconds longer to import.

Common Errors

- **Attempting to import a graphic in an unreadable file format.** XPress cannot import any graphic saved in its native format. For example, an image saved as a Photoshop document will not appear in the Get Picture navigation window. Photoshop images are most often saved as a TIFF or EPS file. Illustrator or FreeHand artwork must always be saved as an EPS.

- **Importing an image saved in the incorrect color mode.** The color mode of a Photoshop image must dovetail with its intended method of output:

  - Full-color images destined for process printing must exist in CMYK or Lab Color mode.

  - Halftones must exist in Grayscale mode.

    —   Line art images must exist in Bitmap mode.

    —   The only time it is appropriate to import a color image in RGB mode is when a document will be printed to a color output device such as an Iris, output as Hi-Fidelity color separations, or output through a color management system that supports RGB. (See "Edit: Preferences: Color Management" in Chapter 6, *The Edit Menu,* for more information.)

- **Importing an image of the incorrect resolution.** If the resolution of any pixel-based image is too high or too low, successful output is not guaranteed. Typically, the resolution of line art ranges from 600 to 1200 pixels per inch, and the resolution of a halftone equals 1.5 to 2 times the target linescreen value.

- **Mistakenly importing a four-color image into a spot-color document.** If your document consists of spot colors (usually chosen from the Pantone library), the graphics you import must contain the same color information. For example, if you import a full-color Photoshop image into a document based on two spot colors, outputting the file results in six plates: one for each spot color, plus cyan, magenta, yellow, and black.

- **Mistakenly importing a spot-color graphic into a four-color document.** If you intend to reproduce your document using only process inks, your graphics must be based on CMYK information. For example, if you import an Illustrator graphic containing two spot colors into a process color document, outputting the file results in six plates: one for each spot color, plus cyan, magenta, yellow, and black. To avoid this, you must open the graphic in the original application and convert the spot colors to CMYK.

- **Importing a graphic containing inconsistent spot-color names.** When working with spot colors, the color names defined in an imported graphic must match the color names in the XPress document. If they do not, the imported colors are added to the Colors Palette, resulting in additional plates when the file is output. One way to avoid this is to import one of these graphics before defining the colors in XPress. Since the colors are automatically added to the Colors Palette, you can use them throughout the rest of the document. If this is impossible, you must change the color names in the graphic using the original application.

- **Importing and scaling an improperly sized pixel-based graphic.** When scanning or generating pixel-based images, always try to make them as close to the desired size as possible. These images cannot be scaled at the same range as vector-based EPS files. Scaling up lowers the effective resolution, which eventually results in pixelized output. Scaling down raises the effective resolution, which eventually leads to slower output times and PostScript errors.

Special Notes

- XPress can import graphics saved in the following file formats: EPS, Photoshop EPS, TIFF, Scitex CT, Windows Bitmap (BMP), JPEG, PICT, and PCX. It is strongly recommended that all print-oriented graphics exist as one of the first five options. If you import and print JPEG images, they must exist at the appropriate resolution and color mode and be set to the lowest compression

File Menu

setting. In other words, don't import JPEGs from your web site and expect them to print properly.

- When you edit a graphic in XPress, you do not alter the contents of the original file; instead, XPress acts as sort of a filter that translates the changes you apply in the document to the output device. On the one hand, this does allow you to make simple changes without opening and changing the original graphic. On the other, the controls are relatively primitive (especially when compared to Photoshop's), and the results are very difficult to proof.

- Occasionally, a gray field appears in the picture box when you import an EPS graphic. This means the file was originally saved with no preview. Since the preview is vital for any accurate positioning or further edits, you must open the graphic in the original application and resave it with the Preview option checked in the EPS dialog.

- A vector-based graphic may contain nonessential elements such as nonprinting guides, stray points, or unwanted shapes pushed off to the side of the work area. XPress recognizes this information as part of the file, and if they exist above or to the left of the intended graphic, the contents of the picture box appear to be offset. To fix this problem, you can reposition the graphic using the Content Tool. However, it is recommended that you open the file in the original application, delete the offending elements, and reimport.

The Get Picture Dialog

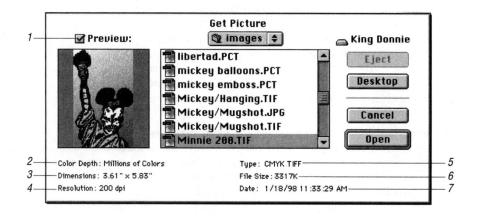

1. **Preview**

   When this box is checked, a thumbnail of the currently selected file appears in the field below.

2. **Color Depth**

   This item displays the bit-depth of the currently selected file. It only applies to pixel-based images. One-bit images are described as "Line Art." Eight-bit images are described as "256 Colors." Twenty-four-bit images are described as "Millions of Colors." Since EPS images cannot be recognized by this feature, they are described as "Unknown."

3. **Dimensions**

   This item displays the width and height of the currently selected file. The unit of measurement is based on the setting in the Edit: Preferences: **Document** dialog.

4. **Resolution**

   This item displays the resolution of the currently selected file. Although it presents this information as "dots per inch," a term more accurately applied to output devices, it refers to the frequency of image pixels (or "ppi").

5. **Type**

   This item displays the color mode and file format of the currently selected file.

6. **File Size**

   This item displays the size of the currently selected file.

7. **Date**

   This item displays the date and time of the last saved modification to the currently selected file.

See Also

Page Tools: **Content Tool**
Picture box tools
Edit: Preferences: **Document**
Edit: **Colors**
Utilities: **Usage**
Photoshop in a Nutshell (File: **Supported File Formats**)
Photoshop in a Nutshell (Image: **Mode**)
Photoshop in a Nutshell (Appendix C)

File: Save Text
(Option-Command) [Alt-Control]-E

Use this command to export a range of text from an XPress document to a separate word processing file.

Common Uses

* **Distributing text to a series of outside resources**. If multiple writers or editors are responsible for the content of a single XPress document, this command allows you to save the desired portions of text into a separate file. This way, additional people can edit or refine copy without referring directly to the document. Later, the text can be imported back into the appropriate place.

- **Exporting text for use in another application.** This command allows you to use text generated or formatted in XPress in another application, such as Word or PageMaker.

- **Exporting text for use in another project.** If you know that you will require text from a current document in a future project, you can save the necessary portions using this command. This way, you do not have to refer to a complex document when it's time to retrieve the text.

- **Exporting information for a database.** If you have generated a series of numbers, names, or similar information delineated by commas or tabs, you can export it into a text file recognizable by your database software.

- **Creating a style sheet template.** When a writer or series of writers generate content for a large project, it is common to provide them a word processing file containing no information but the style sheets used in XPress. This is done by defining the styles in an XPress document, applying each style to a line of text in a single text box, and exporting the text into a Microsoft Word file. If a writer uses this file as a Word template, then all the style sheets will be properly applied when you later import the text using File: **Get Text**.

- **Extracting XPress text for use in an HTML document.** Although you could accomplish this using copy and paste techniques, this method gives you an external text file you can refer to repeatedly, if necessary.

Common Errors

- **Saving text in a file you cannot open in another application.** If your intent is to further edit the exported text, it must be saved in a format recognizable by your software. For example, if you are using a less robust word processing program such as ClarisWorks, you will not be able to open a Microsoft Word file. In this case, you must save the text as ASCII.

- **Failing to preserve the correct style sheet information.** There are two factors to consider when exporting and reimporting style sheets:

  - When using File: **Save Text** to export, all the defined style sheets must be applied somewhere in the selected text box, even if only to a blank paragraph. Any existing style sheet not directly applied will not be included.

  - When reimporting the text, you must turn on the Include Style Sheets option in the File: **Get Text** dialog.

- **Exporting and reimporting locally formatted text.** Only style sheet–based text retains its formatting during exporting. Text that has been formatted manually will lose most of its characteristics.

Special Notes

- This command is only available when a text box is selected and the Content Tool is active.

- XPress can only export and import style sheets using Microsoft Word files. This doesn't mean you have to use MS Word—as long as you use a word processing program that can recognize and write Word files, your style sheets will be safe. Similarly, you can export the actual style tags by saving the text using the XPress Tags option.

- You can only export text from multiple text boxes if they have been linked with the Linking Tool. If you want to create one long text file based on a series of separate stories, you must export them separately and join them in a word processing program.

- The Macintosh version of XPress cannot export text into a Rich Text Format (RTF) file. If this is necessary, save the text as a Microsoft Word file, open it in a program capable of producing an RTF file (such as Word), and resave it from there.

The Save Text Dialog

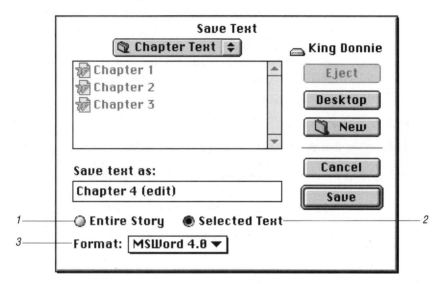

1. **Entire Story**

   When this option is on, XPress exports the entire contents of the selected text box, regardless of whether any text is highlighted. If no text is highlighted (a flashing cursor is present in the text box), this option is automatically chosen and cannot be changed.

2. **Selected Text**

   This option is only available when a range of text has been highlighted using the Content Tool. When this option is on, only the highlighted text is imported.

3. **Format**

   From this pop-up, select the desired format for the exported text file.

See Also

Page Tools: **Content Tool**
Text box tools
File: **Get Text**
Edit: **Style Sheets**

File:Append
(Option-Command) [Alt-Control]-A

This command allows you to import the Style Sheets, Colors, H&Js, Lists, and Dashes & Stripes settings from a saved XPress document into the current document. Since you can *append*, or copy, this information using each of the specific dialogs, this command acts as a shortcut, allowing you to access all settings at once.

Use this command when you are preparing a document that will contain the same settings as a document you have already created. It serves only to save time—the results are the same as if you defined each setting manually, using the appropriate command.

Common Errors

Appending to the default document instead of a specific document. If you choose this command when no documents are open, the information you define becomes the default setting for all subsequent new documents. For example, if you append two spot colors with no open documents, those colors appear in the Color Palette of every document you create from that point on. If this happens, you must access the appropriate dialog—again, with no document open—and delete the unwanted settings. (See "Edit: Preferences" in Chapter 6 for more information.)

Special Notes

- Although you can append the same information using the appropriate Edit Menu commands, this is the only command that allows you to access all settings at once.

- The document you append from can be open when you choose this command. However, it must be saved at least once since defining the settings you wish to append. If the entire document has not been saved, it will not appear in the navigation dialog that first appears when you choose File: **Append**.

- If you attempt to append items that have the same name but different settings as the current document items, the Conflict dialog appears, where you must choose from the following:

  - Clicking Rename opens a dialog that allows you to rename the appended item.

  - Clicking Auto-Rename adds an asterisk before the name of the appended item.

- Clicking Use New replaces the existing settings with the settings of the appended item.

- Clicking Use Existing ignores the appended item, using the existing settings instead.

- When appending a series of conflicting items, checking Repeat For All Conflicts applies the command you select to every item. When unchecked, the Conflict dialog appears for each item.

The Append Dialog

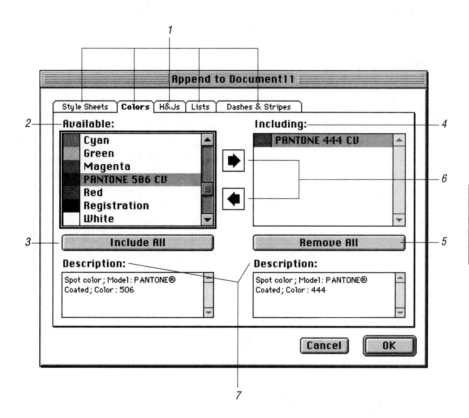

1. **Tabs**

   You must click the appropriate tab to append the desired information. By switching between subjects, you can add settings from all areas.

2. **Available**

   This field displays the available settings of the dialog you choose to append from. The type of settings that appear here depend on the currently selected tab.

To select continuous items, hold down the shift key while clicking. To select noncontinuous items, hold down the (Command) **[Control]** key while clicking.

3. **Include All**

Click this button to move all the settings that appear in the Available field to the Including field.

4. **Including**

This field displays all the currently appended settings.

To select continuous items, hold down the Shift key while clicking. To select noncontinuous items, hold down the (Command) **[Control]** key while clicking.

5. **Remove All**

Click this button to delete the contents currently appearing in the Including field.

6. **Arrows**

Use these buttons to move setting titles from the Available field to the Including field, and back again. For example, to append a style sheet from document A to document B, highlight the desired style in the Available field, and click the right-pointing arrow. The title appears in the Including field and is removed from the Available field. To remove the same style sheet, there is no delete command—instead, you must select it in the Including field and click the left-pointing arrow. The title reappears in the Available field and is removed from the Including field.

7. **Description**

These fields display the characteristics of an item selected in either the Avail able or Including field. If more than one item is highlighted, no information appears. If you are unsure of which items to append, use this feature to double-check the information built into each definition.

See Also

Edit: **Preferences**
Edit: **Style Sheets**
Edit: **Colors**
Edit: **H&Js**

File: Save Page as EPS
(Option-Command-Shift) [Alt-Control-Shift]-S

This command allows you to save the contents of a single XPress page as an EPS file, similar to a graphic created in Illustrator or FreeHand.

Common Uses

- **Importing an XPress page as a graphic element**. After a page has been saved as an EPS, you can import it back into XPress (or another program like Page-

---

Maker) like any other graphic. It can be positioned, scaled, rotated, and flipped, just like any other EPS graphic.

- **Opening an XPress document in another application.** If you wish to access the contents of an XPress page in Illustrator, FreeHand, or Photoshop, you must first save it as an EPS using this command. (See "File: Open" earlier in this chapter for more information.)

Common Errors

- **Failing to provide the typefaces used in saved pages.** When a saved page contains type, those typefaces must be available to the system when the file containing the graphic is output. Unlike Illustrator or FreeHand, XPress has no command to convert type to paths, allowing you to print without the specific typeface.

- **Attempting to open the saved page back into XPress.** Once a page has been saved as an EPS, you cannot open it in XPress using File: **Open**. If you will be editing the file in the future, be sure to retain the original document. Then, if necessary, resave the page as an EPS.

- **Saving pages that contain imported saved pages.** Although you will encounter few problems if you import an EPS page into another XPress document, avoid saving pages that contain these graphics. XPress allows you to do so, but there's no guarantee those files will output successfully.

Special Notes

- A saved page retains all the specific information built into the file, such as traps, kerning, and spot/process color definitions.

- When the EPS file is created, the information of all graphics imported onto the page are built into the file by default. Unlike typefaces, the individual graphics files do not need to be present during output or when the file is opened in another application. This is the sole reason that pages saved as EPS files can grow to such enormous file sizes.

- There is a difference between a page saved as an EPS and a PostScript file generated using File: **Print**. File: **Save Page as EPS** can only save one page at a time. A PostScript file can contain multiple pages and is primarily used as a means to upload the information to a trapping program, impositioning program, or imagesetter RIP.

- When a saved page is imported into another program, it does not display any information placed beyond the page boundaries of the original file. If it is opened in Illustrator, however, this information is clipped by a mask. You can access the hidden portions by choosing Select: **All** and applying Object: Masks: **Release**. If desired, you can increase the clip area using the Bleed value in the Save Page as EPS dialog. Hidden information is still included in the file, however, and could potentially cause output problems.

File Menu

The Save Page as EPS Dialog

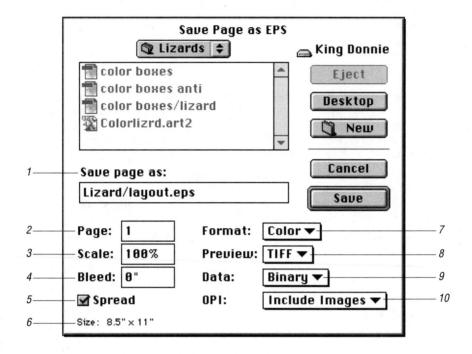

1. **Save Page As**

   In this field, enter the desired name for the saved file. By default, the name appears as the current page number with ".eps" tagged at the end.

2. **Page**

   This field must display the number of the page you wish to convert to an EPS file. By default, XPress enters the number of the page currently active when you choose this command.

3. **Scale** (10 to 100%)

   If desired, save the page at a scale percentage smaller than the original dimensions. A saved page can still be scaled once it has been imported as a graphic.

   It's important to note that any imported pixel-based graphic is subject to the same scaling limitations as in a standard document—when a page is saved as an EPS, this information still exists as pixels and cannot be scaled too high or too low.

4. **Bleed** (0 to 6 inches)

   By entering the value in this field, you increase the clip area that XPress applies to a saved page. Normally, the clip area is based on the page boundaries of the original document. Entering a value greater than 0 expands this area, allowing information extending beyond the page boundaries to display when you import the page as a graphic.

5. **Spread**

When this box is checked, you can save the contents of two facing pages as a single EPS file.

6. **Size**

This item displays the size of the resulting EPS file, including the value entered in the Bleed field.

7. **Format**

The options of this pop-up determine the type of EPS file written to your hard drive:

Color

When this item is chosen, a single EPS file is written that contains all the defined color information.

B&W

When this item is chosen, the color information is stripped out, resulting in a file consisting of only gray tones. If the page will be imported into a document destined for black and white output, choose this option.

DCS

When this item is chosen, this command produces a five-part DCS file consisting of a low-resolutionolution preview and four component files, one each for the cyan, magenta, yellow, and black information. The basic premise is the same as creating a similar file out of a large-sized, high-resolutionolution Photoshop graphic. The small preview is given to a designer to position in a layout, and when the document is later output, it is relinked to the component files. Unlike Photoshop-based DCS files, however, you can open and edit these component files in another program. If this happens, you will not be able to relink and output successfully.

DCS 2.0

When this item is chosen, a file is created that not only keeps track of CMYK information but defined spot colors as well. Although this achieves the same effect as if Color was chosen, certain color management systems or trapping programs may require DCS 2.0 files to work properly.

8. **Preview**

This pop-up determines the type of preview built into the EPS file:

None

When this item is chosen, no preview is added to the file. If you import it as a graphic, a gray field fills the picture box. The graphic will still output.

TIFF

When this item is chosen, a low-resolution TIFF is used for a preview. This is the preferred setting for a graphic that will be viewed on a Windows-based workstation.

PICT

When this item is chosen, a low-resolution PICT is used for a preview. Although they can read EPS files with TIFF previews, this option is the default on Mac-based versions of XPress.

9. **Data**

This pop-up determines how the code representing the file is written to the disk:

ASCII

Choose this item if the file will ultimately be printed directly from a UNIX- or Windows-based workstation, since binary data cannot be sent via a parallel port. If this is the case, you cannot define a TIFF preview—these are binary.

Binary

Most major software packages support this option (the default selection), which results in smaller file sizes, quicker imports, and faster download times than ASCII. If the file will ultimately be processed on a Macintosh or downloaded to a PostScript Level 2 printer in the form of a PostScript file, set this pop-up to Binary.

Clean 8-bit

This option creates a file that can be sent over a parallel port. A sort of ASCII/binary hybrid, it results in a smaller file size than ASCII but can be printed from a UNIX or Windows workstation more successfully than binary. For the safest results, use ASCII.

10. **OPI**

Referring to Open Prepress Interface, the options in this pop-up determine whether the information of all imported graphics will be built into the EPS file, or whether it will simply contain links to the actual files on your hard drive. Adding links is preferable when the imported graphics would result in an inordinately large EPS file, but you must remember to supply the graphics when the document containing the saved page is output.

There are three options:

Include Images

Here, all graphic information on the page is included in the EPS file. This option results in the largest file size and should be chosen if you do not use an OPI server.

Omit TIFF

When you choose this item, any TIFF images on the page are not fully included in the EPS file. Instead, the resulting graphic contains a low-resolution preview and a link to the original image. When using an OPI server, the TIFFs are replaced with OPI information.

Omit TIFF & EPS

When you choose this item, no imported TIFF or bitmap EPS graphics are fully included in the new file. Instead, the resulting graphic contains low-resolution previews and links to the original images. When using an OPI server, these graphics are replaced with OPI information

See Also

File: **Open**
File: **Get Picture**
File: **Print**
Photoshop in a Nutshell (File: **Supported File Formats**)

File: Collect for Output

When you prepare a document for output—particularly if you are sending it to a service provider—you must collect all the disparate elements into a single job folder. These elements include the XPress document, all the imported graphics, and all the pertinent typefaces. To assist in this process, this command automatically places copies of the open document plus all the imported graphic files into a folder of your choice.

A Text Only report is also generated and placed in the folder, which includes the following information: document title, document size, XPress version, page count, page dimensions, required XTensions, document fonts, embedded EPS fonts, imported graphic titles (including file format, file size, dimensions, resolution, and rotation), paragraph and character styles, H&J settings, defined colors, trapping specifications, and the number and names of color plates.

Common Errors

- **Assuming that this command copies the necessary typefaces into the project folder.** This command does not move or copy fonts into the project folder. Other programs or XTensions—such as *FlightCheck* from Markzware—are capable of doing this, but otherwise, you must copy the fonts manually.

- **Attempting this command without enough hard disk space.** It is important to remember that the command does not *move* the necessary graphics files—it places *copies* into the project folder. If you do not have enough available space on your hard drive, the command cannot be completed. To avoid this problem, direct the Collect for Output dialog to a folder on a removable media cartridge, such as a Zip, Jaz, or SyQuest.

- **Attempting this command when graphics are missing or modified.** Before choosing File: **Collect for Output**, use the Utilities: **Usage** dialog to update all the graphics contained in the document. Otherwise, XPress will not be able to locate the files.

Special Notes

- The active XPress document must be saved before you choose this command. If any edits have been made since the last save, you are prompted to save before the command continues.

- To create only the written report of your document statistics, check the Report Only button in the Collect for Output dialog.

- The report is saved as an ASCII text file with XPress Tags included. If you open the report in a basic text-reading application, each paragraph starts with a style sheet tag. To read the report without seeing the tags, import it into another XPress document. The tags are converted to style sheets, and the report appears as a formatted range of text.

File: Document Setup
(Option-Command-Shift) [Alt-Control-Shift]-P

This dialog allows you to change the page dimensions of a document after it has been created. All the settings found in the File: **Document Setup** dialog originally appeared in the File: **New** dialog.

Common Errors

Attempting to apply settings that place page elements off the pasteboard. Unless you have an XTension that expands the pasteboard area above and below a document—such as *Pasteboard XT* from Markzware—the amount you can reduce the size of a document is limited. For example, if an object is placed at the bottom of a letter-sized page, you cannot reduce the height or switch the orientation. If you try, an alert appears, stating "This page size would cause items on master page 'X' to be positioned off the pasteboard." When this occurs, you must enter a larger value, move the offending page elements, or create a new document with the appropriate dimensions.

Special Notes

- This command is not available if a master page is displayed on-screen.

- You cannot access the Facing Pages box if your document contains any facing master pages, regardless of whether those pages contain any information. (If a document was originally created with facing pages, a facing master page automatically appears in the Document Layout Palette.) You must delete all facing master pages before you can access this option.

- Many users refer to this dialog as they attempt to change the column or margin guides. To change those settings, you must go to the appropriate master page and choose Page: **Master Guides**.

The Document Setup Dialog

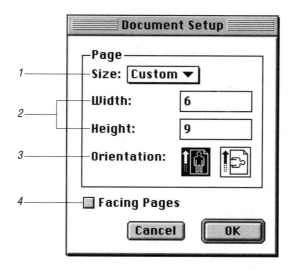

1. **Size**

   This pop-up contains the same five industry standard page sizes as the File: **New** dialog. Choosing an item automatically enters its values in the Width and Height fields.

2. **Width and Height**

   If desired, you can manually enter the new page dimensions in these fields.

3. **Orientation**

   These items allow you to switch back and forth between landscape and portrait formats. Clicking one or the other automatically exchanges the Width and Height values.

4. **Facing Pages**

   If a document was originally created with facing pages, this box appears checked. Unchecking it converts the facing pages to single-sided pages. If a document was created with single-sided pages, this box appears unchecked. Checking it converts the single-sided pages to facing pages.

See Also

File: **New**
Page: **Master Pages**
The Document Layout Palette

File: Page Setup
(Option-Command) [Alt-Control]-P

This command accesses the Setup panel of the File: **Print** dialog. (See the next section "File: Print" for more information.) It's a holdover from earlier versions of XPress, when the setup options existed in a separate dialog.

File: Print
(Command) [Control]-P

This command allows you to print the currently open document to an output device or a file on your hard drive.

Common Uses

Refer to Appendix A for full descriptions of the following:

- Outputting a document composite
- Outputting laser proofs during preflight
- Outputting final separations
- Creating a PostScript file
- Manually tiling a document

Common Errors

- **Failing to provide (or request) the necessary fonts and graphics.** When a project is turned over to a service provider for output, you must supply all the graphics and fonts used in the XPress document. Failure to do so could result in low-resolution images and default fonts appearing in the final printouts. At the very least, it results in lost time as your service provider contacts you for this information. (See "File: Collect for Output" earlier in this chapter for more information.)

- **Outputting unlinked or modified graphics.** Even if all the graphics files used in a document are present, you must make sure the links are updated before outputting. If a link has been broken or a graphic has been edited, an alert appears when you attempt to print, stating that "Some disk files for pictures in this document are missing or have been modified." You have two choices. If you click List Pictures, a version of the Utilities: **Usage** dialog appears, allowing you to update the broken links. If you click OK, the document is output regardless of the picture status, which often results in incorrect printouts. (See "Utilities: Usage" in Chapter 13 for more information.)

- **Attempting to separate incorrectly defined colors.** You cannot tell if a color has been improperly defined until you output laser proofs. Most commonly, an intended spot color separates into CMYK components, or a process color outputs as a spot plate. If this occurs, you must re-edit the color definition. (See "Edit: Colors" in Chapter 6 for more information.)

- **Setting the incorrect PPD file during output.** A PPD, or *PostScript Printer Description* file, communicates information about an output device to XPress. Each output device has its own PPD. To get the best printed results, you must choose the appropriate item from the Printer Description pop-up in the Setup panel of the File: **Print** dialog. If you have only one output device—a laser printer for proofing, perhaps—this only has to be set once. If you switch between multiple printers, you must set (or at least double-check) this pop-up each time.

- **Outputting at the incorrect linescreen value.** The target linescreen value depends on the specific project, as well as the specific output device. If a project will be run on-press at 150 lpi, it must be output to film at that value. However, if you run proofs on a 300 or 600 dpi laser printer, such a high screen frequency results in long print times and dark, difficult-to-read halftones. For laser proofs, use a value between 75 and 90 lpi—but remember to set the target value for final output.

- **Failing to transverse pages when outputting to film.** To save materials when printing to film, set the pages to print side by side instead of end to end. For example, if you output 50 letter-sized pages in *landscape* as opposed to *portrait* orientation, you save over 100 inches of film. When an imagesetter's PPD is chosen in the Printer Description pop-up, you can achieve this effect by clicking the landscape orientation button.

- **Outputting a gradient that is too long, resulting in shade-stepping.** This applies to XPress blends, as well as any gradients produced in imported Illustrator, FreeHand, or Photoshop graphics. Any blend between two colors has a limited number of possible tones. For example, if you create a blend between black and white, up to 254 shades of gray can be generated between them. As you lengthen the gradient, you widen the individual tones. When a gradient extends too far, the tones become visible. The exact point at which banding occurs depends on two things:

  - **The tonal difference between two colors.** For example, a black-to-white gradient can extend to approximately eight inches before banding occurs. A blend between two medium grays contains fewer tones and can only extend a fraction of the distance.

  - **The linescreen value of a printed image.** As you increase the linescreen of a printed document, you reduce the number of tones an output device can reproduce. If the linescreen exceeds a printer's recommended limit, banding will occur—and gradients are the first elements visibly affected.

- **Failing to prepare a document for bleeds.** If a printed piece will contain *bleeds*, or ink printing to the very edge of the final page, you must compensate for this in the XPress document by extending such areas at least 9 points past the page boundary. If this information only extends to the exact edge of the page, there is no latitude when the project is trimmed after running on-press.

- **Outputting an improperly trapped document.** When a project contains abutting colors—particularly if the colors are spot inks—trapping must be considered. Many users simply use XPress' default automatic trap settings, but the resulting values are far too low to be of any tangible use. At the very least, you must raise the default values, or consult with your printer or output specialist for specific advice. It is important to note that trapping does not affect composite printouts—it is only applied to separated documents. In order to proof your traps before final output, you must print separations on at least a 600 dpi laser printer, or output a color composite on a device that supports trapping information, such as a 3M Rainbow. (See "Edit: Preferences: Document: Trapping" in Chapter 6 for more information.)

Special Notes

- You can cycle through the five panels of the Print dialog by holding down the (Command) [**Control**] key and pressing Tab.

- When you construct a facing-page document, it does not automatically mean you should output with the Spreads option turned on. Generally, there are three reasons to output spreads:

  - When you have imposed the pages of a simple document into printer spreads, as opposed to the default reader spreads. In this case, each pair of facing pages should be output onto the same film page. (See Chapter 15, *The Document Layout Palette*, for more information.)

  - When a multipage document contains a center spread or cover spread. In this case, the cover or center page will be printed onto the same film page, allowing you to apply a crossover color or graphic. However, the remaining pages must be output as single pages. To accomplish this, handle the file in sections: output the cover and/or center spread individually with the Spreads box checked, then output the ranges of the remaining pages with the Spreads box unchecked.

  - When the cover or center spread of a project is constructed in a separate document. Often, a user creates this file using the same page dimensions as the original document, then moves a series of pages together using the Document Layout Palette. This reduces the risk of entering miscalculated page dimensions and provides a handy template for creating additional folds or similar design elements. Outputting this document as a spread treats the individual pages as a single film page.

- Although it's impossible to accurately predict a document's output time, you can safely assume that the more pages and color graphics it contains, the longer it will take. Whenever possible, your output environment should include the following:

  - A well-equipped, high-speed workstation to process or spool the file quickly.

  - A PostScript Level 2 (or higher) output device. If your laser printer or RIP dates back to 1992 or earlier and hasn't been upgraded, you will reduce your print times by up to 75% by investing in a new printer.

  - A high-speed network, such as Ethernet. If you are still using dedicated printer cables or phone lines to send your information to an output device, you are only moving about 10KB per second. By upgrading your network, you increase this rate considerably.

- It is possible to *embed* screen information in an imported graphic or build these instructions into the file. For example, a duotone constructed in Photoshop invariably contains custom angles, or a FreeHand file may contain a low screen value as a special effect. Since these graphics must be saved as EPS files, there is no way XPress can override the built-in values, regardless of the screen angles or values you enter in the File: **Print** dialog.

The Print Dialog

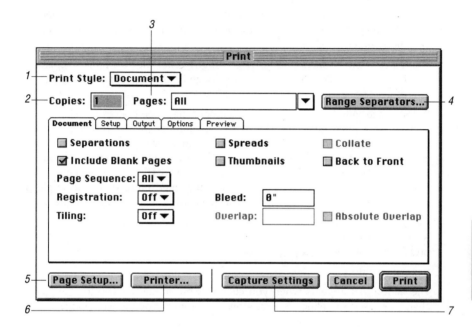

The following print commands are available regardless of the currently selected panel:

1. **Print Style**

   When you create custom print settings using Edit: **Print Styles**, they appear as items in this pop-up. When you select an item other than Document, all five panels assume the style's predefined settings. If you alter any settings after selecting a print style, a bullet appears before the style name, indicating the change. If desired, reset the original style by selecting Document from the pop-up, then the appropriate print style again.

2. **Copies**

   Here, enter the number of times you want your output device to produce the range of pages defined in the Pages field. Unless you check the Collate box in the Document panel, multiple copies of each page are printed at once. For example, when printing five copies of a five-page range, the printer generates five copies of page one, then five copies of page two, and so forth.

3. **Pages**

Here, enter the range of pages you wish to output. XPress defaults to All, meaning that you will output all existing pages of the document. However, you can be more specific:

- To print one specific page, enter the appropriate page number.

- To print a continuous range of pages, enter the page numbers separated by a hyphen. For example, to print pages 2 through 8 of a 12-page document, enter "2-8".

- To print two noncontinuous pages, enter the page numbers separated by a comma. For example, to print page 2 and page 8 of a 12-page document, enter "2, 8".

- To print two noncontinuous page ranges, enter the two ranges separated by a comma. For example, to print pages 2 through 5 and 7 through 10 of a 12-page document, enter "2-5, 7-10".

If the page numbering of your document has been altered using Page: **Section**, you must enter the specific page numbers when printing a single page or a range. For example, if your document starts at page 10 and you attempt to print page 1, an alert appears, stating, "This page range is invalid." To avoid this, enter "10". Or you can force XPress to read absolute page numbers by adding a plus symbol before the page number. For example, if you enter "+1" in a document starting at page 10, XPress outputs the first page of the document.

Also, if a section uses prefixes (such as "B-1" or 14.3"), you must include the prefix when specifying a page range.

4. **Range Separators**

The dialog that appears when you click this button allows you to change the characters used to delineate continuous and noncontinuous page ranges.

5. **Page Setup**

Clicking this button accesses the page setup commands specific to your operating system.

6. **Printer**

Clicking this button accesses the page setup commands specific to your output device. You do not need to access this dialog unless it contains settings or commands not found in the XPress print panels.

7. **Capture Settings**

Ordinarily, if you set a range of print commands and then choose Cancel, you must re-establish the settings the next time you access the Print dialog. If you set a range of commands and click this button, the dialog automatically closes, but the settings are preserved.

The remaining print commands are located in the five tabbed panels:

File: Print: Document Panel

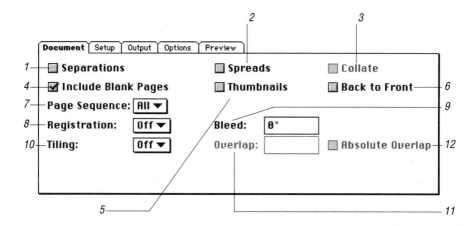

1. Separations

When this box is checked, XPress outputs separations based on the colors defined in the document. When unchecked, XPress outputs a *composite*, or a unseparated printout.

2. Spreads

When this box is checked, XPress removes the boundary that exists between two facing pages. Both pages are printed as one page film, surrounded with crop and registration marks. Check this box only when this effect is needed—otherwise, the page films will be unusable. (See "Special Notes," earlier in this chapter.)

3. Collate

This option is only available when you enter a value greater than 1 in the Copies field. When this box is checked, copies of multipage documents are printed separately, one after the other. This adds considerable time to the printing process, since XPress has to process and print the document once for each copy, instead of once for all copies.

4. Include Blank Pages

When this box is unchecked, XPress doesn't output any pages containing no information. If the entire contents of a page have been suppressed (using either the OPI pop-up in the Options panel or the Item: **Modify** dialog), XPress considers it a blank page as well. When checked, XPress outputs all pages, regardless of their contents.

5. **Thumbnails**

When this box is checked, XPress scales the output down to 12.5% and gangs as many pages as possible on a single printed page. This feature is only intended to provide a quick overview of a document. It is not available when Spreads or Separations is checked, and the processing time is the same as if this item were turned off.

If desired, you can enlarge the thumbnails by entering a value over 100% in the Reduce or Enlarge field in the Setup panel. Again, this is to provide an overview—if you simply want to output smaller page sizes, use only the Reduce or Enlarge field.

6. **Back to Front**

When this box is checked, the printed page order is reversed.

7. **Page Sequence**

This pop-up allows you to print either all the odd numbered pages or all the even numbered pages of a document. This is commonly used to print double-sided pages on a laser printer. By outputting all the odd numbered pages first, you can print the appropriate even numbered pages on the reverse side by placing the printouts in the right position in the printer's paper tray.

8. **Registration**

This pop-up allows you to add crop and registration marks to your printouts. This feature also adds a line of page information in the upper-left corner, including the document name, date and time of printing, page number, and plate color. There are three items:

Off

This option results in no marks or page information.

Centered

This option adds crop marks and page information and places a registration mark on each side of the page, centered top-to-bottom and left-to-right.

Off Center

This option adds crop marks and page information and places an off-centered registration mark on each side of the page.

It is vital that this box is checked whenever you output color separations. Otherwise, there is no indication of plate colors or page numbers, resulting in unusable films.

9. **Bleed (0 to 6 inches)**

By entering a value in this field, you increase the printable range of a document beyond the defined page boundaries. If a Registration option is selected, the crop mark still indicates the original dimensions. This option allows you to handle bleeds in the final printed piece by outputting information beyond the trim line, creating the illusion of ink printing all the way to the edge of the page.

10. **Tiling**

Use this option when you want to output a document larger than the print size of your printer. Rather than scale the document down to fit the limit of your printer, it is printed at actual size in a series of pieces. Most often, this feature is used to output 11 × 17-inch pages (or higher) on a printer only capable of handling letter-sized paper. There are three items in this pop-up:

Off

When this item is selected, no tiling occurs. If the document is too large to be fully printed, the upper-left corner is output.

Manual

When this item is selected, you manually set the information that will appear on each printed page. By positioning the zero coordinates of the rulers, you determine the upper-left starting point of the next printout. Each tile must be set and printed individually. If the document contains more than one page, you must enter the specific page number in the Pages field, or the tile will be applied to all pages in the document.

To preview the position of the tile, switch to the Preview panel.

Automatic

When this item is selected, XPress determines the information that appears on each printed page. All tiles are printed at once. If the document contains more than one page, you must enter the specific page number in the Pages field, or all pages in the document will be automatically tiled.

To prevent any information from being clipped, refer to the Overlap value, which follows.

To preview the auto-tiled areas, switch to the Preview panel. Overlapping areas are marked with gray.

11. **Overlap**

The value in this field determines the amount of overlapping information on auto-tiled pages. This feature makes it easier to align the individual printouts when you tape them together. It defaults to three inches (18p), but most users prefer a lower setting of .5 to 1 inch (3p6 to 6p).

12. **Absolute Overlap**

When this box is unchecked, XPress attempts to keep the page number to a minimum, yet still provide the inserted Overlap value. When checked, XPress adds as many tile pages as necessary to apply the Overlap value.

File Menu

File: Print: Setup Panel

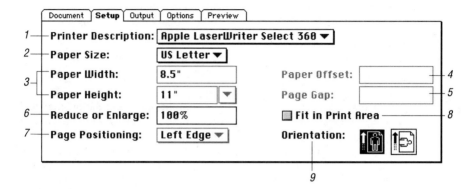

1. **Printer Description**

   From this pop-up, select the PPD of the intended output device. Whenever you switch printers, you must select a new PPD. If your printer is not included here, you must acquire and install the appropriate file. Although you can choose generic PPDs for laser printers, color printers, and imagesetters, you must have a device-specific PPD in order to successfully use the remaining settings in this panel.

2. **Paper Size**

   From this pop-up, choose the intended size of the paper you're printing to. The options that appear depend on the active PPD. When a generic PPD is selected, this setting is determined by the print driver utilized by your operating system. When a specific laser or color printer PPD is selected, all supported paper sizes appear. When an imagesetter PPD is selected, "Custom" appears in the pop-up, and you can edit the Width and Height fields independently. This is because imagesetters are not restricted to physical paper sizes; they print to a roll of film that is later trimmed.

   If the incorrect setting is chosen—for example, US Letter for a tabloid-sized document or a width too narrow for a page printing to film—your printouts may be clipped.

3. **Paper Width and Height**

   When outputting to a device not restricted to paper sizes (such as an imagesetter), you must make sure that the width and height can accommodate the document page size. If it is too narrow, the printouts will be clipped. Consult with your vendor to be certain.

   A good rule of thumb is the width of the page plus two inches. This will accommodate any page information, crop marks, and registration marks. It is important to note that when you transverse pages to film, you automatically print them side by side—here, you must enter the *height* of the document page, plus two inches in the Width field.

4. **Paper Offset**

By increasing the value in this field, you increase the distance between the left edge of the printed information and the left edge of the film. In nearly all instances, the default value is sufficient, since imagesetters automatically offset the pages by .25 to .5 inches to accommodate the grippers that feed the film through.

5. **Page Gap**

By entering a value in this field, you increase the space between two pages on a roll of film.

6. **Reduce or Enlarge**

This option allows you to scale the printed pages up or down. This command affects the entire contents of the document, including text, graphics, and the placement of crop and registration marks. This is a print-specific command; the actual document is untouched.

7. **Page Positioning**

This pop-up determines the placement of information on the printed page. Its affect is most noticeable when printing smaller page sizes onto single-sheet laser printers. There are four options:

Left Edge
This option, the default, begins printing in the upper-left corner of the page.

Center
This option prints the information in the center of the page.

Center Horizontal
This option prints the information in the center of the page, along the top.

Center Vertical
This option prints the information in the center of the page, along the left edge.

8. **Fit In Print Area**

When this box is checked, XPress enters the Reduce or Enlarge percentage necessary to scale the document to fit the item selected in the Paper Size pop-up.

9. **Orientation**

Here, the option you choose depends on the orientation of your document. For example, if you created a letter-sized document in landscape orientation, you must choose the landscape option here before printing. Otherwise, your printout will be clipped. It is important to note that setting an orientation in the File: **New** dialog does not automatically set the orientation in the Setup panel.

To transverse pages for a roll-fed output device, click the landscape option after choosing the appropriate PPD in the Printer Description pop-up. If your output device supplies software that adds a Transverse option elsewhere in the Print panels, ignore the landscape option.

File: Print: Output Panel

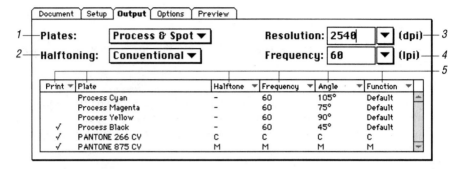

1. Plates

When the Separations box in the Document panel is unchecked, this pop-up appears as Print Colors. Here, XPress attempts to optimize the printing infor-mation based on the type of output device handling the file:

Black & White

> This option is preferred when the output device does not have a method for handling screened information, as is the case with non-PostScript laser printers.

Grayscale

> This option is automatically set when the PPD selected in the Printer Description pop-up is based on a printer that supports halftone screens.

Color Composite

> This option is automatically set when the PPD selected in the Printer Descriptions pop-up is based on a color output device, such as a Canon Color Copier with a Fiery RIP or 3M Rainbow.

When the Separations box in the Document panel is checked, this pop-up appears as Plates. There are two items:

Process & Spot

> When this option is set, XPress separates all process colors and spot colors.

Convert to Process

> When this option is set, XPress converts all existing spot colors to their closest CMYK equivalent. This only occurs during output—it does not affect the color definitions in the actual document.

2. **Halftoning**

This pop-up determines the halftoning method applied to document. It affects the precise screen value and screen angles and, in many cases, the shape of the halftone dots themselves.

Conventional

This setting pertains to the screening information built into XPress. If your output device does not have its own screening software, this is the only option available.

Printer

Imagesetters usually have their own proprietary screening information. For example, AGFA imagesetters are driven by software called *Balanced Screening*, which produces optimal results for the specific technology. This option only appears when outputting to such a device. Selecting it overrides XPress' screening information, letting the appropriate software take over.

3. **Resolution**

This pop-up does not affect the resolution of your image file or the resolution of your output device. However, setting it to the target resolution allows XPress to better process any low-resolution graphics. Also, when printing to low-resolution output devices, XPress doesn't spend time processing any image information unnecessary for adequate output. The options appearing here depend on the available resolutions of the current output device.

4. **Frequency**

In this field, set the target linescreen value for the printed piece. Depending on the PPD set in the Printer Description pop-up, a list of optimal choices—based on the resolution and reproductive range of the device—is accessed from the small pop-up.

The final linescreen for a project run on-press is based on a series of factors, including cost, paper stock, press type, and printing method.

5. **Separation information**

This field displays information about the available document colors:

Print

Each color initially appears with a checkmark, indicating that it can be output. To suppress the printout of a particular plate, click the checkmark next to its name.

Plate

This item displays the names of all document colors. If the Separations box is unchecked in the Document panel, the only color listed is black—printing without Separations checked results in a composite, with no specific color information.

When Separations is checked, this item displays all the colors listed in the document's Colors Palette. It also includes colors not used anywhere in the document, such as blue, green, and red. It is not necessary to suppress the printout of these colors.

The names of colors based on process inks do not appear here. Their color content is represented by the cyan, magenta, yellow, and black items.

Halftone

This item displays the setting chosen from the Halftone pop-up in the Edit: Colors: **Edit Color** dialog. If any of the colors list C, M, Y, or K here, it means that the color shares the same screen information as that particular process color.

Frequency

This item displays the linescreen value entered in the Frequency field. To change a single value, select it, and choose Other from this pop-up. To reset all inks, enter a new value in the Frequency field.

Angle

This item displays the screen angle at which a particular color will output. When Default is listed, the shape is determined by the screening software used by your output device. To change the angle, choose an option here.

Function

This item displays the specified halftone dot shape. When Default is listed, the shape is determined by the screening software used by your output device. To change the shape, choose an option here.

File: Print: Options Panel

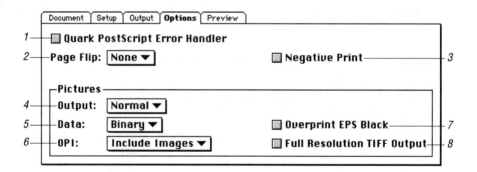

1. **Quark PostScript Error Handler**

   When this box is checked, XPress attempts to keep track of any PostScript error that causes a document to misprint. If such an error occurs, XPress outputs all information processed before the error occurred, then produces a report detailing the location and contents of the page element causing the error. This does assist in isolating and troubleshooting the problem, but it doesn't provide a solution.

2. **Page Flip**

This pop-up determines the *reading* of a film page, or which side of the page contains the silver halide emulsion. The option you choose depends on the method used to reproduce a document on-press, so you should consult with your printer if there is any confusion. There are four options:

None

 The default setting, this results in right-reading, emulsion up film.

Horizontal

 This results in right-reading, emulsion down film.

Vertical

 This produces the same result as Horizontal but is rotated 180˚.

Horizontal & Vertical

 This produces the same result as None but is rotated 180˚.

If you are printing to an imagesetter using its screening software, this option may have no effect—the setting will be applied from a different source.

3. **Negative Print**

When this box is checked, XPress outputs *negative*, or reversed output. If you are printing to an imagesetter using its screening software, this option may have no effect—they typically print negatives by default, and a command to produce positive films is accessed from a different source.

4. **Output**

The items in this pop-up affect the output of imported graphics:

Normal

 When this item is selected, all the information contained in the linked graphics files is sent to the output device, resulting in the highest quality output.

Low Resolution

 When this item is selected, XPress outputs only the imported low-resolution previews representing each graphic. This allows a document to print much more quickly, especially if you only want to produce a quick proof.

Rough

 When this item is selected, no image information is printed—rather, all graphics are replaced with a bounding box. This results in the fastest output time.

5. **Data**

This pop-up determines the type of information sent to the output device:

ASCII

 Choose this item when printing directly from a UNIX- or Windows-based workstation.

Binary

 Most major software packages support this option (the default selection), which results in faster print times than ASCII. If the file will ultimately be processed on a Macintosh or downloaded to a PostScript Level 2 printer in the form of a PostScript file, set this pop-up to Binary.

File Menu

6. **OPI**

   This pop-up determines whether TIFF and EPS graphics are output directly or are substituted with OPI (Open Prepress Interface) comments:

   Include Images
   > Here, all graphic information in the document is output. Choose this option if you are not using an OPI server.

   Omit TIFF
   > When this item is chosen, any TIFF images in the document are replaced with OPI comments.

   Omit TIFF & EPS
   > When this item is chosen, any TIFF or EPS graphics in the document are replaced with OPI comments.

   Consult the documentation of your OPI system for specific substitution details.

7. **Overprint EPS Black**

   This option applies to imported vector-based graphics containing objects colored 100% black. When this box is unchecked, the black objects do not overprint unless the fill or stroke was specifically set to overprint in the original application. When checked, the black objects overprint regardless of the original setting.

8. **Full Resolution TIFF Output**

   When this box is checked, XPress outputs halftone TIFF images at full resolution. When unchecked, the image is downsampled during processing, based on the current linescreen value. Outputting with this option off will reduce output time, but finely detailed images may display the effects of reduced resolution.

File: Print: Preview Panel

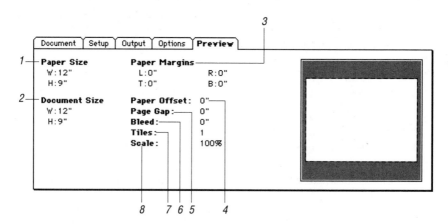

1. **Paper Size**

   This item displays the current selection from the Paper Size pop-up in the Setup panel.

2. **Document Size**

   This item displays the width and height of the open document.

3. **Paper Margins**

   This item displays the restricted print area of the selected output device. For example, laser printers cannot print to the very edge of the page; most can print .2 to .4 inches away. If the output device has no limitation—imagesetters, for example, can print beyond the page boundaries—zeros appear.

4. **Paper Offset**

   This item displays the Paper Offset value entered in the Setup panel.

5. **Page Gap**

   This item displays the Page Gap value entered in the Setup panel.

6. **Bleed**

   This item displays the Bleed value entered in the Document panel. The bleed width displays in the preview thumbnail as a blue frame.

7. **Tiles**

   This item displays the number of pages required to automatically tile a page. If Tiling is turned off or set to Manual, this item displays "1". In the preview thumbnail, the Overlap area defined in the Document panel is highlighted in gray.

8. **Scale**

   This item displays the Reduce or Enlarge value entered in the Setup panel.

File Menu

See Also

Page Tools: **Content Tool**
File: **New**
File: **Collect for Output**
Edit: Preferences: Document: **Trapping**
Edit: **Colors**
Edit: **Print Styles**
Item: **Modify**
Page: **Section**
Utilities: **Usage**
Photoshop in a Nutshell (Special Tools: **Gradient Tool**)

File: Quit
(Command) [Control]-Q

This command forces the operating system to discontinue running XPress. If any open documents are unsaved, you're prompted to Save, Don't Save, or Cancel the entire Quit command.

CHAPTER 6

The Edit Menu

Edit: Undo/Redo
(Command) [Control]-Z

This command works the same as in any other program: selecting it reverses, or "undoes," the last applied command. XPress has only one Undo level, so only the very last command can be reversed. Choosing Undo again reapplies the command. Toggling back and forth between Undo and Redo is the only way to see the before-and-after effect of a command or action to a page element.

Common Errors

Attempting to undo multiple commands. If you are about to apply a series of commands to a document, the following precautions allow you to compensate for the lack of multiple undo levels:

- Save the document before applying the next suite of commands. If unsatisfied with the results, choose File: **Revert to Saved**.

- Make a copy of the document using File: **Save As**, and apply the commands there. If unsatisfied, close the copy, and delete the file. If satisfied, close, delete the original, and continue editing.

Special Notes

- When manually entering text, the amount you can undo depends on the last time you clicked inside the text box to position the cursor. For example, if you type 100 words and then choose Edit: **Undo**, all 100 words are deleted. If you type 50 words, click in the box to reposition the cursor, then type another 50 words, choosing undo only deletes the last 50 words.

- You cannot undo the following commands:

  - **Drawing a text box, picture box, rule, or Bézier path.** The only exception is when you use a tool that draws in polygonal segments, such as the Bézier Text Path and Bézier Picture Box Tools. Here, choosing Edit: Undo removes the most recently placed segment.

  - **Linking or unlinking a chain of text boxes.** To do so, you must apply the Linking Tool or Unlinking Tool, depending on the intended result.

  - **Deleting a series of text boxes from a linked chain.** The boxes reappear when you undo, but they are not relinked. If you delete an entire chain, however, the link is untouched when you undo.

  - **Any File Menu item.** Most of these commands involve writing information to a hard drive or preparing a document for printing, none of which can be undone in any application.

  - **Any Edit Menu item.** The only exceptions are Edit: **Cut** and **Paste**. Choosing undo after cutting restores the cut information; choosing undo after pasting removes the pasted information, restoring any information it may have replaced.

  - **Style: Text to Box.** This only applies if you create a standalone character mask. If you choose this command while holding down the (Option) [Alt] key, which embeds the character mask in the text box, you can select Edit: **Undo** immediately thereafter.

  - **Item: Group/Ungroup.** Instead of choosing undo, you must select the objects and choose Group or Ungroup again.

  - **Item: Lock/Unlock.** Instead of choosing undo, you must select the objects and choose Lock or Unlock again.

  - **Item: Content.** When you convert one type of box to any other, you cannot reverse the command. This is important to note, because if a box contained information when you converted it, you cannot restore it.

  - **Any Page Menu item.** To reverse the values of one of these commands, you must choose another command and enter the appropriate values. For example, if you inserted an incorrect number of pages using Page: **Insert**, you must remove them using Page: **Delete**.

  - **Any View Menu item.** To reverse the effect of one of these commands, you must choose another one from the same menu. For example, if you mistakenly choose View: **50%**, simply select another item. If you mistakenly open a palette, close it.

  - **Any Utilities Menu item.** To reverse the effect of one of these commands, you must open the same command and make the appropriate changes.

Edit Menu

Edit: Cut
(Command) [Control]-X

This command deletes document information from view while copying it to the Clipboard. Later, you can reapply the information using Edit: **Paste**. This command is only available when a page element is selected or when information in a text box or dialog field is highlighted.

Common Errors

- **Using Edit: Cut instead of Edit: Copy.** Copying leaves the selected information intact; cutting removes it from the document.

- **Cutting the contents of a box instead of the entire box, or vice versa.** Depending on the information you want to cut, the appropriate tool must be active. When the Content Tool is active, you can only cut the contents of a selected box. When any other tool is selected, you can cut the entire box, contents included.

Special Notes

Choosing this command is exactly the same as choosing Edit: **Copy** and then pressing the delete key.

See Also

Edit: **Copy**
Edit: **Paste**
Edit: **Show/Hide Clipboard**

Edit: Copy
(Command) [Control]-C

This command saves document information to the Clipboard, a section of "short-term" memory that applications use as an invisible holding area. After copying, you can apply that information to the same document or a different document using Edit: **Paste**. Although this command is called copy, that term only applies to the act of copying to the Clipboard. To actually create a copy of the selected page information on-screen, you must select Edit: **Paste** after using this command.

Unlike Edit: **Cut**, copied information is not removed from the page.

Common Errors

Copying the contents of a box instead of the entire box, or vice versa. Depending on the information you want to copy, the appropriate tool must be active. When the Content Tool is active, you can only copy the contents of a selected box. When any other tool is selected, you can copy the entire box, contents included.

Special Notes

- When placing copied information in the same position on a different page, reset the zero coordinates to 0,0 before copying, and take note of the X and Y coordinates of the selected item in the Measurements Palette. This way, you can re-enter the values after pasting, placing the item in the right position.

- When producing multiple copies, use Item: **Step and Repeat**. This allows you to enter a specific number of copies and offset values—but the information is not copied to the Clipboard.

- When copying more than one page element, the Item Tool must be active. Not only will Edit: **Select All** apply to every element on a page, but you will be able to Shift-click multiple items before copying.

See Also

Page Tools: **Item Tool**
Page Tools: **Content Tool**
Edit: **Cut**
Edit: **Paste**
Edit: **Select All**
Item: **Step and Repeat**
View: **Show/Hide Rulers**

Edit: Paste
(Command) [Control]-P

This command places the contents of the Clipboard in the active document.

Common Uses

Refer to Appendix A, *Common Techniques*, for full descriptions of the following:

- Duplicating text boxes, picture boxes, and lines
- Copying highlighted text from one box to another
- Copying text from one document into another
- Copying text from one application to another
- Pasting the contents of a picture box
- Pasting the contents of a page
- Anchoring a picture box in a text box
- Anchoring a text box in another text box

Common Errors

Pasting graphics copied from other applications. Although XPress does not support dragging and dropping from other graphics applications, it does allow you to copy information in one program (such as Photoshop or Illustrator) and paste it into a picture box. The problem is that any graphic copied from another program can

Edit Menu

only be pasted as a low-resolution preview. No link is made between the document and the original graphic file, nor can one be made using Utilities: **Usage**. Instead of copying and pasting, save the original graphic, and import it using File: **Get Picture**.

Attempting to paste the contents of one box type into another. You cannot paste text into a picture box, nor a graphic into a text box. If you wish to *anchor* the contents of a box into an existing text box, you must copy and paste the entire box, not just the contents.

Special Notes

- When copy/pasting text from one document to another, any style sheets applied to the copied text are automatically added to the second document. When pasting text from another application, no style sheets are retained—instead, XPress applies the setting currently selected in the Style Sheets Palette.

- When copy/pasting a graphic from one document to another, its status in the Utilities: **Usage** dialog is maintained.

- If the Item Tool is active when you paste multiple items, the items remain selected. This is particularly useful if you must immediately enter page coordinates in the Measurements Palette to reposition the items. If any other tool is active, no items are selected after pasting.

See Also

Page Tools: **Item Tool**
File: **Get Picture**
Edit: **Copy**
Edit: **Cut**
Utilities: **Usage**

Edit: Clear

Choosing this command is exactly the same as pressing the (Delete) [**Backspace**] key:

- When the Content Tool is active, you can only clear the contents of a picture box or a range of highlighted text.

- When the Item Tool is active, you can clear any selected box or rule.

Special Notes

- This command is not available if any tool other than the Content or Item Tool is active. Likewise, pressing (Delete) [**Backspace**] in this case has no effect. The only exceptions are tools that draw in polygonal segments, such as the Bézier Text Path and Bézier Picture Box Tools. Here, pressing (Delete) [**Backspace**] removes the most recently placed segment; choosing Edit: **Clear** deletes the entire shape.

- Edit: **Clear** is very similar to Item: **Delete**. Choosing that command, however, removes the entire page element, regardless of the currently active tool.

See Also

Page Tools: **Item Tool**
Page Tools: **Content Tool**
Line Tools: **Bézier Text Path Tool**
Box Tools: **Bézier Picture Box Tool**
Item: **Delete**

Edit: Select All
(Command) [Control]-A

This command automatically selects all possible page information. It's available only in two situations:

- When a text box is selected and the Content Tool is active. Here, choosing this command highlights all the text in a box or chain of linked boxes.

- When the Item Tool is active. Here, choosing this command selects all the boxes and rules on the currently active page.

Special Notes

When the Item Tool is active, Edit: **Select All** works under the following conditions:

- When the active page is one of two facing pages, this command selects the items of both pages.

- In XPress, the active page is the topmost page visible on-screen. If you have scrolled vertically until the dividing line between pages is visible, this command only selects the items on the upper page.

Edit Menu

Publish and Subscribe Overview

Available only on the Macintosh platform, Publish and Subscribe allows you to create a dynamic link between XPress and graphics created in outside applications.

Using this feature, multiple users can access (or *subscribe* to) image files made available over a network. When a graphic is updated in the original program, the changes automatically appear in every document containing it.

Publish and Subscribe never caught on, mainly because it appeals to a very specialized use: editing information embedded in documents shared over a network, using a suite of software that supports this feature. Even then, you'd have to be willing to redefine your work habits to accommodate what is, at best, an unnecessarily complex process.

Publish and Subscribe will never impact its intended market—fast-paced print-publishing systems like magazines and newspapers—but it could enjoy a small

---

resurgence on Mac-driven intranet networks. Here, different users within the same company can update text and images used by time-sensitive corporate documents stored on a central server. These documents remain available electronically to the rest of the company, and whenever one is opened, all the new changes are present.

If your work does not specifically call for this feature, ignore it.

Edit: Subscribe To

This command allows you to link to an *edition*, or a file produced by a graphic application's Publish feature. When you subscribe to an edition, which exists separately from the actual graphic file, a low-resolution preview appears in the selected picture box, just as if you imported it using File: **Get Picture**. The difference is that you can use Edit: **Subscriber Options** to automatically update the graphic whenever the original file is edited. Also, more than one user can access and update an edition file over a network.

Common Errors

Deleting the edition or graphic file. When you subscribe to an edition, you create a link to that file, instead of the original graphic file. (You can see this when you open Utilities: **Usage**.) If the link is broken or if either file is deleted, the image will not output successfully. Similarly, if you send a document containing published editions out of house for processing, you must provide the editions *and* the original files.

Special Notes

XPress can only subscribe to EPS or PICT images. Although Photoshop allows you to publish a TIFF, the resulting edition will not be recognized when you choose this command. Avoid using PICT images whenever possible, especially when working with full-color images.

See Also
> File: **Get Picture**
> Edit: **Subscriber Options**

Edit: Subscriber Options

The items in this dialog determine how XPress interacts with a published edition that was imported using Edit: **Subscribe To**.

Special Notes

When the Content Tool is active, double-clicking a picture box opens this dialog, whether or not Publish and Subscribe was used. If desired, you can click Get Edition Now to update the image if it has been edited since you imported it. You gain no advantage by doing this—in fact, the Utilities: **Usage** dialog lets you do the same thing and displays more information about the graphic file.

The Subscriber Options Dialog

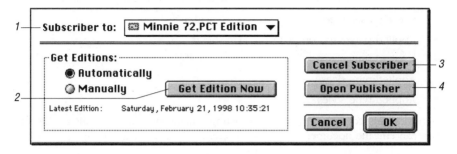

1. **Subscriber To**

   This pop-up displays the name and disk location of the edition.

2. **Get Edition Now**

   Click this button to update the published graphic. When Automatically is selected, XPress updates the image by itself, whenever you make any edits. When Manually is selected, you can only update by clicking Get Edition Now.

3. **Cancel Subscriber**

   Click this button to break the link between the XPress document and the edition.

4. **Open Publisher**

   Click this button to open the published image in the application originally used to create it. If the necessary application isn't already running—and if you have enough RAM—it is launched.

See Also

Edit: **Publish and Subscribe Overview**
Edit: **Subscribe To**
Utilities: **Usage**

Edit: Show/Hide Clipboard

When you choose this command, a small window appears that displays the current contents of the Clipboard. You cannot access or edit this information. To close the window, click its Close button, or choose Edit: **Hide Clipboard**.

Edit: Find/Change
(Command) [Control]-F

Use this command to pinpoint and change the following textual information:

- Specific characters, words, phrases, or sentences
- Applied paragraph or character style sheets
- Applied fonts
- Applied type sizes
- Applied type styles

Choosing this command accesses a floating palette instead of a dialog. This way, you can edit the document directly without having to close anything.

Common Uses

Refer to Appendix A for a full description of how to perform a variable search using the wildcard character.

Common Errors

- **Failing to start a search at the start of a text chain.** When you insert the cursor in a text box, Find/Change begins its search from that point. Unlike spell-checking in a word processing program, however, XPress will not automatically scan the beginning of the text after it gets to the end. To avoid this, do one of two things:
  - Make sure you insert the cursor at the very beginning of the text box or chain.
  - Hold down the (Option) [**Alt**] key to change the Find Next button to read Find First. Clicking this button ensures that XPress starts at the beginning of the story or document.
- **Failing to check the appropriate boxes in the attributes palette.** Because you can change multiple attributes at once, it is important to double-check the settings. Since you cannot undo this command, you would have to attempt to apply the opposite settings to reverse the effect, which is not always possible.

Special Notes

- To search only the contents of a single story, select the text box (or one of the links in a text chain) with the Content Tool. To search the entire document, don't select any text boxes, and check the Document box.
- After entering the appropriate information, click the Resize button in the upper-right corner of the palette to display only the Find and Change buttons.
- If any text flows past the bottom of a text box, this command still works—you simply can't see the items it finds or changes.

- You can enter a series of special characters into this palette, allowing you to include invisible or difficult to target characters in a search:

    – **New paragraph.** Press (Command) [**Control**]-Return, or enter "\p".

    – **New line.** Press (Command-Shift) [**Control-Shift**]-Return, or enter "\n".

    – **Tab space.** Press (Command) [**Control**]-Tab, or enter "\t".

    – **New column.** Press (Command) [**Control**]-Enter, or enter "\c".

    – **New box.** Press (Command-Shift) [**Control-Shift**]-Enter, or enter "\b".

    – **Wildcard.** This character allows you to perform variable searches. (See Appendix A for more information.) Press (Command) [**Control**]-?, or enter "\?".

    – **Backslash.** If you need to affect an actual backslash character, press (Command) [**Control**]-\, or enter "\\".

    The following three items refer to the automatic page number character:

    – Previous text box page number. Press (Command) [**Control**]-2, or enter "\2".

    – **Current text box page number.** Press (Command) [**Control**]-3, or enter "\3".

    – **Next text box page number.** Press (Command) [**Control**]-4, or enter "\4".

The Find/Change Palette (Word Search)

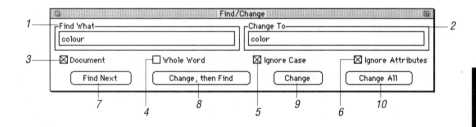

1. **Find What**

    Here, enter the range of text you wish to search for. If desired, you can copy text (including special characters) directly from the document and paste it into this field.

    You can enter a maximum of 80 characters.

2. **Change To**

    The text entered here replaces the text entered in the Find What field. The methods used to perform the replacement depend on the remaining dialog settings. If your intent is only to find text, not replace it, you can ignore this field. (Note that if this field contains no text and you choose a Replace option, you remove all occurrences of the text entered in the Find What field.)

    You can enter a maximum of 80 characters.

3. **Document**

When this box is checked, all document text is included in the search. When unchecked, only the selected text box or chain is included. Although you can uncheck this box when no text boxes are selected, doing so disables all Find and Change buttons.

4. **Whole Word**

When this box is checked, XPress only affects items that match the contents of the Find What field. For example, if you search for the word "mark," XPress only targets instances of that word surrounded by spaces, punctuation marks, or invisible characters.

When unchecked, XPress also affects words that contain the letters entered in the Find What field. For example, if you search for the word "mark," words such as "marksmanship" and "checkmark" are included in the search.

Neither setting fully includes hyphenated words. In this case, only the word entered in the Find What field is affected.

5. **Ignore Case**

When this box is checked, XPress ignores the case of the Find What text when performing the search, affecting all lowercase, uppercase, and initial-cap variations. For example, if you search for the word "box," XPress includes "box," Box," and "BOX." The text used to replace these items is similarly capitalized.

When unchecked, XPress still locates capitalized variations of the Find What text, but only replaces them with the exact contents of the Find What field.

6. **Ignore Attributes**

When this box is checked, XPress pays no attention to any applied typeface, style sheets, type style, or point size. Instead, every occurrence of the Find What text is affected, regardless of its appearance.

When unchecked, the dialog changes to allow you to search and replace specifically formatted text. See the next section, "The Find/Change Palette (Attributes)."

7. **Find Next**

Click this button to locate the next occurrence of the Find What text. It is automatically highlighted, waiting for you to click one of the three Change buttons.

When a text box is selected, XPress begins searching from the position of the flashing cursor. Hold down the (Option) [**Alt**] key to change this button to Find First, allowing you to start searching at the beginning of the selected text box.

When no text box is selected, XPress begins searching at the beginning of the most recently created text box or chain. It then cycles through the remaining stories in the reverse order they were created in.

8. **Change, then Find**

Click this button to replace the currently highlighted Find What text with the contents of the Change To field. XPress automatically highlights the next instance. This option allows you to skip certain items by clicking the Find Next button again.

9. **Change**

Click this button to replace the currently highlighted Find What text with the contents of the Change To field. Instead of finding the next item, XPress disables all the Change buttons, requiring you to either click Find Next again or close the palette.

10. **Change All**

Click this button to replace all instances of the Find What text with the contents of the Change To field. When the Document box is unchecked, only the currently selected text box is affected. When it's checked, this option replaces every occurrence of the Find What text in the document.

The Find/Change Palette (Attributes)

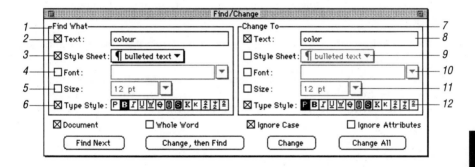

1. **Find What**

Define the formatting attributes you wish to search for in this section. To target an attribute while searching, check its box. To ignore an attribute, leave its box unchecked.

When you check an attribute in this section, you are not required to check the same box in the Change To section. This allows for a wide number of editing variations.

2. **Text**

To search for specific text, check this box, and enter the text in the adjacent field.

If any other Find What boxes are checked, their settings must dovetail with the targeted occurrences of the entered text. For example, if you enter your name in the Text field and check no other boxes, the search targets all occurrences of your name, regardless of formatting. If you check the Size box and set it to 12 pt., the search is limited to your name set in 12 pt. If you also check Font and set it to Helvetica, the search is limited to your name set in 12 pt. Helvetica.

3. **Style Sheet**

To limit the search to a specific style sheet, check this box, and choose it from the pop-up.

The pop-up displays all the style sheets defined in a document, regardless of how many have been applied. If you attempt to search for one that hasn't been applied somewhere, nothing happens.

The No Style item does not appear here. Therefore, you cannot use Find/Change to strip away style sheet information.

4. **Font**

To limit the search to a specific typeface, check this box, and choose it from the pop-up.

This pop-up only displays fonts used somewhere in the document.

5. **Size**

To limit the search to a specific point size, check this box, and enter the desired value.

You can only enter one size at a time. To apply a search to a size range—for example, from 10 to 15 pt.—make sure the remaining settings are correct, and run the search six times: once for each point size.

6. **Type Style**

To limit a search to specific type styles, check this box, and click the appropriate buttons.

By clicking repeatedly, each button can be white, black, or gray. When a button is white, it's *off*, and the style has no impact on the search. When a button is black, it's *on*, and the search only finds text that the style has been applied to. When a button is gray, it acts as a sort of auxiliary style, and is only recognized when any black-button styles have been applied as well. For example:

– If Bold is black, the search is limited to text formatted with the Bold type style.

– If Bold is black and Italic is gray, the search includes text tagged with Bold *and* Bold/Italic, but ignores text formatted only with Italic.

– If Bold and Italic are both black, the search includes only text tagged with Bold/Italic.

– When both items are gray, the search includes all Plain, Bold, Italic, and Bold/Italic text.

These buttons only affect text formatted using the Style: **Type Style** options, whether they were chosen from that menu, the Measurements Palette, or the Define Style Sheet dialog. If you use the actual italic or boldface version of a typeface, this item has no effect on the search.

7. **Change To**

The settings in this section have no impact until you click one of the Change buttons at the bottom of the palette.

To include an attribute in a change, check its box. To leave an attribute untouched, leave its box unchecked.

8. **Text**

When this box is checked, the text entered in this field replaces whatever items are highlighted by the search.

Most often, this option is used to replace text entered in the Find What text field. However, if that box is unchecked and this one is checked, you may be surprised by the results. For example, assume you entered your name in this field and unchecked the Find What text box. If you search for only a particular style sheet, then *all text* the style sheet is applied to is replaced with your name. If you search for a particular font, then *all occurrences* of that font are replaced with your name, and so on.

9. **Style Sheet**

When this box is checked, the chosen style sheet is applied to whatever items are highlighted by the search.

This is particularly useful for changing the formatting of a specific word or phrase, such as a product or company name, throughout an entire document.

10. **Font**

When this box is checked, the chosen font is applied to whatever items are highlighted by the search.

Unlike the Find What font pop-up, this one displays all fonts currently available to your system.

11. **Size**

When this box is checked, the set point size is applied to whatever items are highlighted by the search.

12. **Type Style**

When this box is checked, the selected type styles are applied to whatever items are highlighted by the search.

Like the Find What option, each style can be white, black, or gray—but the results are different:

– When a button is black, that style is applied to the search items, regardless of any previously applied styles.

– When a button is white, that style is stripped away from any of the search items it has been applied to.

– When a button is gray, any occurrences of that style are left alone.

Edit Menu

Edit: Preferences

Every major graphics application has a vast and complex interface. Because the program has so many variables and so many different uses, certain elements can be altered to better suit your working environment. These are called *preferences* and can be changed on the fly whenever XPress is open.

These preferences are stored in the XPress Preferences file, located in the Quark-XPress application folder. To reset all the Preferences at once, delete the file, and let XPress create a new one the next time the program is launched. Also, if the program begins acting inconsistently—certain values keep resetting or the program periodically quits—deleting the preferences file often solves the problem.

Edit: Preferences: Application
(Option-Command-Shift) [Alt-Control-Shift]-Y

Preferences found in the following four panels only affect your XPress application—the information is not built into any document. Therefore, if you move a document from one workstation to another, none of these settings automatically carry over.

The Display Panel

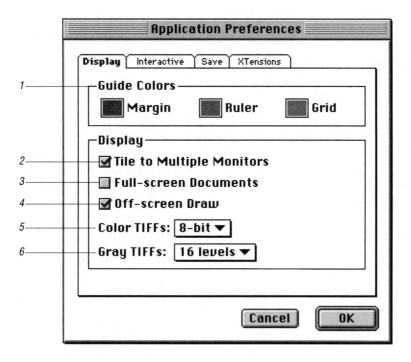

1. **Guide Colors**

   These swatches determine the on-screen color of margin guides, ruler guides, and the baseline grid. To change a color, click the appropriate swatch, and set a value in the color wheel that appears. Change these colors only when they visually conflict with any colored page information.

2. **Tile to Multiple Monitors**

   On a Macintosh configured with more than one monitor, this option allows XPress to expand a document to cover all available screen area. If you only have one monitor, this option has no effect.

3. **Full-screen Documents**

   When this item is checked, clicking the resize box in the upper right of the document window enlarges the window to fill all the available screen space. When unchecked, about a half inch of space is left between the edge of the screen and the left and bottom edges of the window.

4. **Off-screen Draw**

   When checked, this option continually redraws images positioned off-screen—as you scroll, graphics appear to redraw all at once. When unchecked, graphics redraw one at a time. On faster systems, you can barely discern between the two settings. On slower systems, the difference is purely aesthetic—there is no speed gain either way.

5. **Color TIFFs**

   This item determines the on-screen image quality of imported color TIFFs—it does not impact the actual image file or printing. When setting a value, it's a choice between faster redraw times with lower image quality (a lower bit depth), and slower redraw times with higher on-screen image quality (a higher bit depth).

   Changing this setting has no effect on images already present in a document. It only affects images imported from that point on.

   Any images imported with 16-bit or 32-bit previews cannot be edited with the Style Menu commands.

6. **Gray TIFFs**

   This item determines the on-screen image quality of imported Grayscale TIFFs—it does not impact the actual image file or printing. Choosing 16 Colors results in images that refresh more quickly on-screen, while choosing 256 colors results in halftones that nearly match the actual image quality. Users of fast workstations will notice little speed difference between the two settings.

   Changing this setting has no effect on TIFFs already present in a document. It only affects images imported from that point on.

Edit Menu

The Interactive Panel

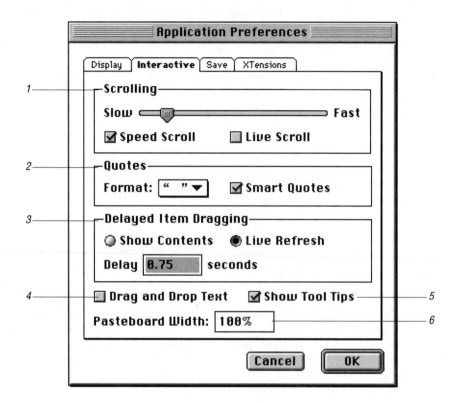

1. **Scrolling**

   These preferences apply to the scroll bars on the right and bottom edge of an XPress document window.

   Slow/Fast

   This slider determines the scroll speed when using the scroll arrows to navigate a document.

   Speed Scroll

   This option grays out images that suddenly appear on-screen during scrolling. Images are redrawn only when scrolling stops, allowing you to proceed more quickly. Otherwise, XPress attempts to redraw images as you scroll, significantly slowing the process.

   Live Scroll

   This option allows you to dynamically scroll through a document by grabbing and moving the page boxes in the scroll bars. Otherwise, you must drag and release the page box before XPress completes the scroll. Access Live Scroll temporarily by (Option) [**Alt**]-dragging the page box.

2. **Quotes**

When the Smart Quotes box is checked, XPress converts any manually entered quote marks to the style set in the Format pop-up. There, you can choose from American, Spanish, and French quotes. Also, imported straight quotes are converted to the item set in the Format pop-up.

3. **Delayed Item Dragging**

When you quickly grab and drag a picture box with the Item Tool, you only see the shape of the box. Delayed item dragging involves holding down the mouse button for a moment before moving the item—this way, you can see the contents of the box as you move it.

Show Contents

This option refreshes the contents of the box less frequently. On one hand, this results in annoying on-screen flickering. On the other, the box can be moved smoothly and consistently, with no jumps or skips.

Live Refresh

This option refreshes the contents of the box you move much more frequently. On one hand, you can see the image in all its detail as you reposition the box. On the other, you cannot move the box smoothly— the demands placed on XPress' memory only allow for the box to move in staggered jumps, making it difficult to work with precision.

Delay (.1 to 5)

This value determines how long you have to hold the mouse button before you can use delayed item dragging. It defaults to .75 seconds, which means you must wait for three quarters of a second before you can see the contents while dragging.

4. **Drag and Drop Text**

This option allows you to reposition a range of highlighted text. Once you select a range, position the cursor over the highlighted area, hold down the mouse button, and drag. An insertion point moves throughout the existing text, indicating the new position of the highlighted text once you release the mouse button.

To copy text instead of moving it, hold down the Shift key as you drag.

You can only drag and drop within a single text box or text chain.

5. **Show Tool Tips**

This option displays the name of a tool whenever the cursor is positioned over an item in the Tool Palette.

6. **Pasteboard Width** (0 to 100%)

The *pasteboard* is the blank work area surrounding a single page or set of facing pages. This option allows you to shrink the overall width, or the area to the right and left of the pages (you can't affect the area above or below). For example, if you enter 75%, the pasteboard area is reduced by 25%.

You can't enter a value over 100% to expand the pasteboard—that requires an XTension such as *PasteboardXT*, from Markzware.

Edit Menu

The Save Panel

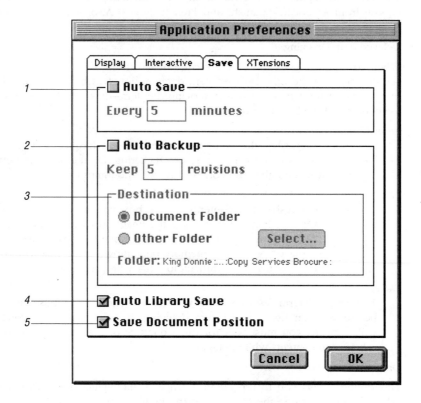

1. **Auto Save** (.25 to 10,000 minutes)

   This feature automatically saves the active document at the specified period of time. Instead of simply triggering File: **Save**, Auto Save creates a temporary duplicate file, placing it in the same folder as the original document. As long as you work without saving, XPress continually updates the Auto Save file instead of the actual document. As soon as you manually choose File: **Save**, the Auto Save file is discarded, and XPress creates a new one.

   This command only kicks in if any edits have been made since the last Auto Save. If a document sits open and untouched, nothing happens.

   To revert a document back to the contents of the Auto Save file instead of the last saved version of a document, hold down the (Option) [Alt] key while choosing File: **Revert to Saved**.

2. **Auto Backup** (1 to 100)

   This feature automatically saves additional copies of the open document. When you choose File: **Save**, XPress first saves the document, then places a copy in the folder targeted by the Destination settings (below). Each one is saved with the same name, with a number tagged at the end—the higher the number, the more recent the backup. Unlike the Auto Save file described previously, these files are not automatically discarded. You must delete them manually.

3. **Destination**

These controls determine the folder that contains the Auto Backup files. When Document Folder is selected, the backups are saved in the same folder as the document they are based on. When Other Folder is selected, you can click the Select button, navigate to your desired folder, and establish that one as the destination.

4. **Auto Library Save**

When this box is unchecked, XPress' libraries are saved only when they are closed. When checked, libraries are saved every time an item is added or a change is made.

5. **Save Document Position**

When this box is checked, XPress remembers the size and on-screen position of a document's window when you open the file again. When unchecked, every document opens in a full or near-full screen window, based on the setting in the Edit: Preferences: Application: **Display** panel.

The XTensions Panel

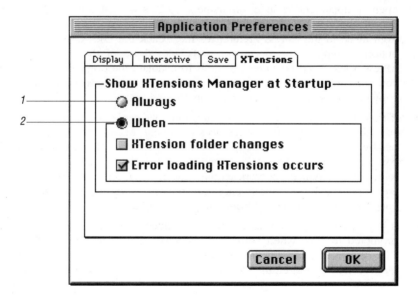

1. **Always**

When this item is selected, the Utilities: **XTensions Manager** dialog appears every time XPress is launched. This allows you to pick and choose the XTensions that will load at startup.

2. **When**

Here, you tell the dialog to open only when it has to: either when XTensions have been added to or removed from the XTensions folder, or when an XTension fails to load correctly.

Edit: Preferences: Document
(Command) [Control]-Y

The preferences in the following five panels can be set in two ways:

- **Default preferences.** Any values changed when no documents are open become the default settings and are automatically applied to each subsequently created document.

- **Document preferences.** If changes are made while a document is open, they affect only that specific document. As soon as the document is closed, the preferences revert back to the default settings. If you find yourself setting and resetting a Document preference, close all documents, and set the preference once more to make it a default.

Special Notes

- Unlike the Application preferences, Document prefs are written into each XPress file. Since these values are often customized by individual users, they're usually inconsistent between copies of XPress. Therefore, when you open a document created on someone else's workstation, a dialog may appear, stating that "Some settings saved with this document are different from those in the XPress Preferences file." Click the Use XPress Preferences button to replace the document prefs with those of the current copy of XPress. Click Keep Document Settings to maintain the original values. Unless you are confident that you need to convert the settings to match the active copy of XPress, always keep the document settings.

- If you work in an environment using multiple copies of XPress, it is often advisable to make all the preferences consistent. Instead of setting these values by hand, focus your attention on one workstation. When the settings are complete, copy the XPress Preferences file into the QuarkXPress application folder on the remaining workstations. The next time those copies of XPress are launched, the new preferences are present. Note that the XPress Preferences file cannot be moved from one platform to another.

- If you open a document and only reset a document preference, you are not prompted to save when you close. However, unless you manually choose File: **Save** before closing the document, the new setting is not remembered the next time you open the file.

The General Panel

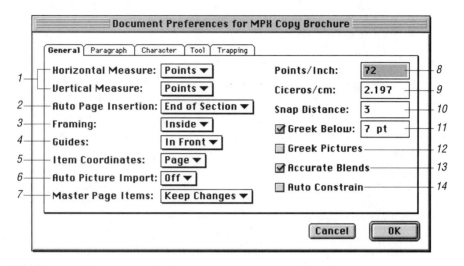

1. **Horizontal and Vertical Measure**

   These pop-ups determine the unit of measurement used by the rulers, the Measurements Palette, and all dialogs. If your work does not call for a specific unit, simply set the one you feel most comfortable with. Choose from Inches, Inches Decimal, Picas, Points, Millimeters, Centimeters, Ciceros, or Agates.

   Ciceros are a European measurement, similar to the picas preferred by the North American and British printing industries. Both are based on points, although the European point is slightly larger (by one one-thousandth of an inch).

   Agates are commonly used by newspapers to measure vertical column length in classified ads. An *agate line* is one column wide by approximately 5.4 points deep.

2. **Auto Page Insertion**

   This pop-up determines the placement of new pages when a large amount of text is imported into an automatic text box. (See "Page: Master Pages" in Chapter 11, *The Page Menu*, for more information.)

   Off

   Here, XPress does not add new pages to accommodate the text. You must manually insert new pages, add text boxes, and perform the necessary linking.

   End of Story

   Here, XPress adds new pages at the end of the active text chain. For example, if a chain runs from page five to page ten, the new pages are inserted following page ten. If master pages are applied, the new pages assume the attributes of the page at the end of the chain.

End of Section

Here, XPress adds new pages after the last page of the current section. If master pages are applied, the new pages assume the attributes of the last page in the section.

End of Document

Here, XPress adds new pages at the end of the document, regardless of its length or number of sections. If master pages are applied, the new pages assume the attributes of the last page in the document.

If a document has only one page, one section, or one story, the last three options result in the same effect.

3. **Framing**

This pop-up determines whether a frame appears on the inside or outside of the picture box edge. Choosing one over the other does not affect the overall width or height of the box—in fact, when Outside is chosen, the picture box shrinks as necessary to maintain the original box dimensions.

The main issue here is trapping. When Inside is chosen, the information inside the box extends all the way underneath the applied frame. For example, if you apply a black frame to a box containing a four-color image, the frame traps the image colors when the file is output and run on-press. When Outside is chosen, the image only extends to the inner edge of the frame, and trapping is not guaranteed. (See "Item: Frame" in Chapter 10, *The Item Menu*, for more information.)

Changing this preference does not affect any frames already applied throughout the document.

4. **Guides**

This pop-up determines the placement of the ruler guides on-screen. When you choose Behind, they appear beneath any existing page elements. When you choose In Front, you can see the guides regardless of any information you have placed on the page. I prefer to keep the guides in front, and press the F7 key to hide and reveal the guides as necessary. (See "View: Show/Hide Guides" in Chapter 12, *The View Menu*, for more information.)

5. **Item Coordinates**

This pop-up determines the display of measurements on the rulers and Measurements Palette. The changes are only apparent when multiple pages are positioned side by side, whether the result of the Facing Pages option in the File: **New** dialog or repositioning pages using the Document Layout Palette. When Page is chosen, the rulers measure each page individually, although repositioning the 0,0 crosshairs on one page automatically repositions them on the other. When Spread is chosen, the multiple pages are treated as one. For example, if you have two letter-sized facing pages, the horizontal ruler extends from 0 to 17 inches, instead of 0 to 8.5, then 0 to 8.5 again. (See "View: Show/Hide Rulers" in Chapter 12 for more information.)

6. **Auto Picture Import**

   This option allows you to automatically reimport modified graphics. When turned off, you must manually select Utilities: **Usage** and update the links from there. When On is chosen, any modified graphics are updated invisibly, with no need to access another dialog, whenever the document is opened. This can be problematic, however—for example, if you edit the size of a graphic and then update the link automatically, you may not notice that it now extends beyond the edge of its picture box. I prefer to check our links manually, at least use the On (verify) option. Here, whenever modified images are detected, an alert appears, asking if you wish to update the items. If you click OK, the Utilities: **Usage** dialog appears, where you manually perform the necessary tasks. (See "Utilities: Usage" in Chapter 13, *The Utilities Menu*, for more information.)

7. **Master Page Items**

   This pop-up determines what happens when you reapply the contents of a master page to a document page using the Document Layout Palette. When Delete Changes is chosen, every master item on the document page is replaced with the contents of the master page, whether or not any of the items have been locally edited. When Keep Changes, the default, is chosen, the locally edited items remain on the document page, and the untouched master items are replaced. (See Chapter 15, *The Document Layout Palette*, for more information.)

8. **Points/Inch** (60 to 80)

   The conventional measurement of a point is a tiny bit bigger than the digital measurement. There are 72.27 points per inch using the traditional method, but for the sake of more intuitive calculations, PostScript-based graphics applications use 72 points per inch. XPress defaults to 72, but if you must change the setting, enter the new value in this field. For example, to make the default point size dovetail with the European Didot system (which uses ciceros instead of picas), enter 67.43 here.

9. **Ciceros/cm** (2 to 3)

   Points that make up a cicero are slightly larger than points that make up a pica. As a result, a cicero is approximately 1 pt. longer than a pica. In an effort to maintain the European measuring standard, XPress defaults to 2.197 ciceros per centimeter. If you must change the setting, enter the new value in this field.

10. **Snap Distance** (1 to 216)

    This item represents the snapping distance of a guide when View: **Snap to Guides** is turned on. The value is measured in *monitor pixels*, as opposed to whatever unit of measurement you have defined. The resolution of most monitors is about 72 pixels per inch, so a snap distance of 6 (the default) is equal to roughly 6 pt., regardless of the current zoom percentage. (See "View: Snap to Guides" in Chapter 12, *The View Menu*, for more information.)

11. **Greek Below** (2 to 720 pt.)

    This option allows you to *greek* text below a certain size, or make it appear on-screen as a series of gray lines. This is particularly useful when a page contains an abundance of small-sized text, which can slow down redraw times considerably. Note that this value pertains to the on-screen size, not the actual point size of the type. For example, if Greek Below is set to 7 pt. (the default), any text set at 6.999 pt. or smaller is grayed out when the current zoom percentage is 100%. When you zoom in to 200%, however, the on-screen type appears larger and is not greeked.

12. **Greek Pictures**

When this box is checked, all imported graphics are *greeked*, or grayed out. This allows for rapid scrolling and document navigation, since XPress does not have to expend any memory redrawing the information. When unchecked, XPress ultimately redraws all the graphic information, based on the settings in the Edit: Preferences: Application: **Display** panel.

When you select a greeked picture with the Item or Content Tool, it temporarily ungreeks, allowing you to view the image.

13. **Accurate Blends**

This setting applies to gradients made with the Blends pop-up of the Color Palette. When unchecked, gradients display less accurately but redraw more quickly. When checked, the on-screen resolution of gradients are increased, resulting in more accurate colors but at the cost of slower redraw times.

14. **Auto Constrain**

When this box is checked, every picture or text box you draw is automatically a constraining item. Any box or line you then draw that fits completely within of one of these boxes cannot be moved beyond its boundaries, just as if you had created a constraining relationship using Item: **Constrain**. (See "Item: Constrain" in Chapter 10 for more information.)

The Paragraph Panel

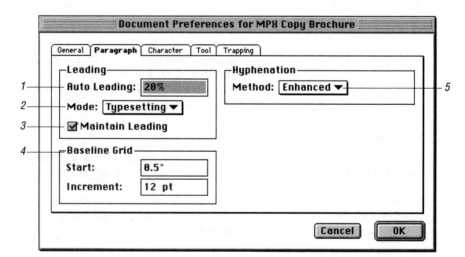

1. **Auto Leading** (1 to 100%)

   This value determines the line spacing of text tagged with a leading value of *auto*. Here, leading is determined by the current point size of the text, plus a specified percentage of that value. For example, if you set type at 100 pt. and the Auto Leading value is 20% (the default), the result leading is 120 pt. Reducing that type to 10 pt. changes the leading to 12 pt. (See "Style: Leading" in Chapter 7, *The Style Menu (Text)*, for more information.)

   Note that the auto leading of a line of text is determined by the largest point size that appears. For example, if a paragraph is set at 12 pt. but a letter or word is set at 24, the line containing the larger characters has a leading of 28.8 pt. (assuming the Auto Leading value is set to 20%). To avoid this, apply a numerical leading value, instead of the *auto* setting.

2. **Mode**

   This pop-up determines the technique used to measure leading. When Word Processing is chosen, XPress measures leading from the tops of capital letters, a method used by many word processing programs. Here, leading is ultimately the result of the cap size, which differs greatly from typeface to typeface. When Typesetting is chosen, XPress measures leading from baseline to baseline. Here, leading remains numerically consistent, regardless of the typeface used.

3. **Maintain Leading**

   This option attempts to maintain consistently aligned baselines within a single text box. It applies primarily to single text boxes divided into multiple columns. For example, if the text of one column is offset by another object containing an Item: **Runaround** value, the lines of text below the object align to the baselines of the neighboring column. This only works if at least one line of text in the column being offset remains above the object.

   When unchecked, the text is offset by the value entered in the Runaround dialog, regardless of the resulting baseline positions.

4. **Baseline Grid**

   These values establish the starting point and spacing of the baseline grid. The Start value determines the amount of space between the top of the page and the first line of the grid. The Increment value determines the spacing between each gridline. (See "View: Show/Hide Baseline Grid" in Chapter 12 for more information.)

5. **Hyphenation Method**

   This pop-up allows you to choose between the different hyphenation standards used by the current and earlier versions of XPress. New documents always default to Expanded, or the set of algorithms used by XPress 4.0. The only time you'll encounter the other options is when you open documents created with XPress 3.3 or earlier. Version 3 used Enhanced, the new method at the time. Versions earlier than 3 used Standard, the very first method built into XPress. When you open one of these documents (and retain the document prefs), the appropriate item appears in this pop-up. To take advantage of the latest hyphenation method, choose it from this pop-up—but be warned that although your text will hyphenate more efficiently, the existing text will probably reflow.

The Character Panel

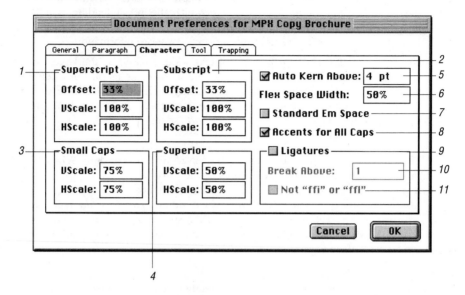

1. **Superscript** (all values: 0 to 100%)

   These values control the offset percentage and scale of any text tagged with the Superscript type style.

   Superscript text is raised from the baseline by a percentage of the established point size, as entered in the Offset field. For example, if you superscript 24 pt. text and the offset value is 33% (the default), the text is raised 8 pt. If the leading is set to auto, however, the superscript text remains in place, while the remaining characters of the line are dropped by the offset percentage. Avoid this by setting a numerical leading value.

   The VScale and HScale values control the vertical and horizontal scaling of the superscript text. When both values are 100% (the default), the character size is not changed when you apply the type style. Many designers prefer to lower the percentages to 75 to 85%, to make the superscript characters more easily discernible against the rest of the text. (See "Style: Type Style: Superscript" in Chapter 7 for more information.)

2. **Subscript** (all values: 0 to 100%)

   These values control the offset percentage and scale of any text tagged with the Subscript type style.

   Subscript text is lowered from the baseline by a percentage of the established point size, as entered in the Offset field. For example, if you subscript 24 pt. text and the offset value is 33% (the default), the text is lowered 8 pt. If the leading is set to auto, however, the subscript text drops by the offset percentage, along with the entire following line. Avoid this by setting a numerical leading value.

The VScale and HScale values control the vertical and horizontal scaling of the subscript text. When both values are 100%, the default, the character size is not changed when you apply the type style. Many designers prefer to lower the percentages to 75 to 85%, to make the subscript characters more easily discernible against the rest of the text. (See "Style: Type Style: Subscript" in Chapter 7 for more information.)

3. **Small Caps** (all values: 0 to 100%)

These values control the vertical and horizontal scaling of lowercase text tagged with the Small Caps type style. When you apply this style, all lower-case letters are changed to capitals and reduced to the percentages entered here. For example, if 24 pt. small cap text is reduced by the default value (75%), lowercase letters appear as 18 pt. If the scale is raised to 85%, lower-case letters appear as 20.4 pt. Many designers prefer a higher horizontal scale—usually 5 to 7%—which results in slightly expanded lowercase small caps. (See "Style: Type Style: Small Caps" in Chapter 7 for more information.)

4. **Superior** (all values: 0 to 100%)

These values control the vertical and horizontal scaling of text tagged with the Superior type style. Regardless of the scale, the offset value of Superior text is the same—the characters are raised from the baseline until they are flush with the tops of the capital letters of that typeface.

5. **Auto Kern Above** (2 to 720 pt.)

When this box is checked, XPress utilizes the kerning information built into each typeface. By entering a value in the accompanying field, you establish a point at which text will not be auto-kerned. This is typically kept at a small point size, because text below 4 or 5 pt. does not benefit from kerning and is not worth the additional processing time it requires to apply the kern pairs. (See "Style: Kerning" in Chapter 7 and "Utilities: Kerning Table Edit" in Chapter 13 for more information.)

6. **Flex Space Width** (1 to 400%)

This value determines the width of a *flex space*, or a special character that acts as a fixed, uneditable distance between two other characters. Its width is based on a percentage of an en space, as it exists at the current point size. The default, 50%, means that a flex space is one half the width of an en space. If desired, enter a value between 1 and 400%.

7. **Standard Em Space**

This option standardizes the XPress em space to the measurement recognized by most word processing and graphics applications. When checked, the width of an em space equals the overall point size. For example, when text is 18 pt., an em space is 18 pt. When unchecked, XPress determines the width of an em space to be the same as two consecutive zeros. Here, the width ulti-mately depends on the typeface, instead of the point size.

Edit Menu

8. **Accents for All Caps**

   When this box is checked, you can add accents to letters tagged with the All Caps style. Also, any lowercase letters containing accents retain them when you apply the type style. When unchecked, you cannot add accents to All Caps text. Also, any existing accents are hidden when you apply the type style. The accents are still there—if you convert back to plain text, they become visible.

   Regardless of whether or not this box is checked, you can add accents to capital letters if the All Caps type style is not applied. (See "Style: Type Style: All Caps" in Chapter 7 for more information.)

9. **Ligatures**

   A ligature is a single type character used to replace two or more letters with conflicting shapes. In XPress, the letters in question are "fi," "fl," "ffi," and "ffl." With many typefaces—especially those containing serifs—the ascender of the letter "f" overlaps the dot of the "i" or the top of the "l," resulting in an awkward artifact. Most typefaces have ligature characters built in, so this problem can be avoided in XPress. When this box is checked, all occurrences of these letter combinations are replaced with the appropriate ligature whenever possible. When unchecked, the individual letters are left alone, and the remaining options are not available.

10. **Break Above** (0 to 100)

    This value determines the tracking value you can apply to a ligature before it splits into its component letters. If the value is 1 (the default), any tracking value above 1 unit splits the letters. If the value is 10, the ligature remains until you apply a tracking value of over 10 units. If desired, enter a value between 0 and 100.

    Avoid setting too high a value here—as you increase the tracking, the spacing between ligature characters does not expand until you exceed the Break Above value.

    Note that this value does not apply to kerning. As soon as you insert the cursor between two ligature characters and increase the kerning, the characters split.

11. **Not "ffi" or "ffl"**

    Check this box to force XPress to ignore all occurrences of "ffi" and "ffl" when automatically inserting ligatures.

The Tool Panel

The following preferences allow you to establish the characteristics of each tool in the Tool Palette. The settings you choose are ultimately based on the needs of your specific work. For a series of recommended preferences for each tool, refer to "Special Notes" in the sections describing the tools in Part I of this book.

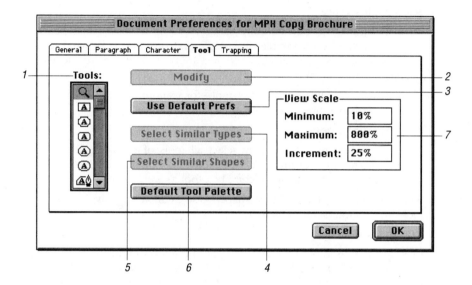

1. **Tools**

   In this scrolling list, select the tool or tools you wish to edit. To select more than one, do one of the following:

   – Hold down the Shift key while clicking to select tools consecutively.

   – (Command) [**Control**]-click to select and deselect tools nonconsecutively.

   – Use the Select Similar Types or Shapes buttons (descriptions follow).

   If any of the remaining panel options do not apply to the currently selected tool, they are rendered unavailable.

   Since the Item and Content Tools have no user-definable settings, they do not appear here.

2. **Modify**

   After selecting a tool, click this button to open the Item: **Modify** dialog, where you set your desired preferences.

   The panels available in the dialog depend on the selected tools—only panels that apply to all selected tools appear. When multiple tools are selected, the first panel is called Group. If the topmost selected tool is a box tool, the

Group panel only offers box preferences, which have no effect on any selected line tools.

If the Zoom Tool is selected in the Tools window—even if other tools are selected as well—the Modify button is not available.

3. **Use Default Prefs**

Click this button to reset the currently selected tool to the original default preferences. To reset all the tool preferences at once, select every tool before clicking Use Default Prefs.

4. **Select Similar Types**

Click this button to automatically select all tools of the same type as the current selection. For example, if a single text box tool is selected, clicking this button selects all remaining text box tools. This allows you to globally establish new prefs for each classification of tools.

If you select two different types of tool—for example, a text box tool and a line tool—this button is not available.

5. **Select Similar Shapes**

Click this button to automatically select all tools of the same shape as the current selection. For example, if the circular text box tool is selected, clicking this button selects the circular picture box tool as well.

If you select two different tool shapes—for example, a polygon and a line tool—this button is not available.

6. **Default Tool Palette**

Click this button to reset the arrangement of the tools in the Tools Palette. For example, if you have chosen a different series of tools from the available flyout palettes, clicking this button resets the palette to the original default.

7. **View Scale**

These values control the magnification range of the Zoom Tool and are only available when the Zoom Tool is selected in the scrolling list. The following options only apply to the act of clicking and (Option) [**Alt**]-clicking with the Zoom Tool—zooming in by dragging with the Zoom Tool is not affected.

Minimum

This value is the lowest percentage you can zoom out to. It defaults to 10% (the lowest possible percentage) and cannot be set higher than the maximum value.

Maximum

This value is the highest percentage you can zoom in to. It defaults to 800% (the highest possible percentage) and cannot be set lower than the minimum value.

Increment

This value determines the increase or decrease in percentage when zooming in or zooming out.

This percentage is an absolute (not relative) value. Assume the Increment value is set to 25% (the default). Clicking with the Zoom Tool simply adds 25 to the current zoom percentage, instead of increasing the percentage by 25% of its current value.

The Trapping Panel

The following preferences determine how XPress automatically traps the colors of a document during output. See Chapter 18, *The Trap Information Palette,* for specific trapping issues and techniques.

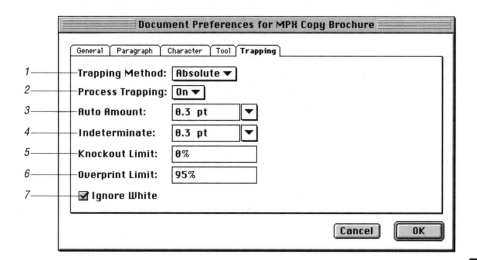

1. **Trapping Method**

   From this pop-up, choose the method used by XPress when applying its automatic trapping values:

   Absolute

   This option applies the trap values entered in the Auto Amount and Indeterminate fields. Object colors are choked or spread based on how light or dark they are in relation to abutting colors. This process is most similar to the techniques used in conventional trapping and is by far the most common choice.

   Proportional

   This option results in more variable (and more difficult to predict) trap values. Essentially, XPress compares the *luminosity,* or brightness, of two neighboring colors and calculates the difference between them. Trap thickness is determined by multiplying that number by the Auto Amount value. For example, if the luminosity of one color is 90%, the other is 30%, and the Auto Amount value is .4 pt., the resulting trap is .24 pt. (.6 × .4 = .24). The basic assumption is that colors differing more widely receive thicker traps, and colors differing less receive thinner traps. Since this does not take actual color content into consideration—not to mention that it's quite difficult to manually calculate luminosity values—it's almost impossible to accurately predict the resulting traps.

Knockout All

This option is the same as turning trapping off. All trapping applied within a document is shut down: the remaining prefs are unavailable, trapping information built into color definitions is ignored, and the Trap Information Palette unchangeably displays all colors as knockouts.

Select this item only when you're positive you want all colors to knock out. For example, some dedicated trapping programs require that no automatic traps be built into the PostScript file generated from a color XPress document. To knock out specific items in a document while trapping others, use the Trap Information Palette.

2. Process Trapping

When this option is turned off, XPress treats each process color as a single component, to be trapped according to its overall lightness or darkness in comparison to a background color.

When turned on, XPress treats the CMYK components of each foreground and background color individually. The manner in which these colors are trapped depends on whether Absolute or Proportional is chosen from the Trapping Method pop-up (see the previous description). This option most often results in smoother process traps, since the chokes and spreads are divided between four separation plates for each trapped color. Unless you receive specific instructions from your printer, leave this option on.

3. Auto Amount (0 to 36 pt.)

This value is the trap width used by XPress' automatic trapping. The default is .144 pt., which is too thin for virtually all methods of on-press reproduction—especially when applied to abutting spot inks. Most presses tolerate between .25 pt. and .5 pt., and certain flexographic print methods can require a width of several points. Many users permanently set this value between .25 pt. and .35 pt., but you should consult with your printer or service bureau before each project is output for optimal values.

This value is only applied to colors or objects not further edited with the Edit: Colors: **Trap Specifications** dialog or Trap Information Palette.

4. Indeterminate (–36 to 36 pt.)

XPress cannot trap the color of a single object with a background of many different (and often conflicting) colors, such as a multicolor blend, imported halftone, or imported full-color image. Instead, it treats these items as one color, called *Indeterminate*. This value behaves the same as Auto Amount and is applied automatically—unless the color of the object receiving the trap has been edited using the Edit: Colors: **Trap Specifications** dialog or Trap Information Palette. Most users set the Auto Amount and the Indeterminate value to the same width.

5. **Knockout Limit** (0 to 100%)

This item sets the cutoff point at which one color may or may not knockout from another. The value is based on a comparison of luminosity values. When it's set to 0% (the default), a color sharing the same luminosity value as the background knocks out. If this value is set to 5%, the tolerance increases: a color with a luminance value with 5% of the background knocks out.

This value only applies to automatic trapping and colors editing using the Edit: Colors: **Trap Specifications** dialog—you can always create manual knockouts using the Trap Information Palette.

6. **Overprint Limit** (0 to 100%)

This item sets the cutoff point at which one color may or may not overprint another. The value is based on a tint percentage. For example, objects colored black always overprint. If the tint of a black object falls below the Overprint Limit, the object cannot overprint—instead, it's trapped using the Auto Amount values. Likewise, if a spot color is set to overprint in the Edit: Colors: **Trap Specifications** dialog, it will not overprint if its tint falls below the Overprint Limit.

This value only applies to automatic trapping and colors editing using the Edit: Colors: **Trap Specifications** dialog—you can always create manual overprints using the Trap Information Palette.

7. **Ignore White**

When this box is checked, the color white (also viewed as the white page background or an area of no ink coverage) is not considered an actual color when automatic trapping is applied. Here, XPress only considers the actual colored background objects when determining trap width.

When unchecked, XPress regards white areas—as well as any other underlying color—as indeterminate and applies the trap width entered in the Indeterminate field.

Edit: Preferences: Index

The following preferences determine the punctuation used by XPress when building an index.

Use the Index Palette to tag words for indexing. To convert those entries to a formatted index, use Utilities: **Build Index**.

Special Notes

• When building an index, XPress uses the index preferences of the currently open document. This can be confusing, especially when indexing multiple book chapters. To establish permanent index prefs, make changes in this dialog with no documents open.

• If you reset these preferences after building an index, you must rebuild the index to see the changes.

The Index Preferences Dialog

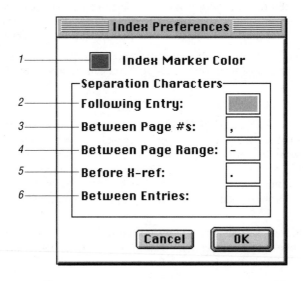

1. **Index Marker Color**

   When adding words to the Index Palette, you must mark them throughout your document or book chapters. Depending on the method used, the marker is either colored brackets or a small, outlined box. By default, the marker color is red—to change the color, click this swatch, and select a new value in the color picker.

2. **Following Entry**

   This item determines the punctuation that immediately follows an index entry. By default, it's a space character, but you should change it to match your required standards.

   For example, the index of this book uses a comma followed by a space. A sample would appear as "EPS graphics, 12, 86–89."

   Another common form is a colon followed by a space. A sample would appear as: "EPS graphics: 12, 86–89."

   Note that when an entry is immediately followed by a cross-reference (no page numbers are listed), the Before X-ref character is used instead.

3. **Between Page #s**

   This item determines the punctuation that separates listed page numbers. By default, it's a comma followed by a space (the most commonly used option).

   For example, in "Enriched black: 220, 290, 350," a comma and space separates each page number. If this value is changed to a semicolon followed by a space, the line would appear as "Enriched black: 220; 290; 350."

4. **Between Page Range**

This item determines the characters used to indicate a range of pages. The most common form is an en dash with no spaces. A sample would appear as: "File Menu: 120–165." A less common form is " to " (note the single space before and after the word). A sample would appear as "File Menu: 120 to 165."

By default, this character is a standard hyphen. However, nearly all typographic standards require that an en dash be used instead. To permanently change this value, close all documents, open the Index Preferences dialog, and enter (Option) [**Alt-Control-Shift**]-hyphen.

5. **Before X-ref**

This item determines the punctuation that immediately precedes a cross-reference. It defaults to a period followed by a space, but other common forms include a semicolon followed by a space, or simply a space.

For example, in "Process inks. See Colors," the cross-reference is preceded by a period and a space.

6. **Between Entries**

In a *run-in* index, which displays an entry and its subentries as a single paragraph, this item determines the punctuation used to separate entries. It defaults to no character, but run-in indexes commonly use a semicolon followed by a space. A sample would appear as: "Spot colors: 180–187; Defining: 181–183; Trapping: 185, 187."

In a *nested* index, which lists all entries and subentries as separate lines, this item determines the ending punctuation of each paragraph. Here, the most common form is no character, which results in no ending punctuation.

See Also

Utilities: **Build Index**
The Index Palette

Edit: Style Sheets
Shift-F11

After you have entered text manually or imported a text file, there are two ways to apply character and paragraph formatting:

- **Format locally.** To format characters or words, highlight a range of text, and choose the desired attributes from the Style Menu or Measurements Palette. To format paragraphs, insert the cursor in the desired paragraph (or highlight a range of paragraphs), and set the desired attributes using the Style (Text): **Alignment**, **Leading**, **Formats**, **Tabs**, and **Rules** dialogs. If a document contains more than just a few words or lines, however, this technique is time-consuming, complex, and often confusing. Every occurrence of text must be manipulated manually, which greatly increases the chances of user error.

- **Define and apply style sheets.** Here, you create a list of predefined character or paragraph attributes. Instead of manually applying individual attributes to format a range of text, you can apply these predefined settings with a simple keystroke or mouse-click. Since all occurrences of a style sheet "read" their information from a single source, you can globally change attributes by editing the style sheet, instead of searching throughout a document for every instance of a particular formatting style. Also, style sheets ensure that a multi-page document is consistently formatted, regardless of how many specific attributes are involved.

This command is only used to create new or edit existing style sheets. Once defined, any style sheet can be applied in three ways: by a keyboard shortcut (as established in the Edit Style dialog), from the Style Menu (Style (Text): **Character Style Sheet** or **Paragraph Style Sheet**), or from the Style Sheets Palette.

For more information on applying style sheets, see Chapter 16, *The Style Sheets Palette.*

Common Uses

Creating the basis for quickly formatting repetitive text-based page elements. These commonly include: variably sized heads (A-heads, B-heads, C-heads, etc.), body text, pull quotes, sidebars, page headers and footers, page numbers, captions, and photo credits.

Refer to Appendix A for full descriptions of the following:

- Formatting run-in heads
- Formatting a series of "Based On" styles
- Deleting an existing style sheet
- Replacing all occurrences of an existing style sheet
- Appending style sheets from an existing XPress document
- Appending style sheets from a Microsoft Word document

Common Errors

- **Using the Normal style sheet.** This style sheet is simply XPress' default font, or the typeface that automatically appears when you begin typing in a text box. It's not suitable for use throughout a document, especially when other style sheets are in use. When a document is opened in another copy of XPress, it's too easy to replace the Normal style sheet of the document with the one defined in the program—which changes all occurrences of Normal-formatted text. Avoid this problem by avoiding the Normal style. Define a new style sheet instead.

- **Combining local formatting with applied style sheets.** Once you begin defining style sheets, take the time to define them for *all* occurrences of text throughout the document. For example, if you add a new repeating page element after defining your styles—a master page header, for example—resist the temptation to duck in and locally format the new item. Either apply an existing style sheet or define a new one.

- **"Tweaking" text on-screen, instead of editing the style sheet.** As you construct a document, you'll probably want to make incremental changes to the text. Although the most intuitive way to determine these changes is to apply them locally to an on-screen sample, it's important to note that locally changing style sheet–formatted text does not affect the original definition. Once you have figured out the new settings, you must return to Edit: **Style Sheets** and redefine the appropriate items.

- **Defining a style sheet with type styles instead of actual typefaces.** Whenever possible, avoid using the Type Style buttons when defining the character attributes of a style sheet. For example, when creating an italic style, select the italicized member of the desired font family instead of clicking the "I" type style. This way, if the appropriate font is not supplied to the person outputting the file, they receive a prompt before printing. Otherwise, all occurrences of the italic style could be replaced with plain text with no warning. (See "Style: Type Style" in Chapter 7 for more information.)

- **Mistakenly choosing New in the Style Sheet dialog when updating a paragraph style.** When editing an existing style, you still have the option of clicking the New button to update the character attributes. This does update the settings, but doing so creates an additional character style sheet based on the paragraph style settings. On its own, this causes no real problem. When you append the styles from another document, however, you end up with a series of unnecessary character styles, which may conflict with the current document settings. Avoid this by clicking the Edit button when updating a style sheet.

Special Notes

- You can define a style sheet by locally formatting a range of text and choosing Edit: **Style Sheets** while the cursor is inserted somewhere within it. Once you choose New: **Paragraph** or New: Character, all locally defined attributes are listed in the Description field. From there, you can name the style and define any additional settings. Once you close the Style Sheet dialogs, however, note that the style sheet is not automatically applied to your original sample. If necessary, you must apply the style sheet manually.

- Although it doesn't appear in the style sheet definition dialogs, an item called "No Style" is always available when you apply the styles throughout a document. Choosing this item strips away any style sheet tag, while leaving the formatting untouched.

- Beyond this command, there are two additional methods of adding style sheets to a document. First, you can copy them from another XPress document using File: **Append** or the Append button in the Edit: **Style Sheets** dialog. Second, XPress can import styles already defined in a Microsoft Word file. (See "File: Get Text" in Chapter 5 for more information.)

- Any style sheets you define with no documents open become XPress defaults and are available in the Style Sheets Palette of all subsequently created documents. When you define style sheets with a document open, they are only available in that particular document.

The Style Sheets Dialog

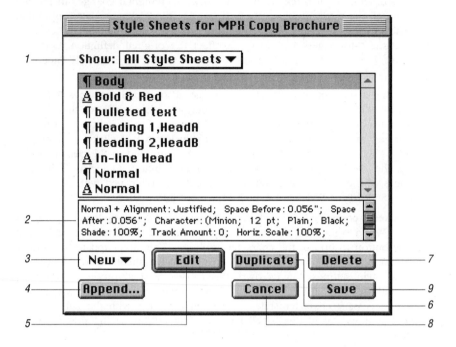

1. **Show**

   This pop-up controls the style sheets that appear in the underlying list:

   — *All Style Sheets* displays every single style sheet defined in the document.

   — *Paragraph Style Sheets* displays every paragraph style defined in the document.

   — *Character Styles* displays every character style sheet defined in the document.

   — *Style Sheets In Use* displays only the paragraph and character styles currently applied somewhere in the document.

   — *Style Sheets Not Used* displays only the paragraph and character styles not applied somewhere in the document.

2. **Style Description**

   This scrolling field displays the attributes of the style sheet currently selected in the above list.

3. **New**

   Click this button, and choose an item from the resulting pop-up to create a new style sheet. Choosing Paragraph opens the Edit Paragraph Style Sheet dialog. Choosing Character opens the Edit Character Style Sheet dialog.

   Double-click this button to open the Edit Paragraph Style Sheet dialog.

4. **Append**

   Click this button to copy style sheets from a saved XPress document. This option is exactly the same as using File: **Append**, only instead of letting you access colors and H&Js as well, you can only access style sheets. (See File: **Append** for more information.)

5. **Edit**

   Click this button to edit the contents of the currently selected style sheet. The appropriate Edit dialog appears, where you change the original style sheet attributes. From there, you can select and edit additional style sheets, or click Save to close the dialog and apply the changes throughout the document.

6. **Duplicate**

   Click this button to produce a copy of the currently selected style sheet. The name of the new style is the original title with "copy" tagged at the end. XPress automatically opens the appropriate Edit dialog, allowing you to immediately make changes.

7. **Delete**

   Click this button to remove the currently selected style sheet. If it hasn't been applied in the document, it simply disappears. If it has been applied, an alert appears, asking "OK to delete this style sheet and replace it with another style sheet wherever it is used?" From the Replace With pop-up, you can choose another defined style sheet or No Style.

8. **Cancel**

   Click this button to close the Style Sheets dialog and ignore any additions or edits.

9. **Save**

   Click this button to save all changes to the style sheets list, close the dialog, and apply any changes throughout the document.

   The Edit Paragraph Style Dialog

Edit Menu

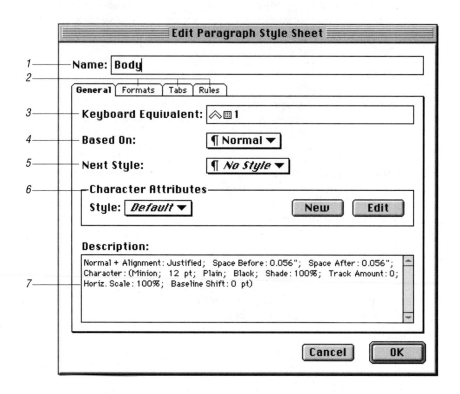

1. **Name**

   When defining a new style sheet, enter its name in this field. "New Style Sheet" initially appears here, but it automatically highlights, allowing you to simply type the new name without manually selecting anything. When editing an existing style sheet, its name appears in this field. If desired, change it.

2. **Panel Tabs**

   You must flip through the Formats, Tabs, and Rules panels when defining style sheet attributes. These panels contain the same information as the Style: **Formats, Tabs,** and **Rules** dialogs. Refer to those items for more specific information. Descriptions of the items on the General panel follow.

3. **Keyboard Equivalent**

   To define a style sheet shortcut, insert the cursor in this field, and apply the desired keystroke. Use the numeric keypad or the F keys (if you have an extended keyboard). Press a single key, or use a combination of the Control/ Option/Command/Shift keys (for Mac), or the Alt/Control/Shift keys (for Windows). For example, if you simply press the F1 key, "F1" appears in the field. If you press (Option-Command) [**Alt-Control**]-F1, the appropriate symbols appear. Pressing the defined key combination while editing text applies the style sheet.

Although many users define single key equivalents, use multiple key combinations whenever possible. While editing text, single key equivalents override any F key commands built into XPress. If you use single numeric keypad equivalents, you cannot use those keys to type numbers.

4. **Based On**

This pop-up displays all currently defined style sheets, plus No Style (the default). Choosing an item here does two things: the attributes of the current style sheet are set to match the base style, and a dynamic link is formed between the two style sheets.

This option allows you to create and control many variations of a single style sheet. For example, if your document contains A-heads, B-heads, and C-heads, chances are they share the same typeface, leading, space before or space after, and other values—the major difference is the point size. Here, you can define the A-head style first, then choose it from the Based On pop-up when defining the remaining two styles. If you later need to change the typeface used by all three head styles, change only the A-head style—the change is automatically applied to the B-head and C-head styles.

Editing the base style affects the linked styles in one of two ways:

– **Shared settings are globally changed**. For example, if the A-head style mentioned shares the same color as the linked styles, changing it also changes the color of the B-head and C-head styles. If only the A-head and B-head styles share the same color, the B-head color changes, and the C-head is untouched.

– **Unshared settings are not globally changed**. If you change a setting in the base style that is different from the linked styles, then only the base style is changed. For example, if you change the point size of the A-head, the B-head and C-head style sheets are not affected.

If you choose an item from the Based On pop-up *after* you define a series of character attributes, they are completely replaced with the settings of the Based On style. As long as you make no additional edits, you can choose (Command) [**Control**]-Z to undo, if necessary.

5. **Next Style**

This pop-up determines the style sheet applied when you create the next paragraph, as you enter text manually. This option has no effect when you apply the style sheet to an existing range of text.

For example, you might set the Next Style for an A-head style sheet to a body text style. This way, after you set the A-head style and type the A-head text, pressing Return automatically shifts the style sheet of the next paragraph to the body text style sheet.

This pop-up displays all currently defined style sheets, but it defaults to Self, meaning that the style sheet remains active as you create new paragraphs.

Edit Menu

6. **Character Attributes**

Each paragraph style sheet contains a built-in character style sheet. This information determines the character attributes of any text receiving a paragraph style sheet.

Style

This pop-up displays all currently defined character style sheets. If one of these contains the character attributes you wish to apply to a paragraph style sheet, choose it. Otherwise, the selected item is Default, and you must set the attributes manually by clicking New or Edit.

New

Click this button to access the Edit Character Style dialog and define the character attributes of the paragraph style. When you use this option, however, XPress creates a new character style sheet in addition to the paragraph style sheet, based on the settings you define.

Edit

Click this button to access the Edit Character Style dialog and define the character attributes of the paragraph style. This option does not result in an additional character style sheet—the settings only apply to the paragraph style.

7. **Description**

This scrolling field displays all the settings of the active paragraph style sheet.

The Edit Character Style Dialog

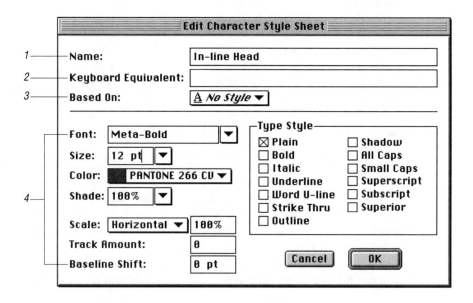

1. **Name**

   When defining a new style sheet, enter its name in this field. "New Style Sheet" initially appears here, but it's automatically highlighted, allowing you to simply type the new name without manually selecting anything. When editing an existing style sheet, its name appears in this field. If desired, change it.

2. **Keyboard Equivalent**

   To define a style sheet shortcut, enter the cursor in this field, and apply the desired keystroke. (This option is described in full in the previous section "The Edit Paragraph Style Dialog.")

3. **Based On**

   This pop-up displays all currently defined character style sheets, plus No Style (the default) and Normal. Choosing a style sheet here does two things: the attributes of the current style sheet are set to match the base style, and a dynamic link is formed between the two style sheets. In the future, when the base style is changed, the linked styles are affected as well. (This option is previously described in full in "The Edit Paragraph Style Dialog.")

4. **Remaining Settings**

   The remaining settings are identical to those found in the Style: **Character** dialog. (See "Style: Character" in Chapter 7 for more information.)

See Also

Page Tools: **Content Tool**
File: **Get Text**
File: **Append**
Style (Text): **Type Style**
Style (Text): **Character**
Style (Text): **Character Style Sheet**
Style (Text): **Formats**
Style (Text): **Tabs**
Style (Text): **Rules**
Style (Text): **Paragraph Style Sheet**
The Style Sheets Palette

Edit Menu

Edit: Colors
Shift-F12

There are five ways to add color definitions to the Colors Palette:

- Import a graphic containing its own color definitions. (See "File: Get Picture" in Chapter 5 for more information.)

- Append colors from an existing XPress document. (See "File: Append" in Chapter 5.)

- Drag a colored item from an XPress library into a new document. (See "File: New: Library" in Chapter 5 for more information.)

- Copy and paste a colored XPress element from one document to another. (See "Edit: Copy" and "Edit: Paste" earlier in this chapter for more information.)

- Define your own colors using the Edit: **Colors** dialogs.

This command is the only place in XPress that gives you complete control over all the variables of a color definition. Defining colors, however, is only the first step in successfully handling color in an XPress document: the second step is applying colors to individual page elements (see Chapter 17, *The Colors Palette*, for more information), and the third is trapping applied colors (see Chapter 18 for more information).

Common Uses

Refer to Appendix A for full descriptions of the following:

- Defining a spot color
- Defining a color based on CMYK components
- Defining a multi-ink color
- Globally replacing an applied color
- Defining a spot varnish

Common Errors

- **Defining a color without referring to a swatch book.** The swatches and color wheels that appear in the Edit Color dialog are half-hearted attempts by XPress to accurately display colors on-screen. The only way to successfully choose a print-destined color is by referring to an actual printed sample. Fortunately, you can purchase printed samples of each color library supported by XPress from the manufacturer or any graphics supply company.

- **Attempting to redefine an imported spot color.** XPress appears to allow you to edit a color imported with EPS artwork. For example, you can choose Edit: **Colors**, select an imported color, and change its name, color content, even its color model. However, doing so results in the graphic outputting to its closest CMYK equivalent—the spot color information is lost, and the color has to be redefined.

- **Misnaming spot colors.** When you choose a spot color from one of the installed libraries, its catalog number—Pantone 185 CV, for example—appears in the Name field. This name also appears in the top left corner of the appropriate film separations when you output a file. By changing the name, you change the name of the resulting seps. If you import graphics containing the same spot color, you could wind up with one spot color divided among two separations. For example, if you define PMS 185 in XPress, change its name to "Red," then import a graphic containing PMS 185, the Colors Palette contains two variations of the same color. All page elements tagged with Red output to seps titled "Red," and the information in the imported graphics output to plates titled "Pantone 185." When using spot colors—particularly when importing graphics—keep all color names the same.

- **Defining colors using inappropriate models.** Although XPress allows you to define colors using upwards of 15 different models, you should make every effort to use only the models that dovetail with your intended printing method. For example, when defining colors for a four-color project, use only the CMYK-based models. Although you can generate CMYK separations from RGB, Lab, or HSB colors, you have no way of accurately predicting the on-press results.

- **Mistakenly adding spot colors to a process-color document.** Adding a spot color to a four-color document results in a fifth color plate during separation. If this is your intention, fine. If you really wanted the closest CMYK equivalent of a spot color, refer to a process-matching swatchbook (such as Pantone ProSim), or at least make sure the Spot Color box is unchecked when you define the color.

- **Mistakenly adding process colors to a spot-color document.** Adding a process color to a one- or two-color document results in CMYK separations during output. When defining spot colors, the Spot Color box must be checked in the Edit Color dialog. Otherwise (with the exception of multi-ink combinations), XPress attempts to produce the closest CMYK equivalent.

Special Notes

- Any colors you define with no documents open become XPress defaults and are available in the Colors Palette of all subsequently created documents. When you define colors with a document open, they are only available in that particular document.

- Although Red, Green, and Blue are default colors, they're not intended for use in an XPress document—they only represent the RGB electron guns used by your monitor to display color. Applying these colors results in additional red, green, or blue plates when the file is separated. To avoid this, open the Edit Color dialog with no documents open, and delete them from the default color list.

- Cyan, Magenta, Yellow, Black, White, and Registration cannot be deleted from the default color list.

- Since Registration appears the same as Black on-screen, it is easy to confuse the two when applying colors. If you apply Registration to a page element, however, the result is 100% coverage of every defined color. For example, applying Registration to a box in a four-color document results in 400% ink coverage—far too much for any printing method. Many users avoid this problem by changing the default on-screen appearance of Registration. With no documents open, choose Edit: **Colors**, double-click Registration, and adjust the color wheel to display a never-used value, such as bright orange or purple. The output values remain the same, but the item is now clearly distinguishable from Black in the Colors Palette.

- To preview how XPress perceives the CMYK percentages of a color library selection, open the Edit Colors dialog, and choose CMYK from the Models pop-up. The values appear in the CMYK fields. If you want to convert a spot

Edit Menu

color to these values, uncheck the Spot Color box, and click OK. To preserve the original definition, click Cancel.

The Colors Dialog

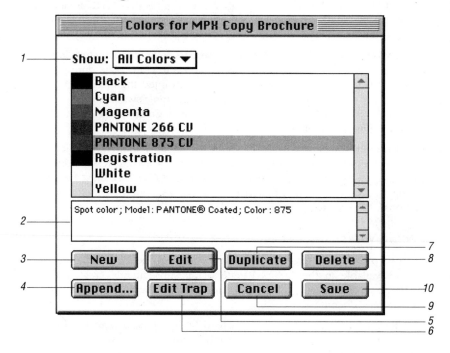

1. Show

This pop-up controls the colors that appear in the underlying list:

— *All Colors* displays every color defined in the document.

— *Spot Colors* displays every color defined with the Spot Colors box checked.

— *Process Colors* displays every color defined with the Spot Colors box unchecked.

— *Multi-Ink Colors* displays color combinations created using the Multi-Ink model.

— *Colors In Use* displays every color currently applied somewhere in the document. When no documents are open, only Black and White appear.

— *Colors Not Used* displays every defined color not applied in the document.

2. Color Description

This scrolling field displays the attributes of the color currently selected in the above list.

3. **New**

   Click this button to open the Edit Color dialog and create a new color.

4. **Append**

   Click this button to copy colors from a saved XPress document. This option is exactly the same as using File: **Append**, only instead of letting you access style sheets and H&Js as well, you can only access colors. (See "File: Append" in Chapter 5 for more information.)

5. **Edit**

   Click this button to open the Edit Color dialog and edit the values of the currently selected color. Afterwards, you can select and edit additional colors, or click Save to close the dialog and apply the changes throughout the document.

6. **Edit Trap**

   Click this button to open the Trap Specifications dialog, where you can build trap behaviors directly into a color definition. (See "The Trap Specifications Dialog" later in this chapter.)

7. **Duplicate**

   Click this button to produce a copy of the currently selected color. The new color name is the original title with "copy" tagged at the end. XPress automatically opens the Edit Color dialog, allowing you to immediately make changes.

8. **Delete**

   Click this button to remove the currently selected color. If it hasn't been applied in the document, it simply disappears. If it has been applied, an alert appears, asking "OK to delete this color and replace it with another color wherever it is used?" From the Replace With pop-up, choose any other defined color. Click OK to replace all occurrences of the deleted color with the selected item.

9. **Cancel**

   Click this button to close the Colors dialog and ignore any additions or edits.

10. **Save**

    Click this button to save all changes to the color list, close the dialog, and apply any changes throughout the document.

The Edit Color Dialog

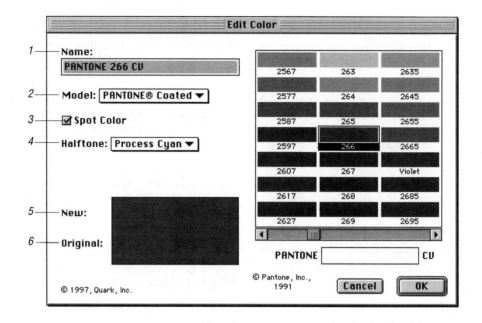

1. **Name**

   This field displays the name of the active color:

   - When you first click the New button in the Edit Color dialog, "New Color" appears here, but the field automatically highlights, allowing you to immediately enter a new name.

   - When you select a color from one of the supported libraries, its name automatically appears here.

   - When defining a process color, you can name it as descriptively as necessary. Since every process variation—including colors selected from process libraries—separates to CMYK plates, changing the color name poses no threat of improper output. Note that many users name process colors by their CMYK components (for example, "50C, 75M, 10Y").

2. **Model**

   From this pop-up, choose the appropriate model for the color you wish to define. Each item uses its own tools and fields to establish the desired values.

   If desired, you can remove unwanted items from this pop-up by removing the appropriate files from the Color folder, inside the QuarkXPress application folder.

RGB (0 to 100%)

Here, you define a color based on red, blue, and green—the colors used by electronic displays such as computer monitors and video screens.

Unlike Photoshop, which uses brightness values (incremental numbers from 0 to 255) to display RGB color, the sliders only allow you to work with light intensity, or percentages from 0 to 100. A value of 0% Red, for example, removes all red information from the color, while a value of 100% displays red at full intensity. Or create a color by clicking on the color wheel to specify a hue and dragging the vertical slider to increase or decrease its overall brightness. As you do so, the sliders and fields display the changes.

To convert Photoshop's brightness values to XPress percentages, divide the value by 256 (for example, 128 ÷ 256 = .5, or 50%). To convert XPress percentages to brightness values, multiply the percentage by 2.56 (for example, 50 × 2.56 = 128).

Avoid this model when specifying a color for print.

HSB (H: 0° to 360°, S: 0 to 100%, B: 0% to 100%)

Here, you define a color based on *hue, saturation,* and *brightness,* a method familiar to any artist who has ever mixed paint.

Hue is the actual color, such as purple, green, or brown. This value is measured in degrees, which determines the color's position around the HSB color wheel. If the color point is in the precise center of the wheel, changing this value has no effect.

Saturation is color intensity. For example, the difference between a soft, pastel pink and a vivid Hi-Liter is the amount of saturation. This value is measured in percentages. A value of 0% *desaturates*, or reduces a hue to its closest gray value. A value of 100% creates the most vivid hue possible, as limited by the brightness setting.

Brightness is overall lightness or darkness of a color. This value is also measured in percentages. A value of 0% reduces any hue to black, the darkest value possible. A value of 100% creates the brightest hue possible, as limited by the saturation setting.

Avoid this model when specifying a color for print.

LAB (L: 0 to 100%, A: −120 to 120, B: −120 to 120)

Here, you define a color using a device-independent model created by the *Commission Internationale d'Eclairage* (or, *CIE*—this model is often referred to as *CIE Lab*).

The L channel represents lightness, or how bright a color is. Values range from 0, which is black, to 100, which is the full intensity of the color.

Ordinarily, "a" represents colors between green and magenta, which oppose each other on the color wheel. Similarly, "b" represents colors between blue and yellow. XPress, however, has its own unique interpretation of the values, and the a and b controls make no intuitive sense. For example, manipulating the a and b sliders can affect color lightness (even though the Lightness value itself is unchanged), which theoretically remains constant unless edited directly. Because of these inconsistencies, Lab values from other programs (such as Photoshop) result in totally different colors when entered in XPress. Also, XPress CMYK to Lab/Lab to CMYK conversions differ considerably from the conversions of other applications.

Avoid this model when specifying a color for print.

CMYK (0 to 100%)

Here, you define a color by entering percentages for cyan, magenta, yellow, and black directly into the corresponding fields. Avoid the color wheel altogether, since you cannot estimate the printed appearance of a process color using on-screen tools.

Use this model only when you are certain of the necessary values. Otherwise, you'll have more success using one of the process color libraries—such as Pantone Process or TRUMATCH—which allow you to choose colors based on actual printed samples.

Multi-Ink

Here, you a create a new color by combining tints of existing colors.

To combine colors, select an ink from the available list. Select a percentage from the Shade pop-up. Select the next ink, and define its desired shade. When you close the Edit Color dialog, the combination appears in the color list as one item consisting of multiple ink values.

The Process Inks pop-up contains two items: CMYK (the default) and Hexachrome. With CMYK, the standard process inks appear in the list below. Select Hexachrome only when combining inks based on Pantone's high-fidelity color system.

Using this option to combine process inks is exactly the same as defining a color using the CMYK model. In fact, you can create a color more quickly using that model than creating a multi-ink combination.

When combining spot colors (or a spot color with a process color), don't be confused by the fact that the Spot Color box is unchecked and unavailable. This model remembers the original color definitions—if a spot color is defined as such, it behaves that way when part of a multi-ink color.

PANTONE Coated

Here, you can choose a predefined color from the Pantone Color Formula Guide 1000, the industry standard spot ink system.

Although this model claims to be geared for coated paper stock, the primary difference between this and its Uncoated counterpart are the initials at the end of the color name (this option uses "CV" instead of "CVU"). Since most graphics applications now use the "CV" naming convention, most users choose this option regardless of whether they print to coated or uncoated stock. Also, these colors display slightly darker on-screen in an attempt to simulate their actual printed appearance.

When choosing one of these inks, the Spot Color box must be checked. Otherwise, XPress outputs the closest CMYK equivalent.

TOYO

This process library is rarely used outside Japan.

DIC

Short for *Dainippon Ink and Chemicals, Inc.*, this is another Japanese color system.

TRUMATCH

This is a highly organized library of over 2,000 CMYK colors. Here, the range of printable color is divided into 50 different hues, each with 40 tints. This allows a designer to choose a lighter or darker version of a color with a minimal shift in color cast.

FOCOLTONE

From the United Kingdom, this library contains 763 CMYK combinations selected for their ability to form a *process bridge*, or share enough color components to reduce the need for trapping.

PANTONE Process

This library contains over 3,000 CMYK combinations.

PANTONE ProSim

Short for *Process Simulation*, this library shows the printed effect of converting Pantone's spot color library to CMYK. This way, you can determine how closely a spot color's CMYK equivalent matches the actual ink.

PANTONE Uncoated

This library contains the same colors as PANTONE Coated, but the letters CVU are added after the color name. Use this library when the spot colors defined in your imported graphics contain the CVU suffix.

These colors display on-screen less vividly than the Coated library in an attempt to simulate their final printed appearance.

When choosing one of these inks, the Spot Color box must be checked. Otherwise, XPress outputs the closest CMYK equivalent.

Hexachrome Uncoated and Coated

These libraries contain 2,000 predefined high-fidelity color combinations. The only difference between the two is the on-screen appearance of the colors—the Coated selections display slightly darker on-screen in an attempt to simulate their final printed appearance.

Neither Hexachrome model allows you to manually enter percentages for the six inks. To do this, use the multi-ink model, and choose Hexachrome from the Process Inks pop-up.

Edit Menu

3. **Spot Color**

   This box determines whether a color separates to its own plate or into process components during output. When checked, a color is treated as a spot ink, even if you selected it from a process library. When unchecked, the color is based on process inks, even if you selected it from one of the Pantone spot-ink libraries.

   Choosing colors from a spot or process library does not automatically set this box. In fact, once you manually click it, the setting remains until you click it again, regardless of the current model. Therefore, you must double-check this box whenever you define a color.

4. **Halftone**

   This pop-up determines the printed screen angle of a spot ink.

   Here, you can only apply the default angles used for the four process inks. New spot colors default to Process Black, which outputs tinted screens at 45°. Choose Process Cyan to set the angle to 105°, Process Magenta for 75°, Process Yellow for 90°. To set your own custom angle, ignore this pop-up, and reset the value in the Output panel of the File: **Print** dialog. This option has no effect on solid (100%) colors.

   Ordinarily, the screen angle of a spot color matters little. If you're not blending spot inks, leave the pop-up set to Process Black—45° is the most visually neutral angle. When blending spot inks using the multi-ink model, however, identical angles result in halftone dots directly overprinting each other. Although mixing spot inks is nowhere near as predictable (or effective) as mixing process inks, you'll have better luck by setting different screen angles: leave the darkest color set to Process Black, and set the lighter color to Process Cyan.

5. **New**

   This swatch displays the current color and changes to reflect your edits as you choose from a library, manipulate a color wheel, or manually enter values. This color appears on-screen when you apply it throughout a document.

6. **Original**

   When editing an existing color, this swatch displays the original value. As you create your color definitions, you can click this swatch at any time to reset the current value to the original.

The Trap Specifications Dialog

Here, you build trapping commands directly into a color's definition. These traps override the automatic trapping values but can be overridden using the Trap Information Palette.

Access this dialog by selecting the color you wish to edit (from the list in the Edit: **Color** dialog) and clicking the Edit Trap button.

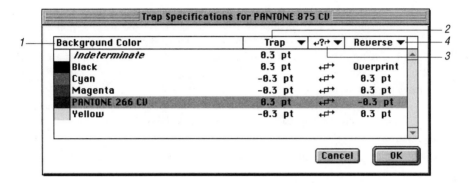

1. **Background Color**

   Here, you re-establish the trapping relationship between the active color and any other currently defined color. For example, if Black is selected in the color list when you open this dialog, you can change the way black elements are trapped when adjacent to specific colors by selecting the colors from this list and adjusting the remaining settings. Although "Background Color" suggests that these traps only take effect when the selected color sits beneath a black element, the —?— and Reverse settings can make the trapping relationships reciprocal (see the descriptions that follow).

   White and Registration do not appear in this list, since these colors cannot be trapped or otherwise adjusted.

2. **Trap**

   In this pop-up, choose from five methods of re-establishing the trap value:

   Default

   With this item set, the results of XPress' automatic trapping preferences display in the underlying list. Positive values indicate a spread; negative values indicate a choke. When you choose a different item, an asterisk appears next to the new value. Choosing Default after setting a new value reverts the color back to the XPress preferences.

   Knockout

   Choosing this item results in no applied trapping whenever the active color is positioned over the background color.

Overprint

Choose this item to force the active color to overprint whenever it overlaps the background color. This option does not override the Overprint
Limit value set in the Edit: Preferences: Document: **Trapping** panel.

Auto Amount (+)

Choosing this item results in a spread, based on the Auto Amount value
set in the Edit: Preferences: Document: **Trapping** panel. If the default trap
is already a spread, this item has no effect. If the default trap is a choke,
it is reversed.

Auto Amount (—)

Choosing this item results in a choke, based on the Auto Amount value
set in the Edit: Preferences: Document: **Trapping** panel. If the default trap
is already a choke, this item has no effect. If the default trap is a spread,
it is reversed.

Custom (–36 to 36 pt.)

Choose this item to manually enter a trapping value. Enter a positive
value to create a spread; enter a negative value to create a choke.

3. —?—

This pop-up determines the relationship between the Trap and Reverse
values:

Dependent Traps

With this item selected, setting a Trap value automatically resets the
Reverse value. Likewise, setting a reverse value automatically resets the
Trap value. When you choose Knockout from one of the pop-ups,
the other value sets to Knockout as well. When you choose Auto Amount
(+) or Auto Amount (–), the other value sets to the opposite amount.
When you enter a Custom value, the other value sets to the opposite
amount.

Choosing Overprint, however, does not automatically set the other value
to Overprint. To establish this relationship, choose Independent Traps
from this pop-up, then choose Overprint from both the Trap and Reverse
pop-ups.

Independent Traps

With this item selected, setting a Trap value has no effect on the Reverse
value. Likewise, setting a Reverse value has no effect on the Trap value.
You must set the pop-ups separately.

4. **Reverse**

Here, you reestablish the trap value whenever the background color is
applied to an element positioned on top of the active color. For example, if
the active color is black and you are editing Pantone 287 CV as the background color, this option allows you to define a new trap value whenever the
foreground element is colored Pantone 287 CV and the background color is
black. Setting a value here simply allows you to avoid opening the Edit Trap
dialog twice for each two-color relationship.

The items in this pop-up are the same as in the Trap pop-up (see the
previous descriptions).

See Also

File: **Append**
File: **Print**
Edit: Preferences: Document: **Trapping**
Style (Picture): **Color**
The Colors Palette
The Trap Information Palette
Photoshop in a Nutshell (Image: **Mode Overview**)
Photoshop in a Nutshell (Image: **Mode**)

Edit: H&Js
(Option-Command) [Alt-Control]-H

This command controls the *hyphenation and justification* settings used by XPress. Although always listed as "H&Js," they are actually two separate functions:

- Hyphenation determines how words break (or hyphenate) at the end of a line. The hyphenation values apply to all text, regardless of the Style (Text): **Alignment** setting.

- Justification controls the spacing between letters and words when Style (Text): Alignment: **Justified** is applied to text.

These settings combine to create a satisfying visual "flow" of words, characters, and spacing throughout columns of text. Inappropriate H&J values result in awkward spacing, such as "rivers" (large gaps between words occurring on several lines in succession), single words stretching across an entire column, or lines too "loose" to read easily.

By default, XPress uses a predefined set of H&J values. This item appears in the H&J list as "Standard" and can be edited, if desired. If you don't define new H&Js, or if you don't set a new H&J item when you define style sheets, the Standard item is automatically applied.

Common Errors

- **Failing to establish H&Js as part of a style sheet definition.** There are two ways to apply H&Js. Insert the cursor in the desired paragraph and choose Style: **Formats,** or set the H&J item as you define your style sheets (in the Formats panel of the Edit: Style Sheets dialog). If you locally apply H&Js, you have no easy way of telling which item is applied to what paragraph. To work with multiple H&Js using the same style sheet settings, create duplicates of the style sheet, reset the H&Js, and add a descriptive word or two to the end of the style sheet name.

- **Manually hyphenating words using the hyphen character.** If you feel a particular word needs to break at the end of a line and XPress' settings fail to make it do so, do not use a "hard" hyphen. Although the word does break and continue on the next line, the hyphen remains inserted in the word if the text reflows. Instead, use a *discretionary hyphen.* Here, if the text flows and the word no longer needs to break, the hyphen disappears. To add a discretionary hyphen, insert the cursor appropriately, and press (Command) [**Control**]-hyphen.

- **Failing to utilize nonbreaking hyphens.** If necessary, XPress breaks a word wherever a standard hyphen exists. Occasionally, you'll want to prevent this from happening. For example, short hyphenated words (such as "hi-fi") and numbers (such as "Figure 5-20") are more easily readable when kept from breaking. Instead of a standard hyphen, use a *nonbreaking hyphen.* Here, the entire hyphenated word is bumped to the next line, instead of breaking on the hyphen. To add a nonbreaking hyphen, press (Command) [**Control**]-=.

Special Notes

- Any H&Js you define with no documents open become XPress defaults and are available in the Style (Text): **Formats** dialogs of all subsequently created documents. When you define or edit H&Js with a document open, they are only available in that particular document.

- Many designers prefer to work with Hyphenation turned off, especially when working with left-justified text. To make this option readily available, create a default H&J called Hyphens Off, and uncheck the Auto Hyphenation box.

- XPress refers to an internal dictionary to decide how to break a particular word. If you use a word not recognized by XPress, it can only use its best guess. When unsatisfied with a word break, add it to XPress' dictionary using Utilities: **Hyphenation Exceptions**.

The H&Js Dialog

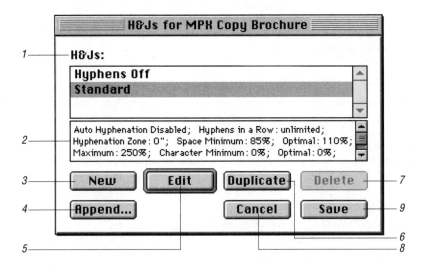

1. **H&Js**

   This scrolling list displays all currently available H&Js, whether they are defaults or document-specific. The Standard item is the XPress default H&J and cannot be deleted.

2. **H&J Description**

   This scrolling field displays the attributes of the H&J currently selected in the above list.

3. **New**

   Click this button to open the Edit Hyphenation and Justification dialog and create a new H&J.

4. **Append**

   Click this button to copy H&Js from a saved XPress document. This option is exactly the same as using File: **Append**, only instead of letting you access style sheets and colors as well, you can only access H&Js. (See "File: Append" in Chapter 5 for more information.)

5. **Edit**

   Click this button to open the Edit Hyphenation and Justification dialog and edit the values of the currently selected H&J. Afterwards, you can select and edit additional H&Js, or click Save to close the dialog and apply the changes throughout the document.

6. **Duplicate**

   Click this button to produce a copy of the currently selected H&J. The new H&J name is the original title with "copy" tagged at the end. XPress automatically opens the Edit Hyphenation and Justification dialog, allowing you to immediately make changes.

7. **Delete**

   Click this button to remove the currently selected H&J. If it hasn't been applied in the document, it simply disappears. If it has been applied, an alert appears, asking "OK to delete this H&J and replace it with another H&J wherever it is used?" From the Replace With pop-up, choose any other defined H&J. Click OK to replace all occurrences of the deleted H&J with the selected item.

8. **Cancel**

   Click this button to close the H&Js dialog and ignore any additions or edits.

9. **Save**

   Click this button to save all changes to the H&Js list, close the dialog, and apply any changes throughout the document.

Edit Menu

The Edit Hyphenation & Justification Dialog

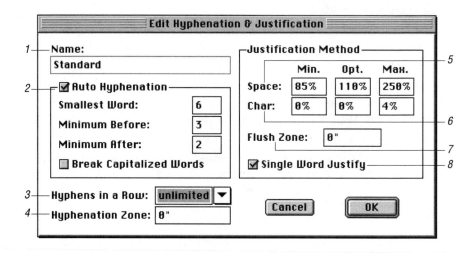

1. **Name**

   When defining a new H&J, enter its name in this field. "New H&J" initially appears here, but it automatically highlights, allowing you to type the new name without manually selecting anything. When editing an existing style sheet, its name appears in this field. If desired, change it.

2. **Auto Hyphenation**

   When this box is checked, XPress hyphenates any text that the H&J is applied to, based on the following values:

   Smallest Word (3 to 20)

   This value determines the minimum number of letters a word can contain and still be hyphenated. The default is 6.

   Minimum Before (1 to 6)

   This value determines the minimum number of letters allowed to exist before an automatic hyphen. The default is 3.

   Minimum After (2 to 8)

   This value determines the minimum number of letters allowed to exist after an automatic hyphen. The default is 2.

   Break Capitalized Words

   When this box is checked, XPress hyphenates words starting with a capital letter, such as names and words at the start of sentences. When unchecked (the default), these words are not hyphenated.

   This option only applies when you capitalize the first letter of a word by holding down the Shift key as you type. Text entered with the Caps Lock key depressed or formatted with Style: Type Style: **All Caps** is not affected.

When Auto Hyphenation is unchecked, this entire feature is turned off, and XPress does not break any words.

3. **Hyphens in a Row** (0 to 7)

This value determines the maximum number of consecutive lines that can end with a hyphen. The default is Unlimited, which imposes no such limit. Typically, the Unlimited option saves the most column space, but at the expense of visual flow. This makes it a common option for frequent publications, such as newspapers. For higher quality publications, many designers reduce this number to 1 or 2, then add any further required hyphens manually (see the "Special Notes" section earlier in this chapter).

The pop-up menu beside this field contains the current value, plus Unlimited. Entering 0 here is the same as choosing Unlimited.

4. **Hyphenation Zone** (0 to column width)

The hyphenation zone is a defined space, measured from the right margin, which allows you to partially limit the occurrence of automatic hyphens. The unit used here is based on the Horizontal Measurement setting in the Edit: Preferences: Document: **General** panel.

For example, assume this value is set to 1 inch. XPress now hyphenates the last word in a line only if one of the following is true:

– The previous word ends before this 1-inch zone. If the previous word falls partially within the zone, the last word is bumped to the next line.

– A point where XPress wants to break the word falls within this zone. If not, the word remains unbroken and bumps to the next line.

5. **Space** (Min: 0 to 500%, Opt: min to max, Max: 85 to 500%)

These values determine the amount of space XPress allows between the words of justified text.

The percentages are based on the standard space width of the applied typeface (created by pressing the spacebar), which vary considerably from font to font. 100% equals the space width built into the typeface.

XPress initially applies the Opt value to word spaces. If the results are insufficient, it adjusts the spaces to fit within the range defined by the Min and Max values. Although spacing may vary from line to line, the same spacing is used on a single line.

For tighter overall spacing, set the Opt value to a lower number, such as 88 to 92%. For looser overall spacing, set this value to a higher number, such as 105 to 115%. To prevent the spaces from becoming awkwardly narrow or wide, keep the Min and Max values at a reasonable range, such as 80% and 150%.

Although XPress never creates a word space below the Min value, it may exceed the Max value if necessary.

6. **Char** (Min: –50 to 100%, Opt: min to max, Max: 0 to 100%)

These values determine the amount of letterspacing allowed by XPress.

That these values appear as percentages is somewhat misleading. Each percentage point is actually the same as a kerning or tracking unit: 1/200 of an em space. However, if Standard Em Space is checked in the Edit: Preferences: Document: **Character** panel, XPress bases its em space value on a percentage of the current point size—and each Char percentage typically results in a slightly smaller space.

XPress initially applies the Opt value. If the results are insufficient, it adjusts the spaces to fit within the range defined by the Min and Max values. Although letterspacing may vary from line to line, the same values are used on a single line.

When any alignment other than Justified is used, XPress only applies the Opt value.

To turn off letterspacing, enter 0% in all three fields. This way, spaces are only applied between words (as defined by the Space values, described previously), instead of characters.

7. **Flush Zone**

This value is similar to the Hyphenation Zone but only applies to the last line in a paragraph. It's a defined space, measured from the right margin, that determines whether the last line is extended to be flush with the right margin (or *force justified*).

If the last word of the last paragraph falls within this space, the line is force justified. If the last word does not, the line is unchanged. The effect is the same as applying Style (Text): Alignment: **Forced** to a paragraph.

8. **Single Word Justify**

When this box is checked, XPress will force-justify any single word falling alone on a single line. This is commonly seen in newspapers. This option does not apply to the last line in a paragraph—here, you must use the Flush Zone or apply Style (Text): Type Style: **Forced**.

When unchecked, single words are left alone and may not extend to the right edge of the column.

Edit: Lists

Use this command to create a list of specific style sheets applied throughout a multipage document. Once created, all lists appear in the Lists Palette. From there, they can be used to compile textual information occurring throughout a document or book—tables of contents, lists of figure titles, and lists of photo captions are good examples.

Lists do little more than copy the written content of text formatted with a specific style sheet. For example, if a style sheet titled "A-Head" is added to a list, this feature tracks all items formatted with that style. When you select the list in the Lists Palette, the text of each A-Head item appears, in the same order as the document text. By creating a new text box and choosing the Build List command, every A-Head item is inserted, along with the appropriate page number, if desired.

Common Errors

- **Adding incorrect style sheets to a list**. List items should only include the style sheets applied to the specific text you want to access. For example, A-Head,

---

B-Head, and C-Head styles are commonly used to create a table of contents. Adding style sheets for body text, however, would defeat the purpose of a TOC.

- **Appending a list containing style sheets with the same name, but different settings.** When you append a list, you also append all the style sheets contained within. If any same-named styles have the same settings, no alert appears, and the style sheet of the current document is used. If any same-named styles have different settings, you have the option of renaming them, using the style of the current document, or using the imported style. Unless you've planned for this ahead of time, you risk replacing one of the style definitions or having redundant styles appear in the list. To avoid this, make sure all same-named styles have identical settings. If not, change the name of one of the styles before appending.

Special Notes

- Any lists you define with no documents open become XPress defaults and are available in all subsequently created documents. When you define or edit lists with a document open, they are only available in that particular document.
- You can add up to 32 different style sheets to a single list. In the Lists Palette, each item can display up to 256 characters.

The Lists Dialog

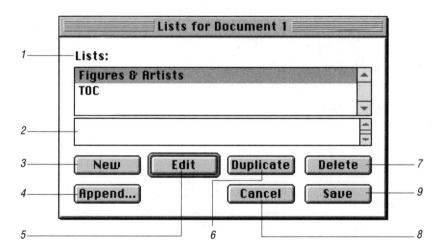

1. **Lists**

   This scrolling list displays all currently available lists, whether they are defaults or document-specific.

2. **List Description**

   This scrolling field displays the style sheets contained in the list currently selected in the above list.

3. **New**

   Click this button to open the Edit List dialog and create a new list.

4. **Append**

   Click this button to copy lists from a saved XPress document. This option is exactly the same as using File: **Append**, only instead of letting you access multiple options, you can only access lists. (See "File: Append" in Chapter 5 for more information.)

5. **Edit**

   Click this button to open the Edit List dialog and edit the content of the currently selected list. Afterwards, you can select and edit additional lists, or click Save to close the dialog and apply the changes throughout the document.

6. **Duplicate**

   Click this button to produce a copy of the currently selected list. The new list name is the original title with "copy" tagged at the end. XPress automatically opens the Edit List dialog, allowing you to immediately make changes.

7. **Delete**

   Click this button to remove the currently selected list. No alert appears, even if the list has been accessed by the Lists Palette. When you click Save, the information is simply no longer available.

   When you delete a list originally appended from another document, the imported style sheets remain in the current document. If necessary, open Edit: **Style Sheets**, and delete them there.

8. **Cancel**

   Click this button to close the Lists dialog and ignore any additions or edits.

9. **Save**

   Click this button to save all new and edited lists and close the dialog. You must use the Lists Palette to update any changes made to existing lists.

The Edit List Dialog

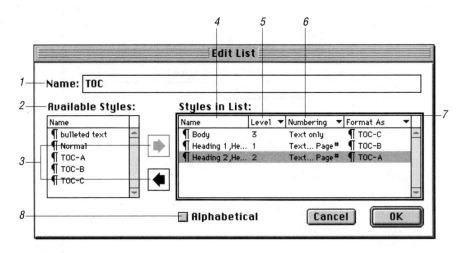

1. **Name**

   When defining a new list, enter its name in this field. "New List" initially appears here, but it automatically highlights, allowing you to type the new name without manually selecting anything. When editing an existing list, its name appears in this field. If desired, change it.

2. **Available Styles**

   This scrolling list displays all style sheets currently defined in the document (character style sheets can't be added to a list, so they do not appear). To select one to add to the list, click it. To select continuous items, hold down the Shift key while clicking. To select noncontinuous items, hold down the (Command) [**Control**] key while clicking.

3. **Arrows**

   To add style sheets to the list, select one or more from the Available Styles window, and click the right-pointing arrow. Double-click an item to achieve the same effect.

   To remove style sheets from a list, select one or more from the Styles in List window, and click the left-pointing arrow. Double-click an item to achieve the same effect.

4. **Name**

   This column displays the name of each style sheet currently contained in the list.

5. **Level**

   This pop-up allows you to indent the items that ultimately appear in the Lists Palette. Items tagged as Level 1 (the default) appear flush left in the Lists Palette field. Each subsequent level results in a larger indent: Level 2 indents an eighth inch, Level 3 a quarter inch, and so forth.

   This has no effect on how the list appears when finally converted into formatted text—rather, it allows you to view the List Palette information as a hierarchy with indented subheadings.

6. **Numbering**

   This pop-up determines whether page numbers are added to the Lists Palette items when they are converted to formatted text. The numbers themselves do not appear in the Lists Palette.

   Text Only
   When this option is set, no page numbering is included when the list is converted to text.

   Text . . . Page #
   Here, the page number is included after each list item when it's converted to text. The number is always preceded by a tab character, to facilitate additional formatting.

   Page # . . . Text
   Here, the page number is included before each list item when converted to text. The number is always followed by a tab character, to facilitate additional formatting.

7. **Format As**

This option allows you to set a style sheet to each list item, to be applied when the Lists Palette information is converted to formatted text. All currently defined style sheets are available.

Since it's rare that a final list or table of contents uses the same style sheets as the actual document, you may need to define the appropriate styles before using this option. For example, in addition to list styles titled "A-Head," "B-Head," and "C-Head," you could define three new styles titled "TOC A-Head," "TOC B-Head," and "TOC C-Head." By setting the appropriate styles in this pop-up, formatting is automatically applied when you build the final list.

Style sheets do not have to be added to the list to be available here.

8. **Alphabetical**

When this box is unchecked (the default), List Palette items appear in the same order as they do in the document: from the top to the bottom of the page, from the first page to the last. When checked, all items appear in alphabetical order, regardless of their Level setting.

See Also

Appendix A
File: New: **Book**
File: **Append**
Edit: **Style Sheets**
Style (Text): **Tabs**
The Style Sheets Palette
The Lists Palette

Edit: Dashes & Stripes

Use this command to create or edit *dashes* (broken line styles) and *stripes* (stacked line styles).

Dashes and stripes can be applied to lines created with the following tools:

- Line Tool
- Bézier Line Tool
- Freehand Bézier Line Tool
- Orthogonal Line Tool
- Text path tools

Once you create a line, apply dashes and stripes using Style (Line): **Line Style** or Item: **Modify**, or by choosing an option from the Measurements Palette.

Common Uses

Refer to Appendix A for full descriptions of the following:

- Creating a dotted line style
- Applying dashes and stripes to a curved text path line
- Creating and applying two-color dashes
- Creating a dash with alternating dots and squared dashes

Common Errors

Defining dash or stripe segments too thin to print. When creating a stripe or a proportional dash, segment thickness is based on a percentage of the current line weight. For example, if a stripe segment has a thickness of 50%, applying the stripe as a 2 pt. line results in the segment appearing as 1 pt. thick. However, if the segment has a thickness of only 5 to 10%, it appears as .1 or .2 pt. thick. While such lines can be accurately printed to film, it's unlikely that a printing press can handle such a light line weight. For the best results, make your thinnest line segments at least 15%.

Special Notes

- Any dashes and stripes defined with no documents open become XPress defaults and are available in all subsequently created documents. When you define or edit dashes and stripes with a document open, they are only available in that particular document.

- When multiple lines are selected, Style (Line): **Line Style** and the Measurements Palette pop-ups are not available. Use Item: **Modify** to apply line styles to more than one line at a time.

- To apply dashes and stripes to a text or picture box, select the box, and choose Item: **Frame**. All line styles are available in the Style pop-up. For the best results when applying a dashed line, make sure the Stretch to Corners box is checked when you define the line style.

Edit Menu

The Dashes & Stripes Dialog

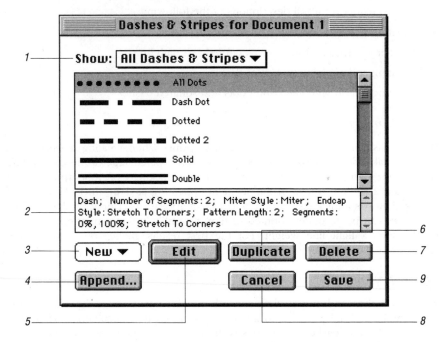

1. Show

This pop-up controls the dashes and stripes that appear in the underlying list:

- *All Dashes and Stripes* displays every setting available to the document.
- *Dashes* displays every dash setting available to the document.
- *Stripes* displays every stripe setting available to the document.
- *Dashes & Stripes In Use* displays only the dashes and stripes currently applied somewhere in the document.
- *Dashes & Stripes Not Used* displays only the dashes and stripes not applied somewhere in the document.

2. Description

This scrolling field displays the attributes of the dash or stripe currently selected in the above list.

3. New

Click this button, and choose an item from the resulting pop-up to create a dash or stripe. Choosing Dash opens the Edit Dash dialog. Choosing Stripe opens the Edit Stripe dialog.

Double-click this button to open the Edit Dash dialog.

4. **Append**

   Click this button to copy dashes and stripes from a saved XPress document. This option is exactly the same as using File: **Append**, only instead of letting you access other settings, you can only access dashes and stripes. (See "File: Append" in Chapter 5 for more information.)

5. **Edit**

   Click this button to edit the contents of the currently selected dash or stripe. The appropriate Edit dialog appears, where you change the original attributes. From there, you can select and edit additional dashes or stripes, or click Save to close the dialog and apply the changes throughout the document.

6. **Duplicate**

   Click this button to produce a copy of the currently selected dash or stripe. The name of the new item is the original title with "copy" tagged at the end. XPress automatically opens the appropriate Edit dialog, allowing you to immediately make changes.

7. **Delete**

   Click this button to remove the currently selected dash or stripe. If it hasn't been applied in the document, the item simply disappears. If it has been applied, an alert appears, asking "OK to delete this dash/stripe and replace it with another dash/stripe wherever it is used?" From the Replace With pop-up, you can choose another defined setting.

8. **Cancel**

   Click this button to close the Dashes & Stripes dialog and ignore any additions or edits.

9. **Save**

   Click this button to save all changes to the Dashes & Stripes list, close the dialog, and apply any changes throughout the document.

Edit Menu

The Edit Dash Dialog

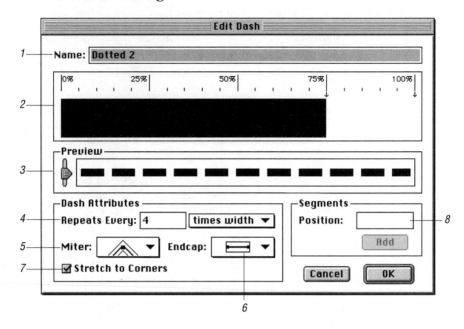

1. **Name**

   When defining a new dash, enter its name in this field. "New Dash" initially appears here, but it automatically highlights, allowing you to type the new name without manually selecting anything. When editing an existing dash, its name appears in this field. If desired, change it.

2. **Ruler**

   Clicking this ruler creates line breaks by determining where the black information starts and stops. You can add and further position as many as nine arrows:

   – When creating a new dash, your first click places a single arrow. This serves to limit the original solid black line.

   – Each additional click actually places *two* arrows, directly on top of each other. Click-drag to separate the arrows. Click-dragging over a black area adds a break; click-dragging over a white area adds a dash.

   – Black always starts at 0%—unless you position an arrow directly at 0%, which resets the starting color to white.

   – To clear all existing arrows, (Option) **[Alt]**-click the ruler.

   – To remove a single arrow, drag it up and off the ruler.

3. **Preview**

   This area displays the current dash settings. Move the vertical slider all the way up to preview the dash at 22 pt. Move it all the way down to preview at 2 pt. It defaults to the center, displaying the preview at approximately 11 pt.

---

4. **Repeats Every**

This option determines how the dash pattern repeats when applied to a line or frame. The pop-up contains two items:

Times width (.01 to 50)

This item results in a *proportional* relationship between the repeating pattern and the applied width—the dashes and spaces enlarge as the line thickness increases. Smaller values in the Repeats Every field reduce the length of the repeating pattern; larger values increase the length.

Points (0 to Repeats Every value)

This item results in an *absolute* relationship between the pattern and applied width. The ruler above changes from percentages to points; the number of points depends on the value entered in the Repeats Every field. Here, the defined pattern repeats at the specified length, regardless of the established line width.

5. **Miter**

This item determines the shape of a dash as it rounds the corner of a box or line. Choose from three items (top to bottom): sharp corner, rounded corner, or beveled corner.

Unlike illustration programs, XPress has no option for *miter limit*, which determines the relative length of sharp-cornered miters at severe angles. Also, there are controls to further affect the rounded and beveled options—their sizes are based purely on the established line width.

6. **Endcap**

This item determines the shape of the exposed ends of each dash. The first item bases the dash shape on the measurements specified by the arrows. The second item rounds the ends of each dash. The third item, of little use, extends each end by one half the applied line width.

7. **Stretch to Corners**

When this box is checked, the repeating pattern is adjusted to conform equally to the corners of a box. This option overrides the Repeats Every value, even if only slightly. When unchecked, the dash repeats according to the Repeats Every value and typically wraps differently around each corner.

8. **Position**

This field allows you to apply arrows to the ruler numerically, instead of by eyeballing and clicking. When creating a proportional dash, enter a value between 0% and 100%, and click Add. When creating an absolute dash, enter a value between 0 and the value entered in the Repeat Every field, and click Add.

Unlike manually inserting arrows, this method places them one at a time. The existing dashes shift to accommodate each new addition.

Edit Menu

The Edit Stripe Dialog

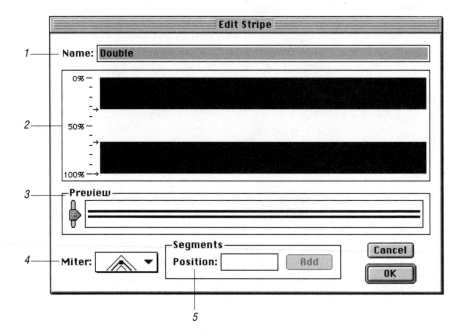

1. **Name**

   When defining a new stripe, enter its name in this field. "New Stripe" initially appears here, but it automatically highlights, allowing you to type the new name without manually selecting anything. When editing an existing stripe, its name appears in this field. If desired, change it.

2. **Percentage Field**

   You can only create proportional stripes, which is not possible with dashes. The thickness of the different line segments is based solely on percentages of the applied line width. For example, if a black segment extends from 0% to 50%, it will appear as 12 pt. thick when the stripe width is set to 24 pt.

   You can add and further position up to 41 arrows:

   - When creating a new stripe, your first click places a single arrow. This serves to limit the original solid black line.

   - Each additional click actually places *two* arrows, directly on top of each other. Click-drag to separate the arrows. Click-dragging next to a black area adds a break; click-dragging next to a white area adds a stripe.

   - Black always starts at 0%—unless you position an arrow directly at 0%, which resets the starting color to white.

   - To remove a single arrow, drag it up and off the ruler.

   - To clear all existing arrows, (Option) [**Alt**]-click the ruler.

3. **Preview**

This area displays the current stripe settings. Move the vertical slider all the way up to preview the stripe at 22 pt. Move it all the way down to preview at 2 pt. It defaults to the center, displaying the preview at approximately.11 pt.

4. **Miter**

This item determines the shape of a stripe as it rounds the corner of a box or line. Choose from three items (top to bottom): sharp corner, rounded corner, or beveled corner.

Unlike illustration programs, XPress has no option for *miter limit*, which determines the relative length of sharp-cornered miters at severe angles. Also, there are controls to further affect the rounded and beveled options—their sizes are based purely on the established line width.

5. **Position**

This field allows you to apply arrows to the ruler numerically, instead of by eyeballing and clicking. Enter a value between 0% and 100%, and click Add.

Unlike manually inserting arrows, this method places them one at a time. The existing stripes shift to accommodate each new addition.

See Also

Line Tools
File: **Append**
Style (Line): **Line Style**
Item: **Modify**
Item: **Frame**
The Measurements Palette

Edit: Print Styles

Print styles are lists of predefined File: **Print** settings. This command allows you to configure a series of print options for a variety of devices and output methods. This way, instead of manually entering all the settings each time you print, you choose the appropriate item from the Print Style pop-up in the File: **Print** dialog.

Examples of print styles could include the following:

- B&W laser, letter-size, composite
- B&W laser, letter, seps
- B&W laser, tabloid, composite
- B&W laser tabloid, seps
- Color laser, letter
- Color laser, tabloid
- Imagesetter, letter, transverse

Special Notes

- Any print styles defined with no documents open become XPress defaults, and are available in all subsequently created documents. When preparing basic print styles for a series of in-house output devices, set them as defaults.

- When you define or edit print styles with a document open, they are only available in that particular document. Designers may often tweak a default print style, configuring it appropriately for a specific document. Make sure the document is open when this occurs.

- When preparing the settings, the Profiles panel is not available—even when Edit: Preferences: **Color Management** is turned on. If you need to adjust these settings when printing a file, load the most appropriate print style in the File: **Print** dialog, then click the Profiles tab and establish the settings manually.

- If multiple workstations are required to use the same print styles, don't bother defining them individually. Instead, set them on one workstation, export the styles into a separate document, and import them into the remaining copies of XPress.

- To reset XPress' default File: **Print** settings, choose Edit: **Print Styles**, and edit the Default item.

The Print Styles Dialog

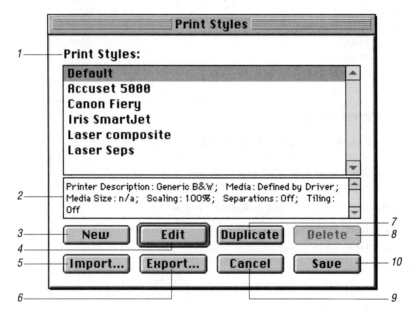

1. **Print Styles**

    This scrolling list displays all currently available print styles. An item called Default is always listed and can't be deleted. This style contains XPress' default print settings.

---

2. **Description**

   This scrolling field displays the attributes of the print style currently selected in the above list.

3. **New**

   Click this button to open the Edit Print Style dialog and create a new print style.

4. **Edit**

   Click this button to open the Edit Print Style dialog and edit the contents of the currently selected item. Afterwards, you can select and edit additional styles, or click Save to close the dialog and make the print styles available in the File: **Print** dialog.

5. **Import**

   Click this button to import print styles that have been exported from another document. In the dialog that appears, you can select one, some, or all of the available styles.

   This command can only recognize exported print style documents.

6. **Export**

   Click this button to export the currently selected print styles into an external XPress document. This file can then be imported into another copy of XPress using this dialog's Import button.

7. **Duplicate**

   Click this button to produce a copy of the currently selected print style. The new name is the original title with "copy" tagged at the end. XPress automatically opens the Edit Print Style dialog, allowing you to immediately make changes.

8. **Delete**

   Click this button to remove the currently selected print style.

9. **Cancel**

   Click this button to close the Print Styles dialog and ignore any additions or edits.

10. **Save**

    Click this button to save all new and edited print styles and close the dialog.

Edit Menu

The Edit Print Style Dialog

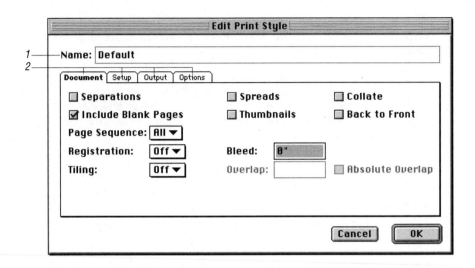

1. **Name**

   When defining a new print style, enter its name in this field. "New Print Style" initially appears here, but it automatically highlights, allowing you to type the new name without manually selecting anything. When editing an existing style, its name appears in this field. If desired, change it.

2. **Panel Tabs**

   The panels available here are identical to the first four panels in the File: Print dialog.

   See "File: Print" in Chapter 5 for more information.

CHAPTER 7

The Style Menu (Text)

The following commands are available in the Style Menu only when a text box is selected and the Content Tool is active.

Style: Font

This submenu displays all typefaces currently available to your operating system. This list is the same one that appears in the Measurements Palette and the Character Attributes dialog.

Fonts are listed alphabetically, by family. Futura, Helvetica, and Times are examples of font families. When a font family contains more than one variation, they're available in an additional submenu. For example, Times Plain, Italic, Bold, and Bold Italic appear in a submenu that extends from the Times item in the initial font list.

This list can only be used to format type locally:

- After highlighting text using the Content Tool, choose a font to change the typeface of the selected range.

- If the cursor is flashing when you choose a font (no text is highlighted), all subsequently entered text appears in the new typeface.

To change the font built into a style sheet definition, choose Edit: **Style Sheets**, and edit the appropriate item.

Special Notes

- Font files simply copied to your hard drive are not recognized by XPress. To appear in this list, fonts must be installed in your system. There are two ways to do this:

- **Install all fonts.** On the Mac, drag all font files into the Fonts folder, located in the System Folder. On Windows, use the Windows Explorer to drag and drop font files from a disk into the Fonts folder. When you relaunch XPress, the new fonts are available. Use this method when you routinely use only a limited number of fonts, and you typically output your own files in-house.

- **Use a font management utility,** such as Symantec's *Suitcase* or Alsoft's *MasterJuggler.* Such software allows you to turn fonts off and on, without having to manually relocate files on your hard drive. Use this method when you routinely accept fonts from clients, turn projects over to a vendor for output, or maintain type libraries of over 100 fonts.

• If you have not defined paragraph or character styles, search and replace all occurrences of an applied font using Edit: **Find/Change** or Utilities: **Usage.**

See Also

Page Tools: **Content Tool**
Edit: **Style Sheets**
Style (Text): **Character**
The Measurements Palette

Style: Size
(Command-Shift) [Control-Shift]-

This submenu displays a list of predetermined type sizes. It also contains an item called Other, which allows you to manually enter a size from 2 to 720 pt. This option is the same one that appears in the Measurements Palette and the Character Attributes dialog.

You're not limited to manually entering size values. To change the point size on the fly, highlight a range of text and use the following shortcuts:

• **Increase size through the preset values.** Press (Command-Shift) [**Control-Shift**]-period.

• **Decrease size through the preset values.** Press (Command-Shift) [**Control-Shift**]-comma.

• **Increase size in 1 pt. increments.** Press (Option-Command-Shift) [**Alt-Control-Shift**]-period.

• **Decrease size in 1 pt. increments.** Press (Option-Command-Shift) [**Alt-Control-Shift**]-comma.

An easy way to remember these shortcuts is to check out the keyboard characters above the comma and period: Less Than (which *decreases*) and Greater Than (which *increases*).

Special Notes

- The size of a drop cap created using Style (Text): **Formats** appears as a percentage. The Measurements Palette reflects this, but the Style (Text): **Size** submenu only displays the original point size. The size first appears as 100%, based on the Character and Line Count values entered in the Paragraph Attributes dialog. To resize a drop cap without changing the Count values, select the character, and enter a value between 10 and 400%.

  You can use the same shortcuts described previously to increase or decrease the size of a drop cap:

  - Instead of resizing through the preset values, the same shortcut cycles through the following: 10%, 14.6%, 18.7%, 20.8%, 25%, 29.2%, 37.5%, 50%, 75%, 100%, 125%, 150%, 200%, 250%, 300%, 350%, and 400%.

  - Instead of resizing in 1 pt. values, the same shortcut increases or decreases the selection by 2.1%.

- You can also scale text up or down by resizing an unlinked text box. This method has a special limitation: you cannot increase the horizontal or vertical scale beyond 400%, the same limit imposed by Style (Text): **Horizontal/Vertical Scale**:

  - (Command) [**Control**]-drag a handle to resize the box and its contents with independent horizontal and vertical scaling.

  - (Command-Shift) [**Control-Shift**]-drag a handle to constrain the box to a square, scaling its contents appropriately.

  - (Option-Command-Shift) [**Alt-Control-Shift**]-drag a handle to proportionately scale the box and its contents.

See Also

Page Tools: **Content Tool**
Style (Text): **Formats**
The Measurements Palette

Style: Type Style

XPress' type styles are a series of 13 predefined character attributes. The options appearing in this list are the same ones available in the Measurements Palette and the Character Attributes dialog.

Apply one or more styles to a range of text using the following techniques:

- **Apply them locally.** Highlight a range of text, and choose an option from the Style (Text): **Type Style** submenu. Once a style is applied, a checkmark appears next to its item in the submenu. When multiple styles are applied, each one is checked.

- **Include them in a style sheet definition.** When creating a character or paragraph style sheet, check the desired type styles in the Character Attributes dialog. This way, they're applied to the selected text whenever you choose the item from the Style Sheets Palette. (See "Edit: Style Sheets" in Chapter 6, *The Edit Menu*, for more information.)

Common Errors

Applying the Bold and/or Italic type styles, then failing to provide the appropriate fonts for output. Most font families contain bold, italic, and bold italic versions. When you apply these styles, XPress automatically knows to use the actual font information during output. However, XPress does not replace any fonts existing in the document. For example, if a paragraph exists in Times Roman and you apply the Italic type style to one or more words, the Times Italic font is not accessed until the document is printed. If Times Italic is not available to your operating system during output, XPress offers no warning. Instead, one of two things happens: all text tagged as Italic defaults to Plain, or XPress attempts to simulate the Italic font, which is never as accurate as using the actual typeface.

This can be confusing, since many decorative fonts don't have bold or italic versions—but when you apply the type style in an XPress document, the text *appears* to be boldfaced or italicized on-screen. Similarly, many fonts have bold and italic versions, but no bold italic version. If both type styles are applied to plain text, they appear to take effect—but if no bold italic version of the font is available, the printed results are unpredictable at best.

To avoid this problem, use the following techniques:

- Be certain that the font in question has bold, italic, and bold italic versions. The quickest way to do this is to check the Style (Text): **Font** submenu: if the versions exist, they appear in the submenu next to the font name.
- After applying the desired type styles, use Edit: **Find/Change** to replace all occurrences of the type style with the appropriate font. This way, if one of the fonts is not present during output, a warning appears. For the best results, execute this method at the very end of a project, after all typeface decisions are final.

Special Notes

- Once you apply type styles, they remain until manually removed. If you change the underlying font, any applied type styles are untouched.
- Multiple type styles can be applied at the same, except the following: Underline and Word Underline, All Caps and Small Caps, Superscript and Subscript. In these cases, you can only choose one or the other. Also, choosing Plain turns off any selected type styles.

Plain
(Command-Shift) [Control-Shift]-P

Plain is the default type style, indicating that no additional characteristics affect the applied typeface. This is true regardless of the current typeface—even if you apply a bold or italic version of a font, the initial type style is Plain. If highlighted text includes any applied type styles, choosing this item removes them.

Bold
(Command-Shift) [Control-Shift]-B

It appears as if this type style accesses the bold version of the current typeface. More accurately, it accesses the *next boldest* version and only when applied to the Regular (or *Roman*) version:

- If a font has only one bold version, applying this type style to the regular version results in bold type during output.

- Many fonts have more than one version heavier than Regular. Futura, for example, includes Heavy, Bold, and Extra Bold versions. Here, applying the Bold type style to Futura Regular results in Futura Heavy—the next boldest version—during output.

- Applying the Bold type style to a font version heavier than Regular results in no change, even if heavier versions are present. For example, applying Bold to Futura Heavy results in Futura Heavy during output, even though it appears bolder on-screen.

- Many fonts have versions lighter than regular. Helvetica Neue, for example, includes Ultra Thin, Thin, and Light versions. Applying the Bold type style to any of these versions results in no change during output, even though they appear bolder on-screen.

To boldface font versions other than regular, apply the Bold type style as needed. Then use Edit: **Find/Change** to substitute a heavier font version for every occurrence of the type style.

Italic
(Command-Shift) [Control-Shift]-I

This type style accesses the italic version of the currently applied typeface. If none is available, XPress attempts to simulate an italicized version, which may or may not match your expectations. To be safe, print a test sheet of the artificial italics to your laser printer before outputting final pages.

Underline
(Command-Shift) [Control-Shift]-U

This type style underlines all characters and spaces. Tab spaces are not affected. The underline thickness is always one-fifteenth the current point size. For example, 60 pt. type receives a 5 pt. underline; 12 pt. type receives a .8 pt. underline. The space between the baseline and the underline is always the same as the line thickness.

Underline is rarely used for design purposes. You can't edit for thickness or position, and the underline unattractively overlaps the descenders of lowercase characters. If your intention is to add emphasis to your text, consider using Italic. If you must create an underline, consider the following:

- If the text requiring an underline is a single paragraph, use Style (Text): **Rules** to add an underline of editable thickness, placement, and color.

- Use the Orthogonal Line Tool to add a manually editable underline. This is only effective on simple text elements, such as banner-sized type. If necessary, Item: **Group** the line and the text box to maintain their relative positions.

Word Underline
(Command-Shift) [Control-Shift]-W

This type style is the same as Underline, only all standard spaces, em and en spaces, tab spaces, and flex spaces are ignored.

Strike Thru
(Command-Shift) [Control-Shift]-/

This type style applies a 1 pt. line through all affected characters (except tab spaces). Strike Thru is used most often as an editorial device, indicating text to be removed from a story.

Outline
(Command-Shift) [Control-Shift]-O

This type style does two things: it sets the text color to white and outlines character shapes with a very thin line. When you change the text color, only the outline is affected; the fill color remains white.

As a special effect, this option is quite limited: you can't change the outline thickness (which is far too thin to trap properly) or the fill color. To create more easily editable outlined text, do one of the following:

- Create the text in an illustration program, such as Illustrator or FreeHand. There, you have full control over fill and stroke values and can build in trap information before saving and importing. For the best results, convert the text to outlines before saving the graphic.

- Set the text in XPress, using the Plain type style. After it's properly adjusted, highlight it, and choose Style (Text): **Text to Box**, which converts the characters to a single merged picture box. Use Item: **Frame** to add different outline styles and thicknesses. Use the Colors Palette to add different fill colors and tints.

Shadow
(Command-Shift) [Control-Shift]-S

This type style adds a hard-edged drop shadow beneath the text.

As a special effect, this option is quite limited. The color of the shadow is always the same—50% black, regardless of the current text color. Also, the offset value of the shadow can't be changed. It's always 5% of the current point size, to the right and down. For example, if you apply Shadow to 100 pt. text, the offset is 5 pt. to the right, 5 pt. down. To create a more effective drop shadow, do one of the following:

- Set the initial type using the Plain type style. Duplicate the text box, and choose Item: **Send to Back**. Set the underlying text to the desired shadow color, and position appropriately using the Item Tool. Item: Group the boxes to maintain their relative position.

- Set the type, and create the shadow in a vector-based illustration program, such as Illustrator or FreeHand.

- To create a soft-edged drop shadow, set the type, and create the effect in a pixel-based program, such as Photoshop. See "The Layers Palette, in *Photoshop in a Nutshell* (O'Reilly) for more information.

- Purchase a utility such as *QX-Effects* from Extensis, which allows you to create a variety of text-shadow effects.

All Caps
(Command-Shift) [Control-Shift]-K

This type style converts all lowercase characters to uppercase. The effect is not the same as typing with the Caps Lock key depressed. That way, you can't change uppercase back to lowercase. Using All Caps, you can always convert text back to lowercase by turning it off. This type style has no effect on uppercase characters created by holding down the Shift key.

Small Caps
(Command-Shift) [Control-Shift]-H

This type style converts all lowercase characters to scaled-down uppercase characters. The default small cap size is 75% of the current point size. Change this value in the Edit: Preferences: Document: **Character** panel.

Superscript
(Command-Shift) [Control-Shift]-=

This type style raises text above the baseline, as determined by the values entered in the Edit: Preferences: Document: **Character** panel. There, you set the offset distance and scale of the superscript characters.

Many users mistakenly use Superscript for such characters as exponents and footnotes. Avoid figuring out your own offset and scale values by using the Superior type style instead (see the description that follows).

Subscript
(Command-Shift) [Control-Shift]-hyphen

This type style drops text below the baseline, as determined by the values entered in the Edit: Preferences: Document: **Character** panel. There, you set the offset distance and scale of the subscript characters.

A common example of subscript characters are the numerals in a chemical equation. To properly format these characters, set the Scale values to 50% and Offset to 15%.

Superior
(Command-Shift) [Control-Shift]-V

In conventional typesetting, *superior* simply refers to any characters raised above the main line of text. In XPress, this type style is preformatted to duplicate the conventional requirements of superscript characters, such as exponents and foot-notes. Superior text is scaled down (according to the values entered in the Edit: Preferences: Document: **Character** panel) and raised so that the tops of the charac-ters are flush with the cap height of the current typeface.

See Also

Page Tools: **Item Tool**
Line Tools: **Orthogonal Line Tool**
Edit: **Find/Change**
Edit: Preferences: Document: **Character**
Edit: **Style Sheets**
Style (Text): **Fonts**
Style (Text): **Text to Box**
Style (Text): **Rules**
Item: **Frame**
Item: **Group**
Item: **Send to Back**
The Measurements Palette
Photoshop in a Nutshell (The Layers Palette)

Style: Color

This submenu displays all items currently available in the Colors Palette. Its use is fairly limited:

- Unlike the Colors Palette, you can only recolor highlighted text. You can't edit the text box or frame color.

- To apply a tint, you have to select a color from this submenu, then choose a value from Style (Text): **Shade**.

There is no functional reason to use this menu item over the Colors Palette or the color values included in a style sheet definition.

Style: Shade

This submenu lets you change the tint value of a highlighted range of text. The preset values range from 0% to 100%, in 10% increments. To set a value not avail-able in the list, choose Other. The Character Attributes dialog opens, where you enter a value in the Shade field.

Style: Horizontal/Vertical Scale

Use this command to expand or compress character shapes. Choosing this command opens the Character Attributes dialog, where you enter a value in the Scale field. You must choose Horizontal or Vertical in the accompanying pop-up—you can't scale in both directions at once. The amount of change is based on a percentage of the current point size—set a value between 25% and 400%.

Typically, there are two reasons to use this effect. You can create compressed or expanded versions of a font by setting a horizontal value between 85% and 130%. Also, to preserve line space at the end of a paragraph, many designers highlight the entire paragraph and set a horizontal value of 97–98%—enough to squeeze the text into place but not enough to cause visible shift in character shape.

Special Notes

- Use the following shortcuts to scale highlighted text on the fly:

    - **Decrease scale in 5% increments.** Press (Command) [**Control**]-[.

    - **Increase scale in 5% increments.** Press (Command) [**Control**]-].

    - **Decrease scale in 1% increments.** Press (Option-Command) [**Alt-Control**]-[.

    - **Increase scale in 1% increments.** Press (Option-Command) [**Alt-Control**]-].

- By default, the preceding shortcuts affect horizontal scale. However, if you use this command to set a vertical scale value first, the shortcuts affect vertical scale.

Style: Kern

In conventional typesetting, *kerning* refers to the process of decreasing the space between two characters (sometimes called a *kern pair*). In XPress, it involves decreasing or increasing the space. Choosing this command opens the Character Attributes dialog, where you enter a value in the Kern field.

This command is only available when you insert the flashing cursor between two characters (when text is highlighted, this item appears as Style (Text): **Track**). Enter a value between –500 and 500 units:

- Each unit is equal to 1/200 of an em space. (See the description of the standard em space in "Edit: Preferences: Character" in Chapter 6 for information.)

- Positive values increase the space between the two characters; negative values decrease it.

The adjustments you make are proportional to the current point size. If you increase or decrease the size of the type, the characters maintain their relative distance.

Special Notes

- When Auto Kern is turned on in the Edit: Preferences: Document: **Character** panel, XPress utilizes the kern pairs that were built into each typeface by its designer. Unless you prefer spending a lot of time adjusting spacing, leave this option on. Automatic kern spaces do not appear as numerical values in the Character Attributes dialog or the Measurements Palette.

- Typically, designers only manually kern larger type (over 24–36 pt., depending on the font). At small sizes, XPress' automatic kerning is almost always sufficient.

Style Menu (Text)

- You can add to the previously described built-in kern pairs using Utilities: **Kerning Table Edit**. There, you change the way XPress displays a particular font—you don't change the parameters of the font itself.

- Use the following shortcuts to adjust kerning on the fly:

  - Decrease kern by 10 units. Press (Command-Shift) [**Control-Shift**]-[.

  - Increase kern by 10 units. Press (Command-Shift) [**Control-Shift**]-].

  - Decrease kern by 1 unit. Press (Option-Command-Shift) [**Alt-Control-Shift**]-[.

  - Increase kern by 1 unit. Press (Option-Command-Shift) [**Alt-Control-Shift**]-].

Style: Track

Similar to kerning, tracking adjusts the character spaces over a range of text. Here, track values affect the spacing to the right of each character. Choosing this command opens the Character Attributes dialog, where you enter a value in the Track field.

This command is only available when text is highlighted (when you insert the flashing cursor between two characters, this item appears as Style (Text): **Kern**). Enter a value between –500 and 500 units:

- Each unit is equal to 1/200 of an em space. (See the description of the standard em space in "Edit: Preferences: Character" in Chapter 6 for information.)

- Positive values increase the spacing; negative values decrease it.

The adjustments you make are proportional to the current point size. If you increase or decrease the size of the type, the characters maintain their relative distance.

Special Notes

- To change the tracking of a single word without affecting the space after it, highlight every letter except the last one.

- You can control the way XPress automatically tracks a font by using Utilities: **Tracking Edit**.

- Use the following shortcuts to adjust tracking on the fly:

  - Decrease track by 10 units. Press (Command-Shift) [**Control-Shift**]-[.

  - Increase track by 10 units. Press (Command-Shift) [**Control-Shift**]-].

  - Decrease track by 1 unit. Press (Option-Command-Shift) [**Alt-Control-Shift**]-[.

  - Increase track by 1 unit. Press (Option-Command-Shift) [**Alt-Control-Shift**]-].

Style: Baseline Shift

This command raises or lowers text from the baseline, or the default "imaginary" line text sits upon. Choosing this command opens the Character Attributes dialog, where you enter a value in the Baseline Shift field.

Adjusting the Baseline Shift is similar to applying the Superscript and Subscript type styles, but with an important difference: those effects can only be set to one offset value (as determined in the Edit: Preferences: Document: **Character** panel), whereas this command can set multiple characters to different offset values.

When text is highlighted, this command only affects the current selection; when the flashing cursor is present, this command affects the subsequently entered text:

- Baseline Shift is measured in points, but the range depends on the current point size. Enter any value up to three times the current point size. For example, when editing 24 pt. text, you can enter a value between –72 and 72 pt.

- Positive values raise text above the baseline; negative values drop text below the baseline.

If you increase or decrease the size of the type, the Baseline Shift changes to maintain proportional offset values.

Style: Character
(Command-Shift) [Control-Shift]-D

The settings in this dialog reflect the first eight items of the Style Menu. The same dialog is accessed when defining a character or paragraph style sheet.

The Character Attributes Dialog

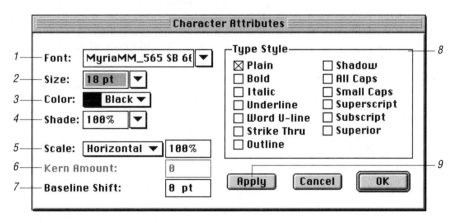

1. **Font**

   See "Style: Font" earlier in this chapter for more information.

---

2. **Size**

   See "Style: Size," earlier in this chapter, for more information.

3. **Color**

   See "Style: Color," earlier in this chapter, for more information.

4. **Shade**

   See "Style: Shade," earlier in this chapter, for more information.

5. **Scale**

   See "Style: Horizontal/Vertical Scale," earlier in this chapter, for more information.

6. **Kern/Track Amount**

   See "Style: Kern" and "Style: Track," earlier in this chapter, for more information.

7. **Baseline Shift**

   See "Style: Baseline Shift," earlier in this chapter, for more information.

8. **Type Style**

   The individual type styles are covered in depth under Style (Text): **Type Style**. Here, each item is preceded by a checkbox. The status of each box depends on the type styles present in a highlighted range of text:

   - **Unchecked.** This indicates that the type style has not been applied. If you check an item, the type style is applied to all highlighted text, in addition to any other type styles present.

   - **Checked.** This indicates that the type style is applied to the entire highlighted range. If you uncheck an item, the type style is removed. Any additionally applied type styles are untouched.

   - **Gray.** This indicates that the type style has been applied to only part of the highlighted range. If you click once on a gray box, it becomes checked, and the type style is applied to the entire highlighted range. If you click twice, it becomes unchecked, and all occurrences of the type style are removed.

9. **Apply**

   Click this button to preview the effect of new Character Attributes settings. If necessary, move the dialog out of the way after clicking. If unsatisfied with the settings, change them. To reset all of them at once, click Cancel, and open the dialog again.

Style: Character Style Sheet

This submenu displays all currently available character style sheets, plus options for No Style and Normal. To apply a character style, select the appropriate letters or words, and choose the desired submenu item.

Special Notes

The contents of this submenu are identical to the Style Sheets Palette. In fact, that palette offers much more efficient methods of applying and manipulating style sheets. Not only can you apply them without accessing a menu item, but certain keyboard-based effects—such as (Option) [**Alt**]-clicking a style to reapply it, or (Command) [**Control**]-clicking to open the Edit: **Style Sheets** dialog—only work using the Style Sheets Palette. The keys have no effect when choosing an item from this submenu.

Style: Text to Box

This command converts highlighted text to a Bézier picture box, while retaining the original character shapes. There are two ways to do this:

• When you simply highlight text and choose the command, a new box appears and the original text is untouched. If necessary, delete the original text after converting.

• When you choose this command while holding down the (Option) [**Alt**] key, the original text is replaced with an anchored picture box.

After applying this command, you can further edit the shape of the characters using XPress' Bézier editing tools. (See Chapter 3, *Line Tools*, for more information.)

Common Uses

Refer to Appendix A, *Common Techniques*, for full descriptions of the following:

• Creating and editing type based on Bézier curves

• Creating and editing an anchored character mask

• Creating character-shaped text boxes

Common Errors

• **Attempting to convert Adobe Type 3 fonts.** You can only convert properly installed Type 1 fonts (when Adobe Type Manager is running) and True Type fonts. Although Type 3 fonts are not produced anymore, many still linger in type libraries that date back before 1990. Fortunately, most of those fonts now have Type 1 counterparts. If necessary, acquire the proper font, or select a different typeface.

• **Attempting to convert fonts with no outline files.** When using PostScript fonts, the outline (or *printer font*) files must be available. This command uses that information to create the Bézier paths.

• **Converting small-sized text.** This command is most effective when applied to large-sized text. Since the result is typically used to import a graphic or create decorative type, the effect is largely lost on characters below 24–36 pt. (depending on the typeface).

- **Attempting to convert text with applied type styles.** The only type styles this command can successfully convert are Bold, Italic, and Bold and Italic applied at the same time. And then, it only works if the appropriate bold, italic, and bold italic font versions are available. If any other type style is applied, an alert appears when you choose this command, stating "Box converted from the highlighted text won't look exactly the same as the text." If you click OK, the resulting box is based on the plain font version, and often has unexpected spacing problems.

- **Failing to set the appropriate box type.** Converted text initially appears as a merged picture box. To change the box type, select it, and choose Item: Content: **Picture** or **None**, depending on its intended use.

Special Notes

- You can only convert one line of text at a time. This is true even if you attempt to convert a single hyphenated word.

- When you simply choose this command to create a separate picture box, you cannot choose Edit: **Undo** afterwards. If necessary, select the new box, delete it, and try again. When you create an anchored picture box, you can undo, provided you make no additional edits before choosing the Undo command.

- When you convert multiple characters, the result is the same as if you created individual character boxes, selected them, and chose Item: Merge: **Union**. To split such a merged picture box into its component characters, select it, and choose Item: Split: **Outside Paths**. (Be sure to avoid choosing the All Paths option—that removes all compound paths from the characters, and you will not be able to "see through" parts of the letter shapes, such as the loop of a capital "P" or lowercase "g.") After splitting, you can import different graphics into each character. If necessary, Item: **Group** the boxes to maintain their relative positions.

- When highlighted characters overlap—if they're tracked very closely together, for example—the converted result is a single box. You cannot separate the characters after converting.

- When you generate a separate character box, it's placed directly below the original text. Although you can use the Item Tool to reposition it, accidentally click-dragging the box edge results in manipulating the path shapes. Avoid this by holding down the (Command) [**Control**] key while dragging with the Item Tool.

See Also

Appendix A (Style: **Text to Box**)
Style (Text): **Type Style**
Item: **Merge**
Item: **Split**
Item: **Content**

Style: Alignment

These commands determine the horizontal alignment of text. The same items are available in the Paragraph Attributes dialog and the Measurements Palette.

Unlike other attributes such as size, color, and type style, these options affect the entire contents of a given paragraph. By default, text is aligned between the left and right edge of a text box (or if the box is subdivided into columns, the left and right column edge). However, if you enter new values for the Left Indent, First Line, or Right Indent in the Paragraph Attributes dialog (Style (Text): **Formats**), alignment is based on the following:

- Text is aligned between the values entered in the Left Indent and Right Indent fields.

- The First Line value offsets the first line of left-, centered,- justified-, and forced-aligned text. It has no effect on right-aligned text. When applied to center-aligned text, any First Line value prevents the text from being truly centered.

For information on vertically aligning text, see "Item: Modify" in Chapter 10, *The Item Menu.*

Left

This item aligns text to the left indent. Conventionally, this is known as "ragged-right" alignment, because while the left edge is flush, the right edge is determined by hyphenation and line breaks.

When Auto Hyphenation is turned on, you can further control how words are broken at the end of a line by establishing a Hyphenation Zone. (See "Edit: H&Js" in Chapter 6 for more information.)

Centered

This item centers lines between the left and right indents.

When Auto Hyphenation is turned on, you can further control how words are broken at the end of a line by establishing a Hyphenation Zone. (See "Edit: H&Js" in Chapter 6 for more information.)

Right

This item aligns text to the right indent. Conventionally, this is known as "ragged-left" alignment, because while the right edge is flush, the left edge is determined by hyphenation and line breaks.

When Auto Hyphenation is turned on, you can further control how words are broken at the end of a line by establishing a Hyphenation Zone. (See "Edit: H&Js" in Chapter 6 for more information.)

Style Menu (Text)

Justified

This item aligns text (except the last line in a paragraph) to the left and right indents.

This is accomplished by expanding or compressing the spaces between words (and, if necessary, characters) to create the most even distribution of text. Set these values in the Edit Hyphenation and Justification dialog. (See "Edit: H&Js" in Chapter 6 for more information.)

Forced

This item is the same as Justified, except the last line in each paragraph extends from the left to the right indent—even if the last line only contains a single word.

Style: Leading

Pronounced "ledding," this value measures the distance between baselines. This is often referred to as "line spacing." Leading can only be applied on the paragraph level.

Common Uses

*   **Using the Auto value.** XPress' default leading value is "Auto" (defined as a percentage in the Edit: Preferences: Document: **Paragraph** panel.) This means that leading is determined by the current point size. For example, if the Auto value is set to 20% and the current point size is 40 pt., the leading equals the point size plus 20%, or 48 pt. As you change the point size, the leading adjusts appropriately, always maintaining the same proportion. To use automatic leading, enter "auto" or 0 in the leading field.

    Most users avoid this option, however—it gives you no numerical control over the leading, and the single Auto Leading percentage does not always translate successfully to different typefaces and different sizes. Also, the auto leading of each line is based on the largest-sized character on each line. If you increase the size of a letter or word, the leading of that line increases as well.

*   **Entering a numerical value.** Here, you enter a specific leading value. If you increase or decrease the size of the type, the leading value remains constant until you manually change it again.

    Enter a value between .001 and 1,080 pt. Most users use points (the default), but you can enter any unit of measurement, provided you include the appropriate abbreviation. For example, you can enter .25" or 1 cm—but XPress automatically converts that value to points when you apply the value.

*   **Entering a relative value.** Here, you set the leading to the current point size of the text, plus a specified amount. For example, if you enter +5 and the current point size is 24 pt., the leading is 29 pt. If you change the size to 18 pt., the leading changes to 23 pt. Likewise, if you enter a negative value, the leading is the current point size minus the specified amount. However, when you enter negative values, the cap height of the lower line cannot overlap the

characters of the upper line. To set leading equal to the current type size, enter +0.

Common Errors

- **Applying different leading values to the same body of text.** Line spacing has a great impact on the overall readability of body text. Some users, in an attempt to conserve space or force text to fit in a specific box size, alter the leading of the last one or two paragraphs. The result is easily picked up by the eye, especially when applied to 10 or 12 pt. text—suddenly, the lines appear cramped (if leading is reduced) or opened (if leading is increased). If you must do this, apply leading consistently throughout the body of text. For the best results, control leading from the style sheet level, instead of trying to affect it manually.

- **Applying too low a value.** If the line spacing is set too low, the descenders of the upper line may overlap the ascenders of the lower line.

Special Notes

- The preferences controlling leading are adjusted in the Edit: Preferences: Document: **Paragraph** panel.

- Use the following shortcuts to control leading on the fly:

  - **Decrease leading in 1 pt. increments.** Press (Command-Shift) [**Control-Shift**]-semicolon.

  - **Increase leading in 1 pt.** increments. Press (Command-Shift) [**Control-Shift**]-apostrophe.

  - **Decrease leading in .1 pt.** increments. Press (Option-Command-Shift) [**Alt-Control-Shift**]-semicolon.

  - **Increase leading in .1 pt.** increments. Press (Option-Command-Shift) [**Alt-Control-Shift**]-apostrophe.

Style: Formats

The settings in this dialog control the formatting of paragraphs. None of the items contained within can affect a single line within an existing paragraph.

Although the Paragraph Attributes dialog contains panels for establishing tabs and rules, those settings are covered under Style (Text): **Tabs** and **Rules**.

Common Uses

Refer to Appendix A for full descriptions of the following:

- Formatting bulleted lists

- Formatting hanging indents

- Copying the attributes of one paragraph to another

- Defining a raised cap

- Defining a raised cap with a hanging indent
- Editing a drop cap
- Creating a graphical drop cap
- Changing the font of a drop cap

Common Errors

- **Locally formatting multiple paragraphs.** If you find yourself using this command to adjust a series of paragraphs, it makes more sense to apply these settings via style sheets. This way, you can easily keep track of any changes, and by referring to the Style Sheets Palette, you can easily tell what attributes are applied to what paragraphs. Otherwise, the only way you can check this information is by inserting the cursor in a paragraph and opening the Paragraph Attributes dialog.

- **Using multiple hard returns to add space between paragraphs.** Many users hit the Return key twice after each paragraph, using the second return to add a space. Not only does this limit the space size to the current leading value, but it often results in spaces appearing at the tops of linked text boxes. For the best results, define a Space Before or Space After value, and only hit the Return key once after each paragraph. This value is most successfully used as part of a style sheet.

Special Notes

- To apply new formatting attributes to a single paragraph, you don't have to highlight any text—just insert the flashing cursor anywhere in the targeted paragraph.

- Each text box has a default Text Inset value of 1 pt. This amount is added to the Left and Right Indent values. To remove the inset, open the Item: Modify: **Text** panel, and enter 0 in the Text Inset field. To remove this value permanently, open the Edit: Preferences: Document: **Tools** panel with no documents open, select the text box tools, and enter 0 in the Text Inset field.

- Another way to add a left indent is to insert the Indent Here character. By inserting the flashing cursor in a paragraph and pressing (Command) [**Control**]-\, the left indent of the remaining lines in the paragraph become flush with the original position of the cursor. To remove the indent, choose View: Show **Invisibles**, and delete the vertical gray bar that represents the Indent Here character.

- When you choose this command, a ruler appears at the top of the currently selected text box. If desired, you can set indents by doing the following:
  - Set the left indent by dragging the lower left triangle. The Left Indent field changes to display the current value.
  - Set the first line indent by dragging the upper left triangle. The First Line field changes to display the current value.
  - Set the right indent by dragging the right arrow. The Right Indent field changes to display the current value.

This ruler spans the distance between the Text Inset values (entered in the Item: Modify: **Text** panel) of a text box or column. You can also use it to apply tabs. (See "Style: Tabs," later in this chapter, for more information.)

The Formats Panel

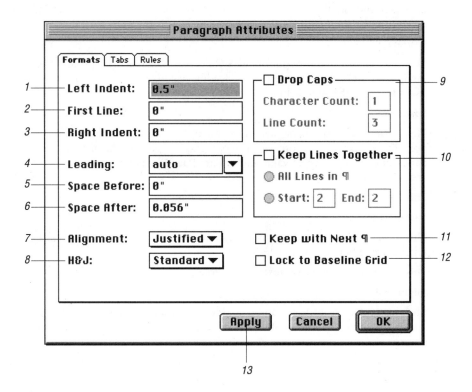

1. **Left Indent**

   This value determines the distance of the left edge of the text from the left edge of the column, text box, or text path.

   The amount here is applied in addition to the Text Inset value entered in the Item: **Modify** dialog. If an inset is applied and you need to indent the text a specific distance, subtract the inset value from the indent amount, and enter that value in the Left Indent field. For example, if you have a 5 pt. text inset and you need a 18 pt. indent, enter 13 pt. in the Left Indent field to compensate for the text inset.

2. **First Line**

   This value determines the distance of the first line of a paragraph from the left indent. If Left Indent is set to zero, you can only enter positive values, which indent the first line to the right. If you enter a Left Indent value, you can enter negative values here, which indent the first line to the left, resulting in a *hanging indent*. When creating a hanging indent, the distance specified in the First Line field cannot exceed the distance in the Left Indent field.

3. **Right Indent**

This value determines the distance of the right edge of the text from the right edge of the column, text box, or text path.

Like Left Indent, this value is applied in addition to the Text Inset value entered in the Item: **Modify** dialog.

4. **Leading**

This item is covered in depth under Style (Text): **Leading**. The pop-up beside the leading field displays the current leading value, plus Auto—you can only use it to apply the Auto setting.

5. **Space Before**

This item adds a space before any paragraph except the first one in a text box. To add a space before the first paragraph, open the Item: Modify: **Text** panel, and enter an offset value under First Baseline. Enter a value between 0 and 15 inches.

This value has no effect on text aligned to a path.

6. **Space After**

This item adds a space after any paragraph except the last one in a text box. Enter a value between 0 and 15 inches.

This value has no effect on text aligned to a path.

7. **Alignment**

Choose an item from this pop-up to set the horizontal alignment of a paragraph. These items are described in depth in "Style: Alignment," earlier in this chapter.

8. **H&J**

This pop-up displays all Hyphenation and Justification settings currently available to the document. See "Edit: H&Js" in Chapter 6 for more information.

9. **Drop Caps**

When this box is checked, XPress converts the first characters of a paragraph into drop caps (sometimes referred to as an *initial caps*). The nature of these characters are defined by the following settings:

Character Count

This value determines how many of the first characters are converted to initial caps. For the traditional single-character drop cap, enter 1. To include more letters, enter a value up to 8.

Line Count

This value determines the size of the initial caps. Rather than attempt to set a point size, enter the number of lines you want the characters to occupy. For example, when the value is 3 (the default), the characters are scaled until they drop three lines down. Enter a value between 2 and 16 lines.

XPress does not measure the size of initial caps in terms of points—rather, it's based on a percentage of the affected characters themselves. (See "Style: Size," earlier in this chapter, for more information.)

10. **Keep Lines Together**

   These controls reduce the possibility of *widows* (the last line of a paragraph appearing at the start of a column) and *orphans* (the first line of a paragraph appearing at the bottom of a column). Most often, this option is applied to body text. Check this box to access the following items:

   All Lines in ¶

   When enabled, this item prevents a paragraph from being split at the end of a column. If it doesn't fit in the available space, the entire paragraph is bumped to the next column.

   Start and End

   When enabled, this option allows a paragraph to be split.

   To prevent orphans, the Start value determines the minimum number of lines XPress allows to appear at the bottom of a column. For example, if the value is 2 (the default), at least two lines of the paragraph are retained at the bottom of the column. If there is not enough space, the entire paragraph is bumped to the next column.

   To prevent widows, the End value determines the minimum number of lines appearing at the top of a column. For example, if the value is set to 2 (the default), XPress will carry over an additional line if a widow occurs.

11. **Keep with Next ¶**

   When this box is checked, the paragraph is forced to flow with the following paragraph into the next linked text box. This feature is useful when two paragraphs cannot be separated. For example, when a subhead appears directly above some body copy, you don't want the subhead to be the last line in a column, with the body copy appearing at the top of the next. If this option was checked when the subhead style sheet was defined, then the subhead automatically flows into the next column.

12. **Lock to Baseline Grid**

   When checked, this item forces the baselines of the text to snap to the grid defined in the Edit: Preferences: Document: **Paragraph** panel. See "View: Show/Hide Baseline Grid" in Chapter 12, *The View Menu*, for more information.

13. **Apply**

   Click this button to preview the effect of new Paragraph Attributes settings. If necessary, move the dialog out of the way after clicking. If unsatisfied with the settings, change them. To reset all of them at once, click Cancel, and open the dialog again.

See Also

Appendix A (Style: **Formats**)
Edit: Preferences: Document: **Paragraph**

Edit: Preferences: Document: **Tools**
Edit: **H&Js**
Style (Text): **Size**
Style (Text): **Alignment**
Style (Text): **Leading**
Style (Text): **Tabs**
Style (Text): **Rules**
Item: **Modify: Text**
View: **Show/Hide Baseline Grid**
View: **Show/Hide Invisibles**

Style: Tabs

Use this command to define a series of *tab stops*, or formatting characters that allow you to jump the text-entry cursor to a specified position by pressing the Tab key.

Tabs can only be applied on the paragraph level. You can position them only between the left and right indents of a column, text box, or text path.

By default, XPress adds invisible left-aligned tab stops every half inch. Although they don't show in the Tabs panel or the ruler that appears over the text box, you can tell they exist by pressing the Tab key: the cursor jumps across the text box in half-inch increments.

To override the invisible tabs, you must define new stops using the Tabs panel. When you apply a single tab, all previous invisible tab stops are ignored in favor of the one you manually place. For example, if you place a tab stop at 1.5 inches, the cursor jumps immediately to that position when you press the Tab key. However, if you press the Tab key again, the cursor continues to jump in half-inch increments. If you place another tab stop at 3 inches, the cursor will jump from 1.5 to 3.

Unless you happen to require a series of half-inch tab stops (which is unlikely), ignore the invisible tabs. Define your own, apply only the number you need, and place them precisely in the required positions.

Common Uses

Refer to Appendix A for full descriptions of the following:

- Creating tables
- Defining tabs with dot leaders

Common Errors

- **Using the spacebar instead of defining tab stops.** Many users, in lieu of tabs, attempt to align multiple items using the spacebar. This has three major shortcomings. First, digital typefaces are not monospaced (like the type set by a typewriter)—each character has its own width and space, which makes it impossible to consistently align using the spacebar. Second, it's difficult to adjust the alignment—you must go back and enter or delete spaces. Third, unlike tab stops, spaces are affected by size changes, font changes, and text reflow—altering any of these throws your alignment out of whack. This is not to mention that using the spacebar is incredibly frustrating and time consuming. By setting tab stops, you never have to (and shouldn't) enter more than one space character in a row.

- **Accidentally changing a newly applied tab stop.** When a tab stop is highlighted in the ruler, clicking different buttons in the Tabs panel changes the type of tab stop. Also, if you attempt to position a new stop by entering a value in the Position field, you only affect the highlighted item. There are two ways to avoid this: clicking the Set button or click-dragging a new tab stop onto the ruler deselects the currently highlighted item.

- **Inserting too many tab stops.** Only enter the exact number of tabs you require.

Special Notes

- When you choose this command, a ruler appears at the top of the currently selected text box. If desired, you can set tab stops by doing the following:

  - Click the appropriate tab style button, and click on the ruler. Drag the stop to reposition it.

  - Click-drag from the desired tab style button to the ruler. Drag the stop to reposition it.

  - To change an existing tab style, click the item once in the ruler to highlight it, then click the appropriate tab style button.

  This ruler spans the distance between the Text Inset values (entered in the Item: Modify: **Text** panel) of a text box or column. You can also use it to set the Left Indent, First Line, and Right Indent. (See "Style: Formats," earlier in this chapter, for more information.)

- Often, you'll need to apply different tab styles to the same body of text. For example, in your body copy, one section may require columns every 2 inches, while another requires dot leaders set at 5 inches. To handle this most effectively, use style sheets. After creating the initial paragraph style for Body Text, duplicate it in the Edit: **Style Sheets** dialog. When editing the duplicate style, choose Body Text from the Based On pop-up, set the desired tab stops, and rename the style descriptively: "Body Text w/ 2-inch tabs," for example. This way, you can easily apply and edit the tabs as needed, plus you can make additional formatting changes, such as Space Before, Space After, or Rules.

- When View: **Show Invisibles** is enabled, tab jumps appear as right-pointing arrows, positioned where you initially pressed the Tab key.

- When you add fill characters (referred to as *leaders*) to a tab space, you can further adjust their size and spacing by highlighting the characters and setting a new point size or tracking value in the Measurements Palette.

- You can enter an automatic right-indent tab stop without opening the Style (Text): **Tabs** panel: insert the cursor in the appropriate position, and press (Option) [**Alt**]-Tab. Any text following this tab aligns flush to the right indent. This tab stop does not appear in the Tabs panel, so it cannot be included in a style sheet definition. To remove it, enable View: **Show Invisibles**, and manually delete the tab symbol.

The Tabs Panel

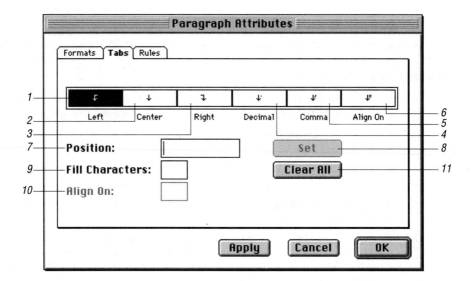

1. **Left**

   After pressing the Tab key, text is left aligned to this tab stop.

2. **Center**

   After pressing the Tab key, text is center aligned to this tab stop.

3. **Right**

   After pressing the Tab key, text is right aligned to this tab stop.

4. **Decimal**

   Essentially, this tab stop aligns on decimals (simply the period character). For example, if you are aligning figures in an accounting balance sheet, "$140.50" and "$5.25" align on the decimal, regardless of the number of characters each item contains. It works by acting as a right-aligned tab until a decimal appears—then from that point, it acts as a left-aligned tab.

   This tab actually aligns on the first-appearing non-numerical character. For example, when you use this tab to align "5p6" and "23p10," the items align on the "p." However, if you attempt to align "5p6.1" and "23p10.5" on the decimal, it still aligns on the "p." In this case, if you insist on aligning to the decimal, use an Align On tab stop (description follows) and align to the period character.

When an item contains no non-numerical character, this tab stop acts the same as a Right tab.

5. **Comma**

This tab stop is identical to the Decimal tab, except it aligns items to the comma character.

6. **Align On**

This tab stop is identical to the Decimal tab, except it aligns to the single character you enter in the Align On field.

7. **Position**

This field performs two functions:

–   To place a tab stop at a specific location, click the appropriate tab style button, enter the desired position in this field, and click Set. The stop automatically appears on the ruler above the text.

–   When dragging a tab stop in the ruler to reposition it, the value in this field shifts to display its current position.

The unit of measurement used here is based on the Horizontal Measure setting in the Edit: Preferences: Document: **General** panel. You can enter different units of measurement, provided you include the appropriate abbreviation after the value.

8. **Set**

After entering a value in the Position field, click this button to apply it to the ruler. After clicking a tab stop in the ruler to highlight it, click this button to deselect the item.

9. **Fill Characters**

If desired, you can specify one or two characters to repeat in the space between a tab character and tab stop. To use this feature, highlight the desired tab stop in the ruler, and enter the necessary characters in this field.

The most common example is a dot leader: by entering a single period here, pressing the Tab key to jump to that stop results in a line of dots connecting to the subsequent text.

To spread out a repeating fill character, enter a single character then a space.

10. **Align On**

This field is available only after clicking the Align On tab button. Here, enter the character you wish to align tabbed item to.

11. **Clear All**

Click this button to clear all manually entered tab stops from the ruler. (Option) [**Alt**]-clicking ruler does the same thing.

Style: Rules

Use this command to apply horizontal lines above or beneath a specified paragraph. Unlike creating rules with any of the line tools, these rules are built into the formatting of the paragraph and flow as necessary through a chain of text boxes.

This command does not effect text on a text path.

Common Errors

Attempting to use this command to underline single words within a paragraph. This command only works on the paragraph level—even if you attempt to create a character style sheet based on a paragraph style that contains a rule, you cannot underline single words. The only options you have for doing this are described under Style (Text): Type Styles: **Underline**.

Special Notes

To create custom lines for use with this command, use Edit: **Dashes & Stripes**. The new additions are available in the Style pop-up in the Rules panel.

The Rules Panel

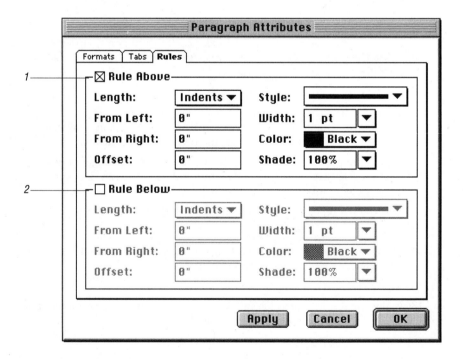

1. **Rule Above**

   When this box is checked, XPress applies a rule above the paragraph. The style of the rule is based on the following settings:

   Length

   This pop-up determines the length of the rule. When Indents is set, the rule extends from the left to the right indent, regardless of the underlying text. When Text is set, the rule only matches the length of the abutting text.

   From Left

   This value adds a space between the left indent and the left edge of the rule. If you increased the Left Indent value using the Paragraph Attributes dialog, you can enter negative values here, if desired.

   From Right

   This value adds a space between the right indent and the right edge of the rule. If you increased the Right Indent value using the Paragraph Attributes dialog, you can enter negative values here, if desired.

   Offset

   This value determines the distance between a paragraph and a rule. Enter either a numerical value or a percentage.

   When you enter a numerical value, the distance is measured from the baseline of the first line to the bottom of the rule. (For Rule Below, it measures from the baseline of the last line to the top of the rule.) Positive values increase the distance up to 15 inches. Negative values decrease the distance—you enter a negative value of up to half the current line width.

   When you enter a percentage, you work with the space that occurs between paragraphs. For example, a value of 50% places the rule directly between two paragraphs. If a Rule Above has an offset of 40%, then 40% of the space between the two paragraphs is placed below the center of the rule. If a Rule Below has an offset of 40%, the 40% of the space is placed above the center of the rule.

   The default value is 0%, which places the rule flush with the abutting text.

   Style

   This pop-up displays all dashes and stripes currently available to the document. To make any changes, choose Edit: **Dashes & Stripes**.

   Width

   This value determines the weight of the rule. Choose from a series of presets, or enter your own value in the available field. Rules can be set between .001 and 864 pt.

   Color

   This pop-up displays all colors currently available in the Colors Palette. To make any changes, choose Edit: **Colors**.

Shade

This value sets the tint of the applied rule color. Choose from a series of presets (in 10% increments), or enter a value between 0 and 100% in the available field.

2. **Rule Below**

When this box is checked, XPress applies a rule below the paragraph. The settings are virtually identical to the ones described under Rule Above.

Style: Paragraph Style Sheet

This submenu displays all currently available paragraph style sheets, plus options for No Style and Normal. To apply a paragraph style, select the appropriate text (or insert the cursor in a paragraph), and choose the desired submenu item.

Special Notes

The contents of this submenu are identical to the Style Sheets Palette. In fact, that palette offers much more efficient methods of applying and manipulating style sheets. Not only can you apply them without accessing a menu item, but certain keyboard-based effects—such as (Option) [**Alt**]-clicking a style to reapply it, or (Command) [**Control**]-clicking to open the Edit: **Style Sheets** dialog—only work using the Style Sheets Palette. The keys have no effect when choosing an item from this submenu.

Style: Flip Horizontal

This command horizontally flips the entire contents of the currently selected text box. The effect is the same as if the text were printed on a transparent page, turned over from left to right.

Special Notes

- This command can be applied in addition to Style (Text): **Flip Vertical**.

- When text applied to a text path is selected, this command changes to Style (Text): **Flip Text**. This command flips text onto the opposite side of the text path. Unlike Flip Horizontal or Vertical, the text does not become a mirror image.

Style: Flip Vertical

This command vertically flips the entire contents of the currently selected text box. The effect is the same as if the text were printed on a transparent page, turned over from top to bottom.

Special Notes

- This command can be applied in addition to Style (Text): **Flip Horizontal**.

- When text applied to a path is selected, this command is not available.

CHAPTER 8

The Style Menu (Picture)

These commands appear in the Style Menu only when a picture box containing an imported graphic is selected and the Item Tool or Content Tool is active.

When you apply these commands, you don't affect the actual contents of the image file. Rather, you change the way that XPress "perceives" the information, as if the image passes through a filter or lens when output.

XPress allows you to tonally edit graphics saved in the following file formats: TIFF, JPEG, PICT, Scitex CT, BMP, PCX, OS/2 Bitmap, PAINT, and PhotoCD. However, the commands you can actually apply depend on the file type, as well as the *bit depth*, or number of colors contained in the graphic. (Refer to the "Special Notes" section in the description of each command for specific limitations.)

These commands are not available when a picture box contains the following graphics:

- **Photoshop EPS.** This includes five-part DCS files.
- **Vector-based graphics.** This includes Illustrator and FreeHand EPS files, as well as object-oriented PICTs.

Special Notes

In order to access these commands, the Color TIFFs pop-up in the Edit: Preferences: Application: **Display** panel must be set to 8 bit when a graphic is imported. If this item was set to 16 bit or 32 bit when a graphic was imported, the Style Menu commands (except Flip Horizontal and Vertical) are not available.

See Also

Edit: Preferences: Application: **Display**
Photoshop in a Nutshell (File: **Supported File Formats**)
Photoshop in a Nutshell (Image: **Mode**)

Style Menu
(Picture)

Style: Color

This submenu displays all items currently available in the Colors Palette. There is no functional reason to use this menu item over the Colors Palette, which allows you to access colors with a swift mouse-click. To add or remove colors, use the Edit: **Colors** dialog.

Special Notes

- Use this submenu to recolor the following image types: TIFF (1-bit and Gray-scale), JPEG (Grayscale), BMP and PCX (1-bit and Grayscale), and PICT (1-bit and Grayscale).

- You can't apply a single color to a full color image. However, XPress allows you to convert a color TIFF to Grayscale when you import it, which you can then recolor from this submenu. To do this, choose File: **Get Picture**, locate the color TIFF, and hold down the (Command) [**Control**] key when you click Open.

See Also

File: **Get Picture**
Edit: **Color**

Style: Shade

This submenu lets you change the tint value of a single-ink image. The preset values range from 0% to 100%, in 10% increments. To set a value not available in the list, choose Other. The Item: **Modify** dialog opens, where you enter a value in the Shade field.

The results of this command depend on the image type affected:

- When you reduce the tint of a 1-bit image, you simply reduce the overall screen value of the one color. For example, if you import black and white line art and set the shade to 10%, it outputs as 10% black.

- When you reduce the tint of a Grayscale image, you reduce all existing half-tone values by the percentage specified in the Style (Picture): **Shade** pop-up. For example, if you choose 40%, 100% black information appears as 40%; 80% values appear as 32%; 10% values appear as 4%. This process is also known as *ghosting.*

- When you reduce the tint of an image after recoloring it with a CMYK color, you reduce each component by the percentage specified in the Style (Pic-ture): **Shade** pop-up. For example, if you apply a 50% shade to a halftone recolored with C: 40, M: 20, Y: 70, K: 10, the new color is C: 20, M: 10, Y: 35, K: 5.

Common Errors

Blowing out highlight information. Many halftones that contain highlight information have been adjusted to accommodate the limitations of a printing press. For example, most presses can reproduce tones between 7% and 92%, so the tonal range of a halftone is compressed to fit between those endpoints. This avoids light tones burning out and dark shadows filling in with solid ink. If a halftone's highlights are over-reduced by lowering its shade value, they will burn out when reproduced on-press. For example, if you apply a 30% shade, you reset all halftone values between 7% and 20% to 2% and 6%—which may not be high enough to print successfully. If you must create a ghost, consider creating it in Photoshop, where you still have control over the minimum highlight value.

Special Notes

Use this submenu to shade the following image types: TIFF (1-bit and Grayscale), JPEG (Grayscale), BMP and PCX (1-bit and Grayscale), and PICT (1-bit and Grayscale).

See Also

> Style (Picture): **Color**
> Item: **Modify**
> *Photoshop in a Nutshell* (Image: Adjust: **Levels**)
> *Photoshop in a Nutshell* (Edit: **Fill**)

Style: Negative
(Command-Shift) [Control-Shift]-hyphen

This command inverts the values of the selected graphic, producing a negative image. The results depend on the image type affected:

- When applied to 1-bit line art, black information becomes white, and white information becomes black.

- When applied to a Grayscale image, the output values are reversed: 100% black becomes 0% black, 90% becomes 10%, 80% becomes 20%, and so forth. The effect is the same as if the original image were inverted in Photoshop.

- When applied to a color image, the results may be unexpected—especially if you have used Photoshop to invert color values. Regardless of the color mode of the imported image, the on-screen preview is RGB—so this command creates an RGB negative, even when applied to a CMYK or Lab Color image. Essentially, this means you have no way of predicting the colors that output. If you must create such a special effect, consider generating it in Photoshop.

Style Menu (Picture)

Special Notes

- You can apply this command to the following image types: TIFF (1-bit, Grayscale, and color), JPEG (Grayscale and color), Scitex CT (Grayscale and color), BMP and PCX (1-bit, Grayscale, and color), PICT (Grayscale and color), and PhotoCD.

- Previous adjustments made using Style (Picture): **Contrast** affect the results of this command.

Style: Contrast
(Command-Shift) [Control-Shift]-C

This command allows you to modify the tone and color content of an imported image.

Common Uses

Refer to Appendix A, *Common Techniques*, for full descriptions of the following:

- Applying simple contrast to an image
- Converting a Grayscale image to black and white line art
- Converting a CMYK image to black and white line art
- Desaturating a color image
- Posterizing to a specific number of levels
- Ghosting a Grayscale image
- Ghosting a color image

Common Errors

Using these commands in lieu of a dedicated image editing program, such as Adobe Photoshop. Style (Picture): **Contrast** is strictly a low-budget editing solution, good for applying simple effects to images where color content or accuracy is not important. The following limitations apply:

- **Original image resolution is largely ignored.** For example, if you convert a 600 pixel-per-inch Grayscale image to black and white, the affected file outputs at roughly 150 ppi. Similarly, finely detailed color images suffer a considerable loss of image quality, especially at higher linescreen values. This alone, in my opinion, is enough to bypass these tools in favor of a more robust image editing program.

- **Corrections are based on a low-res image preview.** Imported graphics always appear on-screen at approximately 72 pixels per inch. To make accurate color decisions, you must have access to every image pixel.

- **You can't accurately judge color values.** Unless you have a rigidly calibrated color editing system, the color you see on-screen is severely affected by factors such as monitor type and room lighting. If you're willing to invest the time and effort to establish such a system, chances are a program like Photoshop is already part of your production process.

- **You can't make numerical corrections.** Photoshop's correcting tools allow you to make corrections based on precise color values, which allow you to better predict the results of your editing decisions. XPress has no such controls.

- **You can't read the adjusted color values.** Photoshop has an on-screen densitometer that displays the numerical values for any part of the image. Also, as you correct, it displays precise before-and-after values. XPress has no such controls.

- **You can't make partial corrections.** The edits you make in XPress can only be applied to the entire image—there is no way to edit a specific part of a file.

- **You can't edit image flaws.** These commands only affect color and tone. Any techniques such as sharpening, blurring, or retouching must be done in another application.

- **You can't save adjustment values.** XPress has no Save/Load command that allows you to apply the same corrections to multiple images. At best, you must write down the adjustment values and apply them manually to each image.

- **You can't control separation values.** Photoshop, for example, allows you to determine UCR/GCR, maximum ink density, and black ink limits when an image is converted to a CMYK file. As soon as you edit such an image in XPress, the relationship between colors is overridden. For example, if you invert a very light CMYK image in XPress, the image becomes extremely dark, because the abundance of black highlights become shadows. You have no control over the ink coverage, which may be too high for the intended press or paper stock.

Special Notes

- You can apply this command to the following image types: TIFF (Grayscale and color), JPEG (Grayscale and color), Scitex CT (Grayscale and color), BMP and PCX (Grayscale and color), PICT (Grayscale and color), and PhotoCD.

- Press (Command) [**Control**]-Z while editing to reset the Picture Contrast Specifications dialog.

Style Menu (Picture)

The Picture Contrast Specifications Dialog

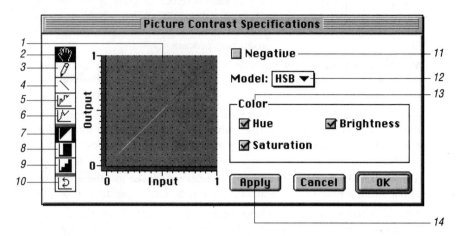

1. **The Input/Output Graph**

   This graph is at the center of all adjustments. The horizontal axis, *Input*, represents the values contained in the imported image. The vertical axis, *Output*, represents the new values applied to the image by this command.

   Each axis appears as a range from 0 to 1. More accurately, 0 equals the lowest possible value of whatever item is selected in the Color section; 1 equals the highest possible value. For example, if CMYK is set in the Model pop-up and only the Cyan box is checked under Color, 0 equals 0% cyan and 1 equals 100% cyan. By adjusting the diagonal curve that bisects the graph, you increase or decrease the amount of information that displays on-screen (and subsequently outputs).

   To facilitate your adjustments, the dotted lines divide the graph into 10% increments. Unfortunately, no readout is available to display positions on the curve.

2. **The Hand Tool**

   Use this tool to drag the currently active curves across the graph. Hold down the Shift key while dragging to constrain its motion vertically or horizontally. Be aware that dragging the curve against the edge of the graph flattens it, as you can see when you drag the curve back again.

3. **The Pencil Tool**

   Use this tool to draw freehand curve modifications. Although many users simply use this tool to create radical tonal shifts, it's also good for making very slight adjustments.

4. **The Line Tool**

   With this tool, click-drag to draw linear modifications. The curve jumps to the point you first click on, and as you drag, the curve straightens. Hold down the Shift key to constrain the line vertically or horizontally.

5. **Add Posterized Points**

   Posterizing refers to reducing the number of tones in an image. Clicking this button places points on the curve at the following values: 5%, 15%, 25%, 35%, 45%, 55%, 65%, 75%, 85%, and 95%.

   Drag one of the points to affect 10% of the tonal range at a time. For example, dragging the point at 55% adjusts the values between 50% and 60%.

   As you drag, the 10% range snaps to a horizontal line, which sets the range to the same value (or posterizes). For example, if you drag the point at 55% up to the 70% line, every value between 50% and 60% resets to 70%.

6. **Add Spike Points**

   Clicking this button places points on the curve at 10% increments. As you drag, the point forms a spike, which redistributes the tones on either side.

7. **Normal Contrast**

   Click this button to reset all curves currently checked in the Color section. To reset a single curve, make sure it's the only one checked.

8. **High Contrast**

   Click this button to add a threshold curve. By default, a vertical adjustment is applied at 30%. For example, when applied to a halftone, all tones lighter than 30% black become white, and all tones darker than 30% turn black. The effect is similar to converting a Grayscale image to black and white line art. To reposition the threshold, select the Hand Tool, hold down the Shift key, and drag horizontally.

9. **Add Posterized Levels**

   Click this button to automatically posterize a curve to six levels: 0%, 20%, 40%, 60%, 80%, and 100%.

10. **Invert Curve**

    Click this button to invert the active curve, resulting in a negative version of the current values. The effect ultimately depends on the items selected in the Color section.

11. **Negative**

    Check this box to edit a negative version of the currently selected image. The curve doesn't change—rather, the effect is the same as if you applied Style (Picture): **Negative**, then chose Style (Picture): **Contrast**.

12. **Model**

    This pop-up determines the types of curve available in the Color section, below. Although you can make corrections based on four different color models, bear in mind that the final correction is based on RGB values, which are then converted to CMYK if the image is separated. See "Mode Overview" in Chapter 10 of *Photoshop in a Nutshell* for more info on color models.

Style Menu (Picture)

13. **Color**

This area displays the different curve options available to adjust an image. To edit a particular curve, check the appropriate box. The items that appear depend on the setting in the Model pop-up:

HSB

Here, you adjust using the Hue, Saturation, and Brightness model. When Hue is checked, the Input/Output bars reflect the spectrum of colors. When Saturation is checked, they reflect overall color intensity. When Brightness is checked, they reflect overall color lightness. When multiple items are checked, their values are edited simultaneously.

RGB

Here, you adjust using the Red, Blue, and Green model. When any particular color is checked, the Input/Output bars reflect the intensity of that color, from none to full strength. When multiple items are checked, you edit their values simultaneously.

CMY

Here, you adjust using the Cyan, Magenta, and Yellow model. When any particular color is checked, the Input/Output bars reflect the intensity of that color, from none to full strength. When multiple items are checked, you edit them simultaneously.

CMYK

Here, you adjust using the Cyan, Magenta, Yellow, and Black model. When any particular color is checked, the Input/Output bars reflect the intensity of that color, from none to full strength. When multiple items are checked, you edit them simultaneously.

14. **Apply**

Click this button to see the adjustments applied to the image without closing the dialog. Pressing (Command) [**Control**]-A does the same thing. To preview as you edit, press (Option-Command) [**Alt-Control**]-A.

See Also

Style (Picture): **Negative**
Photoshop in a Nutshell (Edit: **Fill**)
Photoshop in a Nutshell (Image: **Mode Overview**)
Photoshop in a Nutshell (Image: Adjust: **Levels**)
Photoshop in a Nutshell (Image: Adjust: **Curves**)
Photoshop in a Nutshell (Image: Adjust: **Posterize**)
Photoshop in a Nutshell (Image: Adjust: **Threshold**)
Photoshop in a Nutshell (The Info Palette)

Style: Halftone
(Command-Shift) [Control-Shift]-H

Use this command to define custom halftone screen values.

Common Errors

Recoloring a halftone with a process color, then setting a custom angle. To reproduce properly, process inks output at different angles. If you use Style (Picture):
Color (or the Colors Palette) to apply a process color to a halftone, you can still
access this command. If you set a single custom angle, every color reproducing
that image outputs at the same angle. For the best results, use this command to
affect single-ink halftones.

Special Notes

- You can apply this command to the following image types: TIFF (1-bit and
  Grayscale), JPEG (Grayscale), BMP and PCX (1-bit and Grayscale), and PICT
  (1-bit and Grayscale). This command only affects 1-bit images if a tint has
  been applied using Style (Picture): **Shade**.

- Due to limitations inherent in PostScript, not all screen angles and frequencies can be output. If you enter one of these values, your output device automatically substitutes the closest available value.

- Most often, this command is used to generate special effects, combining custom screen shapes with very low frequencies.

The Picture Halftone Specifications Dialog

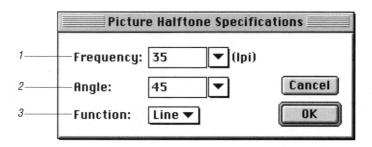

1. **Frequency**

   This item overrides the linescreen value entered in the File: Print: **Output**
   panel. Choose from a list of preset values, or enter your own. If you choose
   Default, XPress uses the linescreen value entered in the Print dialog.

2. **Angle**

This item overrides the screen angle entered in the File: Print: **Output** panel. Choose from a list of preset values, or enter your own. If you choose Default, XPress uses the angle chosen in the Print dialog.

3. **Function**

This item overrides the halftone dot shape entered in the File: Print: **Output** panel. The four standard shapes—Dot, Line, Ellipse, and Square—are listed in the pop-up. The last item, Ordered Dither, produces pattern-dithered output. If you choose Default, XPress applies the shape chosen in the Print dialog.

See Also

File: Print: **Output**
Style (Picture): **Color**
Style (Picture): **Shade**

Style: Flip Horizontal

This command turns the currently selected image over from left to right, like flipping a transparent overlay.

Style: Flip Vertical

This command turns the currently selected image over from top to bottom, like flipping a transparent overlay. The effect is the same as rotating the picture box 180°, then choosing Style (Picture): **Flip Horizontal**.

CHAPTER 9

The Style Menu (Line)

The following commands are available in the Style Menu only when a line is selected. Use the following tools to create lines:

- Line Tool
- Bézier Line Tool
- Freehand Line Tool
- Orthogonal Line Tool
- Orthogonal Text Path Tool
- Bézier Text Path Tool
- Freehand Text Path Tool

See Chapter 3, *Line Tools*, for more information.

Special Notes

- Unlike the Style Menu for text or imported graphics, these commands are available when any tool is active in the Tools Palette. However, if a text path is selected with the Content Tool, the Style Menu displays text editing commands. (See Chapter 7, *The Style Menu (Text)*, for more information.)
- When multiple lines are selected, this menu is not available. However, you can edit more than one line at a time by choosing Item: **Modify** and adjusting the settings in the Group panel.

Style: Line Style

This submenu displays all dashes and stripes currently available to the document. To add custom line styles, choose Edit: **Dashes & Stripes**.

Style:Arrowheads

This submenu contains six arrowhead presets. From top to bottom:

- **Plain Line**. Choose this item to remove any applied arrowheads.

- **Arrowhead on Last Line Point**. Each line has a start and an end: it starts when you first click with the Line Tool, and ends when you release the mouse button. This item places an arrowhead on the point at which you release the mouse button.

- **Arrowhead on First Line Point**. This item places an arrowhead on the point at which you first created the line.

- **Arrowhead on First Line Point, Endcap on Last**. This item places an arrowhead at the start of a line and a primitive "tailfeather" at the end.

- **Arrowhead on Last Line Point, Endcap on First**. This item places an arrowhead at the end of a line and the tailfeather at the start.

- **Double Arrowheads**. This item places identical arrowheads on both ends of the line.

Special Notes

- The size of the arrowhead or tailfeather is based on the weight of the line: thicker lines have larger arrowheads, thinner lines have smaller arrowheads. The smallest possible arrowhead is 9 pt. long and 5 pt. wide—the arrowhead of a 2 pt. line. If you set a line weight below 2 pt., the line changes, but the arrowheads remain at the same size.

- As a design tool, this option is extremely limited. You have no control over the size and shape of the arrowhead or the endcap. And because the flat base of the arrowhead is based on the established line thickness, it becomes obvious if you attempt to apply the larger arrowhead of a very short, heavier line over the end of a thinner line.

- If you must have more control over your arrowheads, use a vector-based illustration program. Adobe Illustrator, for example, has a filter called "Add Arrowheads," where you can choose from 27 different styles and control the size completely. Plus, the arrowhead is based on Bézier curves, which you can edit further, if necessary. As long as you determine the necessary line lengths and thicknesses, you can create custom arrowheads in Illustrator, import them into XPress, and rotate them as necessary.

- If desired, you can convert an arrowhead to editable paths by selecting it and choosing Item: Shape: **Bézier Box**.

Style: Width
(Command-Shift) [Control-Shift]-\

Use this submenu to set the thickness of a line. You can choose from seven preset widths. Or you can choose Other, which opens the Item: **Modify** dialog, where you can enter a width between 0 and 864 points.

Special Notes

- The submenu includes an option called Hairline. When output to an image-setter, a line at this width is .125 pt. thick (.017 inches). A line this thin is good for very little—it can't be trapped, it can barely be detected as a frame or line, and many presses can't even reproduce it accurately. Unfortunately, when printed to a low-resolution laser printer, lines set to Hairline output at roughly .25 pt., a width that poses no real production threat. Many designers don't realize that the line becomes thinner when output at high resolutions, and problems result. To be safe, avoid this item completely. If you want thin rules, set them as low as .25 pt. (preferably .5 pt.).

- Use the following shortcuts to set line width on the fly:

  - **Decrease width by preset value.** Press (Command-Shift) [**Control-Shift**]-comma.

  - **Increase width by preset value.** Press (Command-Shift) [**Control-Shift**]-period.

  - **Decrease width in 1 pt. increments.** Press (Option-Command-Shift) [**Alt-Control-Shift**]-comma.

  - **Increase width in 1 pt. increments.** Press (Option-Command-Shift) [**Alt-Control-Shift**]-period.

Style: Color

This submenu displays all items currently available in the Colors Palette. There is no functional reason to use this menu item over the Colors Palette, which allows you to access colors with a swift mouse-click.

Style: Shade

This submenu lets you change the tint value of a line. The preset values range from 0% to 100%, in 10% increments. To set a value not available in the list, choose Other. The Item: **Modify** dialog opens, where you enter a value in the Shade field.

CHAPTER 10

The Item Menu

Item: Modify

Use this command to further edit picture and text boxes, text paths, and lines. The currently selected item determines the panels that appear in the Modify dialog:

- **Picture Box**. The Box, Picture, Frame, Runaround, and Clipping panels appear.
- **Text Box**. The Box, Text, Frame, and Runaround panels appear.
- **Empty Box**. The Box, Frame, and Runaround panels appear.
- **Text Path**. The Line, Text Path, and Runaround panels appear.
- **Line**. The Line and Runaround panels appear.

Common Uses

Editing multiple items. Most XPress commands can only be applied to a single item. For example, when a single picture box is selected, the commands in the right half of the Measurements Palette allow you to set the graphic's position, angle, skew, scale, and orientation within the box. When more than one box is selected at once, those commands are not available—but they can still be accessed in the Modify dialog.

Special Notes

- Open the Item: **Modify** dialog at any time by double-clicking a box, line, or path with the Item Tool.
- If a selection includes items grouped using Item: **Group**, as well as an item outside that group, Item: **Modify** is not available.
- When multiple items are selected, the Group panel appears in the Modify dialog. When the items are the same type, this panel is substituted for the Box or

Line panel, and your edits are applied to all items. When the items are different types, the number of panels is restricted, and you may not be able to make your desired edits:

– **Picture box and text box.** Only the Group (containing Box settings) and Frame panels appear.

– **Picture or text box and line.** Only the Group panel containing a limited number of Box settings appears.

– **Line and text path.** Only the Group panel containing Line settings appears.

If you need to make more specific edits, select an individual item before choosing Item: **Modify**.

Item: Modify: Box Panel

This panel only adjusts a picture or text box. The contents of either box are not affected.

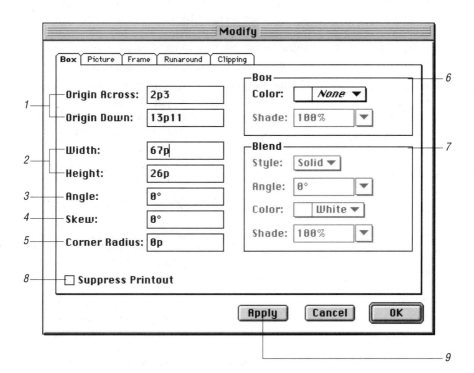

1. **Origin Across and Origin Down**

   These values display the position of the upper-left corner of the box, in relation to the zero points of the ruler. When the zero points are set to the upper-left corner of the page (the default), Origin Across displays the distance of the left edge of the box from the left edge of the page; Origin Down displays the distance of the top of the box from the top of the page.

If the zero points have been set to another part of the page, these values reflect their new position. To use this option accurately, you may need to reset the zero points. (See "View: Show/Hide Rulers" in Chapter 12, *The View Menu*, for more information.)

Reposition a box by entering new values in the Origin fields. To place a box at a specific ruler measurement, enter the new value. For example, if the zero points are in the default position, enter "4" in Origin Across to set the left box edge to 4 inches; enter "2" in Origin Down to set the top box edge to 2 inches.

To move a box a specific distance from its original position, enter a positive or negative amount *after* the current value. For example, to move a box 1.5 inches to the right, enter "+1.5" after the current Origin Across value. Negative values move the box to the left. Similarly, to move a box 1.5 inches down, enter "+1.5" after the current Origin Down value. Negative values move the box up. (This example assumes that the Horizontal and Vertical Measure values in the Edit: Preferences: Document: **General** panel are set to inches. Enter different units of measurement by including the correct abbreviation. For example, if the Measure is set to inches, you can move a box 2.5 picas to the right by entering "+2p6" after the current Origin Across value.)

These items appear in the Measurements Palette when the box is selected.

When an anchored box or line is selected, Align with Text appears instead of the Origin Across and Origin Down fields. Here, you determine how the item appears in a text box in relation to the surrounding text. (See "Edit: Paste" in Chapter 6, *The Edit Menu*, for information on anchoring.) The available settings are as follows:

–   **Ascent**. When enabled, this option aligns the top of the anchored item with the top of the character that immediately follows it.

–   **Baseline**. When enabled, this option (the default) aligns the bottom of the anchored item with the current baseline.

–   **Offset**. Only available when Baseline is enabled, this field allows you to shift the anchored item above or below the current baseline. After such a value is entered, note that the anchored item can still be affected if you highlight it and apply a Style (Text): **Baseline Shift** amount.

2. **Width and Height**

These fields display the current width and height of the selected box. To resize a box to a specific width and height, enter the new values in these fields. To increase the dimensions by a specific amount, enter a positive or negative number *after* the current value. For example, to increase the width by one inch, enter "+1" after the current amount. Negative values decrease the size.

When more than one box is selected, Width displays the distance between the edges farthest to the left and right, and Height displays the distance between highest and lowest box edge. When you increase or decrease the values, all selected boxes are scaled to match the new dimensions.

These items appear in the Measurements Palette when the box is selected.

3. **Angle** (−360° to 360°)

To rotate a box, enter a value between −359° and 359°—when you enter 360°, the box doesn't move. Positive values rotate to the left; negative values rotate to the right.

This option only rotates around the center of a box. When multiple items are selected, this option rotates around their mathematical center. To rotate around a different pivot point, use the Rotation Tool.

This item appears in the Measurements Palette when the box is selected.

4. **Skew** (−75° to 75°)

This option slants a single box across a horizontal axis. The box contents are skewed as well, so the result is a special effect.

After skewing a box, you can set the contents back to their original appearance by going to the Picture or Text panel and entering the opposite skew value. For example, if you skew a picture box by 20°, enter a skew value of −20° in the Picture panel.

To create a slanted box that doesn't affect the contents, use the Bézier Text Box or Bézier Picture Box Tool. If necessary, skew a standard box to the desired degree, then trace it with the appropriate tool. Delete the original box when finished.

5. **Corner Radius** (0 to 2 inches)

This option rounds the corners of the following box types: rectangular, rounded corner, beveled corner, and concave corner. It's not available when round boxes, Bézier boxes, or grouped items are selected.

6. **Box**

These options allow you to set the background color and tint of the selected items. (See "Style: Color" and "Style: Shade" in Chapter 8, *The Style Menu (Picture)*, and see Chapter 17, *The Colors Palette*, for more information.)

If multiple items with different colors are selected, Mixed Colors appears in the Color pop-up. When you choose a single color, it's applied to all selected items. Similarly, if multiple items with different shades are selected, the Shade field is blank. Setting a new value affects all selected items.

7. **Blend**

These options allow you to fill a box with a two-color gradient. If a blend has been applied to a box using the Colors Palette, this area displays the current values (if the selected item has a background color of None, these options are not available):

Style

From this pop-up, choose from six different blend types. A seventh item, Solid, indicates that no blend is applied to the box. As long as Solid appears in the pop-up, the remaining settings are not available.

Angle

This value determines the rotation of the blend. Choose a preset angle from the pop-up, or enter your own value in the field.

Color

This pop-up displays the second color of a blend. When initially creating a blend using the Modify dialog (and the selected item is not colored None), it displays the current box color. To specify a new second color, choose from any item currently available in the Colors Palette. To add or remove colors from this pop-up, use the Edit: **Color** command before opening this dialog.

Shade

This value determines the tint of the second color in a blend.

Blends are covered in depth in Chapter 17.

8. **Suppress Printout**

When this box is checked, neither the box contents nor any applied frames print when the document is output.

9. **Apply**

Click this button to preview the new settings without closing the dialog. Pressing (Command) [**Control**]-A does the same thing.

See Also

Page Tools: **Rotation Tool**
Box Tools: **Bézier Text Box Tool**
Box Tools: **Bézier Picture Box Tool**
Edit: Preferences: Document: **General**
Edit: **Paste**
Edit: **Color**
Style (Text or Picture): **Color**
Style (Text or Picture): **Shade**
Style (Text): **Baseline Shift**
The Measurements Palette
The Colors Palette

Item: Modify: Picture Panel

This panel only adjusts the contents of a picture box. The box itself is not affected.

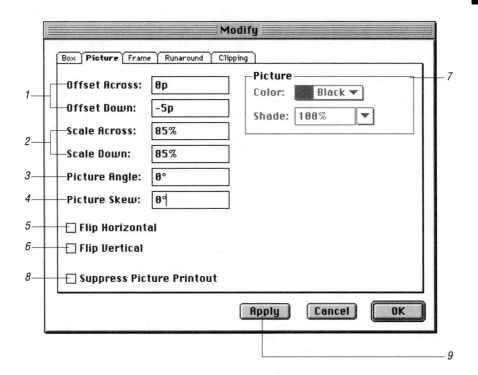

1. **Offset Across and Offset Down**

   These values display the position of a graphic within a box. Offset Across measures the distance between the left edge of the picture and the left edge of the box. Offset Down measures the distance between the top of the graphic and the top of the box.

   When you first import a graphic, it always appears flush to the top and left of the box. To move the image preview down or to the right, enter positive amounts. To move it up or to the left, enter negative amounts. When multiple picture boxes are selected, changing these values affects the contents of each box.

   These items appear in the right half of the Measurements Palette when the box is selected and the Content Tool is active.

2. **Scale Across and Scale Down** (0% to 1000%)

   These values display the current scale of a graphic. Scale Across scales horizontally from the left. Scale Down scales vertically from the right. To scale proportionately, enter equal values in both fields.

   When you first import a graphic, it always appears at 100%. To increase its size in your layout, enter values above 100%. To decrease its size, enter values below 100%.

   These items appear in the right half of the Measurements Palette when the box is selected and the Content Tool is active.

3. **Picture Angle** (–360° to 360°)

   To rotate a graphic within a box, enter a value between –359° and 359°— when you enter 360°, the image doesn't move. Positive values rotate to the left; negative values rotate to the right. This option rotates around the center of the graphic, regardless of its position within a box. The effect is the same when multiple picture boxes are selected.

   This item appears in the right half of the Measurements Palette when the box is selected and the Content Tool is active.

4. **Picture Skew** (–75° to 75°)

   This option slants a graphic across a horizontal axis without affecting the box shape.

   This value can also be used to compensate for a skewed picture box. Enter the opposite skew value here to return the image to its original proportions.

5. **Flip Horizontal**

   When this box is checked, the effect is the same as applying Style (Picture): **Flip Horizontal**: it turns the currently selected image over from left to right, like flipping a transparent overlay.

   This item appears in the right half of the Measurements Palette when the box is selected and the Content Tool is active.

6. **Flip Vertical**

   When this box is checked, the effect is the same as applying Style (Picture): **Flip Vertical**: it turns the currently selected image over from top to bottom, like flipping a transparent overlay. The effect is the same as rotating the picture box 180°, then choosing Style (Picture): **Flip Horizontal**.

   This item appears in the right half of the Measurements Palette when the box is selected and the Content Tool is active.

7. **Picture**

   This option allows you to apply a color and shade value to 1-bit line art or Grayscale images. See "Style: Color" and "Style: Shade" in Chapter 8, *The Style Menu (Picture)*, for more information.

8. **Suppress Picture Printout**

   When this box is checked, the contents of the box do not print when the document is output. However, any applied frames do.

9. **Apply**

Click this button to preview the new settings without closing the dialog. Pressing (Command) [**Control**]-A does the same thing.

See Also

Style (Picture): **Color**
Style (Picture): **Shade**
Style (Picture): **Flip Horizontal**
Style (Picture): **Flip Vertical**
The Measurements Palette
The Colors Palette

Item: Modify: Text Panel

This panel only adjusts the contents of a text box. The box itself is not affected.

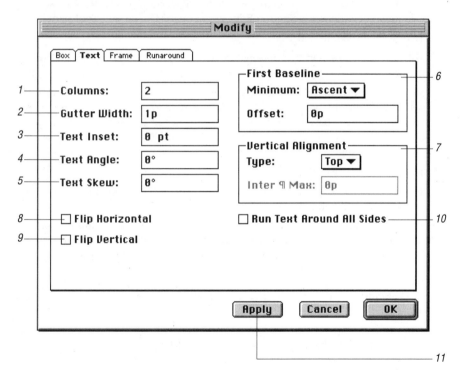

1. **Columns** (1 to 30)

This value subdivides a text box into a series of internal columns. A value of 1 (the default) results in a single column that extends from the left to right edge of the text box.

This item appears in the Measurements Palette when the box is selected.

2. **Gutter Width** (3 to 288 pt.)

This value sets the width between columns created by entering an amount in the Columns field above. The default width is 12 pt.

3. **Text Inset**

This value determines the distance between the edge of a text box and the text. This space only affects the four sides of a box—when a box is divided into columns, the text remains flush with the gutters and only insets from the left, right, top, and bottom box edges.

This space is applied in addition to any Left Indent, First Line, or Right Indent values entered in the Paragraph Attributes dialog (see "Style: Formats" in Chapter 7, *The Style Menu (Text)*, for more information).

The default value is 1 pt., which allows text to display without being partially obscured on-screen by the edges of the box. When text position must be precise, set this value to 0. (If necessary, close all documents, and set this value as a new default using the Edit: Preferences: Document: **Tool** panel.)

4. **Text Angle** (–360° to 360°)

This value rotates text and internal columns with the box, without affecting the box itself.

More accurately, the baselines of the text rotate, but the text still flows to fit within the current box shape. To create a rotated text box containing text with a horizontal baseline, rotate the box using the Item: Modify: **Box** panel, then enter the opposite value here. For example, if you rotate a box by 20°, enter a Text Angle of –20°.

5. **Text Skew** (–75° to 75°)

This value slants the contents of a text box across a horizontal axis. Both text and any internal columns are affected.

To create a slanted text box containing unaffected text and columns, skew the box using the Item: Modify: **Box** panel, then enter the opposite value here. For example, if you skew a box by 20°, enter a Text Skew value of –20°.

6. **First Baseline**

These settings determine the position of the first baseline from the top of a text box:

Minimum
> The items in this pop-up use the current font specifications to determine the placement of the first baseline.
>
> *Cap Height* places the height of an uppercase letter in the first line's largest font size between the first baseline and the box edge (plus any Text Inset value).

Cap + Accent increases the Cap Height space to accommodate any uppercase letters that contain accent characters.

Ascent (the default) uses the ascent value built into the font to determine the space between the first baseline and the box edge (plus any Text Inset value). The *ascent* of a font is the amount required to display the tallest character, as measured from the baseline.

Offset (0 to 48 inches)

This item allows you to set a numerical distance between the baseline and upper box edge (plus any Text Inset value). The default value, zero, represents the current position of the baseline. You can only lower the baseline with this value—you can't set it closer to the box edge.

7. **Vertical Alignment**

These settings control how text is vertically distributed within a text box. You can only adjust the vertical alignment of text in a rectangular box—when any other box shape is selected, this option is not available.

Type

Choose an alignment method from this pop-up.

Top (the default) aligns text to the top of the box, starting from the position of the first baseline.

Centered aligns text between the ascent of the first baseline and the bottom of the box. The current leading value is not affected. Be aware that text is never perfectly centered—to accomplish this, you still have to apply a negative baseline shift value. (See "Style: Baseline Shift" in Chapter 7 for more information.)

Bottom aligns the descenders of the last line to the bottom of the text box (plus any Text Inset value). The current leading value is not affected.

Justified retains the position of the first baseline, places the descenders of the last line flush with the bottom of the box, and adjusts the line spacing to evenly distribute the remaining lines. Here, the current leading value is overridden.

Inter ¶ Max

This item is only available when Justified is chosen in the Type pop-up.

Here, you specify the maximum distance that can appear between vertically justified paragraphs. Occasionally, the space between paragraphs reaches the maximum distance before the text can be distributed to the bottom of the box. When this happens, XPress adjusts the line spacing to complete the desired effect, and the spaces between paragraphs remain at the maximum value.

When set to zero (the default) XPress imposes no limits on the space between paragraphs.

8. **Flip Horizontal**

   When this box is checked, the effect is the same as applying Style (Text): **Flip Horizontal**: it turns the text over from left to right, like flipping a transparent overlay.

   This item appears in the right half of the Measurements Palette when the box is selected and the Content Tool is active.

9. **Flip Vertical**

   When this box is checked, the effect is the same as applying Style (Text): **Flip Vertical**: it turns the text over from top to bottom, like flipping a transparent overlay. The effect is the same as rotating the text box 180°, then choosing Style (Text): **Flip Horizontal**.

   This item appears in the right half of the Measurements Palette when the box is selected and the Content Tool is active.

10. **Run Text Around All Sides**

    When an item containing a Runaround value is placed on top of a text box, the text only flows around the left or right side. When this box is checked, text flows around both sides.

11. **Apply**

    Click this button to preview the new settings without closing the dialog. Pressing (Command) [**Control**]-A does the same thing.

See Also

Edit: Preferences: Document: **Tool**
Style (Text): **Baseline Shift**
Style (Text): **Formats**
Style (Text): **Flip Horizontal**
Style (Text): **Flip Vertical**
Item: Modify: **Box**
The Measurements Palette

Item: Modify: Line Panel

Use this panel to adjust one or more currently selected lines.

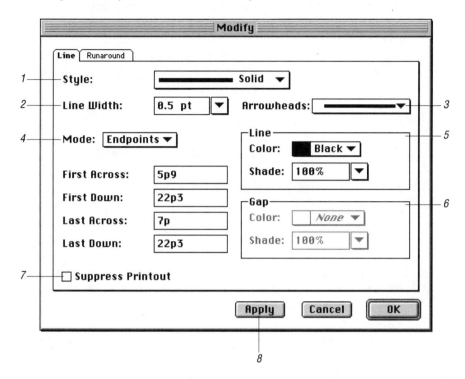

1. **Style**

   This submenu displays all dashes and stripes currently available to the document. To add custom line styles, choose Edit: **Dashes & Stripes**.

   This item appears in the Measurements Palette when a single line is selected.

2. **Line Width** (0 to 864 pt.)

   This item sets the thickness of a line. Choose from seven preset widths, or enter your own value in the field. (See "Style: Width" in Chapter 9 for more information.)

   This item appears in the Measurements Palette when a single line is selected.

3. **Arrowheads**

   This submenu displays five variations of arrowheads and endcaps, plus the default solid line. (See "Style: Arrowheads" in Chapter 9 for more information.)

   This item appears in the Measurements Palette when a single line is selected.

4. **Mode**

This option allows you to precisely reposition a line using numerical values. It's available only when a single straight line or text path is selected. The item chosen from the Mode pop-up determines the measurement fields that appear below. Enter the desired values in these fields to reposition a line.

Endpoints

This item allows you to reposition the first and last points of a line. The *first point* is the point you initially clicked to create a line; the *last point* is the point at which you release the mouse button. The available measurement fields are as follows:

First Across displays the current position of the first point across the horizontal ruler.

First Down displays the current position of the first point down the vertical ruler.

Last Across displays the current position of the last point across the horizontal ruler.

Last Down displays the current position of the last point down the vertical ruler.

First Point

This item allows you to reposition a line based on the current position of the first point. The available measurement fields are as follows:

First Across displays the current position of the first point across the horizontal ruler.

First Down displays the current position of the first point down the vertical ruler.

Angle allows you to rotate the line around the position of the first point.

Length displays the current length of the line. Enter the desired value to increase or decrease the length. The last point moves to reflect the change, and the first point remains stationary (unless you change the First Across or First Down values).

Midpoint

This item allows you to reposition a line based on the current position of the center of the line. The available measurement fields are as follows:

Midpoint Across displays the current position of the midpoint across the horizontal ruler.

Midpoint Down displays the current position of the midpoint down the vertical ruler.

Angle allows you to rotate the line around its mathematical center.

Length displays the current length of the line. Enter the desired value to increase or decrease the length. The first and last points move to reflect the change, and the midpoint point remains stationary (unless you change the Midpoint Across or Midpoint Down values).

Last Point

This item allows you to reposition a line based on the current position of the last point. The available measurement fields are as follows:

Last Across displays the current position of the last point across the horizontal ruler.

Last Down displays the current position of the last point down the vertical ruler.

Angle allows you to rotate the line around the position of the last point.

Length displays the current length of the line. Enter the desired value to increase or decrease the length. The first point moves to reflect the change, and the last point remains stationary (unless you change the Last Across or Last Down values).

These items appear in the Measurements Palette when a single line is selected.

When multiple lines or Bézier lines are selected, however, the Mode pop-up is replaced with the following items:

– **Offset Across and Offset Down.** These items display the current position of the line point farthest to the left and farthest down.

– **Width and Height.** When a Bézier line or text path is selected, these fields display the width and height of the widest and tallest values. When multiple lines are selected, Width displays the horizontal distance between the farthest left and right line points; Height displays the vertical distance between the highest and lowest points.

– **Angle.** To rotate the entire selection, enter a value between –360° and 360°. The line or lines rotate around the mathematical center.

– **Skew.** This item slants the current selection across a horizontal axis. Enter a value between –75° and 75°.

5. **Line**

This option allows you to recolor and tint the currently selected lines. (See "Style: Color" and "Style: Shade" in Chapter 9 for more information.)

6. **Gap**

This item is available only when a dash or stripe is applied to the currently selected line. Here, you apply a second color to a line that fills the existing spaces between dashes or stripes. (See "Edit: Dashes & Stripes" in Chapter 6 for more information.)

Color

This pop-up displays all colors currently available to a document. When None (the default) is set, the spaces are transparent. To fill the spaces with color, choose an item from the pop-up. To add or remove colors, use Edit: **Colors**.

Shade

This option allows you to set the tint of the colored spaces. It has no effect on the original line color. (See "Style: Shade" in Chapter 9 for more information.)

7. **Suppress Printout**

When this box is checked, the selected lines do not print when the document is output.

8. **Apply**

Click this button to preview the new settings without closing the dialog. Pressing (Command) [**Control**]-A does the same thing.

See Also

Edit: **Colors**
Edit: **Dashes & Stripes**
Style (Line): **Color**
Style (Line): **Shade**
Style (Line): **Width**
Style (Line): **Arrowheads**
The Measurements Palette
The Colors Palette

Item: Modify: Text Path Panel

Use this panel to adjust the contents of one or more selected text paths. To change the color and thickness of the actual path, use the Line panel.

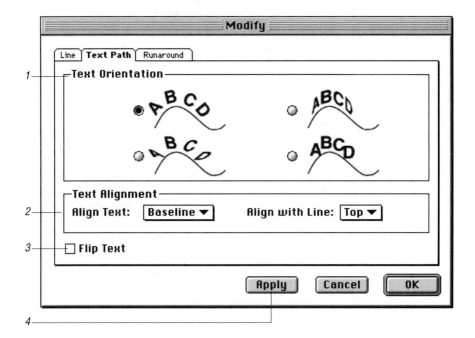

1. **Text Orientation**

   These options determine how XPress displays text on a path created with the Bézier Text Path and Freehand Text Path Tools. They have no effect on text flowing along a straight path.

   Upper Left

   The default option, it forces the text to treat the path as a baseline—characters are rotated as necessary so that the bottom of each is flush with the path. Character shapes are not affected.

   Lower Left

   Two things happen when this option is chosen. First, it rotates each character to treat the path shape as a baseline, like the default option. Second, each character is vertically skewed. The skew angle matches the angle of the path that the lower left of the character sits upon. For example, when the text path is at 30°, a character at that point is vertically skewed 30°.

   As text flows along a steep curve, it may flip horizontally. Assuming a horizontal line is 0°, text is right-reading when a curve is between 90° to the left or right. At values beyond that, the characters flip. At precisely 90°, characters are invisible.

   Upper Right

   Here, text is skewed so that each character stands vertically, but the bottom of each character is flush with the path. No rotation is applied. As with the previous option, the text will flip horizontally when the path angle exceeds 90°.

   Lower Right

   Here, text is not rotated or skewed. Text follows the path, but the baseline for each character remains horizontal. The result is a stair-step effect.

2. **Text Alignment**

   These items determine the placement of text in relation to the text path:

   Align Text

   Here, you choose which part of the characters aligns to the path:

   - *Ascent* places the top of the tallest character flush to the path.

   - *Center* places the midpoint between the ascent and the baseline flush to the path.

   - *Baseline* (the default) places the bottom of the characters flush to the path.

   - *Descent* places any descenders (such as lowercase "y" or "g") flush to the path.

   Align with Line

   This item determines which part of the line text aligns to, based on the Align Text setting. This effect is only apparent when a width and color has been applied to the text path (using the Line panel).

For example, assume the text path is a 12 pt. blue line, and the Align text pop-up is set to Baseline:

- – *Top* aligns the baseline to the top of the line thickness.
- – *Center* aligns the baseline to the actual path.
- – *Bottom* aligns the baseline to the bottom of the line thickness.

3. **Flip Text**

When this box is checked, text flips onto the opposite side of the text path.

4. **Apply**

Click this button to preview the new settings without closing the dialog. Pressing (Command) [**Control**]-A does the same thing.

See Also

Line Tools: **Bézier Text Path Tool**
Line Tools: **Freehand Text Path Tool**

Item: Frame
(Command) [Control]-B

Use this command to apply a border around a picture box, text box, or blank box. You can apply frames to multiple boxes at once, even when they're different types.

Common Uses

Trapping the edges of a four-color image. CMYK images with no frame may *fringe* when reproduced on-press. This means a misregistered plate color is slightly visible beyond the edge of the image. When a black frame is applied to such an image, XPress draws the cyan, magenta, and yellow inks back from the outer edge of the frame (by the Auto Amount value in the Edit: Preferences: Document: **Trapping** panel), which eliminates the possibility of fringe. For the best results, define a frame width of at least .5 pt.

Common Errors

- **Applying one of the bitmap frame options.** The last nine items in the Style pop-up, while certainly decorative, should be avoided if a document will be output to anything but a low-resolution laser printer. These frames are actually pixel-based and don't output well to high-resolution imagesetters. If you must use a decorative frame, create it in a program like Illustrator or Free-Hand, where the results are vector-based, not limited by a set resolution.

- **Reducing the frame width after importing and positioning a graphic.** This is especially problematic when you've applied a fit-to-box command to the image—if the picture box already contains a frame, the image resizes to touch its edge. When you reduce the width, a gap appears between the frame and the image. Whenever you set a smaller frame width, make sure the graphic still extends all the way to the edges of the box.

Special Notes

- A frame can be applied to the inside or the outside of a box, depending on the Frame setting in the Edit: Preferences: Document: **General** panel.

- When using a custom dash as a frame, you can force the dashes and spaces to distribute evenly around each side of a box by checking the Stretch to Corners box in the Edit Dash dialog. (See "Edit: Dashes & Stripes" in Chapter 6 for more information.) The dashes that appear in the Style pop-up by default all have this box checked.

The Frame Panel

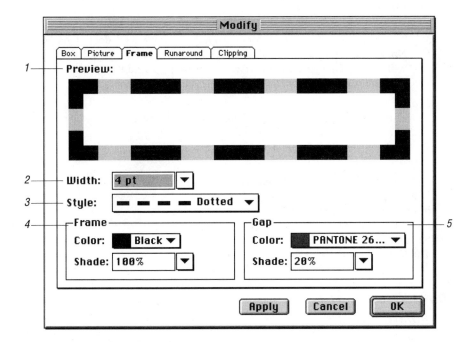

1. **Preview**

   This area displays a preview of the current frame style. It also shows the effect of any applied Gap color. Regardless of the intended width, the preview only displays an 18 pt. frame.

2. **Width**

   This item sets the thickness of a frame. Choose from seven preset widths, or enter your own value in the field. When the value is zero (the default), no frame is applied.

The maximum width is one half the current width or height of the box (whichever is smaller). Of course, the maximum value obscures the entire box contents.

3. **Style**

This submenu displays all dashes and stripes currently available to the document. To add custom line styles, choose Edit: **Dashes & Stripes**.

4. **Frame**

This option allows you to recolor and tint the currently selected lines. (Although you can't recolor a frame using the Style Menu, see "Style: Color" and "Style: Shade" in Chapter 9 for more information.)

5. **Gap**

This item is available only when a dash or stripe is chosen in the Style pop-up. Here, you apply a second color that fills the existing spaces between dashes or stripes. (See "Edit: Dashes & Stripes" in Chapter 6 for more information.)

Color

This pop-up displays all colors currently available to a document. When None (the default) is set, the spaces are transparent. To fill the spaces with color, choose an item from the pop-up. To add or remove colors, use Edit: **Colors**.

Shade

This option allows you to set the tint of the colored spaces. It has no effect on the original line color.

See Also

Edit: Preferences: Document: **General**
Edit: Preferences: Document: **Trapping**
Edit: **Dashes & Stripes**
Style (Line): **Color**
Style (Line): **Shade**
The Colors Palette

Item: Runaround
(Command) [Control]-T

Use this command to create a text wrap effect. A runaround value can be applied to a single box or line and only displaces text when positioned over a text box. If necessary, choose Item: **Bring to Front** after applying a runaround to an item.

Common Errors

Accidentally reflowing text when creating another text or picture box. By default, every text and picture box has a runaround value of 1 pt. If you're not aware of this, any new box positioned even slightly over an existing text box could force the text to reflow. To avoid this, I recommend closing all documents, opening the

---

Edit: Preferences: Document: **Tools** panel, and setting the default runaround value of all boxes to None. This way, you only apply a runaround when you specifically need it.

Special Notes

- To view a Bézier runaround path, choose Item: Edit: **Runaround**. The path displays on-screen in pink.

- To make text flow around both sides of a runaround item, select the text box, open the Item: Modify: **Text Path** panel, and check the Run Text Around All Sides box.

- When a text box or an anchored item is selected, you can only apply an Item runaround. When a line or text path is selected, only None, Item, and Manual appear in the Type pop-up. Manual, like Auto Image, creates an editable Bézier path.

- When applying a runaround to a picture box, the following values appear when you set Embedded Path, Alpha Channel, Non-White Areas, or Same as Clipping in the Type pop-up:

  - **Noise** (–288 to 288 pt.) This value allows you to round off intricately detailed runaround paths. Higher amounts exclude more detail, resulting in a smoother path. Lower amounts include more detail, resulting in a more complex path. (This item is not available when Same as Clipping is set.)

  - **Smoothness** (0 to 100 pt.) This value determines how closely a runaround path surrounds an item. Lower values result in more points used to create the path. Higher values result in fewer points.

  - **Threshold** (0% to 100%). When Alpha Channel is set, this value determines which values of black are included in the runaround path. For example, when 10% is set (the default), black values darker than 90% are included in the path. When 50% is set, only values darker than 50% black are included. Conversely, when Non-White Areas is set, this value uses white as the basis of measurement. For example, when 10% is set, the runaround path ignores all information below 10% black. (When applied to a color image, this value makes a decision based on its Grayscale equivalent.)

The Runaround Panel

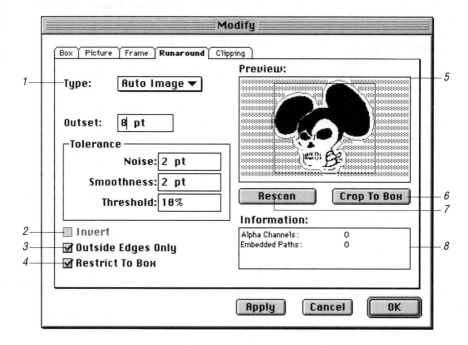

1. Type

Choose the desired runaround method from this pop-up:

None

This option results in no runaround applied to the selected item.

Item

This option results in text that wraps around the box itself—the contents are ignored. When a rectangular box is selected, the fields below determine the offset value for each side. When any other box or a line is selected, a single Outset field is available, where you enter the desired space between the item and the text.

Auto Image

This option ignores the selected box, allowing text to wrap around its contents. An editable Bézier path is created, which you can further manipulate to form the desired shape. The effect is only apparent with images that don't extend all the way to the box edges, such as vector-based illustrations or Photoshop silhouettes. Enter the desired space between the graphic and the text in the Outset field.

Embedded Path

This option wraps text around a path saved in a Photoshop image. For example, if an embedded path is used to create a clipping path in the Clipping panel, this option bases the runaround on the same information. Enter the desired space between the path and the text in the Outset field. (The Tolerance settings are described earlier in this section in "Special Notes.")

If the embedded path is not used as a clipping path, the results are unsatisfactory—since the picture box sits on top of the text box, some text is obscured by the image as it wraps around the path.

Alpha Channel

This option wraps text around an additional mask channel built into a TIFF image. For example, if an alpha channel is used to create a clipping path in the Clipping panel, this option bases the runaround on the same information. Enter the desired space between the channel information and the text in the Outset field. (The Tolerance settings are described earlier in this section in "Special Notes.")

If the channel is smaller than the visible part of the image, however, some of the text will be obscured as it wraps around the shape.

Non-White Areas

This option bases a runaround on the tonal values of the image. By adjusting the Threshold value (described in the previous "Special Notes"), the runaround path is formed by including darker or lighter image tones. Enter the desired space between the path and the text in the Outset field. (The Tolerance settings are described earlier in this section in "Special Notes.")

Same as Clipping

This option is only available after defining a clipping path using the Clipping panel. Here, the runaround is based on the current clipping path. Enter the desired space between the path and the text in the Outset field. (The Tolerance settings are described earlier in this section in "Special Notes.")

Picture Bounds

This option wraps text around a rectangular bounding box that surrounds the contents of a picture box.

User Edited Path

This item appears after a Bézier runaround path has been manually adjusted.

2. **Invert**

Check this box to reverse the effect of the runaround path, allowing text to flow inside.

3. **Outside Edges Only**

When an embedded path contains a shape within a shape (for example, a donut), this option forces XPress to regard only the outer shape. When unchecked, text flows inside the inner shape as well as around the outer shape.

4. **Restrict to Box**

When this box is checked, text ignores any part of a runaround path that extends beyond the edges of a picture box. When unchecked, text is affected by the entire path. The effect is similar to clicking Crop to Box (description follows), but the path itself is not trimmed.

5. **Preview**

This area displays the effect of the current runaround. Sample text appears as gray lines. The picture box appears in blue and the runaround path appears in pink—respectively, these values are based on the Margin and Grid colors in the Edit: Preferences: Application: **Display** panel.

6. **Crop to Box**

If a runaround path extends beyond the edges of a box, this button trims it to match the box dimensions.

7. **Rescan**

Click this button to construct a new runaround path, based on the current settings. If necessary, you must click Crop to Box again.

8. **Information**

This field displays the number of alpha channels and embedded paths contained in an image.

See Also

Edit: Preferences: Application: **Display**
Edit: Preferences: Document: **Tools**
Item: **Clipping**
Item: Modify: **Text**
Item: **Bring to Front**
Item: Edit: **Runaround**

Item: Clipping
(Option-Command) [Alt-Control]-T

Use this command to apply an object-oriented mask to an imported graphic. In a typical clip, information inside the Bézier path remains visible, and information outside the path is rendered transparent. When an image is repositioned, rotated, scaled, or skewed, the clipping path changes as well, maintaining its relative position.

If desired, you can use an XPress clipping path as a runaround path. Set Same as Clipping in the Type pop-up of the Item: Edit: **Runaround** panel.

Common Errors

- **Using this option in lieu of Photoshop clipping paths.** XPress creates clipping paths by auto-tracing existing image information, and it suffers from the same general inaccuracy as any auto-tracing program. Even though you can further edit an XPress path, you only have the low-resolution image preview to use as a guide. When path accuracy is most important, create them using the Pen Tool and Paths Palette in Photoshop. There, you can view the image at full resolution and zoom in to precisely position a Bézier path.

- **Applying a clipping path to an image with a soft or feathered edge.** Clipping paths can only create a hard-edged mask. If you apply this effect to a vignette or anti-aliased silhouette, certain edge pixels will be clipped, based on the Threshold setting in the Clipping panel. As a general rule, these types of images are never clipped; rather, they sit alone, surrounded by white. To apply special background colors, photomontage, or detailed clipping paths, apply these techniques in Photoshop.

Special Notes

- To view an applied clipping path, choose Item: Edit: **Clipping Path**. The path displays on-screen in green.

- When you convert an XPress 3.x document, XPress 4.0 automatically applies a Non-White Areas clipping path to any imported vector-based graphics. The same occurs with Photoshop clipping paths. The XPress paths should be removed, since they trace inaccurately and exclude any white information touching the graphic edge. Unfortunately, you can't edit multiple items with this command. To remove the XPress clipping paths, select each item individually, choose Item: Edit: **Clipping**, and set Item in the Type pop-up.

- Many people create a series of Photoshop paths simply to assist in selections and image editing, and not for use as a clipping path. However, when you import such an image, XPress automatically applies an Embedded Paths clipping path, and the image is unexpectedly clipped. To remove the XPress path, select the item, choose Item: **Clipping**, and set Item in the Type pop-up.

- When you import an image containing a clipping path, XPress automatically applies an additional Embedded Path clipping path. Since XPress uses the same information as the original path, image quality is not hindered. You don't have to remove the XPress clipping path.

- When the original picture box color is white, XPress automatically sets it to None when you apply a clipping path. This allows the underlying information to be visible around the masked item. When the box is set to any other color, the value is not changed when you apply a clipping path.

The Clipping Panel

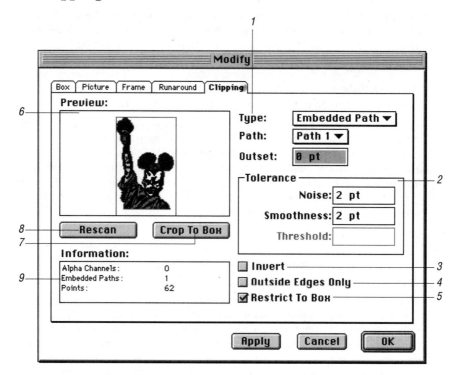

1. **Type**

   Choose the desired clipping method from this pop-up:

   Item

   > This item (the default) results in no clipping path.

   Embedded Path

   > This item uses a path embedded in a Photoshop image as the basis for a clipping path. If the image contains more than one, choose the desired item from the Path pop-up.

   > If a single path contains more than one subpath, this option excludes additional information. For example, if a path consists of a smaller shape within a larger shape, the clipping path reveals only the image that appears between them—pixels outside the larger shape and inside the smaller shape are hidden. Turn this effect off by checking Outside Edges Only (below).

   > To increase or decrease the size of the clipping path, enter a positive or negative value in the Outset field.

   Alpha Channel

   > This item bases a clipping path on an additional mask channel built into a TIFF image. If an image contains more than one additional channel,

choose the desired item from the Alpha pop-up. (See "Select: Save Selection" in *Photoshop in a Nutshell* for specific information on alpha channels.)

To increase or decrease the size of the clipping path, enter a positive or negative value in the Outset field.

Non-White Areas

This option bases a clipping path on the tonal values of the image. By adjusting the Threshold value, the runaround path is formed by including darker or lighter image tones.

To increase or decrease the size of the clipping path, enter a positive or negative value in the Outset field.

Picture Bounds

This item creates a clipping path around the dimensions of the imported graphic, even if it extends beyond the edges of the picture box.

User Edited Path

This item appears after a clipping path has been manually adjusted. This allows you to change the Outset value without affecting the new path shape. If you accidentally set a new clipping path option in the Type pop-up, you must choose Cancel—otherwise, your manual edits are lost.

2. Tolerance

The following values appear when you set Embedded Path, Alpha Channel, or Non-White Areas in the Type pop-up:

Noise (–288 to 288 pt.)

This value allows you to round off intricately detailed clipping paths. Higher amounts exclude more detail, resulting in a smoother but less accurate path. Lower amounts include more detail, resulting in a more complex and slightly more accurate path.

Smoothness (0 to 100 pt.)

This value determines how closely a clipping path surrounds an item. Lower values result in more points used to create the path, which allows it to trace the item more closely. Higher values result in fewer points, resulting in a faster printing but a less accurate path.

Threshold (0% to 100%)

When Alpha Channel is set, this value determines which values of black are included in the clipping path. For example, when 10% is set (the default), black values darker than 90% are included in the path. When 50% is set, only values darker than 50% black are included. Conversely, when Non-White Areas is set, this value uses white as the basis of measurement. For example, when 10% is set, the clipping path excludes all information below 10% black. (When applied to a color image, this value makes a decision based on its Grayscale equivalent.)

3. **Invert**

Check this box to reverse the effect of the clipping path. The image information that was originally transparent is revealed, and the information previously revealed becomes transparent.

4. **Outside Edges Only**

When an embedded path contains a shape within a shape (for example, a donut), this option forces XPress to use only the outer shape as a clipping path. When unchecked, all shapes become part of the clipping path.

5. **Restrict to Box**

When this box is unchecked, the image possessing the clipping path remains within the confines of the picture box, even if the box edges have been adjusted to crop the image. When checked, the entire image displays, regardless of the shape of the box.

6. **Preview**

This area displays the effect of the current clipping path. The picture box appears in blue, and the clipping path appears in green—respectively, these values are based on the Margin and Rulers colors in the Edit: Preferences: Application: **Display** panel.

7. **Crop to Box**

If a clipping path extends beyond the edges of a box, this button trims it to match the box dimensions.

8. **Rescan**

Click this button to construct a new clipping path, based on the current settings. If necessary, you must click Crop to Box again.

9. **Information**

This field displays the number of alpha channels and embedded paths contained in an image, as well as the number of points contained in the current clipping path.

See Also

Edit: Preferences: Application: **Display**
Item: **Runaround**
Item: Edit: **Clipping Path**
Photoshop in a Nutshell (Select: **Save Selection**)
Photoshop in a Nutshell (The Paths Palette)

Item: Duplicate
(Command) [Control]-D

This command generates a duplicate of the currently selected box, line, or text path. Unlike choosing Edit: **Copy** and **Paste**, which always places a duplicate in the center of the screen, this command offsets the new information by the values last entered in the Item: **Step and Repeat** dialog.

Special Notes

- Unlike Edit: **Copy** and **Paste**, it doesn't matter if the Item Tool or Content Tool is active when you choose this command.

- If the selected item has been constrained to a box using Item: **Constrain**, the duplicate items are constrained as well and can't be positioned beyond the boundaries of the constraining item.

- If you duplicate a text box that's part of a linked chain, you duplicate the box as well as all the text in the chain. The text begins at the start of the box (regardless of the original box's position in the chain) and flows beyond the bottom of the box edge.

See Also

Edit: **Copy**
Edit: **Paste**
Item: **Step and Repeat**
Item: **Constrain/Unconstrain**

Item: Step and Repeat

This command allows you to generate a specific number of duplicate boxes, lines, or text paths.

Common Uses

Refer to Appendix A, *Common Techniques*, for a full description of generating horizontal and vertical rules for a form.

Common Errors

Attempting to extend a series of duplicates beyond the pasteboard. If the values entered in the Step and Repeat dialog spread the duplicate items over too great a range, an alert appears, stating "You cannot make that many duplicates using these offsets." The problem is one of two things: either the Repeat Count or one of the offset values is too high. Click OK to close the alert and enter new values.

Special Notes

- If unsatisfied with the results of this command, choose Edit: **Undo** immediately after applying it. The duplicate item disappears, and the original item remains selected, ready for you to choose the command again and enter new values.

- Unlike Edit: **Copy** and **Paste**, it doesn't matter if the Item Tool or Content Tool is active when you use this command.

- If the selected item has been constrained to a box using Item: **Constrain**, the selected item can't be repeated beyond the boundaries of the constraining item.

The Step and Repeat Dialog

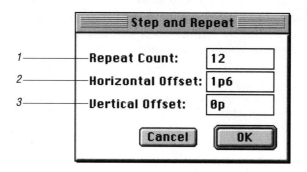

1. **Repeat Count** (1 to 99)

   Here, enter the number of duplicates you wish to generate. Keep in mind that duplicates are created in addition to the original item. For example, if you want 18 vertical lines appearing in a row, select the first line, and enter 17 in this field.

2. **Horizontal Offset** (–24 to 24 inches)

   Here, enter the horizontal space placed between each duplicate. Positive values place duplicates to the right of the original item; negative values place them to the left.

3. **Vertical Offset** (–24 to 24 inches)

   Here, enter the vertical space placed between each duplicate. Positive values place duplicates down from the original item; negative values place them above.

See Also

Edit: **Copy**
Edit: **Paste**
Item: **Duplicate**
Item: **Constrain/Unconstrain**

Item: Delete
(Command) [Control]-K

Choose this command to remove the currently selected items. Unlike pressing the Delete key or choosing Edit: **Clear**, boxes (and their contents) are deleted regardless of the currently active tool.

Common Errors

Using this command to delete a point from a Bézier path. Even when a single point is selected, this command deletes the entire path. To remove a single point or series of points, select them with the Item Tool, and press the Delete key.

See Also

Page Tools: **Item Tool**
Edit: **Clear**

Item: Group
(Command) [Control]-G

This command is available when multiple boxes, lines, and text paths are selected. Most often, items are grouped to maintain their relative positions. For example, when you group an image, caption, and photo credit, you can't accidentally reposition one of the items—when you select one with the Item Tool, the remaining items are selected as well.

Each group has the following characteristics:

- When selected with the Item Tool, a bounding box surrounds the grouped items.

- Reposition an item within a group by holding down the (Command) [**Control**] key while dragging.

- You can edit individual items in a group by selecting them with the Content Tool.

- When a group contains only picture boxes, the Group, Picture, and Frame panels are available in the Item: **Modify** dialog. When a group contains only text boxes, the Group, Text, and Frame panels are available. When a group contains only lines, only the Group panel is available. When a group contains only text paths, the Group and Text Path panels are available. When a group contains a mix of items, only the Group panel is available.

- To remove the group relationship, select the group, and choose Item: **Ungroup**. Any changes made to the items while part of the group are unaffected.

Special Notes

- Resize the items contained in a group using the following techniques:
  - To resize with no constraints, drag one of the bounding box handles. Line width and the contents of text or picture boxes are not scaled.
  - By holding down the (Command) [**Control**] key *after* grabbing one of the handles, you scale line width and box contents along with the items, with no constraints.
  - By holding down the Shift key while dragging, the group snaps to a constrained square. Line width and the contents of text or picture boxes

are not scaled—to scale this information as well, hold down the (Command) [**Control**] key *after* you begin Shift-dragging.

- To proportionately scale the items without affecting line width or box contents, (Option-Shift) [**Alt-Shift**]-drag a handle.

- To proportionately scale the items as well as line width and box contents, (Option-Command-Shift) [**Alt-Control-Shift**]-drag a handle.

• You can group multiple groups by selecting them with the Item Tool and choosing Group again. As you choose Item: **Ungroup**, each group is broken into its component groups. Be aware that when multiple groups are grouped, Item: **Modify** is not available.

• This command is also used before creating a constraining relationship between items. (See "Item: Constrain/Unconstrain," later in this chapter, for more information.)

See Also

Page Tools: **Item Tool**
Page Tools: **Content Tool**
Item: **Modify**
Item: **Ungroup**
Item: **Constrain**

Item: Ungroup

Use this command to remove the relationship between items grouped using Item: **Group**.

This command is available when a group is selected with the Item Tool, or when two or more grouped items are selected with the Content Tool. When multiple groups are selected, this item is not available.

When a group consists of multiple groups, this command only affects the current grouping. To continue ungrouping, select only one of the remaining groups, and choose this command again.

Special Notes

If items in a group have been constrained using Item: **Constrain**, this command removes the constraining as well as the group relationship.

See Also

Page Tools: **Item Tool**
Page Tools: **Content Tool**
Item: **Group**
Item: **Constrain/Unconstrain**

Item: Constrain/Unconstrain

When you *constrain* an item, you limit the range it can be positioned or resized to the confines of a box. When preparing a constraining relationship, the following must occur:

- The edges of the constraining box must completely surround the items you wish to constrain. For the best results, set the box to the exact dimensions you wish to constrain to.

- The constraining box must sit behind the remaining items. If necessary, choose Item: **Send to Back**.

- Group the constraining box and the remaining items by selecting them and choosing Item: **Group**.

After these steps are completed, you can select the group and choose Item: **Constrain**. If any steps are ignored, the command is not available.

To remove the constraining relationship, select the group, and choose Item: **Unconstrain**.

Common Uses

Refer to Appendix A for a full description of how to constrain items to a box.

Special Notes

- Choosing Item: **Ungroup** removes the constraining as well as the group relationship between items.

- To manually reposition a constrained item, hold down the (Command) [**Control**] key, and drag.

- When Auto Constrain is checked in the Edit: Preferences: Document: **General** panel, any item placed on top of a box that completely surrounds it is automatically constrained.

See Also

Edit: Preferences: **Document**
Item: **Group**
Item: **Ungroup**
Item: **Send To Back**

Item: Lock/Unlock

F6 Key

This command locks the currently selected items. Locked items can't be manually repositioned using the Item Tool, nor can an item be resized by dragging its edges or Bézier points. When you attempt to adjust a locked item, the cursor turns into a small padlock.

To unlock one or more locked items, select them, and choose Item: **Unlock**. If your selection includes locked and unlocked items, only Item: **Unlock** is available. To lock all the items, choose Unlock, then choose Lock.

Special Notes

- You can edit the contents of a locked picture box by selecting it with the Content Tool.

- Although you can't manually adjust a locked item, you can reposition, resize, and rotate it using the Item: **Modify** dialog.

See Also

Page Tools: **Item Tool**
Item: **Modify**

Item: Merge

Use this command to convert any combination of selected boxes, lines, or paths into a single Bézier box. This allows you to create complex shapes more easily than using the Bézier line tools. The exact shape that results depends on the item chosen from the Item: **Merge** submenu.

When merging items, the following rules apply:

- You must select more than one item before this command is available.

- The selected item farthest back determines the characteristics of the merged result. For example, if the rear item is a picture box, the image it contains appears in the merged shape. If the rear item is a black line, the background color of the merged shape is black—any existing images in the selected items are deleted.

- When a line or text path is converted to a Bézier box, the width of the new box is the same as the line width. For example, an 8 pt. line becomes an 8 pt. thick box.

- The merged shape can be further adjusted with the Bézier editing tools.

Special Notes

- Change the box type of a merged shape by selecting an item from the Item: **Contents** submenu.

- The merged shape replaces the selected items. To avoid losing the shapes, choose Edit: **Copy** (with the Item Tool active) before merging. Choose Edit: **Paste** after merging to access the original items.

- If the back item is a text box, the merged shape becomes a text box. However, if the merged item contains separate shapes, text won't flow through them. To achieve this effect, split the merged shapes using Item: **Split**, then use the Linking Tool to create a text chain.

See Also

Page Tools: **Item Tool**
Linking Tools
Edit: **Copy**
Edit: **Paste**
Item: **Split**
Item: **Contents**

Item: Merge: Intersection

Here, the merged shape is based on any information overlapping the rear item. Information that doesn't overlap is discarded.

Item: Merge: Union

Here, every selected item is included in the merged shape. When two items overlap, they combine to form one shape. Items that don't overlap remain separate but are part of the merged shape. For example, if you import a picture into a merged item with separate shapes, the same image flows through each shape.

Item: Merge: Difference

Here, the effect is like a cookie-cutter—the rear item is retained, but the shapes of any overlapping items are cut out of it. Use this option to remove part of a line, or to punch holes in a box.

Item: Merge: Reverse Difference

Here, the effect is the opposite of Difference—the shape of the rear item is removed from any overlapping information.

Item: Merge: Exclusive Or

Here, all overlapping information is removed from the final shape. Everywhere two lines or box borders originally crossed, two corner points appear.

Item: Merge: Combine

Here, like Exclusive Or, all overlapping information is removed from the final shape. However, no corner points are added wherever two lines or box borders originally crossed.

Item: Merge: Join Endpoints

This option is only available when two straight lines, Bézier lines, or text paths are selected. In order to join two paths, the following must occur:

- An endpoint of one line must directly overlap an endpoint of the other. If they don't overlap, an alert appears, stating "Endpoints are not close enough to join these lines."

- Two paths can be joined if the distance between endpoints falls within the Snap Distance set in the Edit: Preferences: Document: **General** panel. However, this method is not the most accurate, since both endpoints are repositioned when joined.

Common Errors

Attempting to join two endpoints of the same path. This command can only join the endpoints of two separate paths. To close an open Bézier path, hold down the (Option) [**Alt**] key, and choose Item: Shape: **Bézier Box**. If the endpoints are not touching, they're joined by a straight line. From there, use Item: **Content** to create the desired box type.

Special Notes

When two different line types are selected, the joined line matches the type of line farthest back. For example, if a text path sits behind a line, the joined path is a text path. Likewise, if a line sits behind a text path, the joined path is a line. If necessary, reorient the lines by choosing Item: **Send to Back** or **Bring to Front**.

See Also

   Edit: Preferences: **Document**
   Item: **Send to Back**
   Item: **Bring to Front**

Item: Split

Use this command to divide the following items into separate Bézier boxes:

- Items combined with Item: **Merge** consisting of multiple shapes
- Text converted to boxes using Style: **Text to Box**
- Closed Bézier paths that cross back over themselves

The new, separate boxes replace the original items.

Special Notes

When a merged item of multiple shapes contains a picture, a single image flows through all the shapes. When this item is split, a separate picture appears in each individual box.

Item: Split: Outside Paths

This command divides merged items made up of separate shapes. If one of the items is divided by a smaller shape—such as the inner circle of a donut—the smaller shape is untouched.

For example, assume you have converted the letters "ER" to a box, using Style: **Text to Box**. When you apply this command, the "E" and the "R" become separate boxes, but the loop of the "R" is still fixed and transparent.

When a closed Bézier path crosses over itself, this command divides the path into its separate, visible shapes.

See Also

> Style (Text): **Text to Box**
> Item: **Merge**
> Item: **Split**
> Item: Split: **All Paths**

Item: Split: All Paths

This command splits all closed paths in the currently selected item. If one of the items is divided by a smaller shape, the relationship is removed, resulting in separate shapes.

For example, assume you have converted the letters "ER" to a box, using Style: **Text to Box**. When you apply this command, the "E," the outline of the "R," and the loop inside the "R" become separate boxes.

When a closed Bézier path crosses over itself, the effect is the same as choosing Item: Split: **Outside Paths**.

See Also

> Style (Text): **Text to Box**
> Item: **Merge**
> Item: **Split**
> Item: Split: **Outside Paths**

Item: Send to Back
(Shift)-F5

Use this command to send the currently selected item behind all other items on the page. As you create items, a *stacking order* occurs. The first item appears behind all subsequently created items, until another item is affected by this command.

When a selected item is already the bottom item, this command is not available.

Special Notes

When you hold down the (Option) [**Alt**] key, this command appears as Send Backward. Here, you can send an item one level behind in the current stacking order. Pressing (Option-Shift) [**Alt-Shift**]-F5 does the same thing.

See Also

Item: **Bring to Front**

Item: Bring to Front
F5-Key

Use this command to bring the currently selected item in front of all other items on the page. As you create items, a *stacking order* occurs. The newest item appears in front of all previously created items, until another item is affected by this command.

When a selected item is already the topmost item, this command is not available.

Special Notes

When you hold down the (Option) [**Alt**] key, this command appears as Bring Forward. Here, you can send an item one level behind in the current stacking order. Pressing (Option) [**Alt**]-F5 does the same thing.

See Also

Item: **Bring to Front**

Item: Space/Align
(Command) [Control]-comma

Use this command to automatically align the currently selected boxes, lines, or text paths. If desired, you can insert a specific space between the items, based on the settings in the Space/Align Items dialog.

When used properly, this command relieves you from manually aligning items by placing ruler guides and dragging items with the Item Tool. It's only available when more than one item is selected.

Special Notes

* When boxes are selected, this command pays no attention to the contents. Rather, it's effect is based on the box edges, as specified by the setting in the Between pop-up.

* By setting a series of different options while the Space/Align Items dialog is open, you achieve the affect of applying this command more than once. For example, you can apply a horizontal and a vertical space, and click Apply to preview the effect. Then, without closing the dialog, you can turn off Hori-

---

zontal, vertically distribute the items with a new setting, and click Apply again to see the change. Clicking OK simply closes the dialog after the items are placed where you want them.

The Space/Align Items Dialog

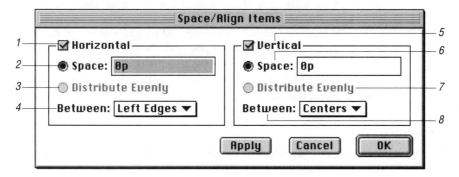

1. **Horizontal**

   When this box is checked, the selected items are repositioned horizontally. This effect is based on the selected item positioned farthest to the left—this item is not moved. If more than one item has the same left boundary, the effect is based on the item closest to the top of the pasteboard.

   When unchecked, the settings are not available.

2. **Space** (0 to 10 inches, or 0 to 1000%)

   When enabled, this option adds a specific horizontal space between the selected items. The application of the space depends on the setting in the Between pop-up.

   When this value is zero (the default), no space is added—the items are aligned flush to the setting in the Between pop-up.

   If desired, enter a percentage instead of an absolute number. Here, the new distribution is based on the space that already exists between items. For example, enter 200% to double the space between two vertical lines.

3. **Distribute Evenly**

   This option is only available when more than two items are selected. When enabled, the items farthest to the left and right aren't moved—however, the remaining items are evenly spaced between them.

4. **Between**

   This pop-up determines the horizontal placement of aligned items:

   Items

   > Here, the selected items align from the right edge of the first item, to the left edge of the next, and so forth. Any value entered in the Space field is inserted between the actual items.

Left Edges

Here, the left edges of the selected items align to the left edge of the first item. Any value entered in the Space field is inserted between the left edges of the selected items.

Center

Here, items are aligned to the center of the first item. Regardless of an item's shape, the center point is determined as the center of a bounding box that surrounds its overall dimensions. Any value entered in the Space field is inserted between the center points of the selected items.

Right Edges

Here, the right edges of the selected items align to the right edge of the first item. Any value entered in the Space field is inserted between the right edges of the selected items.

5. **Vertical**

When this box is checked, the selected items are repositioned vertically. This effect is based on the selected item positioned farthest to the top—this item is not moved. If more than one item has the same top boundary, the effect is based on the item farthest to the left.

When unchecked, the settings are not available.

6. **Space**

When enabled, this option adds a specific vertical space between the selected items. The application of the space depends on the setting in the Between pop-up.

When this value is zero (the default), no space is added—the items are aligned flush to the setting in the Between pop-up.

If desired, enter a percentage instead of an absolute number. Here, the new distribution is based on the space that already exists between items. For example, enter 200% to double the space between two horizontal lines.

7. **Distribute Evenly**

This option is only available when more than two items are selected. When enabled, the items farthest to the top and bottom aren't moved—however, the remaining items are evenly spaced between them.

8. **Between**

This pop-up determines the vertical placement of aligned items:

Items

Here, the selected items align from the bottom edge of the first item, to the top edge of the next, and so forth. Any value entered in the Space field is inserted between the actual items.

Top Edges

Here, the top edges of the selected items align to the top edge of the first item. Any value entered in the Space field is inserted between the top edges of the selected items.

Center

Here, items are aligned to the center of the first item. Regardless of an item's shape, the center point is determined as the center of a bounding box that surrounds its overall dimensions. Any value entered in the Space field is inserted between the center points of the selected items.

Bottom Edges

Here, the bottom edges of the selected items align to the bottom edge of the first item. Any value entered in the Space field is inserted between the bottom edges of the selected items.

Item: Shape

This submenu allows you to change the shape of the following items:

- **Picture Box.** When changing the shape to another box type (including Bézier box), imported graphics are not affected. When converting a box to a line, its contents are deleted.

- **Text Box.** None of the shape options delete the contents of a text box—only the distribution of the text changes. Choosing any of the line options converts the text box to a text path.

- **Line.** When you convert a straight line to a box, the box traces the line's length and thickness. When you convert a curved Bézier line to a box, the box is based on the highest, lowest, leftmost, and rightmost points. When you convert a dashed or striped line to a box, the individual shapes become editable boxes.

- **Text Path.** You can't convert a straight text path to a box—however, you can convert it to another line type. When you convert a curved text path to a box, you create a text box based on the line's highest, lowest, leftmost, and rightmost points. The original text flows inside the box.

This submenu is only available when a single item is selected.

Special Notes

- Whenever a plain line is converted to a box, it becomes an empty box with a background color of None. To change the contents, use the Item: **Content** commands.

- When you convert an item to a standard box shape, the new box has no editable Bézier points—to produce this effect, choose Item: Shape: **Bézier Box** after converting.

- When a box contains a frame, its width and color carry over when the box is converted to a line. For example, if a picture box has a red 6 pt. frame, converting it produces a red 6 pt. line. Conversely, when a line is converted to a box, the line color becomes the frame color—however, the default frame width of a converted box is 0 pt.

- When you convert a box with no frame to a line, the new line has a default thickness of Hairline (or .125 pt.), too thin for most reproductive methods. You must remember to set a heavier line weight after converting.

- When you convert a box to a line, you can't choose Item: **Undo**, nor can you convert it back to the original box dimensions. If there is any doubt, select the box with the Item Tool, and choose Edit: **Copy** before converting.

Item: Shape: Rectangular Box

This option converts the selected item to a rectangular box. (See "Item: Shape" earlier in this chapter for more information.)

Item: Shape: Rounded Corner Box

This option converts the selected item to a rounded corner box. (See "Item: Shape" earlier in this chapter for more information.) The default corner radius is .25 inches, or 18 pt.

Item: Shape: Beveled Corner Box

This option converts the selected item to a beveled corner box. (See "Item: Shape" earlier in this chapter for more information.) The default corner radius is .25 inches, or 18 pt.

Item: Shape: Concave Corner Box

This option converts the selected item to a concave corner box. (See "Item: Shape" earlier in this chapter for more information.) The default corner radius is .25 inches, or 18 pt.

Item: Shape: Elliptical Box

This option converts the selected item to an elliptical box. (See "Item: Shape" earlier in this chapter for more information.)

Item: Shape: Bézier Box

This option converts the selected item to a closed Bézier path. When applied to a box, the box shape doesn't change—but the points making up the box become editable Bézier points.

Special Notes

When applied to a curved or straight line, this option traces its length, shape, and thickness. To convert an open Bézier path to a closed Bézier box, hold down the (Option) [**Alt**] key while choosing this command.

Item: Shape: Line

This option converts the selected item to a non-Bézier line. When applied to a box, the line extends from the upper left to lower right of the item's bounds. (See "Item: Shape" for more information.)

Item: Shape: Orthogonal Line

This option converts a box or curved line to a horizontal or vertical non-Bézier line. (See "Item: Shape" for more information.)

The orientation of the new line depends on the width and height of the selected object. When the width is greater than the height, the new line is horizontal. When the height is greater, the new line is vertical.

When applied to a box, horizontal lines extend from the left-edge center point to the right. Vertical lines extend from the top-edge center point to the bottom. When applied to a curved path, horizontal and vertical lines are placed in the mathematical center of the former path.

This option has no effect on standard diagonal lines.

Item: Shape: Bézier Line

This option converts a box or line to a single, open Bézier path. Although the shape may appear closed after converting a box, the endpoints of the path simply overlap.

Special Notes

To convert a new Bézier line to a text path, leave it selected, and choose Item: Shape: **Text**.

Item: Content

Use the options in this submenu to change the type of the currently selected item. This command is only available when a single item is selected.

Item: Content: Picture

Choose this option to convert a text or empty box to a picture box. This item isn't available when a line or text path is selected.

Item: Content: Text

Choose this option to convert a picture or empty box to a text box. Lines and Bézier paths are converted to text paths.

Item: Content: None

Choose this option to convert a picture or text box to an empty box. Any box contents are deleted. Empty boxes can contain no images or text, but you can apply color, frames, and tints, just like any other box.

When applied to a straight text path, it converts to a standard line. When applied to a curved text path, it converts to a Bézier line.

Item: Edit

The options in this submenu allow you to view and edit any existing Bézier information. This command is only available when a single item is selected.

Item: Edit: Shape
Shift-F4

When this item is checked, you can view and edit the individual points of a Bézier path. When unchecked, these points are hidden—a bounding box surrounds the path, only allowing you to reposition and scale the item.

See Also
> Line Tools: **Bézier Line Tool**

Item: Edit: Runaround
(Option) [Alt]-F4

When this item is checked, you can view and edit the individual points of a Bézier runaround path, created using Item: **Runaround**. By default, runaround paths appear on-screen as pink, but this value can be changed by resetting the Grid color in the Edit: Preferences: Application: **Display** panel.

See Also
> Line Tools: **Bézier Line Tool**
> Item: **Runaround**
> Edit: Preferences: Application: **Display**

Item: Edit: Clipping Path
(Option-Shift) [Alt-Shift]-F4

When this item is checked, you can view and edit the individual points of an XPress clipping path, created using Item: **Clipping**. By default, clipping paths appear on-screen as green, but this value can be changed by resetting the Ruler color in the Edit: Preferences: Application: **Display** panel.

See Also

Line Tools: **Bézier Line Tool**
Item: **Clipping**
Edit: Preferences: Application: **Display**

Item: Point/Segment Type

Use the options in this submenu to convert currently selected Bézier points or segments.

To convert a single point, click it once. To convert multiple points, Shift-click each one. To convert all the points in a path, double-click one point.

To convert a segment, click it once—the points on either side highlight. To convert multiple segments, Shift-click each one. To convert all the segments in a path, double-click one segment.

See Also

Line Tools: **Bézier Line Tool**

Corner Point
(Option) [Alt]-F1

This option converts all selected points to corner points. (See "Bézier Line Tool" in Chapter 3, *Line Tools*, for more information.)

Smooth Point
(Option) [Alt]-F2

This option converts all selected points to smooth points. (See "Bézier Line Tool" in Chapter 3 for more information.)

Symmetrical Point
(Option) [Alt]-F3

This option converts all selected points to symmetrical points. (See "Bézier Line Tool" in Chapter 3 for more information.)

Straight Segment
(Option-Shift) [Alt-Shift]-F1

This option converts a curved segment to a straight segment by hiding the appropriate curve handles. If a point controlling the shape of a segment is symmetrical, it's converted to a corner point. (See "Bézier Line Tool" in Chapter 3 for more information.)

Smooth Segment
(Option-Shift) [Alt-Shift]-F2

This option converts a straight segment to a segment that can be curved. It does this by revealing the curve handles that control the segment's shape, but in such a way that the segment shape is retained until the handles are adjusted. (See "Bézier Line Tool" in Chapter 3 for more information.)

CHAPTER 11

The Page Menu

Page Overview

XPress' central metaphor is a traditional drafting table: project information is arranged on a series of pages, and the pasteboard—the white work area that surrounds each page—represents the table itself. As with conventional paste-up, XPress allows you to use a series of different page types as you construct your documents.

Document Pages

Document pages contain all the information destined for print. After determining the page count of your final project, you must insert that number of document pages. When you first create an XPress file, it contains a single document page. Techniques for handling and editing actual pages are covered in depth elsewhere in this book:

- **Determining document page dimensions.** Enter the desired values in the Width and Height fields of the File: New: **Document** dialog.

- **Inserting new document pages.** Choose Page: **Insert**, and enter the desired number of additional pages in the Insert Pages field, or drag a blank page icon into the page area of the Document Layout Palette.

- **Navigating to a document page.** Use Page: **Go To** and enter the desired number, choose a page from the Go To Page pop-up in the lower left of the document window, or click the desired page number in the Document Layout Palette.

- **Rearranging document pages.** Use Page: **Move**, drag a page icon in the Document Layout Palette, or choose View: **Thumbnails** and drag the thumbnail icons.

- **Deleting document pages.** Use Page: **Delete,** or select a page icon in the Document Layout Palette and click the palette's Delete Page button.

- **Copying document pages.** Open two documents, set them both to View: **Thumbnails,** and drag the desired thumbnails between them.

- **Exporting a document page.** Navigate to the desired page, and choose File: **Save Page as EPS.**

- **Renumbering document pages.** Use Page: **Section** to re-establish page numbering.

- **Printing document pages.** Choose File: **Print.**

Master Pages

Master pages, despite their title, are not actually *pages*—rather, they're *templates* referred to by your document pages.

If you look at any long document, you'll notice that certain items appear on every page. These can include the following:

- Page numbers

- Headers and footers

- Graphics, such as corporate logos in a catalog or annual report

- Lines or rules above, below, or beside the page information

- Empty picture or text boxes, ready to receive information on each document page

Rather than manually place these items on every page in your document, you can place them on a master page. When future document pages are based on this master page, the master page items automatically appear in the appropriate position. This allows you to easily create a consistent look and feel throughout your document. Also, if you need to change this information, you can return to the master page and make the necessary adjustments. The document pages are automatically updated.

It's important to note that although master pages *look* like document pages, they're not the same:

- Master pages are not numbered along with the document pages. By default, each master page is assigned a letter. For example, the blank master page that first appears in a new document is named "A-Master A." Subsequently added master pages are named "B-Master B," "C-Master-C," and so forth. While you can change the name of each master page, the name must still begin with a letter or number, followed by a hyphen.

- You must navigate to a different part of your document to view and edit the pages. Instead of jumping to a specific page number, you must deliberately navigate to a master page to view its contents.

- Most document page-editing commands are not available while viewing a master page. For example, File: **Save Page as EPS,** Page: **Insert,** Page: **Delete,**

Page: **Move**, and Page: **Section** can only be applied to document pages and are therefore grayed out in their respective menus.

However, you can draw boxes, import graphics, enter text, add lines, and otherwise create a page using all the same tools as when you're editing document pages. For the best results, create and format your master pages before adding and designing your document pages. Techniques for handling and editing master pages are covered in depth elsewhere in this book:

- **Adding new master pages.** Drag a blank page icon into the master page section of the Document Layout Palette. (See Chapter 15, *The Document Layout Palette*, for more information.)

- **Assigning master pages.** When inserting new document pages using Page: **Insert**, set the master page you wish to assign in the Master Page pop-up. Or drag a master page icon onto the desired document page in the Document Layout Palette. (See "Page: Insert," later in this chapter, and Chapter 15 for more information.)

- **Removing a master page.** Select the desired master page icon in the Document Layout Palette and click the Delete Page button. (See Chapter 15 for more information.)

- **Adding an automatic text box.** Click the Automatic Text Box option in the File: New: **Document** dialog, or draw a text box on the master page and use the Linking Tool to link it to the broken link icon that appears in the upper left of every document page. (See "Linking Tool" in Chapter 4, *Linking Tools*, and "File: New: Document" in Chapter 5, *The File Menu*, for more information.)

- **Adding automatic page numbers.** Draw a text box in the appropriate position on the master page, and type (Command) [**Control**]-3 to insert the automatic page number character. When this item is viewed on a document page, it displays the number assigned to the page in the Document Layout Palette.

- **Copying master pages to another document.** Assign the master page to a document page, then use View: **Thumbnails** to drag the page to another document. The master page is automatically transferred to the second document. (See "View: Thumbnails" in Chapter 12, *The View Menu*, for more information.)

Single-Sided Pages

When a document contains single-sided pages, only one page at a time initially appears on the pasteboard. This page type is used for documents such as flyers, letters, one-page projects, and posters—any project that will not be bound. In the Document Layout Palette, single-sided pages appear in a vertical row. A single-sided master page only contains one page.

Create a single-sided document by unchecking the Facing Pages box in the File: New: **Document** dialog. The default master page is also single sided. You cannot add facing pages to a single-sided document.

Special notes

Although you can create a multipage spread by positioning single-sided pages side by side in the Document Layout Palette, they're not facing pages. The advantage of working with facing pages is that you can create a left- and right-facing master page, which allows you to design multipage projects more flexibly.

Facing Pages

When a document contains facing pages, a relationship is established between a left page and a right page. For the easiest example, open a book or magazine. All even-numbered pages appear on the left of the binding (or are *left-facing* pages); all odd-numbered pages appear on the right (or are *right-facing* pages).

In the Document Layout Palette, facing pages appear in twos, one on each side of a vertical black line representing the binding. Since "1" is an odd number, the first document page always appears to the right of the vertical line.

Create a facing-page document by checking the Facing Pages box in the File: New: **Document** dialog. The default master page contains two side-by-side pages, allowing you to create a template for the left- and right-facing pages of the document.

Special notes

A facing-page document can also contain a single-sided document and master pages. To see a common example, refer to a book that starts each section or chapter with a separate, decorative page. Here, this page is based on a single-sided master page, while the remaining document pages are based on a facing master page.

Page: Insert

When you first create a document using File: New: **Document**, it contains only one page. Use this command to add the remaining pages your document requires.

Common Errors

- **Adding one extra page.** When adding a specific number of document pages, bear in mind that one page already exists. For example, when creating an eight-page document, insert seven new pages. If you accidentally insert too many pages, you can't undo this command. Instead, use Page: **Delete** to remove them.

- **Incorrectly linking new pages to an automatic text chain.** When adding pages that continue an automatic chain, one of the automatic text boxes must be selected before the Link to Current Text Chain option is available. However, if you check this option when inserting pages in the middle of the chain, the new automatic boxes are linked to the last box in the chain. For example, if an automatic chain covers 16 pages and you insert four linked pages after page 8, the automatic text flows as follows: pages 1 through 8, jump to pages

13 through 20, back to pages 9 through 12. For the best results, make sure the *last* box in the automatic chain is selected.

Special Notes

- You can access this dialog when adding pages in the Document Layout Palette—hold down the (Option) [Alt] key while dragging a master page icon into the page area. There, the settings in the Insert Pages dialog override the manually placed position of the new page.

- If a document has been renumbered using Page: **Section**, you must use the new numbers when specifying the location of the new pages. For example, if a book chapter is sectioned to run from page 35 to 70, you must enter a number between 35 and 70 when using the Insert Page(s) Before or Insert Page(s) After options. Similarly, if the numbering contains a prefix or consists of letters, these values must be entered.

- To use an absolute page number instead of section numbering, enter a plus sign (+) before the desired value. For example, you can insert new pages after the tenth page in the document (regardless of its page number) by entering "+10" in the Insert Page(s) After field.

- Once pages are added to a document, you can further rearrange them using Page: **Move** or the Document Layout Palette.

- You can't create new master pages with this command. You must use the Document Layout Palette.

The Insert Pages Dialog

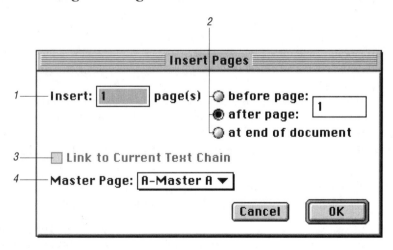

1. **Insert Page(s)** (1 to 100)

   Enter the number of new pages you wish to create in this field. Although you can only add up to 100 pages at a time, each document can contain up to 2,000 pages.

2. **New Page Location**

These options determine the placement of the new pages:

Before Page

When enabled, this option places the new pages before the page number entered in the following field. The page number of the active page appears here by default.

After Page

When enabled, this option places the new pages after the page number entered in the following field. The page number of the active page appears here by default.

At End of Document

When enabled, this option places the new pages at the very end of the document, regardless of the current sectioning or page count.

3. **Link to Current Text Chain**

When a document contains at least one automatic text chain, this option inserts pages that continue the chain. Each new page contains an automatic text box linked to the end of the chain you specify. To make this option available, you must select the last box in the automatic chain you want continued.

Automatic text chains are defined on the master page level—therefore, a document can contain more than one. When you select the last box of an automatic chain, the master page it's linked to appears in the Master Page pop-up. If desired, you can continue the chain using the automatic text box of another master page by selecting the appropriate item in the Master Page pop-up. (See Chapter 15 for more information on master pages and automatic text boxes.)

4. **Master Page**

This pop-up determines which master page, if any, the new pages are based upon.

Blank Single

Here, each new page is a *blank single*, or a single page not based on any master page. This option is available in both single- and facing-page documents.

If you later apply a facing master page to a blank single, it converts to a facing page.

Blank Facing Page

Here, each new page is a *blank facing page*, or a facing page not based on any master page. This option is available only in facing page documents. Whether a new page is a right- or left-facing page depends on its position in the document. For example, placing a new blank facing page after a left-facing page results in a new right-facing page.

If you later apply a single master page to a blank facing page, it converts to a single page.

Master Pages

The Master Page pop-up also displays all master pages currently defined in a document. New pages created with a specific master page set here are based on that information.

This command only allows you to create pages based on one type of master page information at a time. When inserting pages that must be linked to different master page types, you must choose this command more than once, applying the appropriate master page information to the appropriate new pages. (See "Page: Page Overview" in Chapter 11, *The Page Menu*, for more information on page types and master pages.)

See Also

File: New: **Document**
Page: **Delete**
Page: **Move**
Page: **Section**
The Document Layout Palette

Page: Delete

Use this command to remove a range of pages from a document.

Common Errors

Attempting to delete pages containing automatic text chains. If you delete pages containing empty automatic text boxes, the pages are simply removed. If text flows through the automatic chain, the results of this command depend on whether Auto Page Insertion is turned off or on in the Edit: Preferences: Document: **General** panel:

- If it's off, the pages are simply removed. A text overflow symbol appears at the end of the last automatic text box.

- If it's on, the results may be unexpected: new pages are automatically created to accommodate the text flowing through the automatic chain. Avoid this by turning Auto Page Insertion off before using this command.

Special Notes

- If a document has been renumbered using Page: **Section**, you must use the new numbers when specifying which pages to delete. For example, if a book chapter is sectioned to run from page 35 to 70, you must enter a range between 35 and 70. Similarly, if the numbering contains a prefix or consists of letters, these values must be entered.

- To use an absolute page number instead of section numbering, enter a plus sign (+) before the desired value. For example, you can delete the tenth page in the document (regardless of its page number) by entering "+10" in the Delete Page(s) field.

- You can delete pages without accessing this command by using the tools in the Document Layout Palette.

- You can't delete master pages with this command. You must use the Document Layout Palette.

The Delete Pages Dialog

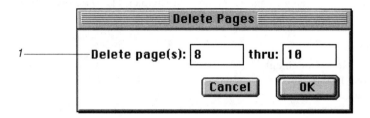

1. **Delete Page(s)**

   Here, enter the page or range of pages you wish to delete. The first field always defaults to the current document page.

   To delete a single page, enter its number in the first field, and leave the second field blank.

   To delete a range of pages, enter the first number in the first field and the last number in the second field.

   To delete a range of pages to the end of the document, you can enter the first number in the first field and "end" in the second field. If desired, you can enter the number of the last document page in the second field instead.

See Also

Edit: Preferences: Document: **General**
Page: **Section**
The Document Layout Palette

Page: Move

Use this command to reposition pages within a document.

Common Errors

Mistakenly moving pages containing a linked text chain. If a text chain (whether manual or automatic) covers a range of pages, moving some of the pages can produce unexpected results. Moving a linked text box does not alter its contents or the original order of linking. For example, assume a linked text chain runs from page 1, to page 2, to page 3. If you place page 3 between pages 1 and 2, the text chain now runs from page 1, to page 3, to page 2. If unsatisfied with the flow of text after moving pages, you may need to unlink the boxes using the Unlinking Tool, then relink them in the desired order with the Linking Tool.

Special Notes

- If a document has been renumbered using Page: **Section**, you must use the new numbers when specifying which pages to move. For example, if a book chapter is sectioned to run from page 35 to 70, you must enter a range between 35 and 70. Similarly, if the numbering contains a prefix or consists of letters, these values must be entered.

- To use an absolute page number instead of section numbering, enter a plus sign (+) before the desired value. For example, you can move the tenth through fifteenth pages in the document (regardless of the page numbers) by entering "+10" thru "+15" in the Move Page(s) fields.

- You can move pages without accessing this command by dragging the page icons in the Document Layout Palette.

The Move Pages Dialog

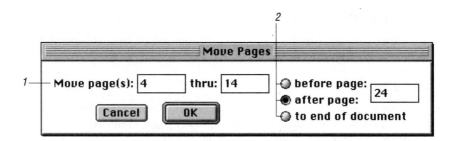

1. **Move Page(s)**

   Here, enter the page or range of pages you wish to move.

   To move a single page, enter its number in the first field, and leave the second field blank.

   To move a range of pages, enter the first number in the first field and the last number in the second field.

   To move a range of pages to the end of the document, you can enter the first number in the first field and "end" in the second field. If desired, you can enter the number of the last document page in the second field instead.

2. **Moved Page Location**

These options determine the new position of the specified page range:

Before Page

When enabled, this option places pages before the page number entered in the following field. The page number of the active page appears here by default.

After Page

When enabled, this option places pages after the page number entered in the following field. The page number of the active page appears here by default.

To End of Document

When enabled, this option places pages at the very end of the document, regardless of the current sectioning or page count.

See Also

Linking Tools
Page: **Section**
The Document Layout Palette

Page: Master Guides

Use this command to reset the column and margin guides originally established in the File: New: **Document** dialog.

Special Notes

- XPress regards column and margin guides as master page items—therefore, this command is only available when a master page is selected from the Page: **Display** submenu or the Document Layout Palette.

- Since a document can contain multiple master pages, it can contain multiple column and margin guide settings as well. You must make sure the appropriate master page is selected before choosing this command.

- The width and height of an automatic text box is based on the margin guides of the master page; whether or not it's divided into columns depends on the number of columns applied to the master page. Changing any of these values alters the automatic text box appropriately.

The Master Guides Dialog

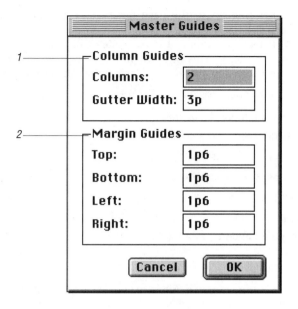

1. **Column Guides**

   These values determine the number of columns and the space between them. (See "File: New: Document" in Chapter 5 for more information.)

2. **Margin Guides**

   These values determine the placement of margin guides, as measured from each of the four page edges. (See "File: New: Document" in Chapter 5 for more information.)

See Also

File: New: **Document**
Page: **Display**
The Document Layout Palette

Page: Section

By default, the page numbering of an XPress document always starts at 1. Also, all automatic page numbers appear as Arabic numerals (1, 2, 3, etc.). This command allows you to establish a new sequence of page numbers in a document. You can also change the type of numerals used—whether to add a prefix to standard page numbers, to change the numbers themselves to roman numerals or letters, or both.

Common Uses

- **Using special characters to number part of a publication.** For example, the introduction of a book is often numbered with lowercase Roman numerals.

- **Adding chapter prefixes to the page numbers of a manual.** Many technical manuals keep page numbers specific to each chapter. For example, the pages in Chapter 4 might run from "4.1" to "4.55," while Chapter 5 starts over at "5.1" and runs to "5.75." This way, whenever a chapter is pulled and updated, it doesn't affect the page numbering of the entire publication.

Refer to Appendix A, *Common Techniques*, for full descriptions of the following:

- Renumbering an entire document
- Partially renumbering a document
- Adding multiple sections to a document
- Removing a section designation
- Including a prefix before page numbers
- Changing page numbers
- Starting page numbering on a left-facing page

Common Errors

- **Failing to track page numbers when manually sectioning multiple documents.** Rather than create an extraordinarily long document, many users split such a project into a series of smaller documents. Once this happens, there are two ways to make sure page numbering stays consistent between documents: use the XPress book feature, or manually establish the numbering range of each document. When manually sectioning your documents, you must constantly be aware of the page range—increasing or decreasing the number of pages in one document does not automatically re-establish the page numbers of the rest.

- **Failing to use the sectioned numbering system when applying page-specific commands.** When a command requires that you enter page numbers, you must use the same format and prefix specified in the Section dialog. For example, if a section runs from page 10 to page 20, you cannot apply a command that affects page 1. Page-specific commands include the following: File: **Print**, File: **Save Page as EPS**, Page: **Insert**, Page: **Delete**, Page: **Move**, and Page: **Go To**. (Refer to the sections in Chapters 5 and 11 describing those commands for more information.)

Special Notes

- The first page of a new section is indicated by an asterisk, as viewed in the Document Layout Palette and page-selection pop-up at the bottom of the document window.

- The page designated to be the start of a new section always retains this setting, regardless of where it's positioned. For example, if the fifth page of an 8-page document is set to start page numbering at 10, the page sequence runs as follows: 1, 2, 3, 4, 10, 11, 12, 13. If the fifth page is then repositioned between the second and third pages, the new sequence runs as follows: 1, 2, 10, 11, 12, 13, 14, 15.

- To access the Section dialog from the Document Layout Palette, click the page icon you want to start the section, then click the page number displayed in the lower left of the palette.

The Section Dialog

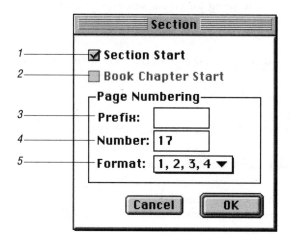

1. **Section Start**

   Check this box to begin a new section, starting at the currently active page. When unchecked, none of the remaining settings are available.

   If the currently active page already starts a new section, unchecking this box removes the designation. If no other sections exist, the page numbering reverts back to XPress defaults.

2. **Book Chapter Start**

   When a document is added to a book created using File: New: **Book**, this box is automatically checked. This feature allows the page numbering of each chapter to run in the order defined in the Book Palette.

   To override this setting—for example, to make the page numbers of an introductory chapter appear in lowercase Roman numerals—check the Section Start box, and define a new section. This is only possible when you close the Book Palette, *then* open the document. As long as the Book Palette is open, this box is checked but unavailable. (See "File: New: Book" in Chapter 5 for more information.)

3. **Prefix** (up to four characters)

Any characters entered here are placed before each automatic page number. For example, if you enter "6.", the page numbers appear as 6.1, 6.2, 6.3, and so forth. If you enter "A–" and the section is set to start at page 25, the page numbers appear as A–25, A–26, A–27, and so forth.

4. **Number** (1 to 9,999)

Assign the first number of the newly established range in this field. For example, if you want a section to start numbering at page 25, enter "25" here.

Enter Arabic numerals, regardless of the item set in the Formats pop-up. For example, if you're using lowercase letters as page numerals, you must enter 10 in the Numbers field to start numbering at "j."

5. **Format**

This pop-up determines the type of numerals used to number pages.

1, 2, 3, 4
   The default, this item uses Arabic numerals.

I, II, III, IV
   This item uses uppercase Roman numerals.

i, ii, iii, iv
   This item uses lowercase Roman numerals.

A, B, C, D
   This item uses uppercase letters. When a document contains more than 26 pages, the numbering goes from Z to AA, AB, AC, and so forth.

a, b, c, d
   This item uses lowercase letters. When a document contains more than 26 pages, the numbering goes from z to aa, ab, ac, and so forth.

See Also

File: New: **Book**
The Document Layout Palette

Page: Previous
Shift-Page Down Key

Choose this command to go to the previous document page. When the first page in a document is active, this command is not available.

Page: Next
Shift-Page Down Key

Choose this command to go to the next document page. When the last page in a document is active, this command is not available.

Page: First
Home Key

Choose this command to go to the first document page. When the first page is already active, this command is not available.

Page: Last
End Key

Choose this command to go to the last document page. When the last page is already active, this command is not available.

Page: Go To
(Command) [Control]-J

This command lets you jump to a specific page number. The number you enter in the Go to Page dialog must fall within the range of the document—otherwise, an alert appears, stating "This page does not exist."

Special Notes

- If a document has been renumbered using Page: **Section**, you must use the new numbers when jumping to a document page. For example, if a section runs from page 35 to 70, you must enter a number between 35 and 70. Similarly, if the numbering contains a prefix or consists of letters, these values must be entered as well.

- To use an absolute page number instead of section numbering, enter a plus sign (+) before the desired value. For example, you can jump to the tenth page in the document (regardless of its page number) by entering "+10" in the Go to Page field.

- You can jump to a specific page by double-clicking the appropriate page icon in the Document Layout Palette.

- You can also jump to a specific page by choosing the appropriate page icon from the page select pop-up in the lower left of the document window.

See Also
Page: **Section**
The Document Layout Palette

Page: Display

This submenu lists all master pages currently available in a document. To display a specific master page, choose the appropriate item from the pop-up. To return to the document, choose Document from the pop-up—you return to the page that was active when you first chose a master page.

Special Notes

- You can jump to a specific master page by double-clicking the appropriate master page icon in the Document Layout Palette.

- You can also jump to a specific master page by choosing the appropriate icon from the page select pop-up in the lower left of the document window.

See Also

The Document Layout Palette

CHAPTER 12

The View Menu

When you create or open an XPress file, the information is displayed in a *document window*. The commands in the View Menu affect how this window displays a document on-screen.

The document window itself contains another set of commands.

Zoom Field

Located in the lower-left corner of the window, this field displays the current zoom percentage. If desired, you can double-click the current value, enter a new percentage, and press the (Return) [**Enter**] key to apply the zoom. Enter a percentage between 10% and 800%.

More commonly, people use the following zoom methods:

- Click or click-drag with the Zoom Tool to zoom in.
- (Option) [**Alt**]-click with the Zoom Tool to zoom out.
- Choose one of the first six View Menu commands to zoom in or out, depending on the current zoom percentage.

Common Errors

Choosing Edit: Undo to reverse a zoom. Although it appears as if you can undo the zoom, you actually undo the last-applied command at the same time. If unsatisfied with the zoom percentage, apply a new one instead of choosing Undo. This rule also applies to the zoom options in the View Menu.

Special Notes

- Macintosh users can highlight the zoom percentage by pressing Control-V.

- When an item is selected, zooming in or out aligns the item to the center of the window.

See Also

Page Tools: **Zoom Tool**
View: **Fit In Window**
View: **50%**
View: **75%**
View: **Actual Size**
View: **200%**
View: **Thumbnails**

Page Select Field and Pop-Up

Located to the right of the zoom field, the page select field displays the currently active document page. You can jump to a specific page by highlighting the value, entering the desired page number, and pressing the (Return) [**Enter**] key. This is particularly helpful when a document contains more than 40 or 50 pages.

You can also jump to a specific page by selecting the appropriate icon in the page select pop-up, which displays every page currently defined in a document.

Special Notes

- To jump to a master page, enter its corresponding letter. For example, to jump to A-Master A (or if you've renamed the master page, "A-Page Title"), enter "a" in the field, and click (Return) [**Enter**].

- To show the document pages as thumbnails, enter "t" in the field, and click (Return) [**Enter**].

- The page number that displays in the page select field depends on the scrolling position of the document. If the upper boundary or lower boundary of the pasteboard is visible, the field displays the number of the upper page. When side-by-side pages appear over the pasteboard boundary, the number of the page farthest to the left displays.

See Also

Page: **Go To**
The Document Layout Palette

Scroll Bars

Like any other window, an XPress document contains scroll bars. These, however, are the least efficient method of scrolling. The most common technique is dragging with the Hand Tool, which you can access at any time by pressing the

---

(Option) [**Alt**] key. (The Hand Tool is disabled whenever the Caps Lock key is depressed.)

Special Notes

Use the following extended keyboard shortcuts to maneuver through a document:

- **Go up one screen.** Press the Page Up key.
- **Go down one screen.** Press the Page Down key.
- **Go to previous page.** Press Shift-Page Up.
- **Go to next page.** Press Shift-Page Down
- **Go to first document page.** Press the Home key.
- **Go to last document page.** Press the End key.

View: Fit in Window
(Command) [Control]-Zero

This command adjusts the zoom to display the entire active page in the document window. The actual percentage depends on the page dimensions. When a page is larger than the current window size, it's scaled below 100% to fit. This allows you to review or edit an entire page at once, at the largest possible scale. Pages smaller than the window are scaled above 100%.

Special Notes

- When you choose this command while holding down the (Option) [**Alt**] key, XPress zooms out to display the entire width of the pasteboard.
- There's no shortcut to fit side-by-side pages in the window. To do this, press (Option-Command) [**Alt-Control**]-Zero to zoom to the pasteboard width, then use the Zoom Tool to drag a box around the page spread.

View: 50%

This command sets the zoom percentage to 50%.

View: 75%

This command sets the zoom percentage to 75%.

View: Actual Size
(Command) [Control]-1

This command sets the zoom percentage to 100%.

Special Notes

- To zoom back and forth between Actual Size and Fit in Window, depress the Caps Lock key and (Option) [**Alt**]-click on-screen. If the Caps Lock key isn't depressed, the Hand Tool appears (see the previous section "Scroll Bars").

- To zoom back and forth between Actual Size and 200%, (Option-Command) [**Alt-Control**]-click on-screen. The Caps Lock key has no effect on this shortcut.

View: 200%

This command sets the zoom percentage to 200%.

View: Thumbnails
Shift-F6

This command is similar to setting a very small zoom percentage—such as 10%— but it's not quite the same:

- You can't edit individual page items. Instead, clicking a page selects the entire page, including its contents.

- Pages with a width or height over 12 inches are scaled below 10% to appear as a thumbnail. This is the only way to view large pages at such a small size.

Because the information is so reduced, this view option is rarely used for reviewing pages. Instead, it allows you to rearrange pages or drag them into another document.

Common Uses

Refer to Appendix A, *Common Techniques*, for full descriptions of the following:

- Using thumbnails to rearrange pages within a document
- Using thumbnails to copy pages to another document
- Using thumbnails to copy master pages to another document
- Using thumbnails to rescue a corrupted document
- Creating temporary thumbnail page numbers

Common Errors

- **Attempting to copy thumbnails to a document set to a different view.** You can only drag thumbnails between documents when *both* documents are set to View: **Thumbnails**. To set all open documents to Thumbnail view, hold down the (Option) [**Alt**] key, and choose View: Window: **Tile Documents**.

- **Attempting to copy thumbnails to an incorrectly sized second document.** When copying thumbnails to another document, the pages of the second document must be *at least* the same size as the original. If the width or height is smaller than the original document, an alert appears, stating "You cannot

---

move a page to a document with a smaller size." If the width and height are greater, the contents of the original page appear in the upper-left corner of the new page. If the width and height are identical, the new pages transfer perfectly.

- **Attempting to copy a facing page to a single-sided document.** When a page is currently linked to a facing master page, it can't be copied to a single-sided document. You must do one of the following before dragging the thumbnail:

  - When dragging the thumbnail into a new document, make sure the Facing Pages box is checked in the File: New: **Document** dialog.

  - Apply a single-sided master page to the page you wish to copy. This is acceptable only if the current master page contains no information—if it does, the information is replaced with the contents of the new master page.

  - Convert the second document to facing pages by choosing File: **Document Setup** and checking the Facing Pages box.

Special Notes

- Use the following techniques to select thumbnails:

  - To select a single thumbnail, click it once.

  - To select contiguous thumbnails, hold down the Shift key while clicking.

  - To select noncontiguous thumbnails, hold down the (Command) [**Control**] key while clicking.

- To mimic the size of thumbnails (while retaining the ability to edit the pages), enter a very low zoom percentage. This reduced size is largely based on the page dimensions. For example, if you set a 5 × 5-inch document to 10%, the pages only appear as half inch squares. If you set a letter-sized document to 10%, it's practically identical to the thumbnail version.

- To jump to the thumbnail of a specific page, choose the appropriate number from the page select pop-up. When you do, the desired thumbnail is placed in the upper-left corner of the window. Beyond this, XPress doesn't indicate a thumbnail's page number in the page select field or Document Layout Palette.

- If a document page is linked to a master page, dragging its thumbnail to another document transfers the master page information as well. The new master page is listed in the Document Layout Palette under the next available letter.

- To print thumbnails, a document doesn't have to be in thumbnail view. Instead, check the Thumbnails box in the File: Print: **Document** panel.

See Also

Appendix A (View: **Thumbnails**)
File: New: **Document**
File: **Document Setup**
File: **Print**
View: **Windows**
The Document Layout Palette

View: Windows

The items in this submenu determine the on-screen layout of multiple open documents.

Special Notes

- Access the Windows submenu by holding down the Shift key and clicking the title bar of the active document.

- Use the following shortcuts to reset the view of all open documents:

  - **Set all views to Fit in Window.** Hold down the (Command) [**Control**] key while choosing Stack Documents or Tile Documents.

  - **Set all views to Thumbnails.** Hold down the (Option) [**Alt**] key while choosing Stack Documents or Tile Documents.

  You can't use these shortcuts when choosing a single document from the View: **Windows** pop-up. You must choose the appropriate setting from the View Menu.

View: Windows: Stack Documents

This command layers the open documents as a sort of cascade, leaving visible about a quarter inch of each window's title bar. The active document is always placed on top of the stack.

View: Windows: Tile Documents

This command resizes the windows so that all of them can be viewed on-screen simultaneously. The active document is always placed in the upper-left corner of the screen.

Special Notes

Many users tile two documents when preparing to copy thumbnails from one document to another. However, XPress always extends two tiled windows horizontally, one over the other. Since thumbnails appear in a vertical row, this is not the most convenient viewing option. For the best results, manually resize the windows so they appear side by side, allowing you to view as many thumbnails as possible. (See "View: Thumbnails," earlier in this chapter, for more information.)

View: Windows: Document List

The lower part of the Windows submenu displays the title of all currently open documents. Select a document to make it active, bringing it all the way to the front.

View: Show/Hide Guides
F7-Key

This command hides and reveals all existing guides. It doesn't remove them from the document. A guide is a nonprinting horizontal or vertical line, similar to a blue line drawn in a conventional page design. This feature is very similar to guides found in Photoshop and illustration programs.

To place a guide, the rulers must be visible and guides must be showing. Create a horizontal guide by clicking and dragging from the horizontal ruler; create a vertical guide by clicking and dragging from the vertical ruler. Since there's no way to constrain the guides to the ruler's tickmarks, you must pay attention to the X or Y value in the Measurements Palette to accurately position the guides.

Depending on how you drag a guide from the ruler, XPress recognizes two types of guide:

- **Page guides** result when you release the mouse button over the page when placing a guide. These guides only appear within the bounds of a single page—they don't extend onto the pasteboard or cross over side-by-side pages. When these guides are used on a master page, they're visible on the document pages.

- **Pasteboard guides** result when you release the mouse button over the pasteboard when placing a guide. These guides extend from one side of the pasteboard to another, and horizontal pasteboard guides cross over all side-by-side pages. When these guides are used on a master page, they're not visible on the document pages.

Regardless of the currently selected tool, you can always drag a guide from the rulers. To reposition an existing guide, however, you must use the Item or Content Tool. If you're using another tool, hold down the (Command) [**Control**] key, and drag. (Command) [**Control**]-dragging a guide does not deselect any currently selected items.

Special Notes

- Set the guide color in the Edit: Preferences: Application: **Display** panel. When specifying a new guide color, you can create dotted black guides by entering 0 in the HSB or RGB fields.

- Remove a single guide by dragging it beyond the edge of the window. Clear multiple guides by (Option) [**Alt**]-clicking the vertical and horizontal rulers. The guides actually removed depend on the current position of the page:

  - When the pasteboard is not visible above or to the left of the page, this technique only removes the page guides.

  - When the pasteboard is visible between the page and the horizontal or vertical ruler, this shortcut only removes pasteboard guides.

- XPress allows you to place guides that are visible only at one specific zoom percentage. Set the desired view, then hold down the Shift key while dragging and placing a guide. For example, if the view is set to Actual Size when you Shift-place a guide, that guide is only visible when the zoom percentage is 100%. At any other value, the guide is hidden.

See Also

Edit: Preferences: Application: **Display**
View: **Show/Hide Rulers**
View: **Snap to Guides**

View: Show/Hide Baseline Grid

This command displays and hides a series of horizontal guides used to consistently align text, lines, and boxes.

This feature is most commonly used to create a *leading grid*, a method of locking the baselines of text in multiple columns to the same series of guides. When this happens, lines of text in neighboring columns are perfectly matched, and the possibility of misaligning them—even if you accidentally nudge a text box—is greatly reduced.

Each document only contains one baseline grid. When designing a project requiring more than one grid setup, you must create separate documents. If necessary, use XPress' bookmaking feature to link the separate documents together. (See File: New: **Book** for more information.)

A baseline grid consists of the following:

- **Starting point.** In the Edit: Preferences: Document: **Paragraph** panel, specify the location of the first guide in the baseline grid, as measured from the top of the page. By default, it starts half an inch down. Any text locked to the baseline grid can't be moved above the first line, regardless of the position of a text box.

- **Grid spacing.** Also in the Edit: Preferences: Document: **Paragraph** panel, specify the distance between grid lines. Since the text locks to this spacing, the value usually equals the leading you wish to apply to the text.

- **Locked baselines.** Text never automatically aligns to a baseline grid—it must be told to. To manually align text to the grid, highlight it, choose Style: **Formats**, and check the Lock to Baseline Grid box. For the best results, check this box when defining style sheets for the text you wish to lock. If you don't want to lock every occurrence of the text, create two style sheets—one that locks and one that doesn't (don't forget to name them descriptively).

Common Uses

Refer to Appendix A for full descriptions of the following:

- Creating a leading grid
- Creating a leading grid with half-increment values
- Assigning text to a leading grid

Common Errors

- **Manually aligning text baselines.** Many users, unfamiliar with leading grids, tediously align their text baselines by dragging ruler guides and nudging text boxes. If you find yourself doing this more than once, your work may be a perfect candidate for the baseline grid.

- **Specifying an incorrect leading value.** If the leading of text locked to the grid exceeds the grid spacing by even a fraction of a point, each line of text snaps to the next grid line. For example, if the grid spacing is set to 14 pt. and the leading is set to 15 pt., the text appears to have a leading value of 28 pt. (When the leading is set below the grid spacing, incidentally, nothing happens.) To increase the leading of locked text, increase the Increment value in the Edit: Preferences: Document: **Paragraph** panel.

- **Assigning an incorrect Space Before or Space After value.** When working with a baseline grid, the spaces you can apply before or after a paragraph (using the Style: **Format** command) are somewhat limited. If the space exceeds the grid spacing, the next paragraph skips to the next grid line before starting. For example, if the grid spacing is 16 pt. and the text has a Space After value of 24 pt., the space between paragraphs is actually 32 pt. For better results, make any Space Before and Space After values equal to the grid spacing.

Special Notes

- Boxes, lines, Bézier paths, and text paths cannot be locked to the baseline grid. However, if View: **Snap to Guides** is turned on *and* the baseline grid is showing, these items will snap to the grid lines as you drag them. To completely constrain their motion to the baseline grid, open the Edit: Preferences: Document: **General** panel, and set the Snap Distance to the same value as the grid spacing. (When you do this, you can still nudge items away from the grid lines using the arrow keys.)

- The color of the baseline grid defaults to pink. To change it, click the Grid swatch in the Edit: Preferences: Application: **Display** panel.

See Also

Appendix A (View: **Baseline Grid**)
File: New: **Book**
Edit: Preferences: Application: **Display**
Edit: Preferences: Document: **General**
Edit: Preferences: Document: **Paragraph**
Style: **Format**
View: **Snap to Guides**

View: Snap to Guides

Turn this command on to create snapping guides. Whenever an item is dragged close enough to a guide (ruler guide, column guide, or margin), it automatically aligns to it. This allows you to quickly and precisely align boxes, lines, and paths. Turn this command off to disable the alignment.

Special Notes

- The snapping distance is determined by the Snap Distance value entered in the Edit: Preferences: Document: **General** panel.

- When positioning a box or closed path, only its outermost edges snap to a guide. When positioning a line or open path, only the endpoints snap.

View: Show/Hide Rulers

This command reveals and hides the horizontal and vertical rulers. The rulers are closely related to X and Y values in the Measurements Palette.

The rulers measure in Inches, Inches Decimal, Picas, Points, Millimeters, Centimeters, Ciceros, and Agates. Establish these units in the Edit: Preferences: Document: **General** panel.

Common Uses

- **Positioning items across the width or height of a document.** In XPress, the position of an item is based on the coordinates of its upper-left corner. When moving an item across the page, this appears as the X and Y values in the far left of the Measurements Palette.

- **Repositioning the Zero Origin.** Click and drag from the criss-cross icon in the upper left of the image, where the two rulers meet. Two crosshairs representing the X axis and Y axis converge on the cursor. Using the rulers or page elements as a guide, release the crosshairs at the desired position. The rulers reflect the change.

- **Placing guides.** Nonprinting guide lines can be dragged from the rulers onto an image. (See "View: Show/Hide Guides," earlier in this chapter, for more information.)

Special Notes

- Regardless of the specified unit, the rulers always measure from the *zero origin*, or the point where the horizontal plane (X) crosses the vertical plane (Y). Once you reposition the zero origin, XPress displays its measurement values slightly differently. If you remember your high school algebra, you'll recall the *Cartesian plane*, which measures the position of a point based on X and Y coordinates. By moving the zero origin and exposing the two axes, you divide the plane into four quadrants. Photoshop mixes positive and negative values to display precise X and Y measurements:

  - **Lower-right quadrant:** positive X and Y values

  - **Lower-left quadrant:** negative X and positive Y values

  - **Upper-left quadrant:** negative X and Y values

  - **Upper-right quadrant:** positive X and negative Y values

- You do not encounter negative measurement values until you move the zero origin. Since it defaults to the upper-left corner, the page exists entirely in the lower-right quadrant, which displays only positive X and Y values.

View: Show/Hide Invisibles

Choose this command to reveal or hide the special nonprinting characters used by XPress to represent spaces, line breaks, tab spaces, and so forth. These characters appear as follows:

- **Word Space**. These appear as a gray dot.
- **Hard Return**. These appear as the paragraph symbol: "¶".
- **Soft Return**. These appear as a left-pointing arrow.
- **Next Column**. These appear as a down-pointing arrow.
- **Next Linked Text Box**. These appear as a double down-pointing arrow.
- **Tab**. These appear as a right-pointing arrow, regardless of their type.
- **Indent Here**. These appear as a gray vertical line.

View Menu

CHAPTER 13

The Utilities Menu

Utilities: Check Spelling

Use the commands in this submenu to spellcheck the text of all or part of a document.

By default, XPress refers to the XPress Dictionary file, which is automatically placed in the XPress folder when you install the application. This file contains approximately 120,000 words, and is referred to in addition to any alternate dictionary specified in the Utilities: **Auxiliary Dictionary** dialog.

Special Notes

- When checking a story, document, or master pages, XPress ignores one-letter words.

- When any of the spellcheck dialogs are open, you can use the following shortcuts:

    – **Lookup.** Press (Command) [**Control**]-L.

    – **Skip.** Press (Command) [**Control**]-S.

    – **Add.** Press (Command) [**Control**]-A.

    – **Done.** Press (Command) [**Control**]-period.

- When you spellcheck a story, document, or master page, the Word Count dialog initially appears, displaying the following information:

    – **Total.** This represents the total number of words scanned by XPress.

    – **Unique.** This represents the number of words checked against the XPress dictionary and any open auxiliary dictionary.

    – **Suspect.** This represents the number of words not recognized by the XPress dictionary or the open auxiliary dictionary.

Utilities: Check Spelling: Word
(Command) [Control]-L

Use this command to check the spelling of a single word. Unless a text box is selected with the Content Tool, this command is not available. It behaves as follows:

- When a single word is highlighted or the flashing cursor is inserted in the middle of a word, only that word is checked.

- When multiple words are highlighted, only the first word is checked.

- When the flashing cursor is inserted just after a word, the word preceding the cursor is checked.

- When the cursor is inserted just before a word, the word following the cursor is checked.

Special Notes

This feature doesn't recognize words separated with a manual hyphen, such as "pocket-sized" or "jet-powered." If you highlight one of these words, XPress only checks "pocket" or "jet." Single words broken by an automatic hyphen are not affected this way.

The Check Word Dialog

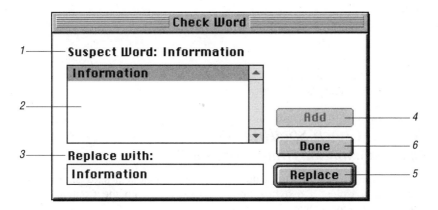

1. **Suspect Word**

   Here, XPress displays the single word being checked. If the spelling of the suspect word matches an entry in the XPress Dictionary, that word appears highlighted in the Dictionary list, below.

2. **Dictionary**

   In this scrolling field, XPress lists the closest matching words in the Dictionary. It's not always accurate—the listed words only begin with the first letter of the suspect word, and XPress only lists up to 10 options. For example, if you've dropped the first letter of "copy," XPress only lists words starting with "o." If the word you need is listed, double-click it, or select it and click Replace.

If the XPress Dictionary contains no closely matching items, this field displays "No similar words found." Here, you must add the word to the dictionary (see the following item "Add"), enter your own spelling (see the following item "Replace With"), or close the dialog.

3. **Replace With**

This field displays the corrected spelling of a word. When you select an item in the Dictionary list, it appears here automatically. Or you can enter your own spelling. When you click Replace, the word entered here replaces the suspect word.

4. **Add**

This button is only available when an auxiliary dictionary is open. Many words, especially abbreviations, are not recognized by the XPress Dictionary. When you add your own words to the Dictionary, XPress doesn't list them as a suspect word during future spellchecks. (See "Utilities: Auxiliary Dictionary," later in this chapter, for more information.)

5. **Replace**

Click this button to replace the suspect word with the corrected spelling in the Replace With field. If the correct spelling appears in the Dictionary list, you can double-click the item.

6. **Done**

Click this button to close the Check Word dialog.

See Also

Utilities: **Check Spelling**
Utilities: **Auxiliary Dictionary**

Utilities: Check Spelling: Story
(Option-Command) [Alt-Control]-L

Use this command to spellcheck the contents of a single text path, single text box, or text chain. Unless a text box or path is selected with the Content Tool, this command is not available.

The Check Story/Document/Masters Dialog

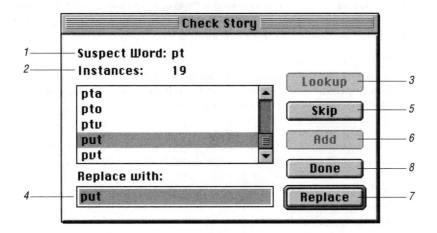

1. **Suspect Word**

   Here, XPress displays the current suspect word. When XPress flags multiple suspect words, it displays them in the same order they appear in the story. As you proceed through the suspect words, the first instance of each one is highlighted in the document, visible behind the open dialog.

   If the spelling of the suspect word matches an entry in the XPress Dictionary, that word appears highlighted in the Dictionary list, below.

2. **Instances**

   Here, XPress displays the number of times a suspect word appears in the story.

3. **Lookup**

   Unlike checking a single word, XPress doesn't list potential spellings for each suspect word. Click this button to display these options in the scrolling list. If XPress has flagged multiple suspect words, you must click this button for each one. To bypass the dictionary options, enter your own spelling in the Replace With field.

4. **Replace With**

   This field displays the corrected spelling of a word. When you select an item in the Dictionary list, it appears here automatically. Or you can enter your own spelling. When you click Replace, the word entered here replaces all instances of the suspect word.

5. **Skip**

   If satisfied with the spelling of a suspect word, click this button to jump to the next one.

6. **Add**

This button is only available when an auxiliary dictionary is open. Many words, especially abbreviations, are not recognized by the XPress Dictionary. When you add your own words to the Dictionary, XPress doesn't list them as a suspect word during future spellchecks. (See "Utilities: Auxiliary Dictionary," later in this chapter, for more information.)

7. **Replace**

Click this button to replace every instance of the suspect word with the corrected spelling in the Replace With field. If the correct spelling appears in the Dictionary list, you can double-click the item.

8. **Done**

Click this button to close the Check Story dialog at any time during the spellcheck. Any words replaced before doing so remain corrected.

See Also

Utilities: **Check Spelling**
Utilities: **Auxiliary Dictionary**

Utilities: Check Spelling: Document
(Option-Command-Shift) [Alt-Control-Shift]-L

Use this command to spellcheck all text in a document, excluding master pages. This command is available only when the Content Tool is active. You don't need to select a text box or path.

Special Notes

The Check Document dialog is identical to the Check Story dialog, described under Utilities: Check Spelling: **Story**.

See Also

Utilities: **Check Spelling**
Utilities: Check Spelling: **Story**
Utilities: **Auxiliary Dictionary**

Utilities: Check Spelling: Masters
(Option-Command-Shift) [Alt-Control-Shift]-L

Use this command to spellcheck all text appearing on your master pages. When a master page is active, Masters appears in the Check Spelling submenu instead of Document. This command is available only when the Content Tool is active. You don't need to select a text box or path.

Special Notes

The Check Document dialog is identical to the Check Story dialog, described under Utilities: Check Spelling: **Story**.

See Also

Utilities: **Check Spelling**
Utilities: Check Spelling: **Story**
Utilities: **Auxiliary Dictionary**
Page: **Display**

Utilities: Auxiliary Dictionary

Use this command to create additional dictionaries, which allow you to add words not included in the XPress Dictionary. This command is also used to open and close existing dictionaries.

Create a new dictionary when your work contains an abundance of words, terms, or abbreviations not recognized by the XPress Dictionary. For example, someone producing a graphic arts book soon realizes that "JPEG," "BMP," and "densitometry" are listed as suspect words whenever the document is spellchecked, even when they're spelled correctly. Although you can easily skip these words in any of the spellcheck dialogs, adding them to an auxiliary dictionary offers two advantages:

- XPress now flags these words only when they're misspelled, reducing the possibility of quickly skipping past one when it's spelled incorrectly.

- When one of these words appears suspect, you can click the Lookup button in the spellcheck dialog to access the proper spelling.

Auxiliary dictionaries are always used in conjunction with the XPress Dictionary file. For information on adding words to a new dictionary, see the next section, "Utilities: Edit Auxiliary."

Special Notes

- Ordinarily, auxiliary dictionaries are document-specific. When you access one while working on a document, it closes when the document is closed and opens again when the document is opened. To use the same dictionary in another document, you must choose this command again.

- Although you can create as many auxiliary dictionaries as you want, you can only open one at a time. Dictionaries are quite small (the 120,000-word XPress Dictionary consumes less than 300KB of disk space), so there's no real reason to create a new one for each document or project. Therefore, many users define one additional dictionary for all their work (see the "Special Notes" item that follows). Multiple dictionaries come into play when a designer must supply a dictionary to another, or when different projects use alternate spellings of specialized terms.

Utilities Menu

- To define a default auxiliary dictionary, close all open documents, choose Utilities: **Auxiliary Dictionary**, and either create a new one or open an existing one. The dictionary is automatically accessed by all subsequently created documents. Note the following conditions:

    - When you open a document originally created and saved with no auxiliary dictionary, the default dictionary is closed. To permanently apply the default dictionary to this document, open the dictionary, and save the document.

    - When you open a document linked to a different dictionary, the default dictionary is overridden.

- Auxiliary dictionaries appear as separate files on your hard drive. To avoid breaking the link between the dictionaries and your documents, keep the files in one place, such as your XPress application folder.

The Auxiliary Dictionary Dialog

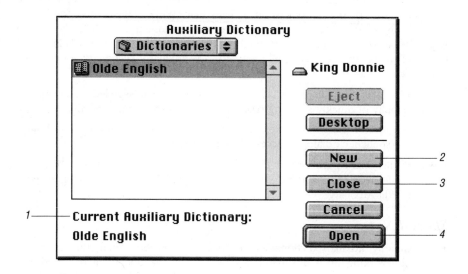

1. **Current Auxiliary Dictionary**

    This field displays the name of the currently open dictionary. If no dictionary is open, "<None>" appears here.

2. **New**

    Click this button to create a new auxiliary dictionary. A navigational dialog appears, allowing you to name the file and place it somewhere on your hard drive.

3. **Close**

    To close the currently open auxiliary dictionary, locate it in the navigational window, select it, and click this button.

4. **Open**

To open an existing auxiliary dictionary, locate it in the navigational window, select it, and click this button.

Utilities: Edit Auxiliary

Use this command to review or alter the contents of the currently open auxiliary dictionary:

- To review the contents of the dictionary, scroll through the list.
- To add a word, enter it in the bottom field, and click the Add button.
- To remove a word, select it in the list, and click the Delete button.

Special Notes

- This command isn't available unless a dictionary has been opened using Utilities: **Auxiliary Dictionary**. If you've defined a default auxiliary dictionary, this command is available in every new document.

- This command isn't always the most efficient way to add words to an auxiliary dictionary. Rather than manually entering word after word, spellcheck the entire document. As long as an auxiliary dictionary is open, you can click the Add button in the spellcheck dialog to add any word not recognized by the XPress Dictionary.

- When adding words to the dictionary, you can't enter spaces, numbers, hyphens, or punctuation marks. If you try, an alert sounds, and the offending characters are highlighted one at a time.

See Also

Utilities: **Auxiliary Dictionary**
Utilities: **Check Spelling**

Utilities: Suggested Hyphenation
(Command) [Control]-H

Choose this command to preview how XPress will break a specific word. Here, you can't change how the word will be hyphenated—rather, you just see how XPress addresses the word, based on the following settings:

- **Edit: H&Js.** First, XPress refers to any H&J setting applied to the word. Depending on the setting, hyphenation may be turned off, capitalized words may or may not be broken, and so forth. (See "Edit: H&Js" in Chapter 6, *The Edit Menu*, for more information.)

- **Utilities: Hyphenation Exceptions.** Next, XPress refers to your custom hyphenation list. If you have entered a specific hyphenation for a word inappropriately broken by XPress, that method is displayed. Note that your hyphenation exceptions can be overridden by the current H&J setting.

- **Edit: Preferences: Document: Paragraph.** If Expanded is chosen from the Hyphenation pop-up in this panel, XPress checks the word against its internal hyphenation dictionary. This dictionary contains far fewer words than the XPress Dictionary used for spellchecking, and the resulting hyphenation can be overridden by the current H&J setting and your list of hyphenation exceptions.

- **The XPress hyphenation algorithm.** If none of the above options affect the currently selected word, XPress displays its "best guess," based on its automatic hyphenation method.

Special Notes

If unsatisfied with the way XPress breaks a word, you have three options:

- **Change the settings of the applied H&J.** Note that this method affects all of the text it's applied to, not just the single word. (See "Edit: H&Js" in Chapter 6 for more information.)

- **Add it to the list of hyphenation exceptions.** Here, you determine your own hyphenation for a specific word.

- **Add a discretionary hyphen.** Here, you manually break a word by inserting the cursor in the appropriate place and pressing (Command) [**Control**]-hyphen.

See Also

Edit: **H&Js**
Utilities: **Hyphenation Exceptions**
Edit: Preferences: Document: **Paragraph**

Utilities: Hyphenation Exceptions

Use this command to create a custom list of hyphenated words. Even with its enhanced hyphenation dictionary and automatic hyphenation algorithm, XPress often breaks a word incorrectly. For example, "prickmedainty" is hyphenated as "prickmedain-ty," instead of the more viable "prick-me-dainty." By adding the correct version to your exceptions list, you ensure that text describing sixteenth-century slang is properly hyphenated.

Common Uses

- **"Protecting" words from hyphenation.** For example, many companies prefer that their title not be hyphenated when it appears in collateral publications. To prevent a word from being hyphenated, add it to your exceptions list with no hyphens.

Common Errors

- **Failing to add a word before saving.** Many users enter a word in the New Entry field and then click Save, assuming the word has been added to the list. Unless you click the Add button before saving, XPress will not recognize your preferred hyphenation.

- **Failing to add all variations of a word.** When you add a single word to the exceptions list, XPress only recognizes the capitalized and noncapitalized versions of that specific spelling. You must manually enter plurals, verb tenses, and other forms of the word to maintain consistent hyphenation. For example, if you enter a custom hyphenation for "nimgimmer," you must also enter one for "nimgimmers," "nimgimmery," "nimgimmerous," and so forth.

Special Notes

- The exceptions list is not saved as an additional file—rather, it's built into the XPress Preferences file. This means that the custom hyphenations are available in every subsequently created document. Also, the list is built into each document. With this in mind, the following circumstances will discard the exceptions list:

  – If the XPress Preferences file is discarded (which often happens when it becomes corrupt), the exceptions list is not available in subsequently created documents.

  – When opening a document created with a different copy of XPress, click Keep Document Settings to retain the exceptions list. If you click Use XPress Preferences, the list built into the document is ignored in favor of the list used by this copy of XPress. Unless the two lists are exactly the same, the words in the document will not hyphenate as intended, which could cause text reflow.

- When creating a custom word break, XPress doesn't allow you to insert a hyphen after the first letter or before the last letter.

- When adding a word, you can't enter numbers, spaces, or punctuation marks.

The Hyphenation Exceptions Dialog

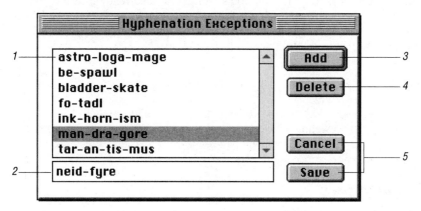

1. **Hyphenation List**

   This scrolling field displays all words currently added to the exceptions list. If no words have been added (or if the hyphenations list has been discarded), "No exceptions" displays here.

2. **New Entry Field**

   In this field, enter the word you wish to hyphenate differently, using hyphens to indicate the desired breaks. For example, entering "phren-ol-o-gy" allows the word to hyphenate between syllables; entering "phren-ology" allows the word to be broken only in half.

   To edit an existing exception, click the word in the scrolling list to make it appear in this field.

3. **Add/Replace**

   When creating a new exception, this button appears as "Add." Click it to add the exception to the list. When editing an existing exception, this button appears as "Replace." Click it to replace the original exception with the corrected form.

4. **Delete**

   To remove an exception from the list, select it in the scrolling list, and click this button.

5. **Cancel/Save**

   Click Cancel to close the dialog and ignore any changes made. Click Save to retain any additions, replacements, or deletions.

See Also

Edit: **H&Js**
Utilities: **Suggested Hyphenation**

Utilities: Usage

Use this command to review the fonts and graphics currently in use by the active document. This information is available under two panels: Fonts and Pictures. When the Color Management Active box is checked in the Edit: Preferences: **Color Management** dialog, a third panel appears: Profiles.

Utilities: Usage: Fonts

This panel displays all fonts currently in use by a document. The fonts listed depend on the currently active page: when a document page is active, it displays fonts appearing on all document pages. When a master page is active, it only displays fonts appearing on the master pages.

Common Uses

Refer to Appendix A, *Common Techniques*, for full descriptions of the following:

- Pinpointing missing fonts
- Substituting for fonts not supplied with a document

Common Errors

- **Assuming this command recognizes imported fonts.** When an imported Illustrator or FreeHand graphic contains an embedded font, this command doesn't recognize their existence. If the font is not open during output, low-resolution character shapes print. For the best results, convert all text to outlines in the original program before saving and importing. Otherwise, you must open the graphic, find out exactly what font is used, and provide it to your output vendor.

- **Using Font Usage to replace fonts, instead of style sheets.** This command allows you to replace all occurrences of a font, even when the current font is recognized by XPress. However, you should only do this as a last resort. If a font is part of a style sheet definition, using this command does not change the style sheet—the effect is the same as if you highlighted the text and selected a new typeface from the Style: **Font** submenu. For the best results, edit the desired style sheets when globally replacing a font.

Special Notes

- This command is quite similar to using the Edit: **Find/Change** command to replace fonts. However, the Find/Change dialog has more flexible settings, which allow you to target specific words, sizes, and type styles. (See "Edit: Find/Change" in Chapter 6 for more information.)

- You can't print the contents of the Fonts panel—but you can print the same information by choosing File: **Collect for Output**, checking the Report Only box, and printing the resulting text file. (See "File: Collect for Output" in Chapter 5, *The File Menu*, for more information.)

- Although this command is frequently used to substitute for a missing font, you can do the same thing when you first open a document containing fonts not currently available to your system. The Missing Fonts dialog appears, which targets the uninstalled fonts and allows you to specify global replacements. (See "File: Open" in Chapter 5 for more information.)

- When characters have been converted to Bézier paths using Style (Text): **Text to Box**, a font is no longer required for output. If the font initially used to create the characters isn't used anywhere else in the document, it doesn't appear in the Fonts panel. (See "Style: Text to Box" in Chapter 7, *The Style Menu (Text)*, for more information.)

The Usage: Fonts Panel

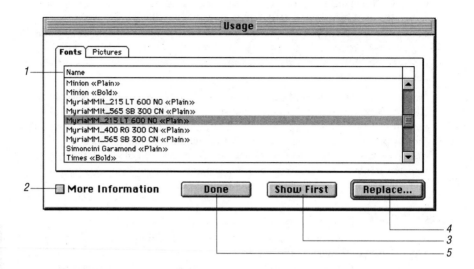

1. Name

Here, XPress lists all fonts currently in use on your document or master pages. Type styles appear in guillemets after the font name. For example, if a word set in Futura Heavy has been italicized, it's listed as "Futura Heavy «Italic»." Remaining occurrences of the font with no type styles applied are listed as "Futura Heavy «Plain»."

Only the Bold, Italic, and Bold/Italic type styles (in addition to Plain) are recognized by the Fonts panel. XPress uses those styles as a cue to substitute the actual bold, italic, or bold italic versions of the font during output. (See "Style: Type Styles" in Chapter 7 for more information.)

When a font used in the document is not available to XPress, its ID number appears in brackets, and it's listed as "unknown." Text formatted with this font will not output properly, so you must do one of two things:

– Close the document, acquire the appropriate font, and open it using your font management utility. This way, when you open the document and print, you're assured that the type will output as expected.

– Select the missing font, and click the Replace button to perform a global replacement. Since it's highly unlikely that the sizing and spacing of the replacement font will match the original, the printed results will not match the expectations of the designer or client.

2. **More Information**

When this box is checked, a scrolling field appears at the bottom of the dialog. It displays the following information about the currently selected list item:

PostScript Name

 The font name, as recognized by your PostScript-compatible output device appears here.

File Name

 The name of the font file, as it appears on your hard drive, appears here.

Type

 The font type (Type 1 PostScript or True Type, for example) appears here.

3. **Show First**

Click this button to highlight the first occurrence of the selected font in the document. (You may need to reposition the Usage dialog for a better view.) After you do, this button changes to Show Next. Click Show Next repeatedly to jump to each occurrence of the font. At any time, hold down the (Option) [**Alt**] key to change Show Next back to Show First.

4. **Replace**

To substitute a font, select an item in the Usage list, and click this button to display the Replace Font dialog. There, choose a new font from the Replacement Font pop-up, and click OK. Only fonts currently available to your system appear in this pop-up.

When substituting a font that appears on both document and master pages, you must perform the replacement on both a document and a master page.

5. **Done**

Click this button to close the Usage dialog. Note that there's no Cancel button to close the dialog while leaving the document untouched. Also, you can't choose Edit: **Undo** after making any changes. If you make an incorrect substitution, you must open the Utilities: **Usage** dialog again and correct your error. Or if you saved the document before making the changes, choose File: **Revert to Saved**.

See Also

Appendix A (Utilities: Usage: **Fonts**)
File: **Open**
File: **Revert to Saved**
File: **Collect for Output**
Edit: **Undo**
Edit: **Find/Change**
Style (Text): **Font**
Style (Text): **Type Style**
Style (Text): **Text to Box**
Utilities: Usage: **Pictures**

Utilities: Usage: Pictures

This panel lists all currently imported graphics. The graphics listed depend on the currently active page: when a document page is active, it displays graphics appearing on all document pages. When a master page is active, it only displays graphics appearing on the master pages.

This command is primarily used to update the *link* that exists between XPress and an imported graphic. When you import a graphic, only a low-resolution preview is placed in the picture box—the information required for successful output remains in the original graphic file. By establishing a link to the file, XPress remembers the location of the graphic and is able to send the information to the output device when a document is printed. When a link is broken, XPress is unable to find the graphic—and only the low-resolution preview can be output.

XPress does attempt to maintain the links. When you print a document, it first checks the location of the graphic when it was originally imported, then the folder the document is saved in. If it doesn't find the graphics files, the links are considered broken.

To avoid this problem, keep the following guidelines in mind:

* Never delete graphics files after importing them.

* Move or rename graphics files as little as possible after importing them.

* If possible, keep all graphics in the same folder. Whenever I can, I keep them in a single folder along with the XPress documents specific to each project. When the project is turned over to an output vendor, I copy the fonts into the folder, ensuring that all the information required for successful output is kept in the same place.

* If you can't pull your graphics into the same folder as you work, use File: **Collect for Output** to gather them together when a project is ready for output.

If any links have been altered when you print a document, an alert appears, stating "Some disk files for pictures in this document are missing or have been modified." When you click the List Pictures button, the Missing/Modified dialog appears, displaying the same link information as the Usage dialog. After updating the necessary links, click the Print button to continue.

Common Uses

Refer to Appendix A for full descriptions of the following:

* Reviewing and re-establishing graphic links

* Jumping to a particular graphic in a long document

Common Errors

- **Ignoring any graphic with a status other than "OK."** When the status of all imported graphics is OK, XPress is able to send all the information to a printer. If you override XPress' warnings that the link information has changed and print the document, the results could range anywhere from low-resolution output, to incorrect positioning, to a PostScript error and mis-printed file.

- **Updating the link of a modified graphic without double-checking its size and position.** For example, if you import a graphic and later edit its size and contents in the original application, its status is listed as Modified. When you update the link, it will appear in a different position in the picture box. After updating a modified graphic, click the Show button to examine the results on-screen.

- **Mistakenly relinking to a new graphic.** When updating a link, XPress allows you to connect to an entirely different graphic file. The effect is the same as selecting an occupied picture box and choosing File: **Get Picture** to import another image. On one hand, this can be quite useful—you can instantly replace every occurrence of a graphic, without manually importing the same file over and over again. On the other, if you accidentally relink to a different graphic, XPress only half-heartedly warns you (when you do, it's initially listed as Modified—when you click Update again, it's listed as OK). Since you can't undo this command, linking to the wrong files wastes precious time, and could result in incorrect printed images.

Special Notes

- If you select a graphic before opening the Usage dialog, the same item is highlighted in the Pictures panel. This allows you to quickly get information about a specific graphic.

- When you update an image link—even when you relink to a different graphic—any Item: Modify: **Picture** settings applied to the picture box (such as image rotation, offset, or color) are retained. If you reimport a graphic using File: **Get Picture**, these settings are discarded.

- The Auto Picture Import option in the Edit: Preferences: Document: **General** panel allows XPress to automatically update modified graphics as soon as a document is opened.

- When more than one missing graphic resides in the same folder, relinking to one displays an alert, stating "Additional missing pictures are located in this folder. OK to update these as well?" Click OK to relink to all the missing graphics in the folder. This alert doesn't appear when updating modified graphics.

- To select contiguous items in the Pictures panel, hold down the Shift key as you click. (Command) [**Control**]-click to select noncontiguous items. This way, you can suppress, unsuppress, or update multiple graphics at once.

The Usage:Pictures Panel

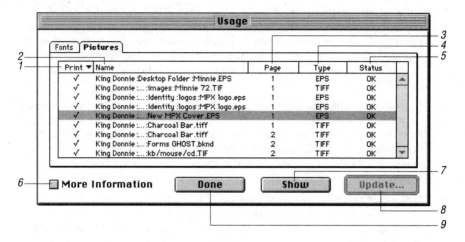

1. **Print**

   This column displays the print status of each graphic. A check indicates the graphic can be printed. No check indicates that a graphic's printout is suppressed. Click the column next to the filename to show or hide a checkmark, or choose Yes or No from the Print pop-up.

   If you've suppressed a graphic by checking the Suppress Printout box in the Item: Modify: **Box** panel *or* the Suppress Picture Printout box in the Item: Modify: **Picture** panel, no checkmark appears. Clicking to add a checkmark overrides the suppression command.

   When you suppress a graphic by hiding its checkmark, XPress automatically checks the Suppress Picture Printout box in the Item: Modify: **Picture** panel.

2. **Name**

   This column attempts to display the location of each graphic by listing the hierarchy of folders. However, if a graphic is more than one or two folders deep, only the hard drive name and the graphic filename fits in the allotted space.

   If you've copied a graphic from another application and pasted it into a picture box, XPress does not refer to a file location or name. "No Disk File" appears instead.

3. **Page**

   This column displays the page number that each graphic appears on.

   If a single graphic crosses over multiple facing pages, this column displays the page number farthest to the left.

   When a graphic is placed entirely on the pasteboard, this column displays the page number closest to the graphic, along with a dagger (†).

4. **Type**

This column displays the file format of each imported graphic.

5. **Status**

This column displays the current link status of each graphic:

OK

> This item indicates that the link is secure, and the graphic can be printed.

Modified

> This item indicates that the graphic has been edited and resaved since it was originally imported into the document. XPress is still aware of its location. You aren't required to update graphics listed as Modified— XPress still outputs the graphic information. However, updating these files allows you to review the edited image on-screen and make any necessary adjustments.

Missing

> This item indicates that the graphic file has been renamed or moved from its original location.

Wrong Type

> This item indicates that the file format of the graphic has been changed. For example, if you import a TIFF and then later resave the image as an EPS, its status displays as Wrong Type. This also occurs if a vector-based graphic replaces a pixel-based graphic of the same name (and vice versa). XPress is still aware of its location.

In Use

> This item indicates that the graphic file is currently open in another application.

No Access

> This item indicates that XPress does not have the access privileges to access the graphic file.

Can't Open

> This item only appears when XPress runs out of memory and cannot display a graphic on-screen. Usually, closing some open documents or allocating more RAM to XPress solves the problem.

6. **More Information**

When this box is checked, a scrolling field appears at the bottom of the dialog. It displays the following information about the currently selected item:

Full Path

> This item displays the entire pathname, or a graphic file's location. If a graphic is listed as Missing, it displays the last known pathname.

File Size

> This item displays the size of the graphic file.

Modification Date

> This item displays the date and time of the last edit made to a graphic.

Dimensions
This item displays a graphic's original width and height—it doesn't display any scaling applied in the document. The units of measurement used are based on the settings in the Edit: Preferences: Document: **General** panel.

When the selected graphic is pixel-based, this item displays its resolution as well.

Color Depth
This item displays the color range of a pixel-based image.

7. **Show**

After selecting a listed item, click this button to force the underlying document to jump to the graphic. It appears in the upper-left corner of the window.

8. **Update**

Click this button to reestablish the link to a graphic. When the status of a graphic is Modified or Wrong Type, the graphic is simply reimported. When the status is Missing, a navigational dialog appears, allowing you to pinpoint the new location of the graphic file. When the status is OK, In Use, No Access, or Can't Open, this button is not available.

9. **Done**

Click this button to close the Usage dialog. Note that there's no Cancel button to close the dialog while leaving the document untouched. Also, you can't choose Edit: **Undo** after making any changes. If you make an incorrect link, you must open the Utilities: **Usage** dialog again and correct your error. Or if you saved the document before making the changes, choose File: **Revert to Saved**.

See Also

Appendix A (Utilities: Usage: **Pictures**)
File: **Revert to Saved**
File: **Get Picture**
File: **Collect for Output**
Edit: **Undo**
Edit: Preferences: Document: **General**
Item: Modify: **Box**
Item: Modify: **Picture**
Utilities: Usage: **Fonts**

Utilities: XTensions Manager

Use this command to enable or disable XTensions.

XTensions are files that add increased functionality to XPress, similar to system extensions or Photoshop plug-ins. A small number are automatically installed with XPress, adding several features covered in this book. However, over the last few years, over 500 XTensions have been written by third-party developers, allowing users to shape their work environments very specifically. Popular third-party XTensions range from preflighting tools, to table generators, to large newspaper- and magazine-publishing systems.

Two things must happen to an XTension before it's recognized by XPress:

* XTension files must be placed in the XTensions folder, located inside the XPress application folder.

* The XTension must be enabled in the XTensions Manager when XPress is launched.

When the XTensions Manager is used to disable an XTension, the file is moved from the XTensions folder to the XTensions Disabled folder, also located in the XPress application folder. The XTensions Manager is only aware of these two folders. If you move an XTension file anywhere else on your hard drive, it doesn't appear in the XTensions Manager and therefore won't be recognized by XPress.

Common Errors

* **Attempting to open a document without enabling the necessary XTensions.** When an XTension is used to generate specialized page information, it must be enabled when the document is opened in the future. For example, when the Cool Blends XTension is disabled, you can't open any document contain- ing two-color blends created from the Colors Palette. Most often, this prob- lem occurs when a designer acquires a third-party XTension, uses it to customize a document, then fails to supply it to the service provider when the project is output. To avoid this problem, copy the necessary XTension onto the disk containing the project information before handing it over for output. Be certain to notify the output technician.

* **Enabling or disabling XTensions without creating a new set.** When you simply turn XTensions on or off, the Set pop-up displays No Set. This temporary set remains active as you quit and relaunch XPress, but as soon as you choose an established item from the Set pop-up, the XTensions Manager forgets the pre- vious settings. To have constant access to a specific configuration of XTen- sions, you must choose Save As after making the appropriate settings. This way, you can choose a configuration whenever you need it, without manu- ally enabling or disabling any XTensions.

* **Editing a current set, assuming the changes are saved.** If you change the set- tings of an established set, the Set pop-up changes to No Set. To permanently change an established set, you must create a new one: select the original set from the Set pop-up, make the changes, choose Save As, and enter the same name as the set you wish to edit. You can't replace any of XPress' default XTension sets.

Special Notes

* The changes you make in the XTensions Manager are not document- specific—the last-established set opens when XPress is launched, regardless of any documents that were open.

- The Edit: Preferences: Application: **XTensions** panel allows you to set the XTensions Manager to open whenever XPress is launched, if desired. This is particularly useful when you use a number of custom-defined sets. To manually open the XTensions Manager on startup, hold down the spacebar while launching XPress.

- Many users simply leave all their XTensions enabled. XTensions consume RAM, however, so if you use a great number, you must allocate more RAM to XPress. If you have a limited amount of RAM (less than 24–32 MB), turn off unneeded XTensions to conserve memory.

- Most XTensions written for earlier versions of XPress have either been rewritten for 4.0 or are still compatible in their original form. If they're not, an alert appears the next time you launch XPress, stating "You have pre-4.0 XTensions that are not compatible with QuarkXPress. See the XTensions Manager for further details." The XTensions are not loaded.

The XTensions Manager Dialog

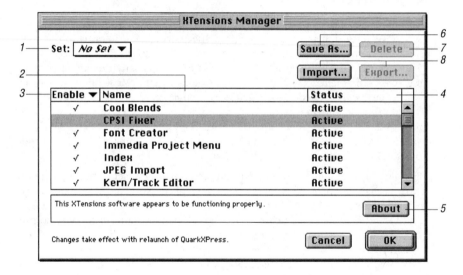

1. **Set**

   This pop-up displays XPress' default sets and any custom sets created by clicking Save As. The XPress default sets are as follows:

   No Set
   > This item appears when you enable or disable XTensions without creating a new set.

   All XTensions Enabled
   > Choose this set to enable all available XTensions the next time XPress is launched.

All XTensions Disabled
> Choose this set to disable all XTensions the next time XPress is launched. Be aware that this strips away many XPress features, and you may not be able to open certain documents.

4.0 Optimized XTensions
> Choose this set to enable only the XTensions written specifically for XPress 4.0.

2. **Name**

This scrolling list displays all XTensions residing in the XTensions and XTensions Disabled folders. If you manually change the contents of these folders while XPress is running, you must relaunch the application to see the changes in the XTensions Manager.

To select an XTension, click it once. To select contiguous items, hold down the Shift key while clicking. To select noncontiguous items, hold down the (Command) [**Control**] key while clicking.

3. **Enable**

This column determines whether an XTension loads when you launch XPress—a checkmark indicates that an item is *enabled* and will load; no checkmark indicates that an item is *disabled* and will not load.

To add or remove a checkmark, click in this column next to the appropriate XTension. You can also select an XTension and choose Yes or No from the Enable pop-up. (When multiple XTensions are selected, this pop-up is the only way to affect all of them at once.)

When an XTension is disabled, its file moves into the XTensions Disabled folder when you quit the application. Likewise, when you enable a disabled XTension, quitting XPress moves the file back into the XTensions folder.

4. **Status**

This column displays the status of each XTension in the XTensions Manager. Enabling or disabling an XTension has no affect on its status until XPress is relaunched.

Active
> This item indicates that the XTension is currently loaded, and new functions are available within XPress.

Not Active
> This item indicates that the XTension is currently disabled.

Error
> This item indicates that XPress could not load the XTension during startup. This occurs when attempting to load an outdated, incompatible XTension, or if any necessary accompanying files can't be located.
>
> The XTension isn't loaded, but it remains enabled. To prevent the error from appearing every time you launch XPress, hide its checkmark in the Enabled column.

Not Found

This item indicates that XPress tried to load an XTension but couldn't find the file. This only occurs when two things happen: an XTension is manually dragged from the XTensions folder, and a custom set is chosen in the Set pop-up that enables that XTension.

If the XTension has been permanently removed, disable the item, and create a new set to prevent the Not Found status from appearing again.

5. **About**

Click this button to display information about the currently selected XTension, including its version, creation date, a brief description of its function, and more. This information appears in a small on-screen window—click the window once to make it disappear.

6. **Save As**

Click this button to save the current configuration of XTensions as a new set. The name you enter in the Save Set dialog will appear in the Set pop-up. If you enter the same name as a currently existing set, a warning appears, asking if it's okay to replace the original set.

7. **Delete**

Click this button to remove the currently established set. No XTensions are enabled or disabled. No Set appears in the Set pop-up, and the same XTensions of the deleted set remain active until you make new changes in the XTensions Manager.

8. **Import/Export**

When you click the Export button, the current configuration of XTensions is saved as a text file bearing the same name as the set. This file can be given to another XPress user, who can access the set by clicking the Import button.

The exported list only contains the names and current status of the Xtensions—no actual XTension files are included. If the exported set contains any third-party XTensions that another user doesn't have, they must be provided. Otherwise, the status of the missing XTensions is listed as Not Found.

Utilities: PPD Manager

Use this command to determine which PostScript Printer Description files are recognized by XPress. The items enabled in the PPD Manager appear in the Printer Description pop-up in the File: Print: **Setup** panel.

PPDs are used by the print driver installed in your operating system to better match the characteristics of your PostScript-compatible output device. Each printer ships with its own PPD—to acquire a PPD (or to get the latest version), contact your printer's manufacturer.

The PPD Manager allows you to ignore unneeded PPDs. The Macintosh operating system, for example, ships with several dozen PPDs. If you only use one or two in-house laser printers, there's no reason you should have to fish through an extensive list every time you output a document.

In fact, if you only use a small number of PPDs, consider deleting the ones you don't need. Even when most of them are not included in the Printer Descriptions pop-up, XPress still scans all the files during startup to see if any changes have been made to the folder. Depending on the number installed (and the horsepower of your computer), this can considerably lengthen the startup time. Use the PPD Manager only when you have access to a large number of different output devices.

Special Notes

- Earlier versions of XPress used PDF (PostScript Description File), as well as PPD, files. These were XPress-specific description files and were stored in the PDF folder, inside the XPress application folder. XPress 4.0 only recognizes PPD files, which means you can no longer use your old PDFs. If necessary, contact your printer's manufacturer for the proper PPD file.

- XPress includes three default descriptions that can't be accessed using this command: Generic B&W (for laser printers), Generic Color (for color printers), and Generic Imagesetter. When one of these is set in the Printer Description pop-up, output is controlled solely by your operating system's print driver.

The PPD Manager Dialog

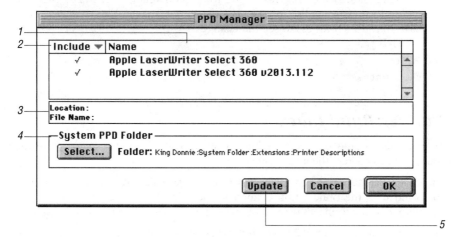

1. **Name**

   This scrolling list displays all PPD files currently installed in your system's Printer Descriptions folder. If you have installed a PPD folder inside your XPress application folder instead (it must be titled "PPD"), any PPDs contained within are listed as well.

   To select a PPD, click it once. To select contiguous items, hold down the Shift key while clicking. To select noncontiguous items, hold down the (Command) [Control] key while clicking.

2. **Include**

This column determines whether a PPD appears in the Printer Description pop-up—a checkmark indicates that a PPD *will* appear; no checkmark indicates that an item *will not* appear.

To add or remove a checkmark, click in this column next to the appropriate item. You can also select a PPD and choose Yes or No from the Include pop-up. (When multiple items are selected, this pop-up is the only way to affect all of them at once.)

3. **Information**

When a single PPD is selected, this field displays its filename and location on your hard drive.

4. **System PPD Folder**

By default, XPress searches for PPDs in your system's Printer Descriptions folder (as well as its own application folder). If you store PPDs anywhere else, you must direct XPress to their exact location. Click this button, and when the System PPD Folder dialog appears, locate the folder containing the PPDs. Be aware that if you redirect XPress to another folder, it no longer recognizes any PPDs stored in your system's Printer Descriptions folder.

5. **Update**

If you've altered the contents of the folder containing your PPDs, click this button to update the list appearing in the PPD Manager. This way, you don't have to relaunch XPress to see the changes.

See Also

File: **Print**

Utilities: Build Index

After all the desired entries have been marked with the Index Palette, use this command to generate the actual index.

The Index Palette entries are compiled in a series of new document pages. This command uses the punctuation defined in the Edit: Preferences: **Index** dialog. It also automatically formats the index, applying up to five different style sheets.

This command is only available when the following occurs:

- The Index Palette is open.

- The document contains a master page with an automatic text box that the new index can flow into. (Technically, this command is *available* when no such master page exists—but choosing it only brings up an alert, describing the need for the master page.)

Common Uses

Refer to Appendix A for full descriptions of the following:

- Formatted nested index example
- Formatted run-in index example

Common Errors

- **Failing to define a new master page before building an index.** It's highly likely that an index will be formatted differently than the rest of the document. For a simple example, examine this book: each page in the main text flows in a single column, with headers at the top of each page; the index pages have double columns with no headers. The index master page should contain an automatic text box, so that new pages will automatically insert to accommodate the text of the index. When you build the index, set this page in the Master Page pop-up.

- **Failing to define new style sheets before building an index.** Although second-, third-, and fourth-level entries appear indented in the Index Palette, they do not automatically indent when you build a nested index. To create this effect, you must build this information into the different paragraph styles that you apply in the Level Styles section of the Build Index dialog. If you apply document style sheets to the index, you can't edit them to create the necessary formatting—if you do, you change the document text they're applied to as well.

- **Editing a project after it has been indexed.** Index page numbers are not linked to the source documents. If you edit a document after building the index, the page numbers will not automatically update. Similarly, if you add any new entries to the Index Palette, they do not automatically appear in the existing index. In both cases, you must rebuild the index.

- **Rebuilding a locally formatted index.** If you make localized changes to an index, they're not remembered if you rebuild it. If you must build a new index, uncheck the Replace Existing Index box. This way, you can refer to the old index while locally formatting the new one. When formatting is complete, delete the pages containing the old index.

Special Notes

An index cannot be generated into a separate document. Instead, it creates new pages, based on the master page set in the Master Page pop-up. To place the index in a new document, you drag the thumbnails of the index into a new document containing the same page dimensions (be sure to set the page numbering appropriately using Page: **Section**). At the very least, when indexing a book, make the final chapter active before choosing Utilities: **Build Index**.

The Build Index Dialog

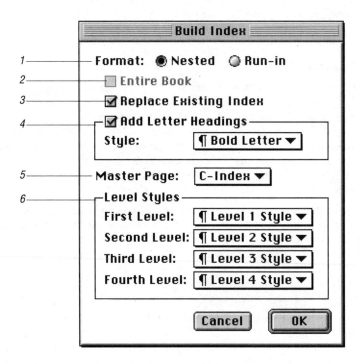

1. **Format**

   These options determine the type of index generated:

   Nested

   > A nested index lists all first-level entries, each with up to three levels of subentries. All entries appear as a single line. (This book contains a nested index.)

   Run-in

   > A run-in index only contains two entry levels, displayed in the form of a single paragraph. The first-level entry starts each paragraph; any subentries, regardless of their level, flow after the initial entry, in the order they appear in the Index Palette entries list.

2. **Entire Book**

   If the active document is part of a book, turn this option on to index all book chapters. If this option is turned off, only the active document is indexed. If a document is not part of a book, this option is not available.

3. **Replace Existing Index**

If an index has already been built, turn this option on to replace it with a new index. To create a second index, usually for purposes of comparison—turn this option off. The pages of the second index appear after the original index.

4. **Add Letter Headings**

Check this box to add a formatted letter heading before each alphabetical section of the index. By default, the Style pop-up lists the first paragraph style that appears in the Style Sheets Palette.

Note that index entries starting with numbers, such as "50% gray" or "8-ball," do not receive a letter heading. If they haven't been realphabetized using the Index Palette's Sort As field, they will appear at the very start of the index. You must manually enter and format a heading, such as "Numbers," after building the index.

5. **Master Page**

In this pop-up, choose the master page that the new index pages will be based on. Only master pages containing an automatic text box will appear—otherwise, XPress would not be able to generate all the pages necessary to contain the index.

6. **Level Styles**

Here, choose the style sheets that will be applied to the index. By default, all pop-ups list the first paragraph style that appears in the Style Sheets Palette.

First Level

In a nested index, this style formats all first-level entries. In a run-in index, however, this is the only pop-up available. This is because run-in entries and their subentries exist in the same paragraph.

Second Level

In a nested index, this style formats all second-level entries.

Third Level

In a nested index, this style formats all third-level entries.

Fourth Level

In a nested index, this style formats all fourth-level entries.

See Also

Appendix A (Utilities: **Build Index**)
File: New: **Book**
Edit: Preferences: **Index**
Edit: **Style Sheets**
Page: **Page Overview**
Page: **Section**
View: **Thumbnails**
The Index Palette

Utilities: Tracking Edit

Each font contains its own *tracking table*, or default character spacing specified by the font's designer. This value isn't always satisfying, so XPress allows you to adjust the tracking, depending on your needs:

- **Manual adjustments.** Here, you adjust the spacing of a highlighted word, line, paragraph, or story using the Style: **Track** command or the tracking controls in the Measurements Palette.

- **Style sheet adjustments.** Here, you build a tracking value into a style sheet definition. This way, text is tracked evenly wherever it appears in the document.

However, if you consistently apply the same tracking values to the same typeface, consider using this command to adjust its tracking table. This way, the font automatically appears at the desired spacing, without the need for additional adjusting. For example, to a designer's eye, Futura Heavy type set over 24 pt. may always require a tracking value of –5 units. If you use this font frequently, edit Futura Heavy's tracking table to change the default value to –5 whenever the font appears at 24 pt. or larger.

Common Uses

Refer to Appendix A for full descriptions of the following:

- Applying a single-value tracking edit
- Tightening tracking as point size increases
- Loosening tracking as point size increases

Common Errors

- **Deleting or ignoring the new tracking values.** Tracking table edits are saved in the XPress Preferences file. When a document contains an edited font, the new values are included in the document preferences, which allows the tracking table to be read by other copies of XPress:

  - If you delete the XPress Preferences file (which often happens when the file becomes corrupt), you lose any changes made to the tracking tables. Unfortunately, there's no way to export the changes into a separate text file, as there is with Kern Table edits. To preserve your changes, back up the XPress Preferences file. Or, if necessary, keep a written record of the new tracking values.

  - When a document is opened in a different copy of XPress, a warning appears, indicating that the document preferences differ from the current XPress settings. To preserve any included tracking tables, you must click the Keep Document Settings button. If you don't, any affected fonts revert back to their original spacing, resulting in text reflow.

Special Notes

- This feature is only available when the Kern/Track Editor XTension is loaded.

- This command only affects how XPress reads, displays, and outputs a particular font—the font files themselves are not changed.

- In a document, a font's initial tracking value is always 0—even when the tracking table has been edited. For example, assume you've changed the default tracking of Futura Heavy to –5. When the font appears in a document, the Track Amount field in the Character Attributes dialog and Measurements Palette displays 0, not –5. If you manually set the tracking to –5, the actual tracking is –10.

- Tracking table edits only take effect when text is larger than the Auto Kern Above value, established in the Edit: Preferences: Document: **Paragraph** panel.

The Tracking Edit Dialog

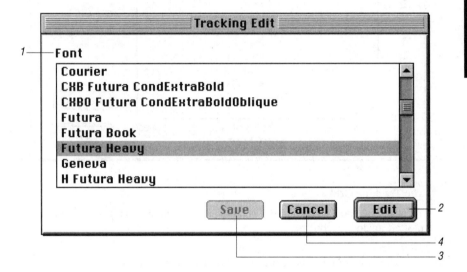

1. **Font**

   Select the font you wish to edit from this scrolling list. Note that every font currently available to XPress appears here—if you wish to adjust the default tracking of an entire font family, you must edit each font individually.

   If desired, type the first one or two letters of the font to jump to the appropriate item.

2. **Edit**

   After selecting the desired font, click this button to open the Edit Tracking dialog.

3. **Save**

   After closing the Edit Tracking dialog, click this button to save the new default tracking values.

4. **Cancel**

   Click this button to close the Tracking Edit dialog, ignoring any tracking table edits.

The Edit Tracking Dialog

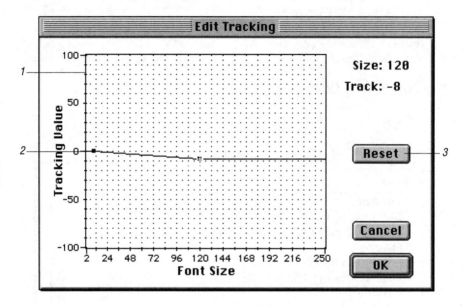

1. **The Tracking Grid**

   This grid is the heart of the Tracking Edit command. Here, two values are plotted against each other:

   Font Size

   The horizontal axis represents the size of a font, and ranges from 2 to 250 pt. Text larger than 250 pt. receives the same tracking value as 250 pt. text. Text smaller than the Auto Kern Above amount is tracked at the original default value (see the previous "Special Notes" section).

   Tracking Value

   The vertical axis represents the new default tracking value. Tracking units here are the same as those described under Style: **Track**—each one is 1/200 of an em space. Although you can manually track text from –500 to 500 units, this command only allows you to track between –100 and 100.

2. **Tracking Curve**

By default, the curve rests at 0, indicating the font's built-in tracking. By repositioning the curve, you establish new tracking values for different font sizes. Click the curve to add as many as four points. As you drag a point, the current Size and Track values display in the upper-right corner of the dialog.

– To apply the same tracking adjustment to all sizes, click and drag a single point. For example, if you drag the entire curve down to –5 and save the adjustment, every occurrence of the font appears to be tracked at –5 units, regardless of its size.

– To apply a tracking value that loosens or tightens as the font size increases, you must position at least two points. For example, if you place one point at Size: 12, Track 10 and another at Size: 72, Track –10, tracking is applied as follows:

All text 12 pt. and below receives a tracking value of 10.

All text 72 pt. and above receives a tracking value of –10.

Text between 12 and 72 pt. is tracked more tightly as the size increases: 27 pt. text is tracked at 5, 42 pt. text is tracked at 0, 57 pt. text is tracked at –5, and so forth.

3. **Reset**

Click this button to remove all points and reset the tracking curve to 0.

See Also

Appendix A (Utilities: **Tracking Edit**)
Edit: Preferences: Document: **Paragraph**
Style: **Track**
The Measurements Palette

Utilities: Kerning Table Edit

Every font contains its own *kerning table*, or default series of kern pairs specified by the font's designer. Without these built-in spacing values, the font would be *monospaced*, like letters created with a typewriter.

Most kerning tables contain between 100 and 500 predefined pairs. The font designer typically focuses on the most commonly occurring letter pairs, such as "St," "Re," "un," and so forth. However, since each character set can produce upwards of 40,000 unique pairs, it's possible that the spacing of certain kern pairs specific to *your* work are unsatisfactory.

For example, no font contains a predefined kern spacing between an apostrophe and "Q." Therefore, if the name "O'Quinn" appears frequently in your work—especially at sizes above 24 pt.—its likely you have to manually kern the two characters. If this word consistently appears in the same font, you can use this command to add a new kern pair, removing the need to manually adjust the space.

Many experienced typesetters can intuitively edit a kerning table, without performing a series of tests. If you're not sure of the exact changes you wish to make, apply a manual kern adjustment between the desired characters *before* opening this command. Write down the necessary changes, and refer to them when editing the kerning table.

Common Uses

Refer to Appendix A for full descriptions of the following:

* Adjusting an existing kern pair in a kerning table

* Adding a new kern pair to a kerning table

Common Errors

* **Editing the Bold, Italic, or Bold/Italic style of a font.** The Kerning Table Edit dialog displays four options for each font: the actual font, plus the font with the Bold, Italic, and Bold/Italic type styles applied. However, only the actual font (listed as "«Plain»") contains the built-in kern pairs. If you attempt to edit the type style versions, no pairs are available—you can only add new pairs. Since XPress outputs the actual Bold, Italic, and Bold/Italic font versions when you apply these type styles, choose the appropriate item in the Kerning Table Edit dialog. For example, to edit Futura Bold kern pairs, select "B Futura Bold «Plain»."

* **Deleting or ignoring the new kern pairs.** Kerning edits are saved in the XPress Preferences file. When a document contains an edited font, the new pairs are included in the document preferences, which allows them to be read by other copies of XPress:

  – If you delete the XPress Preferences file (which often happens when the file becomes corrupt), you lose any changes made to the kerning tables. To preserve your changes, back up the XPress Preferences file, or export the pairs into a text file and save them in a separate folder.

  – When a document is opened in a different copy of XPress, a warning appears, indicating that the document preferences differ from the current XPress settings. To preserve any included kerning tables, you must click the Keep Document Settings button. If you don't, any affected fonts revert back to their original spacing, resulting in text reflow.

Special Notes

* This feature is only available when the Kern/Track Editor XTension is loaded.

* This command only affects how XPress reads, displays, and outputs a particular font—the font files themselves are not changed.

* In a document, a kern pair's initial spacing is always 0—even when the kerning table has been edited. For example, assume you've changed the space between Futura Heavy's "S" and "t" to –15 kern units. When you type the letters and insert the cursor between them, the Kern Amount field in the Charac-

ter Attributes dialog and Measurements Palette displays 0, not −15. If you manually kern the pair to −5, the actual value is −20.

- Kern pair edits only take effect when text is larger than the Auto Kern Above value, established in the Edit: Preferences: Document: **Paragraph** panel.

- Although you can create kern pairs between numbers, automatic page numbers cannot be automatically kerned. XPress sees each automatic page number as a single character, even if it contains two, three, or more numerals. If you're completely unsatisfied with the way these numbers are kerned, you have two options:

  - Choose a font with less noticeable spacing problems.

  - On each page, replace each automatic page number with manually entered characters. If your document contains a large number of pages (more than 24), this is probably unrealistic. Also, if you insert, delete, or reposition any of the pages after replacing the automatic numbers, they will not change to reflect the new page numbering.

The Kerning Table Edit Dialog

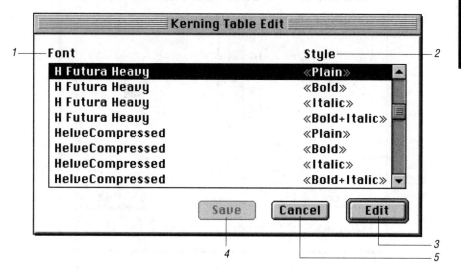

1. **Font**

   Select the font you wish to edit from this scrolling list. Note that every font currently available to XPress appears here—if you wish to adjust the kerning table of an entire font family, you must edit each font individually.

   If desired, type the first one or two letters of the font to jump to the appropriate item.

2. **Style**

   Unlike the Tracking Edit dialog, each font is listed four times: one for the Plain version (the actual font file) and three more, representing the same font with the Bold, Italic, and Bold/Italic type styles applied to it. Only the Plain version of each font contains the kerning table, so be sure to select the appropriate item. (See the previous "Common Errors" section.)

3. **Edit**

   After selecting the desired font, click this button to open the Edit Kerning Table dialog.

4. **Save**

   After closing the Edit Kerning Table dialog, click this button to save the new default kern pairs.

5. **Cancel**

   Click this button to close the Kerning Table Edit dialog, ignoring any kerning table edits.

The Edit Kerning Table Dialog

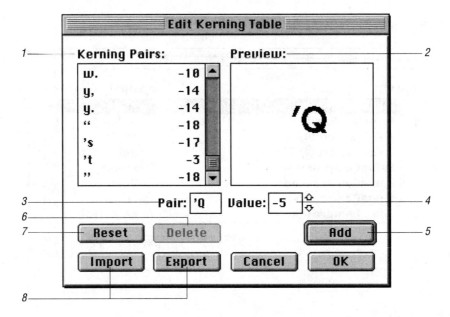

1. **Kerning Pairs**

   This scrolling field lists the current kerning table, including the pairs defined by the font designer as well as any changes you have already applied using this command. To edit an existing pair, scroll down the list, or type the two letters. If a pair has not been added to the list, you must enter it in the Pair field.

   The values on the right indicate the current kern space between each pair. Kerning units here are the same as those described under Style: **Kern**—each one is 1/200 of an em space.

Note that at the start of many kerning tables, many pairs seem to contain only one letter. These pairs actually consist of an empty space and *then* a letter, which allows you to affect the spacing before a word starting with that letter.

2. **Preview**

This area displays the spacing of the currently selected kern pair. Since the characters only appear at roughly 34 pt. (at screen resolution), I don't recommend basing your final decisions on this preview. Instead, print samples of the corrected pairs, at different sizes, to a high-resolution output device.

3. **Pair**

This field displays the kern pair currently being adjusted. When you select a pair from the Kerning Pairs list, it automatically appears here. To edit a new pair, manually enter the characters.

4. **Value**

This field displays the current kern space. To change this value, highlight the field, and enter a new one. Or use the arrows to increase or decrease the amount.

Although you can manually kern a pair between –500 and 500 units, this command only allows you to enter a value between –100 and 100.

5. **Add/Replace**

After editing a kern pair, you must click this button to add the new values to the kerning table. When adding a new pair to the list, this button appears as Add. When editing an existing pair, this button appears as Replace—clicking it replaces the original kern space with the new amount.

6. **Delete**

Click this button to remove the kern pair currently selected in the Kerning Values list. Immediately after you do this, the characters and their spacing still appear in the Pair and Value fields—if you've accidentally deleted the wrong pair, you can still click Add to reinsert it in the list. As soon as you select another pair, the values are lost.

7. **Reset**

Click this button to reset the kerning table back to the font's default. Any new pairs or adjustments made using this command are stripped away. This button is only available when a kerning table has been edited.

8. **Import/Export**

To write the contents of the Kerning Values list to an external text file, click the Export button. There are three reasons to do this:

- It creates a backup of your adjustments, in case you must delete your XPress Preferences file.

- You can give the kerning table edits to another designer using the same font on a different copy of XPress.

- You can import the new pairs and adjustments of one font into the kerning table of a different font. This is not a perfect solution, however, because character shapes can differ greatly from font to font. This technique works best on very similar fonts, such as two thin sans serif typefaces. Even then, certain pairs may require additional adjustment.

To import a kerning table, click the Import button, and locate the exported text file.

See Also

Appendix A (Utilities: **Kerning Table Edit**)
Edit: Preferences: Document: **Paragraph**
Style: **Kern**
The Measurements Palette

PART III

Palettes

This section covers the XPress palettes, in the order they appear under the View Menu. The only exception is the Toolbar, which is covered in the four chapters of Part I.

CHAPTER 14

The Measurements Palette

The Measurements Palette gives you immediate access to the commonly used Style Menus and Item: **Modify** commands, using a series of editable fields, buttons, and pop-ups. The available options depend on the currently selected items.

Reveal and hide the Measurements Palette by pressing the F9 key. XPress always remembers the last position of this palette when you quit and relaunch the application.

At all times, this palette is divided in half:

- **Single picture box selected.** The options on the right of the palette affect the actual box, similar to the Item: Modify: **Box** panel. The options on the left affect the box contents, similar to the Item: Modify: **Picture** panel.

- **Single text box selected.** The options on the right affect the actual box, similar to the Item: Modify: **Box** panel. The options on the left affect the text within the box, similar to many of the commands on the Style Menus.

- **Single line selected.** The options on the left affect the orientation of the line, similar to the Item: Modify: **Line** panel. The options on the right affect the line's style, similar to many of the commands on the Style Menus.

- **Multiple items selected.** The options on the left affect the orientation of the items, similar to the Item: **Group** panel. No options are available on the right.

- **Bézier item selected.** The options on the left affect the orientation of the item, similar to the Item: Modify: **Box** panel (for a closed Bézier shape) or the Item: Modify: **Line** panel (for an open Bézier path). The options on the right affect the currently selected point, curve handle, or segment. The Item: **Point/Segment Type** commands appear, as well as precise measurement fields not available anywhere else.

Common Errors

- **Entering a value that positions an item off the pasteboard.** For example, if you enter too great an X or Y value, an alert appears, stating "The item cannot be positioned off the pasteboard." When you click OK, you must change the incorrect value (which XPress highlights in the Measurements Palette) before you can go back to editing the document. Otherwise, the alert continues to appear whenever you click the page.

- **Attempting to affect the content of multiple picture boxes or lines.** The commands in the right half of the palette are only available when a single item is selected. As long as all the selected items are the same thing, however, you can open the appropriate Item: **Modify** panel and edit them simultaneously.

- **Attempting to highlight an entire negative value by double-clicking the field.** When you double-click a negative value, the minus sign is not included. If you're not paying attention, enter a positive value, and press Return, the result is a negative value. If you enter a new negative value, the result is a number with two minus signs ("−−2.5," for example), which XPress regards as an incorrect value. To avoid this, make sure the entire value is selected, when necessary.

Special Notes

- When entering values on the left side of the palette, you must press the Enter or Return key to apply the change. When entering values on the right, changes are applied by pressing Enter or Return or by moving to a different field.

- Every Measurements Palette adjustment can be reversed by immediately choosing Edit: **Undo**.

- Each palette field can contain values accurate to three decimals, or thousandths of a unit. If you enter a fourth decimal—2.1117, for example—XPress rounds up or down to the nearest thousandth (in this case, 2.112). This rounding is only for display purposes; XPress still remembers the actual four-decimal value.

Copying and Pasting Measurements

You can Edit: **Copy** and **Paste** values between Measurement Palette fields. This is useful when copying and pasting an item from one document to another, and its page position must be the same. After pasting the item, leave it selected, and return to the original document. Select the original item, highlight the X value, and choose Edit: **Copy**. Return to the second document, highlight the current X value, and choose Edit: **Paste**. Do the same for the Y value.

Of course, if desired, you can simply write down the original X and Y values and manually enter them in the second document.

Adding or Subtracting Absolute Values

To add or subtract from a field value, enter a positive or negative amount *after* the current value. For example, assume the Horizontal and Vertical Measure pop-ups in the Edit: Preferences: Document: **General** panel are set to inches. To move a box exactly 2.5 inches to the right, select the box, insert the cursor after the current X value, enter "+2.5", and press Return. To move the box to the left, enter "–2.5".

To move the item using a different unit of measurement, you must include the correct abbreviation:

- To move the box 2.5 inches to the right, enter "+2.5"".

- To move it 2.5 picas, enter "+2p6".

- To move it 2.5 points, enter "+2.5 pt".

- To move it 2.5 centimeters, enter "+2.5 cm".

- To move it 2.5 millimeters, enter "+2.5 mm".

- To move it 2.5 ciceros, enter "+2c6".

- To move it 2.5 agates, enter "+2.5 ag".

As long as you include the right measurement abbreviation, you can enter any unit in the palette fields. After you press Enter or Return to apply the value, XPress automatically converts it to the unit set in the Edit: Preferences: Document: **General** panel.

Entering Proportional Values

To increase or decrease a value by a percentage of the current amount, enter an asterisk (*), then the percentage in the form of a decimal. For example, to reduce the width of a box by 80%, enter "*.8" after the current W value. To increase the horizontal offset position by 1.5 times, enter "*1.5" after the current X value.

Similarly, you can divide the current value by entering a forward slash (/), then the divisor. For example, if the length of a line is 10 inches, entering "/2" divides 10 by 2, resulting in a 5-inch line.

Measurements Palette Shortcuts

Use the following Measurements Palette shortcuts:

- Press (Option-Command) [**Alt-Command**]-M to highlight the first palette field. If the Measurements Palette is hidden, this shortcut displays it, then highlights the first field.

- When any palette field is active, press the Tab key to highlight successive fields. Press Shift-Tab to highlight fields in reverse order.

- Press (Command) [**Control**]-period at any time to exit the palette without applying any changes.

Text Box Measurements

The following options appear when you select a text box. The items on the right are only available when the Content Tool is active.

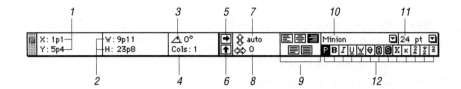

1. **X and Y**

   These fields indicate the position of the box's upper-left corner (known as the *origin*), as measured against the horizontal and vertical rulers. Two things will change these values: manually moving the box, or repositioning the *zero origin* of the ruler guides. If desired, you can move a text box by entering new values in these fields. Positive X values move to the right; negative values move to the left. Positive Y values move down; negative values move up.

   The X and Y fields are identical to the Origin Across (X) and Origin Down (Y) fields in the Item: Modify: **Box** panel. (See Chapter 10, *The Item Menu*, for more information.)

2. **W and H**

   These values indicate the width and height of the box. When you manually resize a text box with the Item or Content Tool, these values change to reflect the new dimensions. If desired, you can precisely resize a text box by entering new values in these fields. You can't enter negative values here.

   The W and H fields are identical to the Width and Height fields in the Item: Modify: **Box** panel. (See Chapter 10 for more information.)

3. **Angle**

   This value indicates the selected box's current angle of rotation. Any value other than 0° (no rotation) pivots the box around its center. Values between 0° and 360° rotate the box counterclockwise. Values between 0° and –360° rotate clockwise. XPress automatically converts values to range between –180° and 180°.

   The Angle field here is identical to the Angle field in the Item: Modify: **Box** panel. (See Chapter 10 for more information.)

4. **Cols**

   This value indicates the number of internal columns present in a text box. The value must be set to at least one.

The Cols field is identical to the Column field in the Item: Modify: **Text** panel. (See Chapter 10 for more information.)

5. **Flip Horizontal**

Click this button to horizontally flip the entire contents of a text box. Only the actual box is affected. For example, if you select a linked box and click this button, text only flips when it flows into this box.

This button is identical to Style: **Flip Horizontal**. (See Chapter 7, *The Style Menu (Text)*, for more information.)

6. **Flip Vertical**

Click this button to vertically flip the entire contents of the text box. Like Flip Horizontal, it only affects the currently selected box.

This button is identical to Style: **Flip Vertical**. (See Chapter 7 for more information.)

7. **Leading**

This field indicates the current *leading*, or line spacing. This value is only applied on the paragraph level—for example, if you attempt to adjust the spacing of a single word or line within a paragraph, every line in the paragraph is affected.

Unlike using the menu command, this option allows you to make adjustments on the fly. To increase leading in 1 pt. increments, click the up-pointing arrow. To decrease it in 1 pt. increments, click the down-pointing arrow. To increase or decrease in .1 pt. increments, hold down the (Option) [**Alt**] key as you click.

This option is identical to Style: **Leading**. (See Chapter 7 for more information.)

8. **Kern/Track**

When the flashing cursor is inserted between two characters, this field indicates the current *kerning*, or space between the pair. When text is highlighted, this field indicates the current *tracking*, or overall word spacing.

Unlike using the menu commands, this option allows you to make adjustments on the fly. To increase kerning or tracking in 1 pt. increments, click the right-pointing arrow. To decrease in 1 pt. increments, click the left-pointing arrow. To increase or decrease in .1 pt. increments, hold down the (Option) [**Alt**] key as you click.

This option is identical to Style: **Track** and **Kern**. (See Chapter 7 for more information.)

9. **Alignment**

These buttons indicate the current text alignment. From left to right, they are Left Aligned, Center Aligned, Right Aligned, Justified, and Force Justified. These settings are only applied on the paragraph level—for example, if you attempt to center-align a single word or line within a paragraph, every paragraph line is affected.

Measure- ments

These options are identical to the Style: **Alignment** commands. (See Chapter 7 for more information.)

10. **Font**

This field indicates the current font. There are two ways to change the font from the palette:

— Choose a new item from the pop-up, which displays all currently installed fonts.

— Highlight the current font name, and type the new font you wish to use. (The new font must be installed.) To quicken this method, press (Option-Command-Shift) [**Alt-Control-Shift**]-M to automatically highlight the font field. Typing the first couple of letters of the font name is usually enough to jump to the desired font. If you have an extensive font list, you can use this technique to jump to a specific letter. For example, if you enter "z" in the field and then choose the pop-up, the list has automatically scrolled down to the end.

This option is identical to Style: **Font**. (See Chapter 7 for more information.)

11. **Size**

This field displays the current font size. To establish a new size, choose a preset value from the pop-up, or highlight the field and enter a new amount.

This option is identical to Style: **Size**. (See Chapter 7 for more information.)

12. **Type Styles**

These options display the currently available type styles. From left to right, they are Plain, Bold, Italic, Underline, Word Underline, Strike Thru, Outline, Shadow, All Caps, Small Caps, Superscript, Subscript, and Superior. Applied styles are highlighted in black.

These options are identical to the Style: **Type Style** commands, and the type style buttons in the Style: **Character** dialog. (See Chapter 7 for more information.)

See Also

Page Tools: **Item Tool**
Page Tools: **Content Tool**
Style (Text): **Font**
Style (Text): **Size**
Style (Text): **Type Style**
Style (Text): **Track** and **Kern**
Style (Text): **Character**
Style (Text): **Alignment**
Style (Text): **Leading**
Style (Text): **Flip Vertical**
Style (Text): **Flip Horizontal**
Item: Modify: **Text**
Item: Modify: **Box**

Anchored Box Measurements

Anchored box palette items are available only when the following occurs:

- A text or picture box is anchored in a text box. (See "Edit: Paste" in Chapter 6, *The Edit Menu*, for more information.)

- The anchored item is selected (not highlighted) with the Item or Content Tool.

The two new items in this palette determine how the anchored item aligns to the baseline it rests upon. The X and Y fields are not available.

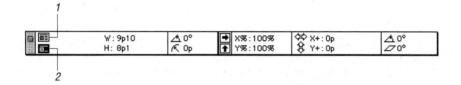

1. **Ascent**

   Click this button to align the top of the anchored box to the baseline it rests upon. If the item dips into the lines below, the text attempts to flow around it.

   This option is identical to the Ascent button available in the Item: Modify: **Box** panel when an anchored item is selected. (See Chapter 10 for more information.)

2. **Baseline**

   Click this button to align the bottom of the anchored box to the baseline it rests upon. This option is only recommended for items anchored in the first line of a text box. If the item extends into any lines above, the text does not reflow—rather, the anchored item appears to rest on top of the text, obscuring it.

   This option is similar to the Baseline button available in the Item: Modify: **Box** panel when an anchored item is selected. (See Chapter 10 for more information.)

Special Notes

When an anchored item is selected with the Content Tool, the options on the right side of the palette are fully available.

See Also

   Edit: **Paste**
   Item: Modify: **Box**

Picture Box Measurements

The following options appear when you select a picture box. The items on the right are only available when the Content Tool is active.

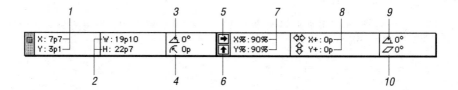

1. **X and Y**

   These fields indicate the position of the box's upper-left corner (known as the *origin*), as measured against the horizontal and vertical rulers. Two things will change these values: manually moving the box, or repositioning the *zero origin* of the ruler guides. If desired, you can move a picture box by entering new values in these fields. Positive X values move to the right; negative values move to the left. Positive Y values move down; negative values move up.

   The X and Y fields are identical to the Origin Across (X) and Origin Down (Y) fields in the Item: Modify: **Box** panel. (See Chapter 10 for more information.)

2. **W and H**

   These values indicate the width and height of the box. When you manually resize a picture box with the Item or Content Tool, these values change to reflect the new dimensions. If desired, you can precisely resize a picture box by entering new values in these fields. You can't enter negative values here.

   The W and H fields are identical to the Width and Height fields in the Item: Modify: **Box** panel. (See Chapter 10 for more information.)

3. **Angle**

   This value indicates the box's current angle of rotation. Any value other than 0° (no rotation) pivots the box around its center. Values between 0° and 360° rotate the box counterclockwise. Values between 0° and –360° rotate clockwise. XPress automatically converts values to range between –180° and 180°.

   The Angle field here is identical to the Angle field in the Item: Modify: **Box** panel. (See Chapter 10 for more information.)

4. **Corner Radius**

   This value indicates the corner radius of the box. When the value is 0, the corners are not affected. When you enter a value between 0 and 2 inches, the corners of a rectangular box become rounded, and the corners of a shaped box become more exaggerated. (This option is not available when a round or Bézier picture box is selected.)

The Corner Radius field here is identical to the Corner Radius field in the Item: Modify: **Picture** panel.

5. **Flip Horizontal**

Click this button to horizontally flip the contents of a picture box.

This button is identical to Style: **Flip Horizontal**. (See Chapter 8, *The Style Menu (Picture)*, for more information.)

6. **Flip Vertical**

Click this button to vertically flip the contents of the picture box.

This button is identical to Style: **Flip Vertical**. (See Chapter 8 for more information.)

7. **X% and Y%**

These fields indicate the current scale of the imported graphic—the box dimensions are not affected. Changing the X% value scales horizontally, starting from the left edge of the graphic. Changing the Y% value scales vertically, starting from the top edge of the graphic.

By entering a value between 10% and 100%, you decrease the original size of the imported preview. By entering a value between 100% and 1000%, you increase the size. To avoid potential printing problems, pixel-based images should not be scaled up or down by more than 20%.

Unless you're creating a visual effect, the X% and Y% field should be set to the same value when scaling. This way, the graphic retains its original proportions. When using this palette, most users highlight the X% field, enter the desired scale, hit the Tab key, then enter the same value in the Y% field.

The X% and Y% fields are identical to the Scale Across and Scale Down fields in the Item: Modify: **Picture** panel. (See Chapter 10 for more information.)

8. **X+ and Y+**

These fields indicate the position of an imported graphic, as measured from the top and left edge of the picture box. Unlike the X and Y fields on the left of the palette, these values have nothing to do with the horizontal or vertical rulers.

These values are set to 0 when you first import a graphic, indicating that it's flush with the top and left edges of the box. If you reposition the graphic by dragging with the Content Tool, the values change to reflect the new position.

To offset a graphic to the left, enter a positive amount in the X+ field; negative values offset to the right. To offset a graphic down, enter a positive amount in the Y+ field; negative values offset up. To offset in any direction in 1 pt. increments, click the appropriate horizontal or vertical arrow. To offset in .1 pt. increments, hold down the (Option) [**Alt**] key as you click. To reset a graphic to its original position, enter 0 in both fields.

The X+ and Y+ fields are identical to the Offset Across and Offset Down fields in the Item: Modify: **Picture** panel. (See Chapter 10 for more information.)

Measure-ments

9. **Picture Angle**

   This value indicates a graphic's angle of rotation within its picture box. Any value other than 0 (no rotation) pivots the image around its center, regardless of its position in the box. Values between 0° and 360° rotate the graphic counterclockwise. Values between 0 and –360° rotate clockwise. XPress automatically converts values to range between –180° and 180°.

   The Picture Angle field here is identical to the Picture Angle field in the Item: Modify: **Picture** panel. (See Chapter 10 for more information.)

10. **Picture Skew**

    This value indicates the skew angle of a graphic within its picture box. This value doesn't affect the box itself. By entering a value between –75° and 75°, you slant the graphic horizontally, across its center.

    The Picture Skew field here is identical to the Picture Skew field in the Item: Modify: **Picture** panel. (See Chapter 10 for more information.)

See Also

Style (Picture): **Flip Horizontal**
Style (Picture): **Flip Vertical**
Item: Modify: **Box**
Item: Modify: **Picture**

Line Measurements (Endpoints)

The following options appear when you select a line and set Endpoints in the Mode pop-up. All options are available, regardless of whether the Item or Content Tool is active.

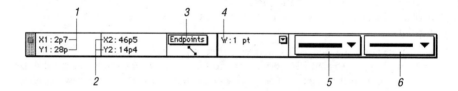

1. **X1 and Y1**

   These fields indicate the position of the line's first endpoint (the one first placed when you created the line), as measured against the horizontal and vertical rulers. Two things will change these values: manually moving the line, or repositioning the *zero origin* of the ruler guides. If desired, you can move the first endpoint by entering new values in these fields. Positive X1 values move to the right; negative values move to the left. Positive Y1 values move down; negative values move up. Since these fields don't affect the last endpoint, changing the values changes the shape and orientation of the line.

The X1 and Y1 fields are identical to the First Across (X1) and First Down (Y1) fields in the Item: Modify: **Line** panel, when Endpoints is set in the Mode pop-up. (See Chapter 10 for more information.)

2. **X2 and Y2**

These fields indicate the position of the line's last endpoint (the point where you released the mouse button when creating the line), as measured against the horizontal and vertical rulers. If desired, you can move the last endpoint by entering new values in these fields. Positive X2 values move to the right; negative values move to the left. Positive Y2 values move down; negative values move up. Since these fields don't affect the first endpoint, changing the values changes the shape and orientation of the line.

The X2 and Y2 fields are identical to the Last Across (X2) and Last Down (Y2) fields in the Item: Modify: **Line** panel when Endpoints is set in the Mode pop-up. (See Chapter 10 for more information.)

3. **Mode Pop-up**

This pop-up determines the fields that appear in the left half of the Measurements Palette when a line is selected. The effect of each item—Endpoints, First Point, Midpoint, and Last Point—are described in full under the appropriate sections of this chapter.

4. **Width**

This field displays the current line thickness. To set a new width, choose a preset amount from the pop-up, or enter a value in the field.

This option is identical to Style: **Width**. (See Chapter 9, *The Style Menu (Line)*, for more information.)

5. **Line Style**

This pop-up displays all dashes and stripes currently available in the document. All lines default to solid black—to apply a new style, choose one from the pop-up.

This option is identical to Style: **Line Style**. (See Chapter 9 for more information.) To define custom dashes or stripes, you must use Edit: **Dashes & Stripes** before they appear here.

6. **Arrowheads**

This pop-up displays the five arrowhead options XPress can apply to a line. To apply one, choose it from the pop-up.

This option is identical to Style: **Arrowheads**. (See Chapter 9 for more information.)

See Also

Page Tools: **Item Tool**
Page Tools: **Content Tool**
Edit: **Dashes & Stripes**
Style (Line): **Line Style**
Style (Line): **Width**
Item: Modify: **Line**

Line Measurements (First Point)

The following options appear when you select a line and set First Point in the Mode pop-up. All options are available, regardless of whether the Item or Content Tool is active.

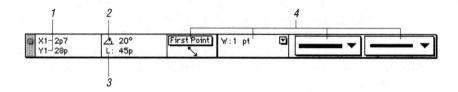

1. **X1 and Y1**

   These fields indicate the position of the line's first endpoint (the one first placed when you created the line), as measured against the horizontal and vertical rulers. Two things will change these values: manually moving the line, or repositioning the *zero origin* of the ruler guides. If desired, you can move the first endpoint by entering new values in these fields. Positive X1 values move to the right; negative values move to the left. Positive Y1 values move down; negative values move up. Since these fields don't affect the last endpoint, changing the values changes the shape and orientation of the line.

   The X1 and Y1 fields are identical to the First Across (X1) and First Down (Y1) fields in the Item: Modify: **Line** panel, when Endpoints is set in the Mode pop-up. (See Chapter 10 for more information.)

2. **Angle**

   This value indicates the line's current angle of rotation, as measured against the horizontal plane. Changing this value pivots the line around its first point. Values between 0° and 360° rotate the line counterclockwise. Values between 0° and –360° rotate clockwise. XPress automatically converts values to range between –180° and 180°.

   The Angle field here is identical to the Angle field in the Item: Modify: **Line** panel, when First Point is set in the Mode pop-up. (See Chapter 10 for more information.)

3. **Length**

   This value indicates the line's current length. If you resize a line by dragging one of its endpoints, this field changes to reflect the new length. When you resize a line by entering a value here, only the last point moves.

   The Length field here is identical to the Length field in the Item: Modify: **Line** panel, when First Point is set in the Mode pop-up. (See Chapter 10 for more information.)

4. **Remaining Items**

The Mode pop-up, Width field, and style pop-ups are described in the previous section, "Line Measurements (Endpoints)."

See Also

Item: Modify: **Line**

Line Measurements (Midpoint)

The following options appear when you select a line and set Midpoint in the Mode pop-up. All options are available, regardless of whether the Item or Content Tool is active.

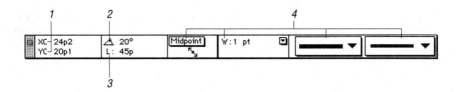

1. **XC and YC**

These fields indicate the position of the line's mathematical center, as measured against the horizontal and vertical rulers. Two things will change these values: manually moving the line, or repositioning the *zero origin* of the ruler guides. If desired, you can move the midpoint by entering new values in these fields. Positive XC values move the line to the right; negative values move to the left. Positive YC values move down; negative values move up.

The XC and YC fields are identical to the Midpoint Across (XC) and Midpoint Down (YC) fields in the Item: Modify: **Line** panel when Midpoint is set in the Mode pop-up. (See Chapter 10 for more information.)

2. **Angle**

This value indicates the line's current angle of rotation, as measured against the horizontal plane. Changing this value pivots the line around its center. Values between 0° and 360° rotate the line counterclockwise. Values between 0° and –360° rotate clockwise. XPress automatically converts values to range between –180° and 180°.

The Angle field here is identical to the Angle field in the Item: Modify: **Line** panel when Midpoint is set in the Mode pop-up. (See Chapter 10 for more information.)

3. **Length**

This value indicates the line's current length. If you resize a line by dragging one of its endpoints, this field changes to reflect the new length. When you resize a line by entering a value here, both endpoints are moved closer to or away from the midpoint.

The Length field here is identical to the Length field in the Item: Modify: **Line** panel when Midpoint is set in the Mode pop-up. (See Chapter 10 for more information.)

4. **Remaining Settings**

The Mode pop-up, Width field, and style pop-ups were described previously "Line Measurements (Endpoints)."

See Also

Item: Modify: **Line**

Line Measurements (Last Point)

The following options appear when you select a line and set Last Point in the Mode pop-up. All options are available, regardless of whether the Item or Content Tool is active.

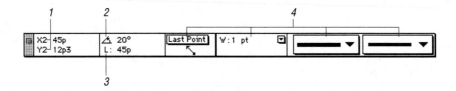

1. **X2 and Y2**

   These fields indicate the position of the line's last endpoint (or the point where you released the mouse button when creating the line), as measured against the horizontal and vertical rulers. If desired, you can move the last endpoint by entering new values in these fields. Positive X2 values move the last point to the right; negative values move to the left. Positive Y2 values move down; negative values move up. Since these fields don't affect the first endpoint, changing these values changes the shape and orientation of the line.

   The X2 and Y2 fields are identical to the Last Across (X2) and Last Down (Y2) fields in the Item: Modify: **Line** panel when Last Point is set in the Mode pop-up. (See Chapter 10 for more information.)

2. **Angle**

   This value indicates the line's current angle of rotation, as measured against the horizontal plane. Changing this value pivots the line around its last point. Values between 0° and 360° rotate the line counterclockwise. Values between 0° and –360° rotate clockwise. XPress automatically converts values to range between –180° and 180°.

The Angle field here is identical to the Angle field in the Item: Modify: **Line** panel when Last Point is set in the Mode pop-up. (See Chapter 10 for more information.)

3. **Length**

This value indicates the line's current length. If you resize a line by dragging one of its endpoints, this field changes to reflect the new length. When you resize a line by entering a value here, only the first point moves.

The Length field here is identical to the Length field in the Item: Modify: **Line** panel when Last Point is set in the Mode pop-up. (See Chapter 10 for more information.)

4. **Remaining Items**

The Mode pop-up, Width field, and style pop-ups were described previously in "Line Measurements (Endpoints)."

See Also
Item: Modify: **Line**

Bézier Path or Shape Measurements

The following options appear when you select an entire Bézier path or shape. The options on the left are available regardless of whether the Item or Content Tool is active. The options on the right depend on the selected item:

- **Bézier Line.** Here, the line style options are available. (See "Line Measurements (Endpoints)" earlier in this chapter for more information.)

- **Text Path.** When the Item Tool is active, the line style options are available. (See "Line Measurements (Endpoints)" earlier in this chapter for more information.) When the Content Tool is active, the text editing options are available. (See "Text Box Measurements" earlier in this chapter for more information.)

- **Bézier Text Box.** When the Item Tool is active, no additional options are available. When the Content Tool is active, the text editing options are available. (See "Text Box Measurements" earlier in this chapter for more information.)

- **Bézier Picture Box.** Whether the Item or Content Tool is active, the picture editing options are available. (See "Picture Box Measurements" earlier in this chapter for more information.)

- **Empty Bézier Box.** No additional options are available.

- **Bézier Point or Segment.** Whether the Item or Content Tool is active, the Bézier editing options appear. (See the next section, "Bézier Point, Segment, or Handle Measurements," for more information.)

Measurements

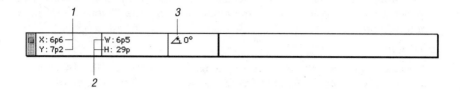

1. **X and Y**

   The X value indicates the position of the point or segment farthest to the left. The Y value indicates the position of the point or segment closest to the top of the page. Both values are measured against the horizontal and vertical rulers.

   Four things will change these values:

   — Manually moving the entire item

   — Repositioning the *zero origin* of the ruler guides

   — Dragging a single point beyond the leftmost or topmost edge of the path or shape

   — Dragging a single segment beyond the leftmost or topmost edge of the path or shape

   When you enter new values in these fields, you move the entire item. Positive X values move to the right; negative values move to the left. Positive Y values move down; negative values move up.

   When a path is selected, the X and Y fields are identical to the Origin Across (X) and Origin Down (Y) fields in the Item: Modify: **Line** panel. When a shape is selected, the fields are identical to the Origin Across (X) and Origin Down (Y) fields in the Item: Modify: **Box** panel. (See Chapter 10 for more information.)

2. **W and H**

   These values indicate the width and height of the path or shape. To determine these values on an irregular path or shape, XPress draws an invisible rectangular box around the item. Width is regarded as the distance from the left to right, and height is the distance from top to bottom.

   When you enter a width value, the item is horizontally scaled from the leftmost edge. When you enter a height value, the item is vertically scaled from the topmost edge.

   When a path is selected, the W and H fields are identical to the Width and Height fields in the Item: Modify: **Line** panel. When a shape is selected, the fields are identical to the Width and Height fields in the Item: Modify: **Box** panel. (See Chapter 10 for more information.)

3. **Angle**

   This value indicates the item's current angle of rotation. Any value other than 0° (no rotation) pivots the item around its center. Values between 0° and 360° rotate the box counterclockwise. Values between 0° and –360° rotate clockwise. XPress automatically converts values to range between –180° and 180°.

When a path is selected, the Angle field is identical to the Angle field in the Item: Modify: **Line** panel. When a shape is selected, the field is identical to the Angle field in the Item: Modify: **Box** panel. (See Chapter 10 for more information.)

See Also

Page Tools: **Item Tool**
Page Tools: **Content Tool**
Item: Modify: **Box**
Item: Modify: **Line**

Bézier Point, Segment, or Handle Measurements

The following options appear in the right side of the palette when you select a Bézier point or segment. When you select multiple paths or segments, the fields are blank. Enter values to affect the orientation of all selected items.

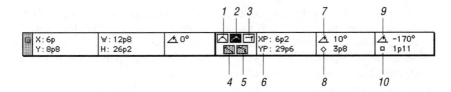

1. **Symmetrical Point**

   Click this button to convert a smooth or corner point to a symmetrical point, similar to choosing Item: Point/Segment Type: **Symmetrical Point**. When a segment is selected, this button converts the points on either end. (See "Bézier Line Tool" in Chapter 3, Line Tools, for more information.)

2. **Smooth Point**

   Click this button to convert a symmetrical or corner point to a smooth point, similar to choosing Item: Point/Segment Type: **Smooth Point**. When a segment is selected, this button converts the points on either end. (See "Bézier Line Tool" in Chapter 3 for more information.)

3. **Corner Point**

   Click this button to convert a symmetrical or smooth point to a corner point, similar to choosing Item: Point/Segment Type: **Corner Point**. When a segment is selected, this button converts the points on either end. (See "Bézier Line Tool" in Chapter 3 for more information.)

4. **Straight Segment**

   Click this button to convert a curved segment to a straight segment, similar to choosing Item: Point/Segment Type: **Straight Segment**. (See "Bézier Line Tool" in Chapter 3 for more information.)

5. **Curved Segment**

   Click this button to convert a straight segment to a curved segment, similar to choosing Item: Point/Segment Type: **Smooth Segment**. (See "Bézier Line Tool" in Chapter 3 for more information.)

6. **XP and YP**

   These fields indicate the position of the currently selected point, as measured against the horizontal and vertical rulers. Two things will change these values: manually moving the point, or repositioning the *zero origin* of the ruler guides. If desired, you can move a point by entering new values in these fields. Positive XP values move to the right; negative values move to the left. Positive YP values move down; negative values move up.

7. **Diamond Handle Angle**

   This field indicates the current angle of the diamond-shaped curve handle. A value of 0° results in the handle extending horizontally from the point. Values between 0° and 360° pivot the handle counterclockwise around the point. Values between 0° and −360° pivot clockwise. XPress automatically converts values to range between −180° and 180°.

8. **Diamond Handle Distance**

   This value indicates the length of the diamond-shaped curve handle, or the distance from the diamond to the point. When you drag the diamond, the value changes to reflect the new distance. When you enter a value in the field, the diamond moves toward or away from the point, which in turn changes the shape of the segment.

9. **Square Handle Angle**

   This field indicates the current angle of the square-shaped curve handle. A value of 0° results in the handle extending horizontally from the point. Values between 0° and 360° pivot the handle counterclockwise around the point. Values between 0° and −360° pivot clockwise. XPress automatically converts values to range between −180° and 180°.

10. **Square Handle Distance**

    This value indicates the length of the square-shaped curve handle, or the distance from the square to the point. When you drag the square, the value changes to reflect the new distance. When you enter a value in the field, the square moves toward or away from the point, which in turn changes the shape of the segment.

See Also

Line Tools: **Bézier Line Tool**
Item: Point/Segment Type: **Symmetrical Point**
Item: Point/Segment Type: **Smooth Point**
Item: Point/Segment Type: **Corner Point**
Item: Point/Segment Type: **Straight Segment**
Item: Point/Segment Type: **Smooth Segment**

Multiple Item Measurements

The following options appear when you select multiple items. Although you can't affect the contents of these items from the Measurements Palette, if they're all the same type—all lines or all picture boxes, for example—you can affect them by opening the appropriate Item: **Modify** panel.

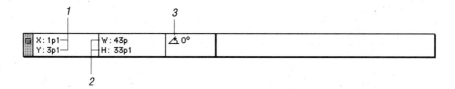

1. X and Y

XPress draws an invisible bounding box around the selected items. The X value indicates the position of the left edge of this box, as measured against the horizontal ruler. The Y value indicates the position of the top edge of the box, as measured against the vertical ruler. If desired, you can move the items by entering new values in these fields. Positive X values move the items to the right; negative values move to the left. Positive Y values move down; negative values move up.

The X and Y fields here are identical to the Origin Across (X) and Origin Down (Y) fields in the Item: **Group** panel. (See Chapter 10 for more information.)

2. W and H

These values indicate the width and height of the bounding box surrounding the items. Changing the Width value scales the items horizontally, starting from the left edge. Changing the Height value scales the items vertically, starting from the top edge. The contents of a picture box or text box are not affected.

The Width and Height fields here are identical to the Width and Height fields in the Item: Modify: **Group** panel. (See Chapter 10 for more information.)

3. **Angle**

This field allows you to rotate the selected items. Any value other than 0° (no rotation) pivots the items around the center of the bounding box. Values between 0° and 360° rotate counterclockwise. Values between 0° and –360° rotate clockwise. XPress automatically converts values to range between –180° and 180°.

The Angle field here is identical to the Angle field in the Item: Modify: **Group** panel. (See Chapter 10 for more information.)

See Also

Item: **Group**

Zero Origin Measurements

The following values appear when you reposition the zero origin of the ruler guides. (See "View: **Show/Hide Rulers**" in **Chapter 12, The View Menu,** for more information.)

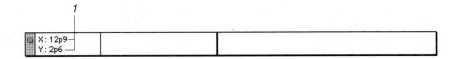

1. **X and Y**

   When repositioning the zero origin, these values indicate the position of the crosshairs, as measured against the horizontal and vertical rulers. These values are based on the current position of the zero origin.

See Also

   View: **Show/Hide Rulers**

Ruler Guide Measurements

The following values appear as you drag a guide from the vertical or horizontal ruler.

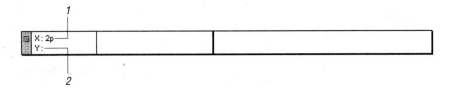

1. **X**

   When dragging a guide from the vertical ruler, this field indicates its position, as measured against the horizontal ruler. If necessary, reset the zero origin before placing a guide.

2. **Y**

   When dragging a guide from the horizontal ruler, this field indicates its position, as measured against the vertical ruler. If necessary, reset the zero origin before placing a guide.

See Also

   View: **Show/Hide Guides**
   View: **Show/Hide Rulers**

CHAPTER 15

The Document Layout Palette

The Document Layout Palette allows you to instantly access your document's pages and master pages.

To display the Document Layout Palette, press the (F10) [**F4**] key. XPress always remembers the last position of this palette when you quit and relaunch the application.

Common Uses

Refer to Appendix A, *Common Techniques*, for full descriptions of the following:

- Creating a basic printer-spread imposition
- Establishing multipage spreads
- Preparing pages with bleeds for output
- Preparing pages with crossovers for output

Common Errors

- **Imposing pages containing automatic page numbers.** When you move an auto-numbered page, the number changes to reflect the page's new position in the document. This is acceptable if your actual intention is to renumber the page. However, if you use the palette to impose pages for output, it causes problems. For example, if you move page 8 next to page 1 to create printer spreads in an 8-page document, the autonumbered 8 changes to 2. To fix this, add hard page numbers: highlight the auto number, and manually enter the desired page number.

- **Attempting to undo a Document Layout Palette command.** None of the actions you can perform with this palette can be reversed by choosing Edit: **Undo**. This is problematic. Attempting to manually reverse a complex technique—such as creating impositions or moving blocks of pages—often causes more problems than it solves, especially if you're unfamiliar with the process. Before performing complex techniques, save the document. This way, you can choose File: **Revert to Saved** to reverse your efforts if necessary.

Special Notes

- There's no specific limit on the number of pages you can place side by side in a spread—as long as their total width doesn't exceed 48 inches.

- This palette only affects pages within a document. For information on dragging master or document pages to another document, see "View: Thumbnails" in Chapter 12, *The View Menu.*

See Also

Appendix A (**The Document Layout Palette**)
View: **Thumbnails**
Edit: **Undo**

Palette Controls

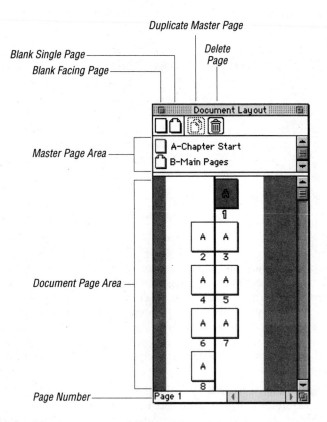

Duplicate Master Page

Delete Page

Blank Single Page

Blank Facing Page

Master Page Area

Document Page Area

Page Number

The Document Layout Palette consists of the options shown in the figure. Most have a counterpart elsewhere in the XPress menus, as noted in the "See Also" sections in the discussion of each one.

Document Page Area

This area displays all document pages in their order of appearance. Each page is represented by a rectangular icon, consisting of the following:

* **Master page letter.** If a page is linked to a master page, a letter appears in the center of the icon. This letter corresponds to the prefix of a master page's name. If a page is not based on a master page, no letter appears.

* **Page number.** The numbers below each icon indicate their order of appearance in the document. When you renumber a document using Page: **Section**, the page numbers here reflect the change. When pages contain automatic page numbers, they reflect the palette numbers. These numbers can be confusing: for example, if you drag page 8 between pages 3 and 4, the palette numbering doesn't change—although the page order is different, the numbers still run consecutively.

When you first add pages to a single-sided document, they appear in a vertical stack. When you first add pages to a facing-page document, they appear in reading order. A vertical black line representing a binding bisects the palette: odd-numbered pages appear on the right, even-numbered pages appear on the left.

Common Uses

* **Selecting pages.** You must select a page before moving, duplicating, or deleting it from the palette:

    - To select a single page, click its icon once.
    - Shift-click to select consecutive pages.
    - (Command) [**Control**]-click to select nonconsecutive pages.

* **Jumping to a specific page.** There are two ways to jump to a page: double-click its icon, or click once on the page number.

* **Moving a single page.** To reposition a page within a document, drag it to the desired position.

    In a single-sided document, the following rules apply:

    - When you drag a page between two other pages, the cursor changes to a down-pointing arrow. When you release the page, the dragged page is placed between the two pages.

    - When you drag a page to the left of another page, the cursor changes to a left-pointing arrow. When you release the page, you create a two-page spread: the dragged page appears on the left, the second page appears on the right.

    - When you drag a page to the right of another page, the cursor changes to a small page icon. When you release the page, you create a two-page spread: the dragged page appears on the right, the second page appears on the left.

Document Layout

In a facing-page document, the following rules apply:

–   When you drag a page to the left of page 1, the cursor changes to a left-pointing arrow (you must place the cursor directly over the vertical line). When you release the page, the dragged page becomes the new page 1, bumping the subsequent pages.

–   When you drag a page to the left of a two-page spread, the cursor changes to a left-pointing arrow. When you release the page, the dragged page becomes the new left-facing page in the spread, bumping the subsequent pages.

–   When you drag a page between two facing pages, the cursor changes to a left-pointing arrow. When you release the page, the dragged page becomes the new right-facing page in the spread, bumping the subsequent pages.

–   When you drag a page to the right of two facing pages, the cursor changes to a small page icon. When you release the page, you create a three-page spread.

•   **Moving multiple pages.** To move multiple pages, select them using the techniques described above and drag them to the desired position. Pages selected nonconsecutively appear in consecutive order after being moved—otherwise, the rules are the same as when moving a single page (above).

See Also

Page: **Page Overview**
Page: **Move**
Page: **Go To**
Page: **Section**

Master Page Area

This area displays all master pages currently available in the document. Single-sided master pages are preceded by a single-page icon. Facing master pages are preceded by a facing-page icon. If necessary, drag down the double-line bar beneath the master pages to reveal more of them.

To create a new master page, see "Blank Single and Blank Facing Page," later in this chapter.

Common Uses

•   **Jumping to a master page.** To access the contents of a master page, double-click its item in the master page area. This is the same as choosing the master page from the Page: **Display** pop-up.

•   **Renaming master pages.** Each master page is assigned a capital letter prefix: "A-," "B-," "C-," and so forth. (When a document page is linked to a master page, this letter appears in the corresponding palette icon.) To rename a master page without changing the prefix, click its name field (it automatically highlights), and enter a new name up to 64 characters long. To change the prefix, enter a new first character followed by a hyphen.

- **Rearranging master pages.** To move an item in the master page area, drag it to the desired location. Make sure the cursor changes to a down-pointing arrow, indicating its new position in the list. If you drag one master page on top of another (the second one highlights), you replace the contents of the second master page with the contents of the first.

- **Inserting a new document page based on a master page.** You can add one page at a time by dragging the desired master page icon into the document page area. Before releasing the mouse button, the cursor changes to indicate the position of the new page in the current layout. (Don't release the mouse button if one of the document pages is highlighted.) The new page is automatically based on the master page.

  This technique is the same as choosing Page: **Insert**, entering 1 in the Insert field, and setting the desired master page in the Master Page pop-up. To access the Insert Page dialog, hold down the (Option) [**Alt**] key while placing a new page.

- **Reapplying the same master page.** When you edit a master page item on a document page, it becomes a *localized* page element. For example, if you reposition a line that was originally part of a master page template, XPress regards the line as if you created it on the document page level. To restore the original master page items, drag the same master page onto the document page icon, releasing it when the icon highlights. The following occurs:

  - Master page items edited on the document page level reappear.
  - The edited master page item remains on the page. If necessary, delete it.
  - Master page items that haven't been edited are untouched.

- **Applying a new master page.** To base a document page on a different master page, drag the desired master page onto the appropriate page icon, releasing it when the icon highlights. For example, if you drag the B-Master B icon over a page linked to A-Master A, three things happen:

  - The contents of A-Master A are removed from the page.
  - The contents of B-Master B are applied to the page.
  - The letter on the page icon changes from A to B, indicating that the document page is now based on B-Master B.

See Also

Page: **Page Overview**
Page: **Insert**

Blank Single and Blank Facing Page

On their own, these icons don't represent any existing pages—rather, you must *drag* them into the document page area or master page area to achieve an effect. The plain icon represents a *blank single* page, or a nonfacing page not based on a master page. The icon with the folded corners represents a *blank facing* page not based on a master page. The blank facing icon is only available when the following occurs:

- The document is originally created with the Facing Pages box checked in the File: New: **Document** dialog.
- You convert a single-sided document to a facing-page document by checking the Facing Pages box in the File: **Document Setup** dialog.

Common Uses

- **Inserting a new blank page.** You can add one page at a time by dragging the desired page icon into the document page area. Before releasing the mouse button, the cursor changes to indicate the new page's position in the current layout. Do not release the mouse button if one of the document pages is highlighted.

  This technique is the same as choosing Page: **Insert**, entering 1 in the Insert field, and setting Blank Single (or Blank Facing Page) in the Master Page pop-up. To access the Insert Page dialog, hold down the (Option) [**Alt**] key while placing a new page.

- **Inserting a new master page.** To create a new single-sided master page, drag the blank single icon into the master pages area. To create a new facing master page, drag the blank facing icon. Do not release the mouse button until the cursor changes to a down-pointing arrow—the list will scroll, if necessary.

- **Changing an existing blank facing page to a blank single page.** Drag the blank single icon directly on top of the document page icon, releasing the mouse button when it highlights.

- **Changing an existing blank single page to a blank facing page.** Drag the blank facing icon directly on top of the document page icon, releasing the mouse button when it highlights.

- **Removing an applied master page.** If a document page is currently linked to a master page, you can break the link by dragging a blank icon directly on top of the document page icon, releasing the mouse button when it highlights. All master page items are removed, while nonmaster page items are untouched.

- **Clearing the contents of a master page.** When you drag a blank page icon onto an item in the master page area (making sure it highlights), two things happen:

  - An alert appears, asking if it's okay to replace the master page with the blank page. Click OK to remove the contents of the master page.

  - If you drag a blank page icon that differs from the master page type—for example, when you drag a blank single onto a facing master page—you change the master page type as well as remove its contents.

See Also

File: New: **Document**
File: **Document Setup**
Page: **Page Overview**
Page: **Insert**

Duplicate Master Page

To duplicate a master page, select the desired item in the master page area, and click this button. The new master page contains the exact contents of the original. The name doesn't duplicate—instead, the next available prefix is used. For example, if two master pages already exist, a duplicate is named "C-Master C," regardless of what the other two are titled.

This option is not available when a document page is selected.

See Also

Page: **Page Overview**

Delete Page

Click this button to remove the currently selected master or document pages.

When you delete a master page currently in use, every document page based on it converts to a blank page (no letters appear on the palette icons). The master page information is removed from each page, but the page-specific information remains untouched.

When you delete a document page, you also delete its contents. The remaining document pages are affected as follows:

- In a single-sided document, the pages following the deleted page bump up.

- When you delete a left- or right-facing page, you change the orientation of the pages that follow. For example, if you delete page 4 of a facing-page document, page 5 becomes page 4, which converts it from a right-facing to a left-facing page; page 6 becomes page 5, which converts it from a left-facing to a right-facing page; and so forth. If the pages are based on a facing master page, this can wreak havoc with your page layouts. To avoid this effect, do one of the following:

  - If possible, delete the right-facing page as well as the left. This way, the orientation of the following pages is not affected.

  - Insert a blank page in the location of the one you just deleted, bumping the following pages back into their original orientation.

Special Notes

When you delete a page, an alert appears, asking if its okay. To bypass the alert, (Option) [**Alt**]-click the Delete button.

See Also

Page: **Delete**

Page Number

This field displays the number of the currently highlighted palette icon. When no pages are highlighted, it displays the number of pages in the document.

Click this field to access the Page: **Section** dialog.

See Also
Page: **Section**

CHAPTER 16

The Style Sheets Palette

The Style Sheets Palette displays all paragraph and character style sheets currently available in the document. It serves two purposes:

- You can *apply* style sheets by clicking the desired item in the palette. This is similar to choosing an item from the Style: **Character Style Sheet** or **Paragraph Style Sheet** submenus, but here, the styles are accessed much more easily. (See "Applying Paragraph Styles" and "Applying Character Styles" later in this chapter.)

- You can *review* applied styles by inserting the flashing cursor in a body of text and noting the item that highlights in the palette. This status report is particularly useful when you have many styles that appear the same on-screen, but have different "invisible" settings, such as tab stops.

There are five ways to add items to the Style Sheets Palette:

- **Define new styles**. By choosing Edit: **Style Sheets**, you can create the style sheets you need one by one.

- **Append existing styles**. By choosing File: **Append** (or clicking the Append button in the Edit: **Style Sheets** dialog), you can import styles that exist in a second document.

- **Copy and paste text from a different document**. When you Edit: **Copy** and **Paste** text from one document to another, any style sheets applied to the text are added to the Style Sheets Palette. Note that additional styles may appear, depending on the Based On or Next Style settings of the pasted style sheets. Also, if a pasted style has the same name but different settings as an existing style, a conflict dialog appears. (See "Edit: Paste" in Chapter 6, *The Edit Menu*, for more information.)

- **Drag formatted text from a library**. If a library item contains text formatted with style sheets, they are added to the palette when you drag the item onto a page. The way these style sheets are added is similar to copying and pasting text from another document. (See "File: New: Library" in Chapter 5, *The File Menu*, and "Edit: Paste" in Chapter 6 for more information.)

- **Importing the style sheets in a word processing document.** For example, if you import a Microsoft Word document and check the Include Style Sheets button in the Get Text dialog, any styles defined in the file are added to the Style Sheets Palette. The same is true if you import an XPress Tags file. (See "File: Get Text" in Chapter 5 for more information.)

Reveal and hide the Style Sheets Palette by pressing the F11 key. XPress always remembers the last position of this palette when you quit and relaunch the application.

Special Notes

- The items in this palette are not available unless the Content Tool is active and a text box is selected.

- To access the Edit: **Style Sheets** dialog, (Command) [**Control**]-click an item in the Style Sheets Palette. Although the name you initially clicked is highlighted in the dialog's Style Sheets list, you can select any other style and click the Edit button, or ignore the list and create a new style.

- When you apply a style sheet, XPress simply tags a range of text with the style sheet name. The style's characteristics can be changed at any time using the Edit: **Style Sheets** command. Whenever you edit a style sheet, all text it has been applied to changes to reflect the new formatting settings.

See Also

Page Tools: **Content Tool**
File: New: **Library**
File: **Get Text**
File: **Append**
Edit: **Paste**
Edit: **Style Sheets**
Style: **Character Style Sheet**
Style: **Paragraph Style Sheet**

Applying Paragraph Styles

Paragraph style sheets can only be applied on the paragraph level. XPress considers a paragraph to be any words that exist between two hard returns. In this light, it doesn't matter if a paragraph contains a single letter or spans multiple pages in a chain of text boxes.

To apply a paragraph style from the Style Sheets Palette, click the Paragraph symbol (¶) to the left of the style, or click the style sheet name. Text is affected in the following ways:

- When the flashing cursor is inserted in the text, the entire paragraph is formatted by the style sheet. If the flashing cursor is present but no text is present, subsequently entered text is formatted by the applied style sheet.

- When a paragraph or words within a paragraph are highlighted, the entire paragraph is formatted by the style sheet.

- When multiple paragraphs are highlighted, even if some are partially highlighted, they are all formatted.

- If type styles have been applied to words within a paragraph, they remain when you apply a different paragraph style sheet.

- If any character style sheets have been applied within a paragraph, they remain after you apply a different paragraph style sheet.

Special Notes

- When you import a raw text file (such as ASCII), the imported text is automatically tagged with the current paragraph style:

  - If you draw a text box and import text without applying a style, the text is tagged with Normal, or XPress' default style.

  - If you apply a style called "Body Text" before choosing File: **Get Text**, all imported paragraphs are tagged with the Body Text settings.

  - When you import into a box that already contains text, the active style at the position of the flashing cursor is applied to the new text.

- When you import a locally formatted word processing file (one that doesn't contain style sheets), the formatting is retained. The applied style is No Style. The same thing occurs when you import a word processing file containing style sheets without checking the Include Style Sheets box in the Get Text dialog.

Locally Formatting a Paragraph Style

After applying a paragraph style, you can further format the text locally. For example, you can highlight a range of text and apply type styles, change the color, change the point size, and so forth. XPress recognizes this formatting, but the way that it indicates it can be confusing. For example, assume that a single word within a paragraph has been italicized by choosing Style: Type Style: **Italic**:

- If you highlight the entire paragraph, a plus sign (+) appears next to the style sheet name in the palette, indicating that formatting other than the style sheet definition has been applied somewhere in the selected range.

- If you insert the flashing cursor in the italicized word, the plus sign (+) appears next to the style sheet name.

- If you insert the flashing cursor anywhere else in the paragraph, the plus sign (+) does not appear.

You can apply different style sheets to paragraphs containing local formatting, but the results depend on the technique you use:

- If you simply apply a different paragraph style, the local formatting is untouched. The plus sign (+) now appears next to the name of the new style, indicating that the local formatting still exists.

Style Sheets Palette

- If you (Option) [**Alt**]-click a different style, all local formatting is removed as the new style is applied. This technique is the same as choosing No Style, then applying the new style sheet.

- If you (Option) [**Alt**]-click the current style, all local formatting is removed. This technique is the same as applying No Style, then applying the original style again.

Special Notes

- (Option) [**Alt**]-clicking a paragraph style removes any applied character styles, along with the local formatting. If the new paragraph style has a corresponding character style, then both items are highlighted in the palette. If the new paragraph style has no corresponding character style, then no item is highlighted in the character style section of the palette.

Applying Character Styles

Character style sheets can be applied to single letters, words, or sentences within a paragraph.

To apply a character style from the Style Sheets Palette, click the Character symbol (A) to the left of the style, or click the style sheet name. Text is affected in the following ways:

- If the flashing cursor is inserted in a word, the character style has no effect. However, if you enter text immediately after applying the style, it's formatted by the character style settings.

- Any highlighted characters are formatted by the style.

- If the leading of a paragraph is set to a numerical value (instead of "auto"), a character style does not affect the line spacing, regardless of its size.

- If type styles have been applied to the highlighted text, they remain after you apply the character style.

- Applying a character style sheet does not remove the underlying paragraph style. In fact, when you highlight a word formatted by a character style, both styles are highlighted in the Style Sheets Palette.

Special Notes

- When you import a raw text file (such as ASCII), the imported text is automatically tagged with the current character style:
  - If you draw a text box and import text without applying a style, the text is tagged with Normal, or XPress' default style.
  - If you apply a character style called "Inline Heads" before choosing File: **Get Text**, all imported characters are tagged with the Inline Heads settings.
  - When you import into a box that already contains text, the active style at the position of the flashing cursor is applied to the new text.

- When you import a locally formatted word processing file (one that doesn't contain style sheets), the formatting is retained. The applied character style is No Style. The same thing occurs when you import a word processing file containing style sheets without checking the Include Style Sheets box in the Get Text dialog.

Locally Formatting a Character Style

After applying a character style, you can further format the text locally. For example, you can highlight a range of text and apply type styles, change the color, change the point size, and so forth. XPress recognizes this formatting, but the way that it indicates it can be confusing. For example, assume a single word within an inline head character style has been italicized by choosing Style: Type Style: **Italic**:

- If you highlight the entire inline head, a plus sign (+) appears next to the character style name in the palette, indicating that formatting other than the style definition has been applied somewhere in the selected range.

- If you insert the flashing cursor in the italicized word, the plus sign (+) appears next to the character style name.

- If you insert the flashing cursor anywhere else in the inline head, the plus sign (+) does not appear.

You can apply different character styles to the selected range containing local formatting, but the results depend on the technique you use:

- If you simply apply a different character style, the local formatting is untouched. The plus sign (+) now appears next to the name of the new style, indicating that the local formatting still exists.

- If you (Option) [**Alt**]-click a different style, all local formatting is removed as the new style is applied. This technique is the same as choosing No Style, then applying the new style sheet.

- If you (Option) [**Alt**]-click the current style, all local formatting is removed. This technique is the same as applying No Style, then applying the original style again.

Style Sheets Palette

The Style Sheets Palette

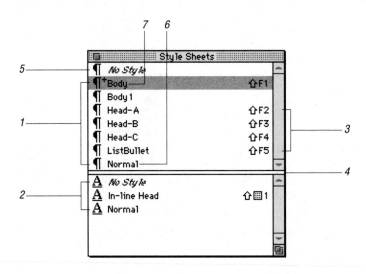

1. **Paragraph Style Sheets**

   This section of the palette lists all currently available paragraph styles. To apply a style, click the desired item (see "Applying Paragraph Styles" earlier in this chapter).

   When editing text, the currently applied style is highlighted. If you select a range of text containing more than one paragraph style, the paragraph symbol (¶) of each style is grayed.

2. **Character Style Sheets**

   This section of the palette lists all currently available character styles. To apply a style, highlight a range of text, and click the desired item (see "Applying Character Styles" earlier in this chapter).

   When editing text, the currently applied style is highlighted. If you select a range of text containing more than one paragraph style, the character symbol (A) of each style is grayed.

3. **Keyboard Equivalent**

   This column displays the keyboard equivalent of a style sheet, if one was defined when the style sheet was created. Pressing the key combination listed here is the same as clicking the item in the palette.

4. **Palette Divider**

   This double line separates the paragraph and character style sheets. To enlarge a section, drag this divider up or down. You can hide all but the first three paragraph styles; you can hide all but the first four character styles.

5. **No Style**

This built-in palette item appears at the start of the paragraph and character style lists. It's not a style sheet—rather, clicking this item removes the style sheet tag, while leaving the formatting untouched.

For example, if you apply a paragraph style called "Body Text," then click No Style, the text doesn't appear to be changed. However, if you later edit the Body Text style sheet and save the changes, the No Style text will not change to reflect the new settings.

XPress regards No Style text as if it were locally formatted. If you apply a style sheet to text tagged as No Style, all formatting—including type styles, colors, different sizes, and so forth—is completely replaced with the style sheet settings.

To simultaneously choose No Style while applying a new style sheet—thereby removing all local formatting—(Option) [**Alt**]-click the desired style.

6. **Normal**

This item represents XPress' default style sheet, existing so the program has a starting point for formatting text. Most often, appears on two occasions:

– When you draw a text box and manually enter text.

– When you draw a text box, choose File: **Get Text**, and import a word processing document without checking the Include Style Sheets box.

To maintain better control of your text, don't attempt to edit this style sheet to format your text. If necessary, create a new style.

7. **Local Formatting Indicator**

The plus sign (+) indicates that text within the applied style has been locally formatted. (See "Locally Formatting a Paragraph Style" and "Locally Formatting a Character Style," earlier in this chapter, for more information.)

Special Notes

• **Auto-Renamed Style.** The asterisk (*) in the **Style Sheets** Palette indicates that a conflicting style name has been automatically renamed by XPress. This only occurs when the style sheet conflict dialog appears (when appending same-named styles or importing text with style sheets named the same as current document styles), and you click the Auto-Rename button.

The Style Sheets Palette Pop-Up

To access this small pop-up, Macintosh users must hold down the Control key and click the specific style sheet they wish to affect. Windows users must right-click the style sheet. The "Style Sheet Name" that appears in each command depends on the actual item you click in the palette.

Edit "Style Sheet Name"

When you click a paragraph style, this command opens the Edit Paragraph Style Sheet dialog. When you click a character style, it opens the Edit Character Style Sheet dialog. The current style is active in the dialog, allowing you to immediately edit its settings. When you close the dialog, the new settings are applied to every occurrence of the applied style sheet.

Choosing this command is the same as choosing Edit: **Style Sheets**, selecting a style from the list, and clicking the Edit button.

Duplicate "Style Sheet Name"

When you click a paragraph style, this command opens the Edit Paragraph Style Sheet dialog. When you click a character style, it opens the Edit Character Style Sheet dialog. It actually creates a new style sheet, based on the settings of the selected style (the style name appears in the Name field, followed by "copy"). Once the dialog is open, establish the new settings, and rename the style, if necessary. When you close the dialog and save the changes, the new style appears in the Style Sheets Palette.

Choosing this command is the same as choosing Edit: **Style Sheets**, selecting a style from the list, and clicking the Duplicate button.

Delete "Style Sheet Name"

Choose this command to remove the style sheet from the palette:

- If the style hasn't been applied in the document, an alert appears, asking if it's okay to delete the style sheet. Click OK to delete.
- If the style has been applied, an alert appears, asking "OK to delete this style sheet and replace it with another style sheet wherever it is used?" You must choose a replacement style sheet from the Replace With pop-up before clicking OK.

Choosing this command is the same as choosing Edit: **Style Sheets**, selecting a style from the list, and clicking the Delete button.

New

Choose this command to create a new style sheet. The Edit Paragraph Style Sheet or Edit Character Style Sheet dialog appears, depending on the type of style you originally clicked.

Choosing this command is the same as choosing Edit: **Style Sheets**, selecting a style from the list, and picking an option from the New pop-up.

CHAPTER 17

The Colors Palette

The Colors Palette displays all colors currently available in the document. It serves two purposes:

- You can *apply* a color by selecting an item and clicking the desired swatch in the palette. The available palette controls differ slightly to reflect a selected text box, picture box, or line. This is similar to using the Style (Picture): **Color** or **Shade** submenus, but here, the colors are accessed much more easily.

- You can *review* applied colors by selecting an item, clicking the appropriate palette control, and noting the color that highlights in the palette. This status report is particularly useful when you have many colors that appear similar on-screen, such as series of TRUMATCH tints.

There are five ways to add items to the Colors Palette:

- **Define new colors.** By choosing Edit: **Colors**, you can define the colors you need one by one.

- **Append existing colors.** By choosing File: **Append** (or clicking the Append button in the Edit: **Colors** dialog), you can import colors that exist in a second document.

- **Import a graphic containing defined colors.** For example, if you import an Illustrator graphic containing two spot colors, they are automatically added to the palette. Once added, you can apply the same colors to any XPress item. (See "File: Get Picture" in Chapter 5, *The File Menu*, for more information.)

- **Copy and paste an item from a different document.** When you Edit: **Copy** and **Paste** an item from one document to another, any applied colors are added to the palette. (See "Edit: Paste" in Chapter 6, *The Edit Menu*, for more information.)

- **Drag a color from a library.** If a library item contains defined colors, they are added to the palette when you drag the item onto a page. (See "File: New: Library" in Chapter 5 for more information.)

Reveal and hide the Colors Palette by pressing the F12 key. XPress always remembers the last position of this palette when you quit and relaunch the application.

Common Uses

Refer to Appendix A, *Common Techniques*, for full descriptions of the following:

- Recoloring text
- Recoloring a frame
- Recoloring a box
- Recoloring an imported image
- Recoloring a line
- Creating reversed type
- Adding enriched blacks to the default Colors Palette
- Creating a one-color blend
- Creating a two-color blend
- Creating linear blends with more than two colors
- Blending into enriched black
- Masking a blend with a line art image
- Masking multiple blends with a line art image
- Creating a spot varnish plate

Common Errors

- **Attempting to color multiple items using the Colors Palette.** When you select multiple items, only a limited number of palette controls are available:
  - When multiple picture or text boxes are selected, you can only recolor their frames and background. When only picture boxes are selected, you can edit their contents by using the Item: Modify: **Picture** panel.
  - When multiple text paths are selected, you can only recolor the path.
  - When multiple lines and boxes are selected, you can only change the background color. Doing so changes the color of the lines as well.
- **Coloring difficult-to-trap items.** Although you can recolor practically everything on a document page, you must remember that any colors destined for on-press reproduction must be trapped. Certain items, such as small text on a colored background or very thin lines, are difficult to trap properly, and certain guidelines must be followed. (See Chapter 18, *The Trap Information Palette*, for more information.)
- **Manually coloring text.** Whenever possible, include text color as part of your style sheet definitions. Not only does this save you time, it reduces the possibility of applying color incorrectly. (See "Edit: Style Sheets" in Chapter 6, and see Chapter 16, *The Style Sheets Palette*, for more information.)

Special Notes

- To access the Edit: **Colors** dialog, (Command) [**Control**]-click an item in the Colors Palette. Although the name you initially clicked is highlighted in the dialog's list, you can select any other color and click the Edit button, or ignore the list and create a new color.

- The Colors Palette doesn't indicate whether a color was defined as spot or process. The best way to confirm a color's separation type is to open the Edit: **Colors** dialog, double-click the color in question, and check the Spot Color box.

- Once a color appears in the palette, you can't override its separation type by importing, appending, or copy/pasting the same color. For example, suppose the Colors Palette currently contains Pantone Reflex Blue defined as a process color. If you import a graphic containing Reflex Blue as a spot color, it's treated as a process color. To change the separation type, you must choose Edit: **Colors**, double-click the appropriate item, and change the Spot Color setting.

- If desired, you can apply colors by dragging a colored swatch from the palette onto a box, line, or path. You don't have to select anything—as you move the swatch over an item, its color temporarily changes. When you release the swatch over an item, the color is applied. This is an inefficient technique, however, because you can only affect line color and a box's background color.

See Also

File: New: **Library**
File: **Get Picture**
File: **Append**
Edit: **Paste**
Edit: **Colors**
Edit: **Style Sheets**
Style (Picture): **Color**
Style (Picture): **Shade**
Item: Modify: **Picture**
The Style Sheets Palette
The Trap Information Palette

Swatch List

The palette's swatch list displays the colors you define or import, as well as XPress' defaults. When applying a color, click the appropriate swatch or color name.

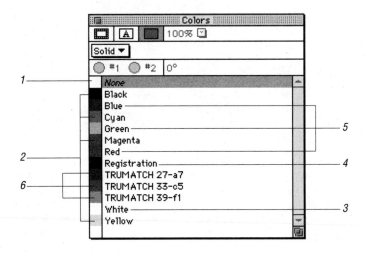

1. None

This item represents no color information whatsoever. Any item tagged with None is transparent. It's only available in two instances:

—   **When coloring a line.** When you first create a text path, for example, it's transparent—this way, only the text following the path is visible.

—   **When coloring the background of a box.** When the background is set to None, a picture or text box is transparent. This allows text, vector-based illustrations, and images masked with a clipping path to be positioned over underlying colors or images.

2. CMYK

Cyan, Magenta, Yellow, and Black are always available in the Colors Palette. They can't be deleted or edited. Their presence allows XPress to readily receive process graphics or convert spot colors to their process components during output. Also, when you choose a color from a process library in the Edit Color dialog, these built-in colors mean that you don't have to define cyan, magenta, yellow, and black individually—they're automatically used by XPress to reproduce the desired ink combinations.

Don't apply these colors from the palette unless you want a tint of only one specific ink. To create CMYK combinations, define a Multi-Ink color or choose an item from a process library.

If your document contains only spot colors, XPress ignores these colors during output.

3. **White**

Another default palette item, this color is actually a knockout command. Wherever it's applied, no ink appears on the final printed piece. Some applications—such as PageMaker—call this color "Paper."

4. **Registration**

Another default palette item, this color applies full ink coverage of all document colors. For example, in a four-color document, it applies C:100, M: 100, Y: 100, and K: 100. In a spot-color document, it applies 100% values of each spot color.

Although it appears black in the palette, do not use this item to color your page elements. In a four-color project, the ink density—400%—is far too high, and in a spot-color project, the resulting color is unpredictable at best. Instead, this color is used by XPress to generate crop and registration marks, which are output at 100% on each separation plate. Apply this color manually only when creating your own crop or registration marks.

5. **RGB**

Red, Green, and Blue appear by default and represent how XPress interprets the values of the RGB electron guns used by your monitor to display color.

Although they exist as spot colors and can be separated, they should be avoided—or better yet, removed from the default palette:

– When used as spot colors, the resulting separation plates do not contain a proper spot ink name, which can lead to confusion during press set-up and reproduction.

– When converted to process colors, Red separates at roughly M: 100, Y: 100; Green separates at roughly C: 77, Y: 100; Blue separates at roughly C: 100, M: 96—values that hardly come close to matching their on-screen appearance.

6. **Defined Colors**

When you define your own colors using the Edit Colors dialog, the names you enter in the Name field are listed alphabetically in the palette.

See Also

Edit: **Colors**
Style (Picture): **Color**

Colors Palette

Cool Blends

Available only when the Cool Blends XTension is loaded, this option allows you to fill a box with a two-color gradient. The Cool Blend palette controls only appear when coloring the background of a box.

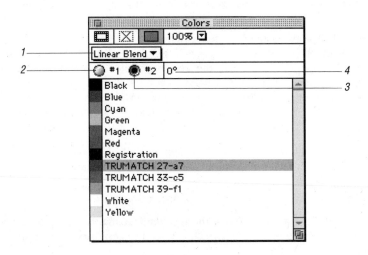

1. **Blend Pop-Up**

   This pop-up defaults to Solid, indicating that no blend is currently applied. To create a blend, choose one of the remaining options:

   Linear Blend
   > This option creates a blend that extends from left (color #1) to right (color #2).

   Mid-Linear Blend
   > This option creates a blend that starts in the middle of the box (#2) and extends to the left and right (#1).

   Rectangular Blend
   > This option creates a blend from a small interior rectangular shape (#2) to the outer edges of the box (#1).

   Diamond Blend
   > This option creates a blend from a small interior diamond shape (#2) to the outer edges of the box (#1).

   Circular Blend
   > This option creates a blend between a small interior circle (#2) to the outer edges of the box (#1).

   Full Circular Blend
   > This option is similar to Circular Blend, but the actual gradient area extends to outer edges of the box.

---

2. **#1**

   To set the first color of a blend, click this button, and select an item from the palette. If a background color has already been applied to the box, it automatically becomes color #1.

3. **#2**

   To set the second color of a blend, click this button, and select an item from the palette. When you first click the button, the color is set to the same as #1.

4. **Angle** (-360° to 360°)

   This value indicates the current rotation of the blend. Positive values rotate counterclockwise. Negative values rotate clockwise.

Common Errors

- **Overextending a gradient.** If a blend is too long, it will not reproduce smoothly. When the range of tones cannot accommodate the length of the gradient, shade-stepping occurs during output. (See "File: Print" in Chapter 5 for more information.) For the best results, keep the following guidelines in mind:

  - Blends running from 100% to 0% should not extend farther than seven or eight inches.

  - Blends with a reduced range—100% to 30% or 40% to 0%, for example— must have a shorter length to avoid banding.

  - The higher the linescreen value, the fewer number of tones can be reproduced—and the likelihood of a long gradient banding increases.

  Note that the advent of PostScript Level 3-compatible output devices will greatly increase the possible length of a printed gradient.

- **Creating a blend between spot inks.** Regardless of the ink types you choose, it's difficult to predict the final printed appearance of a blend. Generally, you'll have more success creating a blend between two process colors—since process inks are transparent, they create new colors when combined. On the other hand, spot inks are opaque. When you create a blend between them, the overprinting halftone spots result in muddy, unpredictable, and often unappealing colors. For the most predictable results, use one-color blends when working with spot inks.

- **Applying a blend to a box containing a Grayscale TIFF.** When this occurs, XPress replaces the lighter values in the image with the blend color defined as ink #1. Ink #2 has no affect on the image. In short, this looks bad, outputs poorly, and reproduces unpredictably.

Special Notes

- To apply a single blend that extends across multiple boxes, select all the boxes, and choose Item: Merge: **Union**. When you apply the blend, XPress treats the separate shapes as a single box. (See "Item: Merge" in Chapter 10 for more information.)

Colors Palette

- When the Accurate Blends box is checked in the Edit: Preferences: Document: **General** panel, blends appear more smoothly on-screen but take longer to redraw. When unchecked, the blends appear less smoothly but redraw more quickly. This option only affects 8-bit (256) color monitors.

See Also

File: **Print**
Edit: Preferences: Document: **General**
Item: **Merge**

Colors Palette (Text Box)

Use the following options to color a selected text box.

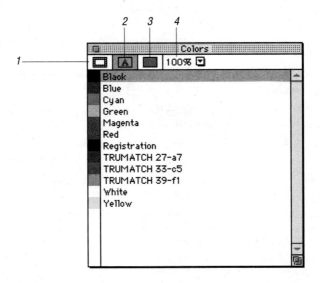

1. **Text Box Frame Color**

   To recolor the box's frame, click this option, and select a color from the list below. If a frame has already been applied, the new color is immediately apparent. If no frame has been applied, no color appears—but when you open the Item: **Frame** panel, the applied color is set in the Frame Color pop-up.

2. **Text Color**

   To recolor text, highlight a range, click this option, and select a color from the list below. If you select a color while the flashing cursor is present, the color is applied to subsequently entered text.

3. **Background Color**

   To recolor the entire text box, click this option, and select a color from the list below. This only affects the box—no text is recolored, even if it's highlighted.

When you set the background color to None, you can see beyond the text to any underlying information.

4. **Shade** (0% to 100%)

This value indicates the tint of the current frame, text, or background color. There are two ways to set a new tint: choose a preset value from the pop-up, or enter your own value in the field.

See Also

Item: Modify: **Text**

Colors Palette (Picture Box)

Use the following options to color a selected picture box.

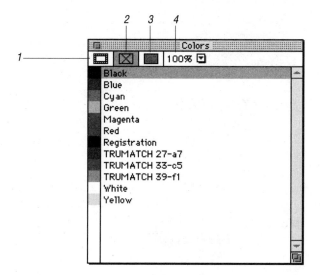

1. **Picture Box Frame Color**

   To recolor the box's frame, click this option, and select a color from the list below. If a frame has already been applied, the new color is immediately apparent. If no frame has been applied, no color appears—but when you open the Item: **Frame** panel, the applied color is set in the Frame Color pop-up.

2. **Picture Color**

   To apply a single color to an imported graphic, click this option, and select a color from the list below.

   This option is only available when the picture box contains one of the following image types: TIFF (1-bit and Grayscale), JPEG (Grayscale), BMP and PCX (1-bit and Grayscale), and PICT (1-bit and Grayscale).

You can't apply a single color to a full color image, any vector-based EPS, or any Photoshop EPS.

3. **Background Color**

To recolor the entire picture box, click this option, and select a color from the list below.

If the image is vector-based or masked by a clipping path, setting this value to None allows you to see beyond the graphic to any underlying information.

If the image is a full-color scan, vector-based graphic, or 1-bit line art, it's not affected by the background color. However, if the image is 8-bit Grayscale, setting a background color other than white may affect the lighter pixels.

4. **Shade**

This value indicates the tint of the current frame, picture, or background color. There are two ways to set a new tint: choose a preset value from the pop-up, or enter your own value in the field. (See "Style (Picture): Shade" in Chapter 8 for more information.)

See Also

Style (Picture): **Shade**
Item: Modify: **Picture**

Colors Palette (Text Path)

Use the following options to color a selected text path.

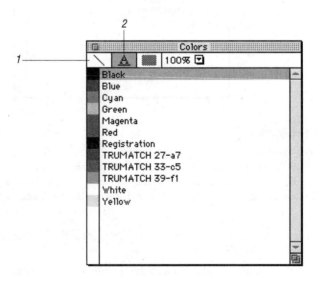

1. **Path Color**

   To recolor a text path, click this option, and select a color from the list below. By default, a text path is .125 pt. thick with a color of None. After applying a new color and width, you may want to change the path's position in relation to the text using the Item: Modify: **Text Path** panel.

2. **Text Color**

   To recolor text aligned to a path, highlight a range, click this option, and select a color from the list below. If you select a color while the flashing cursor is present, the color is applied to subsequently entered text.

See Also

Item: Modify: **Text Path**

Colors Palette (Path/Line)

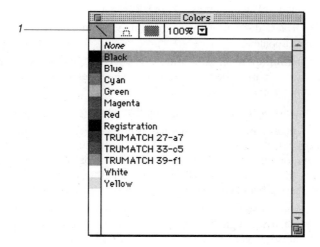

1. **Line/Path Color**

   To recolor a line or path, click this option, and select a color from the list below.

CHAPTER 18

The Trap Information Palette

The Trap Information Palette serves two purposes:

- You can *review* the current trapping value of an item by selecting it and examining the palette.
- You can *manually apply* new traps by selecting an item and entering the desired values in the palette. (This is sometimes referred to as *object-level* or *item-to-item* trapping.)

You can examine or manually trap only one item at a time.

Trapping is a time-honored conventional prepress technique and applies only when different colors abut one another during reproduction. To compensate for any misregistration that may occur on-press, the color of one object is slightly expanded into the adjacent color. By creating this thin overlap, you prevent tiny gaps from appearing between colored objects in your printed piece.

In XPress, traps are based on a relationship between an item and the color positioned beneath it. (Although this color is referred to as the item's *background color*, don't confuse it with the background color of a box. As far as trapping is concerned, a background color can be a four-color image, the color of a line, or multiple shapes, as long as they appear beneath another item.)

For a simple example, suppose a document contains two spot inks: red and blue. If a red line sits above a blue box, the shape of the line knocks out of the box by default. If the line is lighter than the background, the red ink will expand slightly into the blue (or the line *spreads*). If the line is darker than the background, the blue ink will expand slightly into the red (or the line is *choked*). If the concepts of spreads and chokes seem confusing, remember that lighter colors always expand into darker colors. This results in the least-noticeable overlapping of colors.

Trapping values are only generated when a document is separated. When determining the necessary values, XPress follows a hierarchy:

- First, it checks the default automatic trapping values, as entered in the Edit: Preferences: Document: **Trapping** panel.

- Second, it checks to see if the default trapping values of the document differ from the application defaults.

- Third, it checks for custom trapping values built into a color definition. This is done by selecting a color in the Edit: **Colors** dialog, clicking the Edit Trap button, and creating new color-to-color relationships in the Trap Specifications dialog. These override the automatic trapping values.

- Finally, it checks for trapping values applied with the Trap Information Palette. These override the automatic trapping as well as any values built into a color definition.

No matter which trapping method is used, you can only trap information generated in XPress: boxes, text, frames, lines, and paths.

Common Uses

Refer to Appendix A, *Common Techniques*, for full descriptions of the following:

- Trapping with a process bridge
- Using enriched blacks
- Trapping EPS graphics before importing into a document
- Creating XPress-based duotones
- Creating a semi-transparent drop shadow

Common Errors

- **Attempting to trap an imported image.** XPress can't trap the colors of any imported image—even line art or halftones recolored in a document. Vector-based graphics must be trapped in their original application. Pixel-based images can only be forced to knockout or overprint.

- **Over-scaling a trapped EPS graphic.** When you scale a vector-based graphic in XPress, you also scale any applied trap widths. For example, if a graphic contains .3 pt. traps, scaling it to 40% reduces the width to .12 pt.—too thin for most reproduction methods. If you scale it to 200%, the widths increase to .6 pt., which may result in visible overlaps. To avoid this, scale the graphic *before* applying the traps and importing into XPress.

- **Attempting to trap a bitmap frame.** XPress can trap frames consisting of solid lines, dashes, or stripes. However, it can't trap the built-in decorative frames, or any frame generated by the Frame Editor. These are bitmap images and can only be forced to knockout or overprint.

Special Notes

- When an item is not positioned over any other colors, its trap value automatically sets to Overprint. There is no need to change this setting.

- There's no button or switch to "turn off" XPress' trapping controls. However, if you open the Edit: Preferences: Document: **Trapping** panel and set Knockout All in the Trapping Method pop-up, no automatic, color-specific, or manual traps are applied. This is usually required when prepping a document to be process by a dedicated trapping program, such as Adobe TrapWise.

- When you drag colored items from a library or paste them from another document, their original trapping values are affected as follows:

  - If no manual traps were applied to the original item, trapping is determined by the Auto Amount settings in the Edit: Preferences: Document: **Trapping** panel of the current document.

  - If the original color had a built-in trap specification, this value only transfers if the color doesn't already exist in the current document. If a color with the same name already appears in the Colors Palette, the original trap specifications are ignored in favor of the current color.

  - If a manual trap was applied to the original item, it carries over to the current document.

- If you're familiar with creating traps in Illustrator or FreeHand, it's important to note that XPress applies trap widths differently. In an illustration program, traps are based on an overprinting stroke. Because strokes straddle the path they're applied to, the trap value equals one half of the stroke width. For example, a .6 pt. stroke results in a .3 pt. trap. In XPress, no such divisions are required—when you specify a .3 pt. trap, the result is a .3 pt. trap.

- XPress doesn't output trapping information when printing composites. To proof your traps, you must print separations on at least a 600 dpi laser printer. Very few color output devices—3M's *Rainbow* is a notable example—include trapping when printing composites.

See Also

Appendix A (**The Trap Information Palette**)
File: **Print**
Edit: Preferences: Document: **Trapping**
Edit: **Colors**

Overprinting Black

One hundred percent black is the only color that successfully overprints. In other words, when black is printed on top of other inks, it remains black. (When any other color ink overprints—spot or process—the result is always a new color.)

Therefore, black items don't need to be trapped. XPress understands this and auto-matically sets the following information to overprint:

- Black type
- Black lines
- Black frames
- Black boxes
- Imported 1-bit line art

As soon as any of these items are recolored, the overprint command is removed.

Special Notes

- With vector-based illustrations, it's best to set your blacks to overprint or knockout in the original application. However, you can force all the black information to overprint during output by checking the Overprint EPS Black box in the File: Print: **Options** panel. This command has no effect on Photo-shop EPS files or black tints.

- If you don't want a black item to overprint, think twice before setting it to knockout. Remember: knockouts receive no trapping whatsoever. To create the impression of a knockout black, apply a negative trap width (at the very least, set Auto Amount (—) in the Trapping pop-up). This creates a trap by choking the black shape with the underlying colors.

- Because of ink transparency, large areas of process black fail to conceal underlying inks or paper grain very well. For example, if you place a black box over a four-color image, the underlying shapes are slightly visible after printing on-press. To compensate for this shortcoming, you can add cyan, magenta, or yellow components to the black, enriching it for better coverage. (See "Using Enriched Blacks" in Appendix A for more information.)

See Also

Appendix A (**The Trap Information Palette**)
File: Print: **Options**

Trapping White

Although white items don't receive any ink during printing, XPress still considers white a separate color. Therefore, white items can be affected by trapping commands:

- By default, all white items knockout.
- If you trap a white item, no ink overlap occurs—rather, positive values expand the item, and negative values contract it. For example, if you draw a 6 pt. white line over a colored background, it knocks out, resulting in a 6 pt. line during output. If you apply a trap of .5 pt., each side of the line expands by .25 pt. during output, resulting in a 6.5 pt. line. A trap of −.5 pt. contracts each side by .25 pt., resulting in a 5.5 pt. line.

- If a white item is set to overprint, it simply doesn't appear during output. The underlying colors are not affected.

Trapping to Multiple Colors

When a single-colored item abuts more than one color, XPress traps the item as follows:

- If the underlying colors have positive trapping values, XPress spreads the item by the smallest of the values. For example, this occurs when a light-colored item is placed above darker colors.

- If the underlying colors have negative trapping values, XPress chokes the item by the smallest value. For example, this occurs when a dark-colored item is placed above lighter colors.

- If the underlying colors are a mix of positive and negative values, XPress applies the Indeterminate value, as entered in the Edit: Preferences: Document: **Trapping** panel.

- If an item is placed over a blend created from the Colors Palette, XPress applies the Indeterminate value.

- If an item is placed over a four-color image, XPress applies the Indeterminate value.

- If an item is placed over a Grayscale halftone or 1-bit line art, XPress applies the Auto Amount value.

- If an item is placed over a vector-based graphic—whether color or black and white—XPress applies the Indeterminate value.

Special Notes

- When determining the positive or negative values, XPress first refers to the auto trap settings, then checks the trap relationships built into the color definitions. (See "The Trap Specifications Dialog" in Chapter 6, *The Edit Menu*, for more information.)

Trapping Pop-Up

Each item in the Trap Information Palette is controlled by the Trapping pop-up, which contains the following options:

- **Default**. When this option appears, no manual trapping has been applied. Instead, the selected item is trapped according to the values entered in the Trap Specifications dialog or the Edit: Preferences: Document: **Trapping** panel, in that order. The current trap value displays in the field to the right of the pop-up.

- **Overprint**. When this option appears, the selected item overprints the underlying colors.

- **Knockout.** When this item appears, the selected item knocks out of the underlying colors.

- **Auto Amount (+).** When this item appears, the selected item is spread by the current Auto Amount value, entered in the Edit: Preferences: Document: **Trapping** panel.

- **Auto Amount (–).** When this item appears, the selected item is choked by the current Auto Amount value, entered in the Edit: Preferences: Document: **Trapping** panel.

- **Custom.** When you choose this option, the field to the right of the pop-up changes to Knockout. From there, you can enter your own trap value from –36 pt. to 36 pt. (in .001 increments). Negative values choke; positive values spread. As long as this option is chosen, you can continue to edit the value as desired.

See Also

Edit: Preferences: Document: **Trapping**

Palette: Trapping a Text Box

The following options appear when a text box is selected.

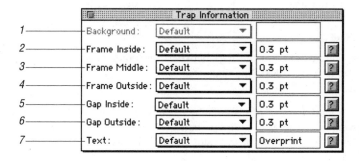

1. **Background**

   This option indicates the current trap applied to a colored box. It's only available when a box doesn't have a frame.

2. **Frame Inside**

   The Frame values are only available when the selected box contains a frame.

   This option indicates the trap between the inner edge of the frame and the background color of the text box. If the background is set to None, this option indicates the trap between the inner edge of the frame and any other underlying colors.

Trap
Information

3. **Frame Middle**

This value is available when the following frame types are applied to the box:

- **Stripes.** When a frame contains multiple stripes, this value indicates the trap between the inner frame edges and the underlying colors.

- **Dashes.** When a frame contains dashes, this value indicates the trap between the endcaps of each dash and the underlying colors.

- **Dots.** When a dashed frame consists of only dots (in other words, no horizontal lines exist between the endcaps), this is the only option available. This value indicates the trap between each dot and the underlying colors.

This option is not available when a solid frame is selected.

4. **Frame Outside**

This option indicates the trap between the outer edge of the frame and the underlying colors.

5. **Gap Inside**

The gap options are available only when a dashed frame contains a gap color, as specified in the Item: **Frame** panel. Note that trapping between the dashes and the gap color is controlled by the Frame Middle option. Striped frames containing a gap color are also controlled by Frame Middle.

This option indicates the trap between the inner edge of the gap color and the background color of the text box. If the background is set to None, this option indicates the trap between the inner edge of the frame and any other underlying colors.

6. **Gap Outside**

This option indicates the trap between the outer edge of the gap color and any underlying colors.

7. **Text**

This option is only available when text is highlighted. It indicates the trap between colored text and the background color of the box. If the background color is None, it indicates the trap between text and any underlying colors.

Palette: Trapping a Picture Box

The following options appear when a picture box is selected:

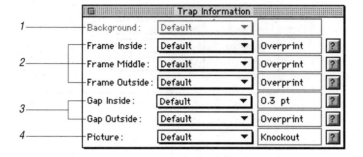

1. **Background**

   This option indicates the current trap applied to a colored box. It's only available when a box doesn't have a frame.

2. **Frame Options**

   The Frame values are only available when the selected box contains a frame.

   The Frame Inside option indicates the trap between the inner edge of the frame and the background color or the contents of the box. Otherwise, the options are the same as those described previously in "Palette: Trapping a Text Box."

3. **Gap Options**

   The gap options are available only when a dashed frame contains a gap color, as specified in the Item: **Frame** panel.

   When a gap is applied to a dashed frame, Gap Inside indicates the trap between the gap color and either the box's background color or its contents. Otherwise, the options are the same as those described previously in "Palette: Trapping a Text Box."

4. **Picture**

   This option is not available when the box contains a vector-based or Photoshop EPS. When you import any other pixel-based image, the pop-up displays Knockout by default. The only other option you have is setting the image to overprint.

Palette: Trapping a Line or Path

The following options appear when a line or path is selected:

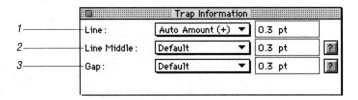

1. **Line**

   When a solid line is selected, this value indicates the trap between the line edges (including the ends of the line) and any underlying colors.

   When a striped line is selected, this value only indicates the trap between the outermost edges of the line and the underlying colors; the inner edges are controlled by the remaining options.

   When a dashed line is selected, this value only indicates the trap between the outer dash edges and the underlying colors.

2. **Line Middle**

   When a solid line is selected, this option is not available.

   When a striped line is selected, this value indicates the trap between the inner line edges and any underlying colors. When a gap color is applied, it indicates the trap between the gap color and the line color.

   When a dashed line is selected, this value indicates the trap between the dash endcaps and the underlying colors.

3. **Gap**

   This option is only available when a striped or dashed line contains a gap color, as specified in the Item: Modify: **Line** panel.

   On a striped line, this value only indicates the trap between the exposed ends of the line and the underlying colors. When a single arrowhead is applied, this value only affects the gap color on the opposite end of the line. When a striped line has arrowheads on both ends, this option is not available.

   On a dashed line, this value indicates the trap between the outer edges of the gap color and the underlying colors. The trap between the gap color and the dash endcaps is controlled by the Line Middle option.

Special Notes

XPress has difficulty trapping dashed lines with rounded endcaps. When automatic trapping is used, only the endcaps are trapped. When you attempt to manually trap the line, the following occurs:

- Changing the Line value in the Trap Information Palette only affects the very first and very last endcap in the line. The outer edges of the line and the remaining endcaps are not affected.

- Changing the Line Middle value has no effect on the dash endcaps.

- When you change the Line and Line Middle values, the results depend on the colors involved. If both the line and the underlying colors are process, the line edges and endcaps are affected. If the line is a spot color and the underlying colors are process (or vice versa), only the endcaps are affected. If both colors are spot colors, the Auto Amount value is applied.

- On a dotted line, automatic trapping fully traps the first and last dot but only affects the endcaps of the remaining dots. To manually trap a dotted line, you must set both the Line and Line Middle values—and even then, only the first dot, last dot, and remaining endcaps are affected.

Palette: Trapping a Text Path

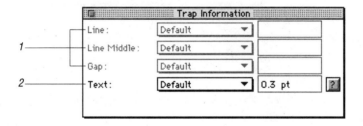

1. **Line, Line Middle, Gap**

   These options are identical to the ones described previously in "Palette: Trapping a Line or Path."

2. **Text**

   This option is only available when text is highlighted. It indicates the trap between colored text and the underlying colors.

Default Trap Pop-up

When an item hasn't been manually adjusted in the Trap Information Palette, the Default Info button appears to the right of each available option. Click and hold this button to review the current status of the item's trap settings. As soon as you apply a new trap value, this button is no longer available, since the default settings are overridden.

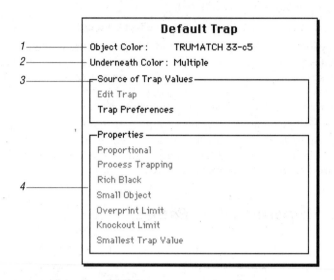

1. **Object Color**

   This displays the color of the currently selected item.

2. **Underneath Color**

   When the selected item is placed over a single color, the color name appears here.

   When the item is placed over multiple colors, one of two options appear:

   — *Multiple* appears here if the trap values of the underlying colors are all positive or all negative.

   — *Indeterminate* appears here if the trap values of the underlying colors are both positive and negative, if the underlying item is a blend, if the underlying item is an imported full-color image, or if the underlying item is an imported vector-based graphic.

3. **Source of Trap Values**

   This section indicates the source of the default trap settings:

   Edit Trap

   This indicates that the current trap value results from changes made in the Edit: Color: **Trap Specifications** dialog. Either the object color or the underlying color (or both) have been edited.

   Trap Preferences

   This indicates that the current trap value results from the default auto trap settings, as entered in the Edit: Preferences: Document: **Trapping** panel.

4. **Properties**

This section indicates the auto trap settings currently affecting the selected item. Active options appear in black; inactive options are grayed out.

Proportional

This appears when an item is being trapped by XPress' proportional trapping algorithm. This only occurs when Proportional Trapping is turned on (in the Edit: Preferences: Document: **Trapping** panel) and the colors have not been edited in the Trap Specifications dialog.

Process Trapping

This appears when an item is being trapped by XPress' process trapping algorithm. This only occurs when Process Trapping is turned on (in the Edit: Preferences: Document: **Trapping** panel), the colors involved are process colors, and the selected item has only one underlying color.

Rich Black

This appears only when an item colored with an enriched black is selected. It indicates that XPress will apply a *keepaway* value to the item, or draw the component colors slightly back from the black edge.

Note that this only occurs when an enriched black is defined using the CMYK mode—if you define an enriched black as a Multi-Ink color, this property is grayed out. (See "Using Enriched Blacks" in Appendix A for more information.)

Small Object

This appears when a line less than 10 pt. or text less than 24 pt. is selected, indicating that XPress will apply a reduced trapping value to preserve the object shape. This only occurs when the object and underlying colors are process.

Overprint Limit

This appears when a color has been set to automatically overprint another color (using the Trap Specifications dialog), but the tint of the selected item falls below the Overprint Limit value, as entered in the Edit: Preferences: Document: **Trapping** panel.

Knockout Limit

This appears when a color has been set to automatically knock out from another color (using the Trap Specifications dialog), but the luminance of the selected item falls below the Knockout Limit value, as entered in the Edit: Preferences: Document: **Trapping** panel.

Smallest Trap Value

This appears when multiple underlying colors trap in the same direction (the values are all positive or all negative). Here, XPress applies the smallest of the values to the selected item. (For more information, see "Trapping to Multiple Colors," earlier in this chapter.)

CHAPTER 19

The Lists Palette

The Lists Palette displays all lists currently available to a document or book.

Lists are used to compile text formatted with specific paragraph style sheets. For example, if a defined list contains a single style sheet titled "Captions," the Lists Palette will track all formatted captions in a document or book, in their order of appearance. If a list contains multiple styles—a chapter title, section names, and subheadings, for example—you can use the Lists Palette to generate a hierarchical outline, similar to a table of contents.

Available lists can come from the following sources:

- **Create new lists using Edit: Lists.** Each list contains a user-specified series of style sheets, their level of appearance in the Lists Palette, and any formatting that occurs once the final list is generated.

- **Copying lists defined in other documents.** This is done by choosing File: **Append** or by clicking the Append button in the Edit: **Lists** dialog.

- **Synchronizing chapters in a book.** When you click the Synchronize button in the Book Palette, the lists in the master chapter are appended by the remaining book chapters. If lists in the remaining chapters are named the same as lists in the master chapter (but have different settings), synchronizing matches the list settings to the master chapter.

Show or hide the Lists Palette by pressing (Option) [**Control**]-F11. XPress always remembers the last position of this palette when you quit and relaunch the application.

Common Uses

Refer to Appendix A, *Common Techniques*, for full descriptions of the following:

- Compiling a table of contents
- Compiling a list of figures

- Compiling a list of figures and captions
- Compiling a list of authors and artists
- Building a formatted list
- Defining lists for a multichapter book

Common Errors

- **Incorrectly compiling lists for a book.** The master chapter must contain the lists (and their component style sheets) that you want to apply to the chapters of a book:

  - If the master chapter contains no lists, you can't select a book list in the Show Lists For pop-up.

  - If the master chapter contains a list not built into the remaining chapters, updating it in the Lists Palette only compiles information from the master chapter. To compile from the remaining chapters as well, you must synchronize the book before clicking Update.

  - If the remaining chapters contain a list with the same name but different settings as the master chapter, each document is compiled according to the settings of its own version of the list. To compile according to the master chapter list, you must synchronize before clicking Update.

- **Building a list before properly inserting the flashing cursor.** When you generate a list by clicking the Build button, it appears wherever the cursor is located. For the best results, create a new text box, and insert the cursor before building a list.

- **Attempting to compile single words.** Lists only recognize paragraph style sheets—you can't compile a word tagged with a character style. Therefore, you can compile a single word only if it exists as a one-word paragraph. To compile a list of single words, use the Index Palette instead.

- **Failing to maintain accurate page numbers.** When you build a list that inserts a page number after each item, the numbers are not linked to the actual document text. Therefore, they can become inaccurate in two ways:

  - If you later edit the source document, bumping paragraph styles to different pages, the list will be inaccurate. When this happens, you must build a new list.

  - If you build a list into a text box linked to the source text, the new information will likely bump paragraph styles to different pages. When this happens, the original page numbers appear in the built list—they're not based on the reflowed text.

- **Attempting to compile style sheets not included in a list.** When you click Update or Build, XPress only recognizes the style sheets included in the current list:

  - If you apply No Style to text formerly tagged with a list style sheet, the text will not be included when you generate a list.

   — If you delete a list style in the Edit: **Style Sheets** dialog and replace it with
another style, the replacement style is only recognized by the Lists Palette
if it's included in the list's definition.

Special Notes

• Once a list is updated, the Lists Palette can be used as a handy "jump-to"
command. When you double-click a list item, XPress jumps to the appropriate page, highlighting the item. When you double-click an item in a book list,
XPress opens the necessary document before jumping to the right page.

• By default, list items are generated in their order of appearance in a document or book. To create an alphabetized list, you must click the Alphabetical
button in the Edit List dialog.

See Also

Appendix A (**The Lists Palette**)
File: New: **Book**
File: **Append**
Edit: **Lists**

Palette Controls

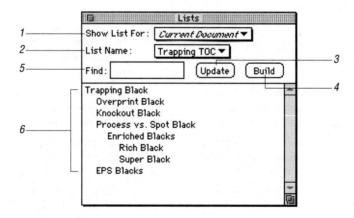

1. **Show List For**

Choose Current Document from this pop-up to access the lists available in an
open document. Choose the name of a book to access the lists available to
the book.

2. **List Name**

This pop-up displays the individual lists available to the document or book, whichever is set in the Show Lists For pop-up. To use the settings of a specific list, choose it from this pop-up.

3. **Update**

Click this button to compile text formatted with the style sheets of the current list. The compiled items appear in the List Items field below. Note that this list doesn't automatically update—if you change the settings of a list or edit a document or book, you must click this button again to compile an updated list.

4. **Build**

Click this button to copy the current list items to an active text box. This text is formatted with style sheets chosen in the Format As pop-up in the Edit List dialog. For the best results, update the list before clicking Build.

5. **Find**

This field allows you to locate a particular list item:

–   When you type the first few letters of the desired item, the palette jumps to the first occurrence of those letters, regardless of the currently high-lighted item.

–   When multiple items share the same name, the palette will only jump to the first occurrence.

6. **List Items**

This scrolling field displays the most recently updated list items. To indent certain style sheet occurrences, you must choose a value from the Level pop-up in the Edit List dialog.

CHAPTER 20

The Index Palette

Use the Index Palette to specify the following information before building a formatted index:

- The individual words or topics listed in the index (known as *entries*)
- Second-, third-, or fourth-level entries (known as *subentries*)
- The page number or page range of each entry and subentry
- Cross-references to other entries

When finished, you can generate the index using Utilities: **Build Index**. That command determines the index type, inserts the necessary punctuation, refers to a predefined master page, and applies the desired style sheets.

While these commands do make the process more efficient, there is no way to fully automate the indexing process. You must still manually tag each entry and subentry, define your own style sheets, and determine your own cross-references.

This palette is only available when the Index XTension is loaded in the XTensions Manager.

Common Uses

Refer to Appendix A, *Common Techniques*, for full descriptions of the following:

- Adding an index entry
- Adding multiple page numbers for a single entry
- Resorting a new index entry
- Resorting an existing index entry
- Adding second-, third-, and fourth-level subentries
- Applying a character style to a page number
- Cross-referencing a current index entry

- Cross-referencing a new index entry
- Placing a cross-reference in parentheses
- Indexing multiple chapters in a book

Common Errors

- **Attempting to index multiple documents.** XPress can only index multiple documents when they're chapters in the same book. If you create indexes for individual documents—even if you've used Page: **Section** to number the pages appropriately—there's no way to compile the separate indexes into one.

- **Compiling nonprinting entries.** If a marked entry has been positioned or affected in such a way that prevents it from appearing in a printed piece, it will not number properly when you build the index. Most commonly, this results when an entry is on the pasteboard or flows past the boundaries of a text box. A dagger (†) will appear next to the entry's page number in the Index Palette. When you build the index, the dagger appears next to the formatted page number. Refer to the Index Palette to find the page number of the offending word, fix the layout problem, and rebuild the index.

  Note that marked words obscured by another page element are not tagged with a dagger in the Index Palette or the formatted index. No warning appears when you build the index.

Special Notes

- For the best results, you must decide whether you're creating a nested or run-in index before using the Index Palette. A nested index allows you to specify up to four formatting levels, each one existing as a single paragraph. A run-in index only uses two levels: one for the entry, one for all the subentries. Additional levels are ignored, since the entry and subentries appear in the same paragraph.
- You can't add same-level entries that have the same page number.
- To specify the index marker color and punctuation used in an index, refer to Edit: Preferences: **Index**.

See Also

Appendix A (**The Index Palette**)
Edit: Preferences: **Index**
Utilities: **Build Index**

Palette Controls

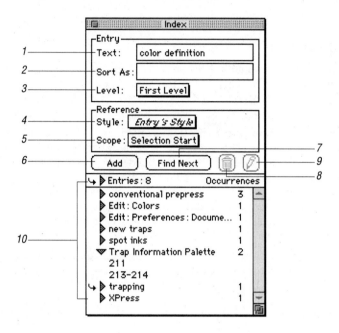

1. Text

This field displays a new or current entry. There are three ways to make text appear in this field:

- Highlight text in the document.

- Insert the cursor and manually type an entry.

- Select an existing index entry from the palette.

An entry can contain up to 255 characters. When you highlight a range of text, only the first 255 characters appear. For the best results, remember that this field should display an entry exactly as you want it to appear in the index.

2. Sort As

This field allows you to override the alphabetical arrangement of an entry. This is often used to reposition first-level entries that begin with a number. By default, such entries are placed at the very start of the index. For example, "50% gray" is placed before words beginning with "A." If you enter "fifty percent gray" in the Sort As field, the entry appears in the "F" section of the index, as if the entry were actually spelled out. (The spelling of the index entry doesn't change; only its order in the index changes.)

3. **Level**

This pop-up allows you to create a hierarchy of entries and subentries. Items tagged as First Level are considered index entries; the remaining levels specify subentries.

Before creating a subentry, you must place the Entries List Arrow beside the correct entry.

Subentries must appear in hierarchical order. For example, you can't jump from a first-level to a third-level entry.

4. **Style**

This pop-up allows you to apply a character style sheet to all the page numbers listed for a specific entry or subentry. Only styles currently available in the document appear here.

A common example is italicizing or boldfacing a page number that contains an illustration.

5. **Scope**

Use this pop-up to establish an entry's page number or range. It also contains the palette's cross-reference command.

It's important to note that these options only take effect when they're selected *before* adding an entry to the Index Palette. When you select an existing entry and set a new item in this pop-up, nothing happens. To change the setting of an existing entry, you must select the entry's *page number*, click the Edit button, then choose a new setting.

Selection Start

When this item is set, the Index Palette lists the page number that contains the open bracket of the entry's index marker.

Selection Text

When this item is set, the palette lists the page numbers from the open to the close bracket of the entry's index marker. When both markers appear on the same page, a single page number is listed; when they appear on different pages, a page range is listed.

To Style

When this item is set, the palette lists the page numbers from the index marker's open bracket to the first occurrence of a specific style sheet after the close bracket. Set the desired style sheet in the pop-up that appears to the right when you select this item. All currently available paragraph styles appear, along with Next (which lists the page numbers to the next new paragraph style).

Specified # of ¶s

When this item is set, the palette lists the page numbers from the index marker's open bracket through a specified number of paragraphs past the close bracket. Set the desired number in the field that appears to the right when you select this item.

To End Of

When this item is set, the palette lists the page numbers from the index marker's open bracket to either the end of the current story or the end of the document. Set the desired item in the pop-up that appears to the right when you select this item.

Suppress Page #

When this item is set, the palette lists no page number for the entry. Most often, this is used for first-level entries that contain no specific number—rather, the underlying subentries contain the page references.

X-ref

When this item is set, the added information is listed as a cross-reference in the currently selected entry. In the pop-up that appears to the right, choose whether the reference is preceded by "See," "See also," or "See herein."

Cross-references appear in two instances: when you want the reader to refer to an index entry *in addition* to the one they've looked up, or you want them to refer to an entry *instead* of the one they've looked up.

6. **Add**

Click this button to add the currently highlighted text to the Index Palette. The way it appears—and the role it plays—depends on the settings in the top half of the palette.

When adding a first-level entry, it's listed alphabetically in the palette. When adding a subentry, you must position the Entries List arrow next to the appropriate item.

7. **Find Next**

When the flashing cursor is inserted in a text box, click this button to jump to the next indexed word, which automatically highlights. When a range of text is highlighted, XPress jumps to the first indexed word appearing after the range.

8. **Delete Entry**

To delete an entry or subentry, select it, and click this button. If an item has any subentries, they're deleted as well. All cross-references to a deleted item are removed.

9. **Edit Entry**

Click this button to change the content of the currently selected entry. To change the spelling of an entry, click the actual entry, then click the Edit button, then enter the new information in the Text field. To change the page numbering, turn down the entry's triangle, select the page number, then click the Edit button.

Double-clicking an item in the palette is the same as selecting it and clicking the Edit button.

10. **Entries List**

This scrolling field lists all the current index entries of document. It contains the following:

Entries

First-level entries appear flush to the left of the list. Second-level entries are indented an eighth of an inch; third-level entries, a quarter-inch; fourth-level entries, three-eighths of an inch.

Arrow

Use this arrow to specify the location of a second-, third-, or fourth-level entry. When a current entry will receive a subentry, click to the left of its triangle to place the arrow. Set the desired item in the Level pop-up, then click Add.

Triangle

Click this icon to display an entry's page numbers and cross-references. Note that cross-references do not display the jump phrase applied with the X-ref pop-up—these are only generated when you build the index.

Page Numbers

An entry's page numbers are only visible when its triangle is turned down. Each number or range appears on its own line. To jump to a specific occurrence in the document, double-click the desired page number. Double-clicking a page number also activates the Edit button, allowing you to change the settings in the Scope pop-up.

Cross-References

An entry's cross-references are only visible when its triangle is turned down. They're listed above the entry's page numbers. To jump to the first appearance of a cross-reference, double-click it in the palette. Double-clicking a cross-reference also activates the Edit button, allowing you to change the settings in the Scope pop-up.

Occurrences

This column displays the number of times each entry has been marked in a document for indexing.

PART IV

Appendixes

Each appendix in this section further expands information covered in the main text.

Appendix A: Common Techniques

The techniques in this section are referred to in the "Common Uses" sections in the main text. I've selected these items for two reasons:

- They best illustrate the proper use of a particular tool or command.
- They represent the dominant techniques and issues required by an advanced XPress user.

To make finding a technique easier, the appendix uses the same structure as the chapters in the book: first the tools are listed, then the menu commands, and then the palettes.

Appendix B: XPress Shortcuts

This section lists over 300 keyboard shortcuts. These items also follow the organization of the book. Each section contains the shortcuts used by a particular toolset, menu, or palette, and appear in the same order as the chapters of the book. Within each section, shortcuts for each tool and command follow the same order as the items discussed in each chapter.

APPENDIX A

Common Techniques

Chapter 1, Page Tools

Rotation Tool

Rotating a single item around a specific point

1. Select a single item with the Item or Content Tool.
2. Determine the pivot-point of the rotation, whether over or outside the selected item. If necessary, mark the location with a hori
3. zontal and vertical ruler guide.
4. After selecting the Rotation Tool, click the pivot-point. Do not release the mouse button.
5. Drag away from the pivot-point, then drag clockwise or counterclockwise as needed.

Rotating a series of duplicate items around the same point

1. Select the desired items with the Item or Content Tool.
2. Determine the pivot-point of the rotation, whether over or outside the selected item. If necessary, mark the location with a horizontal and vertical ruler guide.
3. After selecting the Rotation Tool, click the pivot-point. Do not release the mouse button.
4. Drag away from the pivot-point, then drag clockwise or counterclockwise as needed.

Selecting and rotating a series of items in quick succession

This technique doesn't require selecting any items before rotating:

1. (Option) [**Alt**]-click the Rotation Tool.

2. Click-drag the first item, and rotate as desired. When you release the mouse button, the Rotation Tool remains selected.

3. Click-drag the remaining items as needed.

4. When finished, manually choose the next desired tool.

Chapter 2, Box Tools

Text Box Tool

Use the following keystrokes to insert special characters in a text box. Any characters listed as "n/a" are usually available in separate pi fonts.

Formatting characters

Character	Macintosh	Windows
Open single quote (')	Option-]	Alt-[
Close single quote (')	Option-Shift-]	Alt-]
Open double quote (")	Option-[	Alt-Shift-[
Close double quote (")	Option-Shift-[	Alt-Shift-]
Em dash (—)	Option-Shift-hyphen	Control-Shift-+
Nonbreaking em dash	Option-Command-=	Alt-Control-Shift-=
En dash (–)	Option-hyphen	Alt-Control-Shift-hyphen
Nonbreaking hyphen	Command-=	Control-Shift-hyphen
Discretionary hyphen	Command-hyphen	Control-=

Special symbols

Character	Macintosh	Windows
Copyright (©)	Option-G	Alt-Shift-C
Dagger (†)	Option-Shift-T	Alt-Shift-T
Double dagger (‡)	Option-Shift-7	Alt-035
Paragraph (¶)	Option-7	Alt-Shift-7
Registered (®)	Option-R	Alt-Shift-R
Trademark (™)	Option-2	Alt-Shift-2
Section (§)	Option-6	Alt-Shift-6
Cent (¢)	Option-4	Alt-0162
Pound (£)	Option-3	Alt-0163
Yen (¥)	Option-Y	Control-Alt-hyphen
One half	n/a	Control-Alt-7

Character	Macintosh	Windows
One quarter	n/a	Control-Alt-6
Three quarters	n/a	Control-Alt-8
Infinity (∞)	Option-5	n/a
Multiplication (×)	n/a	Control-Alt-=
Division (÷)	Option-/	n/a
Square root (√)	Option-V	n/a
Greater than or equal to (≥)	Option->	n/a
Less than or equal to (≤)	Option-<	n/a
Not equal to (≠)	Option-=	n/a
Rough equivalence (≈)	Option-X	n/a
Plus or minus (±)	Option-Shift-=	Alt-077
Logical not (¬)	Option-L	Control-Alt-\
Per mil (‰)	Option-Shift-R	Alt-0137
Degree (°)	Option-Shift-8	Alt-0176
Function (*f*)	Option-F	Alt-0131
Integral (∫)	Option-B	n/a
Variation (∂)	Option-D	n/a
Beta (ß)	Option-S	Alt-0223
Mu (μ)	Option-M	Alt-0181
Pi (Π)	Option-Shift-P	n/a
Pi (π)	Option-P	n/a
Sigma (Σ)	Option-W	n/a
Omega (Ω)	Option-Z	n/a

Common Techniques

Foreign characters

When inserting accented characters on a Macintosh, you must type the listed shortcut, then the single desired letter. For example, to insert "ü", press Option-U, then the letter "u".

If working in Windows, you can set the keyboard layout to United States-International (in the Windows Control Panel, click the Keyboard icon, then the Language panel's Properties button). This way, you can enter the desired accent signifier, then the letter. For example, to insert à, type "`", then the letter "a".

Character	Macintosh	Windows
Á	Option-E, then A	Alt-0193
á	Option-E, then a	Alt-0225
À	Option-`, then A	Alt-0192
à	Option-`, then a	Alt-0224
Ä	Option-U, then A	Alt-0196
ä	Option-U, then a	Alt-0228

Character	Macintosh	Windows
Ã	Option-N, then A	Alt-0195
ã	Option-N, then a	Alt-0227
Â	Option-I, then A	Alt-0194
â	Option-I, then a	Alt-0226
Å	Option-Shift-A	Alt-0197
å	Option-A	Alt-0229
Æ	Option-Shift-'	Alt-0198
æ	Option-'	Alt-0230
Ç	Option-Shift-C	Alt-0199
ç	Option-C	Alt-0231
É	Option-E, then E	Alt-0201
é	Option-E, then e	Alt-0233
È	Option-`, then E	Alt-0200
è	Option-`, then e	Alt-0232
Ë	Option-U, then E	Alt-0203
ë	Option-U, then e	Alt-0235
Ê	Option-I, then E	Alt-0202
ê	Option-I, then e	Alt-0234
Í	Option-E, then I	Alt-0205
í	Option-E, then i	Alt-0237
Ì	Option-`, then I	Alt-0204
ì	Option-`, then i	Alt-0236
Ï	Option-U, then I	Alt-0207
ï	Option-U, then i	Alt-0239
Î	Option I, then I	Alt-0206
î	Option-I, then I	Alt-0238
Ñ	Option-N, then N	Alt-0209
ñ	Option-N, then n	Alt-0241
Ó	Option-E, then O	Alt-0211
ó	Option-E, then o	Alt-0243
Ò	Option-`, then O	Alt-0210
ò	Option-`, then o	Alt-0242
Ö	Option-U, then O	Alt-0214
ö	Option-U, then o	Alt-0246
Õ	Option-N, then O	Alt-0213
õ	Option-N, then o	Alt-0245
Ô	Option-I, then O	Alt-0212
ô	Option-I, then o	Alt-0244
Ø	Option-Shift-O	Alt-0216
ø	Option-O	Alt-0248

Character	Macintosh	Windows
Œ	Option-Shift-Q	Alt-0140
œ	Option-Q	Alt-0156
ß	Option-S	Alt-0138
Ú	Option-E, then U	Alt-Control-Shift-U
ú	Option-E, then u	Alt-Control-U
Ù	Option-`, then U	Alt-0217
ù	Option-`, then u	Alt-0249
Ü	Option-U, then U	Alt-Control-Shift-Y
ü	Option-U, then u	Alt-Control-Y
Û	Option-I, then U	Alt-0219
û	Option-I, then u	Alt-0251
Ÿ	Option-U, then Y	n/a
ÿ	Option-U, then y	n/a
¡ (open exclamation)	Option-1	Alt-Control-1 (or Alt-0161)
¿	Option-Shift-/	Alt-Control-/ (or Alt-0191)
«	Option-\	Alt-Control-[(or Alt-0171)
»	Option-Shift-\	Alt-Control-] (or Alt-0187)

Bézier Picture Box Tool

Creating a single picture box from multiple Bézier shapes

To create a picture box with a complex shape, you're not restricted to drawing the entire thing with the Bézier tools. Instead, you can create a smaller series of boxes, rotate and position them as desired, and apply one of the Item: **Merge** options. For example, to create a box consisting of a series of symmetrical shapes, do the following:

1. Draw *one* of the repeating shapes with the desired Bézier box tool.

2. Use Edit: **Copy/Paste** or Item: **Step and Repeat** to generate the number of shapes the box will contain.

3. Position the items appropriately by dragging with the Item Tool.

4. Select all the boxes.

5. Choose Item: Merge: **Union** (see Figure A-1).

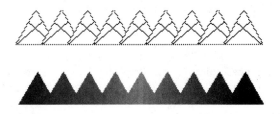

Figure A-1: Repeating and merging multiple Bézier shapes

NOTE

When aligning boxes with straight edges, remember that they must overlap slightly if you want the shapes to interact. It's not enough that one box out-line is positioned *directly* on top of another—the boxes must overlap by at least one monitor pixel.

Chapter 3, Line Tools

Bézier Line Tool

Use the following techniques when drawing a Bézier line.

Drawing a line consisting of straight segments

1. Click with the Bézier Line Tool to place a single corner point. Do not drag as you click.

2. Continue clicking to place a series of points. Each time you click, a straight segment joins the new point with the previous point.

3. After creating the desired segments, choose the Item or Content Tool. The path deactivates, converting to a line.

NOTE

If you use this technique to create a polygonal box, there are two ways to convert the path to a box: click the point you initially placed, or select the Item or Content Tool. The latter method automatically closes the path, re-sulting in a box.

Drawing a basic curved path

To create a curved line, you must drag as you place each point. Click-dragging results in a symmetrical point, with locked and parallel curve handles. There are several ways to utilize these handles as you draw the line.

To start a curved line from a corner point, do the following:

1. Click to place a single point.

2. Click-drag the next point. As you drag, the diamond-shaped handle (moving away from the cursor) affects the curve of the new segment; the square-shaped handle affects the curve of the next segment, which appears when you place the next point.

To start a curved line from a symmetrical point, do the following:

1. Click-drag to place a single point. No segment initially appears—rather, as you drag, the square-shaped handle will affect the curve of the next segment.

2. Place the next point. If you simply click to place a corner point, the segment is only affected by the square handle of the previous point. If you click-drag to place a symmetrical point, the new segment is affected by the previous point's square handle as well as the new point's diamond handle.

NOTE

Don't be misled by the diamond-shaped handle that appears when you click-drag the first point of a line. In other applications (as well as XPress' Bézier box tools), that handle affects the segment that appears when you click the path's initial point to close a shape. However, you can't do this with the Bézier Line Tool, so this handle has no effect. Even if you convert an open line to a closed shape (by choosing Edit: Shape: **Bézier Box**), the two endpoints are joined by a straight segment, whatever this handle's position.

Common Techniques

Joining two open paths

To convert two Bézier lines to a single line, do the following:

1. Determine the two endpoints you want to join.

2. Place the endpoint of one line directly over the endpoint of the other. Do this by dragging one of the points (which edits the shape of the line) or by dragging the entire line (which maintains its shape).

3. Select both lines with the Item or Content Tool. You don't have to select the individual endpoints.

4. Choose Item: Merge: **Join Endpoints**. If the endpoints are spaced too far apart, the command will not work (an alert appears).

Often, you'll want to join two lines by adding a third path between them. This allows you to maintain both the position and shape of the original two lines:

1. Begin drawing the third path by clicking directly on the appropriate endpoint of the first line.

2. Complete the third path by placing a point directly on the endpoint of the second line.

3. Select all three paths with the Item or Content Tool.

4. Choose Item: Merge: **Join Endpoints**.

TIP

You can't join a Bézier line's endpoint to a standard line's endpoint. However, there are two ways around this. First, you can create the straight line using the Bézier Line Tool. Second, you can convert a standard straight line to a Bézier line by selecting it and choosing Item: Shape: **Bézier Line**.

Scaling a path

To scale a path without affecting the current line width, do the following:

1. Select the path, and uncheck the Item: Edit: **Shape** option. Now, the path is surrounded by a bounding box.

2. Drag one of the box handles to resize the entire path with no constraints. Shift-drag to snap the bounding box to a perfect square. (Option-Shift) [**Alt-Shift**]-drag to maintain the current proportions.

To scale a path as well as its line width, you must do the following:

1. Select the path, and uncheck the Item: Edit: **Shape** option.

2. Draw a small item, such as an empty box, over the middle of the path (the size and shape of the box doesn't matter).

3. Select both items, and choose Item: **Group**. The group is surrounded by a bounding box.

4. By holding down the (Command) [**Control**] key when dragging one of the box handles, the path width increases or decreases as you resize. (Command-Shift) [**Control-Shift**]-drag to snap the box to a perfect square. (Option-Command-Shift) [**Alt-Control-Shift**] to maintain the current proportions.

5. Leaving the items selected, choose Item: **Ungroup**.

6. Delete the small item, and continue editing.

Converting an open path to a closed shape

1. Select the open path.

2. Hold down the (Option) [**Alt**] key, and choose Item: Shape: **Bézier Box**. If you simply choose this command, the new box traces the actual path, resulting in a thin and winding box.

Converting a closed shape to an open path

1. Select the closed shape.

2. Choose Item: Shape: **Bézier Line**. Although the shape still appears closed, it's not—the endpoints simply overlap.

3. Activate the Item: Edit: **Shape** option. This allows you to view and edit the new Bézier points.

NOTE

The location of the endpoints is not immediately evident. When you convert a rectangular box, the endpoints are located in the lower-left corner. With an elliptical box, they're located at the bottom. With a Bézier box, the first and last points you originally drew become the endpoints.

Bézier Text Path Tool

Applying text to a closed shape

To apply text to a closed shape, you must first convert the shape to an open path:

1. Select the shape.

2. Choose Item: Shape: **Bézier Line**.

3. Choose Item: Content: **Text** to convert the path to a text path.

4. Activate the Item: Edit: **Shape** option, allowing you to view and edit the new Bézier points.

5. Activate the Content Tool. If the path is already selected, the flashing cursor appears at the location of the first endpoint. If the path is not already selected, click it once with the Content Tool.

6. Enter and format text as desired.

Figure A-2: Applying text around a circular shape

Applying text above a circular shape

1. Create an elliptical text box. Shift-drag the box to create a perfect circle, if desired.

2. Choose Item: Shape: **Bézier Line** to draw a text path.

3. Activate the Content Tool to insert the flashing cursor at the start of the text path (it will be located at the bottom of the circle).

4. Choose Style (Text): Alignment: **Centered** to position the flashing cursor at the top of the circle.

5. Enter and format text as desired (see Figure A-2).

Applying text above and below a circular shape

1. Create an elliptical text box. Shift-drag the box to create a perfect circle, if desired.

2. Duplicate the box by choosing Item: **Step and Repeat**. Enter 0 in the Horizontal and Vertical Offset fields.

3. Leaving the new box selected, choose Item: Shape: **Bézier Line** to convert it to a text path.

4. Activate the Content Tool to insert the flashing cursor.

5. Choose Style (Text): Alignment: **Centered** to place the flashing cursor at the top of the circle.

6. Enter and format the text as desired (see Figure A-3).

Figure A-3: Placing text at the top of the first circle

7. Click in the middle of the circular shape to select the underlying text box.

8. Choose Item: Shape: **Bézier Line** to convert it to a text path.

9. Leaving the path selected, enter 180° in the Angle field of the Measurements Palette. (Do not use the Rotation Tool.)

10. Activate the Content Tool to insert the flashing cursor.

11. Choose Style (Text): Alignment: **Centered** to place the flashing cursor at the bottom of the circle.

12. Enter the desired text. It appears upside down, flowing in the wrong direction.

13. Open the Item: Modify: **Text Path** panel, and check the Flip Text box. The text flows in the right direction but appears on the inside of the path (see Figure A-4).

14. Highlight the text by choosing Edit: **Select All**.

15. Apply a negative baseline shift value to nudge the text to the outside of the text path. Press (Option-Command-Shift) [**Alt-Control-Shift**]-hyphen to make this adjustment on the fly. For the best results, lower the baseline until the tops of any uppercase characters are flush with the text path (see Figure A-5).

Figure A-4: Text applied to the second circle, after flipping it using the Item: Modify: Text Path panel

Figure A-5: The bottom text after adjusting the baseline shift, before (l) and after adjusting tracking

16. Apply your final character formatting to both text paths. If you can only select the path on top, use the Item: **Send to Back** and **Bring to Front** commands to rearrange the layers.

17. Select both text paths with the Item Tool. Drag a marquee around a portion of the paths to select without clicking.

18. Choose Item: **Group** to lock the items together, maintaining their relative position.

TIP

When you apply the baseline shift to the text below the circle, the characters will begin to spread apart. You may need to tighten the tracking to
make the spacing appear the same as the text above the circle.

Chapter 4, Linking Tools

Linking Tool

Use the following commands to create a chain of text boxes.

Creating a text chain on a single page

To link two text boxes, do the following:

1. Draw two empty text boxes.

2. Select the Linking Tool.

3. Click the first box in the chain (or the box that will contain the beginning of
   the text).

4. Click the second box of the chain. The Tool Palette automatically reverts to
   the Item or Content Tool, depending on which one was last active.

NOTE

If one of the text boxes already contains text, it automatically flows to the
first box in the chain. If both boxes contain text, XPress will not allow you
to link the boxes.

To link more than two text boxes on the same page, do the following:

1. Draw the necessary text boxes.

2. Hold down the (Option) [**Alt**] key, and select the Linking Tool.

3. Click the first box of the chain.

4. Click the remaining boxes in the desired order of the chain.

5. When finished, select the Content Tool, and enter or import the desired text.

Creating a text chain on multiple pages

To link two boxes on different pages, do the following:

1. Draw the necessary text boxes.
2. Navigate to the page containing the first box in the chain. (Use Page: **Go To**, the Document Layout Palette, or the Go To Page pop-up in the lower left of the document window.)
3. Select the Linking Tool.
4. Click the first box in the chain.
5. Leaving the Linking Tool active, navigate to the page containing the second box.
6. Click the second box in the chain. The Tool Palette automatically reverts to the Item or Content Tool, depending on which one was last active.

To link more than two boxes on different pages, do the following:

1. Draw the necessary text boxes.
2. Navigate to the page containing the first box in the chain. (Use Page: **Go To**, the Document Layout Palette, or the Go To Page pop-up in the lower left of the document window.)
3. Hold down the (Option) **[Alt]** key, and select the Linking Tool.
4. Click the first box in the chain.
5. Navigate to the page containing the second box in the chain.
6. Click the next box.
7. Continue navigating to the appropriate pages and clicking the boxes in the desired order.
8. When finished, select the Content Tool, and enter or import the desired text.

Adding a new first box to an existing chain

1. Draw the new box in the desired position.
2. Select the Linking Tool.
3. Click the new box.
4. Click the first box of the current chain. If necessary, navigate to the appropriate page. If the chain already contains text, it begins flowing from the upper left of the new box.

Adding a new box to the middle of an existing chain

1. Draw the new box in the desired position.
2. Select the Linking Tool.
3. Click the box in the current chain that will appear before the new box.

4. Click the new box to insert it into the chain. If necessary, navigate to the appropriate page. There's no need to click any subsequent boxes—they're automatically linked.

Adding a new box to the end of an existing chain

1. Draw the new box in the desired position.

2. Select the Linking Tool.

3. Click the last box in the current chain.

4. Click the new box to add it to the end of the current chain. If necessary, navigate to the appropriate page.

Creating an automatic text box on a single-sided master page

To include an automatic text box in the default master page of a new single-sided document, do the following:

1. Choose File: New: **Document** to open the New Document dialog.

2. Uncheck the Facing Pages option. This produces a single-sided master page.

3. Check the Automatic Text Box option. This adds the autolinked text box to the master page.

4. After setting the remaining page dimensions, click OK to create the new document.

To add an automatic text box to an existing document, do the following:

1. In the Document Layout Palette, drag the blank-single icon into the master page area. This creates a new single-sided master page.

2. Navigate to the new master page. Do this by choosing the desired page from the Page: **Display** submenu or the Go To Page pop-up, or by double-clicking the new master page icon in the Document Layout Palette.

3. Draw the desired text box on the master page.

4. Select the Linking Tool.

5. Click the broken-link icon in the upper-left corner of the master page.

6. Click the text box.

7. Return to the document pages, and continue editing.

NOTE

To import text into the new automatic text box, you must use Page: **Insert** to add at least one new page to the document. If using the new master page to format an index, set the appropriate item in the Master Page pop-up of the Build Index dialog.

Creating an automatic text box on a facing master page

To include an automatic text box in the default master page of a new facing-page document, do the following:

1. Choose File: New: **Document** to open the New Document dialog.

2. Check the Facing Pages option. This produces a facing master page.

3. Check the Automatic Text Box option. This adds the autolinked text box to the master page.

4. After setting the remaining page dimensions, click OK to create the new document.

To add an automatic text box to an existing document, do the following:

1. In the Document Layout Palette, drag the blank-facing icon into the master page area. This creates a new facing master page.

2. Navigate to the new master page. Do this by choosing the desired page from the Page: **Display** submenu or the Go To Page pop-up, or by double-clicking the new master page icon in the Document Layout Palette.

3. Draw the desired text boxes on the left- and right-facing master pages.

4. Select the Linking Tool.

5. Click the broken-link icon in the upper-left corner of the master page.

6. Click the text box on the left-facing page.

7. Click the broken-link icon in the upper-left corner of the right-facing page.

8. Click the text box on the right-facing page.

9. Return to the document pages, and continue editing.

WARNING

When editing a facing master page, you cannot link two boxes on different pages. You can only link boxes to the link icon or to other boxes.

Creating an automatic text box consisting of multiple boxes

You cannot create separate, individual automatic text boxes on a single master page. However, the same automatic text box can consist of multiple boxes on the same page. Following the same techniques described previously, create a new master page, and draw the desired boxes. Then do the following:

1. Select the Linking Tool. When working on a master page, you don't have to (Option) [**Alt**]-select the tool to leave it active.

2. Click the broken-link icon in the upper-left corner of the master page.

3. Click the first box in the automatic chain.

4. Click the remaining boxes in the desired order (see Figure A-6).

5. Choose the Item or Content Tool, and return to the document pages. When you import text into the new automatic box, it flows through each box on the page before flowing to the next page.

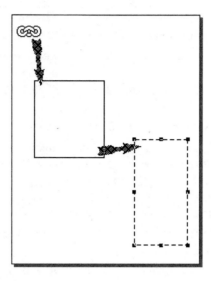

Figure A-6: The linking order of an automatic text box consisting of multiple boxes

---

TIP

To create an automatic text box consisting of symmetrical columns, don't create multiple boxes. Instead, add internal columns to a single box by entering a value in the Cols field of the Measurements Palette. Link the box to the master page as described previously.

Adding a "Continued on" jump line

Use the following technique to generate a jump line that automatically refers readers to text continued on another page. For the best results, a multipage text chain must exist before using this technique:

1. Navigate to the text box that will contain the jump line.

2. At the bottom of the column, draw a text box the same width as the linked box.

3. Position this box at the very bottom of the column. It must overlap the linked text box. If other text boxes are positioned near or underneath the linked box, adjust the layers so the linked box is closest to the jump box.

4. Leaving the box selected, choose Item: **Bring to Front**. (For this command to work properly, the jump box must sit above the linked box.)

5. Choose Item: **Runaround**, and set Item in the type pop-up. This ensures that the jump box will not obscure any underlying text.

6. Enter the desired text of the jump line. For example, type "Continued on page" or "See page" (see Figure A-7).

7. Press (Command) [**Control**]-4 to insert the next page number character. If the underlying box is linked to a box on a different page, that page number appears. If the underlying box is not linked to another box, <None> appears.

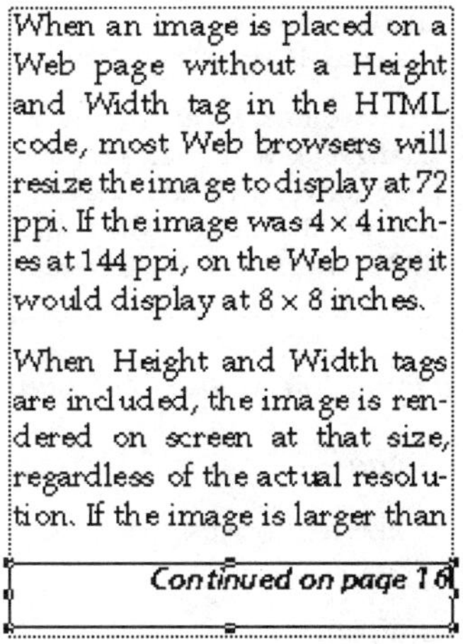

When an image is placed on a Web page without a Height and Width tag in the HTML code, most Web browsers will resize the image to display at 72 ppi. If the image was 4 x 4 inches at 144 ppi, on the Web page it would display at 8 x 8 inches.

When Height and Width tags are included, the image is rendered on screen at that size, regardless of the actual resolution. If the image is larger than

Continued on page 16

Figure A-7: Adding a "jump to" line at the bottom of a linked text box

---

NOTE

As long as the underlying box remains linked, the inserted page number will "know" the location of the text box in the chain. For example, if you insert additional pages between the two text boxes, the jump to number will update appropriately.

Adding a "Continued from" jump line

Using the same steps described previously, draw a box at the start of the desired linked box. Enter the desired text—for example, "Continued from page"—and press (Command) [**Control**]-2 to insert the previous page number character (see Figure A-8).

Continued from page 1

the specified size, image data is discarded when it is displayed. When the image is smaller, image data must be generated on-the-fly to make up the missing space. Not only can this take longer to download and display, but it results in an unacceptible loss of quality.

The two formats are not interchangable, and will produce very different results, depending on the image. GIFs and JPEGs work best for different

Figure A-8: Adding a "jump from" line at the top of a linked text box

Including a text path in a chain

Text paths can be linked just like text boxes. To force text to flow from a box into a path, do the following:

1. Draw the desired box and path.

2. Select the Linking Tool.

3. Click the text box.

4. Click the text path.

5. Enter or import the desired text. When the text reaches the bottom of the box, it flows directly to the path. If desired, you can continue the chain, adding more boxes or paths (see Figure A-9).

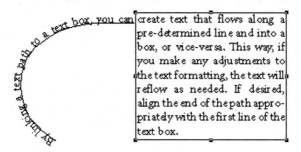

create text that flows along a pre-determined line and into a box, or vice-versa. This way, if you make any adjustments to the text formatting, the text will reflow as needed. If desired, align the end of the path appropriately with the first line of the text box.

By linking a text path to a text box, you can

Figure A-9: Text flowing from a text path to a text box

Chapter 5, The File Menu

File: New: Library

Use the following techniques to create, organize, and implement XPress libraries.

Creating a new library

1. Choose File: New: **Library**.

2. In the New Library dialog, enter a descriptive name. To easily identify the library file later on, include the word "Library" in the name, or add a three-letter extension such as ".lib" or ".qxl" (the Windows extension).

3. Place the file in an easily retrievable location, such as a folder named "Libraries."

4. Click OK. A Library palette appears on-screen, ready to receive new items.

Opening a library

1. Choose File: **Open**.

2. In the navigation window, locate an existing library, and select it.

3. Click Open. The appropriate Library palette appears on-screen, in its last-known position.

Adding items to a library

There are two methods to add items to a library. First, you can use the Edit: **Cut**, **Copy**, and **Paste** commands:

1. Choose the Item Tool.

2. Select an item in the open document.

3. Choose Edit: **Cut** or **Copy**.

4. Click in the open library to determine the position of the new item. To add between existing items, click between them to reveal the two triangles. To replace an existing item, click to highlight it.

5. Choose Edit: **Paste**.

Second, you can drag items directly into the palette:

1. Choose the Item Tool.

2. Select an item in the open document.

3. Drag the items onto the Library palette. Two triangles appear, indicating the location of the new addition. The cursor changes to a pair of eyeglasses.

4. Release the mouse button.

Adding text to a library

Before text can be added to a library, it must first exist in a text box. If the text has been locally formatted, the character attributes are retained. If the text has been formatted with a style sheet, the style definition is retained—but when the text is later retrieved, the way XPress handles the style sheet depends on the open document:

- If the document does not contain the applied style sheet, it's automatically added to the Style Sheets Palette.

- If the document contains a style sheet of the same name, the library text adopts the style sheet of the current document. However, the attributes of the original style sheet are untouched—the result is the same as if you locally formatted the text.

Adding graphics to a library

Before a graphic can be added to a library, it must first exist in a picture box. If the graphic has been scaled, cropped, rotated, or otherwise adjusted, the settings are retained. The way XPress handles graphic links, however, depends on the following:

- If the graphic link was broken when it was added to the library (its status was listed as Missing in the Utilities: Usage: **Pictures** panel), it remains broken when the graphic is retrieved.

- If the link was unbroken when it was added (its status was listed as OK), it remains established only if the original graphic file has not been moved or deleted.

Adding combinations of page elements to a library

1. Select multiple items with the Item Tool.

2. Drag the selection onto the Library palette, as described previously.

TIP

To add the layout of an entire page to a library, select all the items with the Item Tool. You can do this by choosing Edit: **Select All**, but the results depend on whether the active page is a single page or part of a multipage spread. If the page is part of a spread, the items of *every* page in the spread are selected, and therefore added to the library.

Retrieving items from a library

1. Use File: **Open** to open the desired library file.

2. Locate the desired item in the Library Palette.

3. Drag the item from the palette onto the document page.

Labeling items in a library

Label library items to further organize them in the palette:

1. Double-click a palette item to open the Library Entry dialog.
2. Enter a new label in the Label field, or choose an existing label from the pop-up.
3. Click OK.

Labels are not visible in the Library Palette. To utilize them, you must use the palette's Labels pop-up:

- To display every item in the library, set All in the Labels pop-up.
- To display only the items tagged with a specific label, choose the desired label from the pop-up. A checkmark appears next to the active label in the pop-up.
- To hide the items tagged with a specific label, choose the desired label from the pop-up again. The checkmark disappears.
- To display multiple labels, select them in order from the pop-up. Mixed Labels appears in the pop-up.
- To display only the items that have not been labeled, choose Unlabeled from the pop-up.

TIP

If any label other than All has been set in the pop-up, choosing another label results in Mixed Labels. For example, if "Line Art" is currently listed in the pop-up, choosing "Color Images" displays the items labeled "Color Images" in addition to the items labeled "Line Art." This can be confusing, especially if you want to completely switch from one label to another. To do this, set All in the pop-up, then choose the desired label.

Repositioning items in a library

To relocate an item within the same library, drag its thumbnail. The two triangles appear, indicating its new position when you release the mouse button.

Removing items from a library

1. Click the desired item in the palette.
2. Choose Edit: **Cut** or Edit: **Clear**, or press the Delete key. This action cannot be reversed.

Dragging items between libraries

To copy items from one library to another, do the following:

1. Open both libraries using File: **Open.**

2. Drag the item that you wish to copy directly into the library you wish to receive it.

TIP

To remove an item from one library and place it in another, select its thumbnail, and choose Edit: **Cut.** Click in the second library to determine the new addition's location, and choose Edit: **Paste.**

File: New: Book

Use the following techniques when creating and organizing a multichapter book.

Creating a book of chapters with consecutive page numbering

Before creating the actual book, make the following preparations:

- Create the individual documents. These will be treated as separate chapters by the Book Palette.

- Determine each chapter's name, number, and order of appearance in the book.

- Determine the overall design requirements of the book. This includes page dimensions, single/facing page layout, style sheets, custom lines, H&Js, and colors. The first chapter of the book should receive these settings, since it will ultimately become the master chapter of the book, forming the basis that all remaining chapters will follow.

- Save all documents in an easily retrievable location.

To create a book based on these separate files, do the following:

1. Choose File: New: **Book.** In the New Book dialog, name the book, and save it in an easily retrievable location.

2. Click OK. The Book Palette appears on-screen.

3. Click the Add Chapter button. In the navigation window that appears, locate the first chapter of the book. The first chapter you add automatically becomes the master chapter.

4. Click the Add Chapter button again to add the next chapter. As you can see in the palette's Pages column, the next chapter is automatically sectioned to create consecutive page numbering.

5. Continue clicking the Add Chapter button to add the remaining chapters.

Defining a new master chapter

1. Select the desired chapter in the Book Palette.

2. Click the M column beside the chapter. The M appears, and the chapter title appears in bold lettering.

NOTE

When you define a new master chapter, the remaining chapters are not automatically synchronized. If necessary, you must still click the Synchronize button.

Synchronizing a book

To synchronize the book chapters to the current master chapters, click the Synchronize button.

There are two reasons to synchronize:

- After initially adding chapters to a book, synchronizing ensures that the style sheets, colors, and H&J settings of the master chapter are available in the remaining chapters.

- If you change these settings in the master chapter while editing the book, synchronizing ensures that the changes are applied to the remaining documents.

WARNING

If you change these settings in any chapter other than the master chapter, synchronizing removes the changes—remember, the master chapter is used as the basis for this command. To apply these changes to the rest of the book, you must redefine this chapter as the new master chapter (as described previously) before synchronizing.

Creating a book with sectional page numbering

When you add chapters to a book, they're automatically sectioned—the first page of each document is tagged as Book Chapter Start in the Section dialog. If you only want sequential page numbering throughout all the chapters, there's no need to create additional sections.

Often, you'll need to alter the numbering of each chapter. For example, you may want an introductory chapter to be numbered with lowercase Roman numerals. Or you may want each page number preceded by the chapter number (2-11, 3.18, and so forth). In these cases, you'll need to resection the individual chapters:

1. Open the desired chapter.

2. Navigate to the first page of the document.

3. Choose Page: **Section**. In the Section dialog, Book Chapter Start is checked but grayed out.

4. Check the Section Start box.

5. Enter the desired changes. If changing the number format of the chapter, choose an option from the Format pop-up. If adding a prefix, enter it in the Prefix field (don't forget the hyphen, period, or whichever character will fall between the prefix and the page number).

6. Click OK, and save the document. The Book Palette displays the new numbering (see Figure A-10).

7. Repeat as necessary for any remaining chapters.

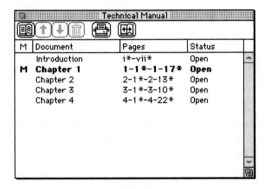

Figure A-10: Multiple sections displayed in the book palette

NOTE

To remove a manually added section and revert the chapter to the palette's default consecutive numbering, do the following: open the chapter, navigate to the first page, choose Page: **Section**, and check the Book Section Start box. Repeat as necessary for the remaining chapters.

Editing the style sheets of a book

To uniformly edit the style sheets of a book, do the following:

1. Edit the existing style sheets in the master chapter.

2. Click the Synchronize button. The new settings take effect wherever the style sheets have been applied.

If you delete a style sheet in the master chapter, synchronizing does not remove the style sheet from the remaining chapters. Although this technique is often used to remove a style sheet and uniformly replace it with another throughout a single document, it will not transfer to other chapters. You'll have to delete the style sheet in each document.

Editing the H&Js of a book

To uniformly edit the H&Js of a book, do the following:

1. Edit the existing H&Js in the master chapter.

2. Click the Synchronize button. The new settings take affect wherever the H&J settings have been applied.

If you delete an H&J in the master chapter, synchronizing does not remove it from the remaining chapters. Although this technique is often used to remove an H&J and uniformly replace it with another throughout a single document, it will not transfer to other chapters. You'll have to delete the setting in each document.

Editing the colors of a book

To uniformly edit the settings of colors that already exist in a book, do the following:

1. Edit a color in the master chapter. Do not change its name.

2. Click the Synchronize button. The new settings take effect wherever the colors have been applied.

If you delete a color in the master chapter, synchronizing does not remove it from the remaining chapters. Although this technique is often used to remove a color and uniformly replace it with another throughout a single document, it will not transfer to other chapters. You'll have to delete the color in each document.

Since you can only synchronize existing colors if you don't change their names, this may not be the most efficient technique. On one hand, if the chapters contain a process color named "Brown," you can change the CMYK components at any time to create a lighter or darker shade. When you synchronize, the Brown settings in each document are replaced with the new values. However, if the book contains a spot color you must keep the color names accurate.

Outputting a book

To print a single chapter, do the following:

1. Select the chapter in the Book palette.

2. Click the Print button.

3. Establish the desired settings in the Print dialog, and click OK.

To print consecutive chapters, do the following:

1. Shift-click the chapters in the Book Palette.

2. Click the Print button.

3. Establish the desired settings in the Print dialog, and click OK.

To print nonconsecutive chapters, do the following:

1. (Command) [**Control**]-click the desired chapters in the Book Palette.

2. Click the Print button.

3. Establish the desired settings in the Print dialog, and click OK.

To print all chapters, do the following:

1. Click the first chapter in the Book Palette.
2. Shift-click the last chapter to select them all.
3. Click the Print button.
4. Establish the desired settings in the Print dialog, and click OK.

File: Open

Opening a PageMaker document in XPress

You must install an XTension, such as *PM2Q* from Markzware, that allows you to convert PageMaker documents into fully operational XPress files.

It is possible to open an XPress document in another application. With the exception of PageMaker, you can only open one page at time in the remaining industry standard graphics applications. The program in question determines the necessary technique.

Opening an XPress document in PageMaker

You must use *QuarkXPress Converter*, a standalone application available for free from Adobe's web site, to convert an XPress document into a fully operational PageMaker file.

Opening an XPress document in Illustrator

Use File: **Save Page as EPS** to save the page as a noneditable EPS document. In Illustrator choose File: **Open**, and locate this file. The page elements are fully editable with Illustrator's tools and commands. It's important to note that the page boundaries of the XPress document are represented by an identically sized box filled with white—depending on your reasons for opening the file in Illustrator it may be more convenient to select and delete this box.

Opening an XPress document in FreeHand

Use File: **Save Page as EPS** to save the page as a noneditable EPS document. In FreeHand, choose File: **Open**, and locate this file. The resulting information can be scaled, rotated, and positioned, but the elements cannot be individually edited. If you absolutely must access this information in FreeHand, you will have more success by opening the image in Illustrator first, saving the file as an Illustrator EPS, and opening that file in FreeHand.

Opening an XPress document in Photoshop

After saving the page as an EPS, there are two ways to bring this information into Photoshop. First, you can simply choose File: **Open** from within Photoshop and choose the appropriate XPress document. From there, Photoshop *rasterizes* the image, or converts it into the pixels it requires. This may not be the most effective way, however, since you can only import the entire size of the page, and any area not occupied by a page element converts to nontransparent white. For the best results, open the XPress EPS file in Illustrator delete the box representing the page boundaries, save it as an Illustrator EPS, and open *that* file in Photoshop. This way, the page elements are surrounded with transparent pixels, allowing you a more flexible basis for image editing.

File: Get Text

Supported Macintosh text file formats

Format	Macintosh	Windows	Extension
ASCII	Yes	Yes	.TXT
ClarisWorks 4.0	No	No	.CWK
Corel WordPerfect 3.x	Yes	No	.WP3
HTML	No	No	.HTM
MacWrite II	Yes	No	none
MacWrite Pro	Yes	No	none
MS Word 98	No	No	.DOC
MS Word 6.0	Yes	Yes	.DOC
MS Word 5.x	Yes	No	.DOC
MS Word 4.x	Yes	No	.DOC
MS Works 3.0	No	No	none
MS Works 2.0	Yes	No	none
RTF	Yes	Yes	.RTF
WordPerfect 2.x	No	No	.WPD
WriteNow 3.0	Yes	No	none

Supported Windows text file formats

Format	Macintosh	Windows	Extension
ASCII	Yes	Yes	.TXT
ClarisWorks 4.0	No	No	.CWK
Corel WordPerfect 8.x	No	No	.WPD
Corel WordPerfect 7.x	Yes	Yes	.WPD
Corel WordPerfect 6.x	Yes	Yes	.WPD
HTML	No	No	.HTM
Lotus Ami Pro 3.0	No	No	.SAM
Lotus Ami Pro 2.0	No	Yes	.SAM
Lotus Word Pro 96	No	No	.LWP
MS Word 97	No	No	.DOC
MS Word 95	Yes	Yes	.DOC
MS Word 6.0	Yes	Yes	.DOC
MS Word 2.0	No	Yes	.DOC

Format	Macintosh	Windows	Extension
RTF	Yes	Yes	.RTF
WordPerfect 5.x	No	Yes	.WP
WordPerfect 4.x	No	No	.WP
WordStar	No	No	.WS
XyWrite III Plus	No	Yes	.XY

File: Print

Outputting a document composite

When you output a composite, you print a document with no separations or registration marks. All "colors" are printed on the same page, reproducing as closely as possible a piece reproduced on-press. This is most often done on laser printers and color printers. Composites are very rarely printed to imagesetters. To output a composite, follow these steps:

1. Choose File: **Print**.

2. In the Document panel, uncheck Separations.

3. Set the Registration pop-up to Off.

4. In the Setup panel, set the target printer in the Printer Description pop-up.

5. If printing to a laser printer, set the desired linescreen in the Output panel's Frequency field. Ordinarily, this field defaults to the target printer's optimal value. Change the value only if necessary.

6. Click Print.

NOTE

Note that lower resolution laser printers cannot reproduce the same screen values of high-resolution imagesetters—because of their larger printer dot sizes, high screen values result in longer output times, darker images, and reduced gray tones. When printing to a 300 dpi device, set a value up to 65–75 lpi. On a 600 dpi device, set a value up to 85–90 lpi. On a 1200 dpi device, set a value up to 110–120 lpi.

Outputting separations

When outputting a document for on-press reproduction, you must create *color separations*. Here, the color information of each document page is printed onto its own color plate, which is then used by your print shop to create the press plates that apply ink to paper. There are four types of color separation:

- **One color.** Here, a document contains only one color usually either black or a single spot color. When outputting a black and white file, you only need to output a composite (as described previously). When outputting a single spot color you must produce a color separation (as described in the procedure that follows).

- **Spot colors.** Here, a document contains a series of single ink definitions. When output, each document page separates into one color plate for each spot ink.

- **Process colors.** Here, the document colors are based on combinations of cyan, magenta, yellow, and black ink percentages. When output, each document page separates into four color plates—one for each process ink.

- **Process and spot colors.** Here, the document contains CMYK colors (such as imported full-color images) as well as single ink definitions (such as a corporate logo's metallic ink). When output, each document page separates into four color plates (for the CMYK inks), plus as many as necessary for each spot ink.

To output separations, follow these steps:

1. Choose File: **Print**.

2. In the Document panel, check Separations.

3. In the Registration pop-up, choose Centered or Offset. This option is important—otherwise, the separated plates will not contain color names, crop marks, or registration marks.

4. In the Setup panel, set the target printer in the Printer Description pop-up.

5. In the Output panel, set the desired linescreen in the Frequency field. If unsure of the value, consult your print shop.

6. Set the desired option in the Plates pop-up. (See File: **Print** for full descriptions of this and the remaining Print dialog settings.)

7. Click Print.

Outputting laser proofs during preflight

Before turning a document over to a vendor for final output, it is highly recommended that you first output a laser composite and laser separations. This serves the following purposes:

- The composite allows the output specialist to preview the document pages, without scrolling through the document on-screen. If necessary, mark this printout with any special notes or requests.

- The separation proves that your document can be successfully separated on a PostScript output device. If you cannot produce the separations on your own printer, the chances are good that the service bureau will encounter the same problems. This also allows you to double-check color definitions, font selections, graphic information, trapping widths (if your printer is at least 600 dpi), and other issues that simply aren't apparent in a composite printout. If you fail to supply laser seps when you send a project to a service bureau, you may be required to sign a "run blind" waiver, absolving the vendor of responsibility for incorrectly constructed documents. In short, you will have to pay for any unusable film.

Use the steps described in the previous techniques to output laser composites and separations. Note that your laser printer may be too small to output the document's page dimensions. For example, you may be producing an 11 by 17-inch piece, but your laser printer only handles letter-sized paper. If this is the case, you have two options: reduce the scale of the printouts (in the Reduce or Enlarge field of the Page Setup panel), or tile the printouts (by selecting an option from the Tiling pop-up of the Document panel).

Creating a PostScript file

Occasionally, you'll need to print your document into a single file, instead of sending the information directly to an output device. This is usually done for three reasons:

- The document must be processed by a separate program. For example, programs like Adobe TrapWise and page imposition software require PostScript files.

- A designer wants a project printed without having an output technician responsible for opening the document, installing the fonts, linking the graphics, and so forth. When created properly, PostScript files are completely self-contained—they possess the fonts, graphics, and XTensions information required for proper output—and can be downloaded directly to an output device.

- It is extremely rare that a service bureau will output Windows-based documents to an imagesetter from a PC. Instead, the project is usually saved as a PostScript file, copied onto a Mac workstation, and downloaded to the printer.

NOTE

There are obvious disadvantages to sending a PostScript file, as opposed to standard documents, to a service bureau for output. Once created, these files cannot be opened or edited. If any incorrect settings are present, they cannot be repaired by the service bureau. Instead, the client assumes full responsibility for any unusable film pages that result. If unsure of what file type to provide, contact your output vendor.

When creating a PostScript file, follow this checklist:

- Make sure you have enough space on your hard drive or removable media to contain the file.

- Turn on all fonts used by the document, as well as any fonts embedded in imported EPS files.

- Double-check (and if necessary, reestablish) all graphic links in the Utilities: Usage: **Pictures** panel.

- Activate the appropriate printer driver.

- Establish the settings in the File: **Print** panels—just as if you're generating final output—including color separation commands, registration marks, and line-screen value.

- Set the output destination to *file*, not *printer*.

- Name the file appropriately.

- Make sure your output vendor supports your type of removable media.

To create a PostScript file from a Macintosh workstation, do the following (these steps assume you're using LaserWriter 8.x, Apple's standard PostScript level 2-compatible driver):

1. Choose File: **Print**.

2. In the five Print dialog panels, establish the desired output settings.

3. Instead of clicking the Print button, click Printer.

4. In the dialog that appears, set File in the Destination pop-up.

5. Click Save.

6. In the dialog that appears, set PostScript Job in the Format pop-up.

7. Click Binary.

8. If you're certain the file will be downloaded to a PostScript Level 2-compatible output device, click Level 2 Only. If unsure, click Level 1 Compatible. For the best results, contact your output vendor—Level 1 files can take considerably longer to print on a Level 2 device.

9. Set All But Standard 13 in the Font Inclusion pop-up.

10. In the navigation window, locate the final destination of the file.

11. Click Save. You return to the File: **Print** dialog.

12. Click Print to generate the file.

Before creating a PostScript file from a Windows workstation, you must set the PostScript level:

1. Choose Start: Settings: **Printers** to access the Printers dialog.

2. Double-click the desired PostScript printer.

3. Choose File: **Properties**, and select the PostScript panel.

4. Click Advanced.

5. If you're certain the file will be downloaded to a PostScript Level 2-compatible output device, click Use PostScript Level 2 Features. If unsure, click Use PostScript Level 1 Features. For the best results, contact your output vendor—Level 1 files can take considerably longer to print on a Level 2 device.

6. Click Tagged Binary Communications Protocol or Pure Binary Data. Consult your vendor for the desired setting.

7. Click OK.

Common Techniques

To generate the actual file, you must create a virtual printer:

1. Choose Start: Settings: **Printers** to access the Printers dialog.

2. Double-click the Add New Printer icon to access the Add Printer Wizard.

3. Select the output device that the file will ultimately output to. If asked whether the device is a local or network printer, choose either option (it doesn't matter which one you choose).

4. In the Available Ports dialog, choose FILE: (Creates a file on disk).

5. Name the virtual printer descriptively, such as "Print to File" or "PostScript File." This item will now appear in the Print dialog's Printer pop-up. Once selected, the open document will print into a PostScript file.

6. If necessary, create virtual printers for every output device you'll use that requires PostScript files.

Manually tiling a document

The Tiling pop-up's Manual option allows you print a specific part of a page. This is particularly helpful when outputting a document too large for your laser printer. While this option takes a little more time and manual effort than Automatic tiling, it gives you much more precise control over the printed results. Follow these steps:

1. Navigate to the first page you want to output.

2. Set the zero origin of the ruler guides to the upper-left corner of the page. XPress will output the page information to the lower right of the origin—or the upper-left corner of the page. (Note that you cannot place the origin above or to the left of the document bounds.)

3. Choose File: **Print**.

4. In the Document panel, set Manual in the Tiling pop-up.

5. Set the desired page range. If you print all pages, XPress will output the upper-left corner of every page. To limit the tile to the current page, enter its number in the Pages field.

6. Click Print.

7. When the screen clears, set the zero origin to the next starting point. (You may want to refer to the first printout before doing this.)

8. Repeat as necessary until the entire page or pages are tiled.

NOTE

XPress doesn't begin tiling at the *exact* location of the zero origin. Instead, it begins about a quarter inch above and to the left, in an attempt to create a thin overlap with the previous tile.

Chapter 6, The Edit Menu

Edit: Paste

Duplicating text boxes, picture boxes, and lines

1. Select the desired items with the Item Tool.

2. Choose Edit: **Cut** or **Copy**.

3. Choose Edit: **Paste**. The new item appears in the center of the document window. To position duplicate items more accurately, use Item: **Step and Repeat** or Item: **Duplicate**.

Copying highlighted text from one box to another

1. Highlight a range of text with the Content Tool.

2. Choose Edit: **Cut** or **Copy**.

3. Select another text box, and insert the flashing cursor in the desired location.

4. Choose Edit: **Paste**.

NOTE

All copied text is tagged with a style sheet, even if it's only Normal or No Style. If you paste into an area formatted with the same style sheet, the text retains the original style. If you paste into an area tagged with a different style, the copied text retains its original formatting, but it adopts the different style sheet. (In the Style Sheets Palette, a plus sign (+) appears next to the current style listing, indicating that it regards the pasted text as locally formatted.)

Copying text from one document into another

To copy an entire text box, follow these steps:

1. In the first document, select the desired text box with the Item Tool.

2. Choose Edit: **Cut** or **Copy**.

3. Switch to the second document.

4. Choose Edit: **Paste**. The new box appears in the center of the document window.

NOTE

If the text is formatted with a style sheet identical to one in the second document, the style is retained. If the copied text is formatted with a style sheet not contained in the second document, that style is added to the Style Sheets Palette when you paste. If the copied text is formatted with a style sheet named the same but formatted differently as one in the second document, the pasted text retains its original formatting but adopts the style sheet of the second document. (In the Style Sheets Palette, a plus sign (+) appears next to the current style listing, indicating that it regards the pasted text as locally formatted.)

To copy highlighted text, follow these steps:

1. In the first document, highlight a range of text with the Content Tool.

2. Choose Edit: **Cut** or **Copy**.

3. In the second document, select a text box, and insert the flashing cursor in the desired location.

4. Choose Edit: **Paste**.

NOTE

If the text is formatted with a style sheet identical to one in the second document, the style is retained. If the copied text is formatted with a style sheet not contained in the second document, that style is added to the Style Sheets Palette when you paste—but if you paste into a range of existing text, the pasted text adopts the current style sheet. (In the Style Sheets Palette, a plus sign (+) appears next to the current style listing, indicating that it regards the pasted text as locally formatted.) If you paste into a new text box, the original style is retained.

Copying text from one application to another

1. Highlight a range of text in another application.

2. Switch to the desired XPress document.

3. Select a text box, and insert the flashing cursor in the desired position.

NOTE

When copying and pasting, XPress cannot retain any style sheets created in another program. When you paste into a new text box, the text is formatted with the Normal style sheet. When you paste into text formatted with another style, the new text fully adopts the current style.

Pasting the contents of a picture box

1. Select a picture box with the Content Tool.

2. Choose Edit: **Cut** or **Copy**.

3. Select another text box, leaving the Content Tool active.

4. Choose Edit: **Paste**. The graphic retains its internal rotation, scale, coloring, and position values.

NOTE

When copying and pasting a graphic to another document, XPress remembers the graphic's current link status. For the best results, make sure the status is OK (in the Utilities: Usage: **Pictures** panel) before copying.

Pasting the contents of a page

1. Reset the rulers' zero origin.

2. Use the Item Tool to select the entire contents of a page. If desired, you can choose Edit: **Select All**—provided that you're aware that this command selects every item on a multiple-page spread.

3. Choose Edit: **Copy**.

4. Note the X and Y coordinates in the Measurements Palette.

5. If pasting the page contents in another document, switch to the desired file (if necessary, reset the zero origin). If pasting the page in the same document, navigate to the desired page (if necessary, add a new page using Page: **Insert**).

6. Leaving the Item Tool active, choose Edit: **Paste**.

7. Enter the noted X and Y coordinates in the Measurements Palette to place the page elements in their original position.

NOTE

Although you can duplicate pages using this technique, you can do it much more efficiently by dragging thumbnails. (See "View: Thumbnails," later in this appendix for more information.)

Anchoring a picture box in a text box

To have a small graphic flow with the text in a box or chain, you must *anchor* the image. Follow these steps:

1. Select the desired graphic with the Item Tool.
2. Choose Edit: **Cut** or **Copy**.
3. Select the text box that will contain the graphic with the Content Tool.
4. Insert the flashing cursor in the desired location.
5. Choose Edit: **Paste** (see Figure A-11).

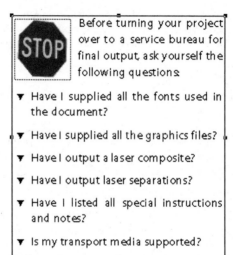

Figure A-11: An anchored picture box with a Right and Bottom runaround of 10 pt.

Use the following techniques to edit the anchored picture box:

- To alter the alignment of the text in relation to the box, select the picture box with the Item Tool, open the Item: Modify: **Box** panel, and choose an **Align with Text** option.
- To edit the contents of the picture box, click it with the Content Tool.
- To add a runaround value to the box, select it with the Item Tool, and choose Item: **Runaround**.
- To delete the anchored box, insert the flashing cursor just after it in the text box, and press Delete.

Anchoring a text box in another text box

To flow a separate text box through a larger text box or chain, you must *anchor* the box. Follow these steps:

1. Select the desired text box with the Item Tool.
2. Choose Edit: **Cut** or **Copy**.
3. Select the text box that will contain the anchored box with the Content Tool.
4. Insert the flashing cursor in the desired location.
5. Choose Edit: **Paste**.

Use the following techniques to edit the anchored text box:

- To alter the alignment of the text in relation to the box, select the anchored box with the Item Tool, open the Item: Modify: **Box** panel, and choose an Align with Text option.

- To edit the contents of the anchored box, click it with the Content Tool, and highlight the desired text.

- To add a runaround value to the box, select it with the Item Tool, and choose Item: **Runaround**.

- To delete the anchored box, insert the flashing cursor just after it in the text box, and press Delete.

Anchoring a line in a text box

To flow a line through a text box or chain, you must *anchor* the line. Follow these steps:

1. Select the desired line with the Item Tool.
2. Choose Edit: **Cut** or **Copy**.
3. Select the text box that will contain the anchored line with the Content Tool.
4. Insert the flashing cursor in the desired location.
5. Choose Edit: **Paste**.

Use the following techniques to edit the anchored line:

- To edit the line, click it with the Item or Content Tool, and make the desired changes.

- To add a runaround value to the line, select it with the Item Tool, and choose Item: **Runaround**.

- To delete the anchored line, insert the flashing cursor just after it in the text box, and press Delete.

Common Techniques

NOTE

If your intent is to place a rule above, below, or between paragraphs, use the Style (Text): **Rules** command instead.

Anchoring a vertical rule in a text box

Although XPress allows you to anchor a vertical line in a text box, it doesn't allow you to alter the alignment of the text in relation to the line, as it does with anchored boxes. For example, you cannot insert an anchored line that abuts the left indent of the text. However, you can partially simulate this effect by anchoring a picture box:

1. Draw a vertical box at the desired length and thickness. (The minimum thickness is 1 pt.)

2. Select the box with the Item Tool.

3. Choose Edit: **Cut** or **Copy**.

4. Select the text box that will contain the graphic with the Content Tool.

5. Insert the flashing cursor in the upper left of the text box.

6. Choose Edit: **Paste**.

7. Select the anchored box with the Item Tool.

8. In the Item: Modify: **Box** panel, click Ascent under Align with Text.

9. In the Runaround panel, enter a Right Offset value (see Figure A-12).

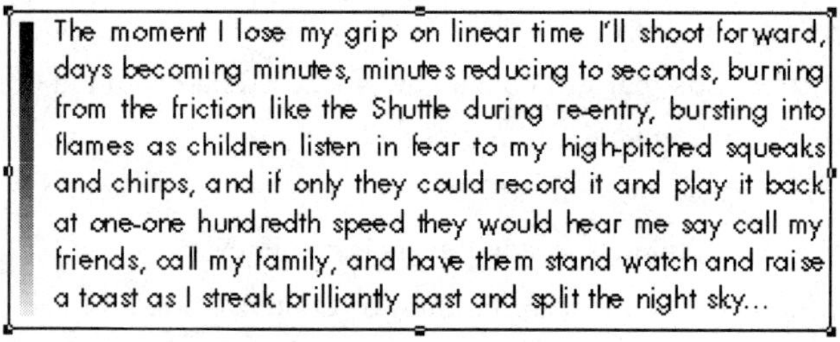

The moment I lose my grip on linear time I'll shoot forward, days becoming minutes, minutes reducing to seconds, burning from the friction like the Shuttle during re-entry, bursting into flames as children listen in fear to my high-pitched squeaks and chirps, and if only they could record it and play it back at one-one hundredth speed they would hear me say call my friends, call my family, and have them stand watch and raise a toast as I streak brilliantly past and split the night sky...

Figure A-12: An anchored vertical box, after setting Align to Text and adding a Right runaround of 10 pt.

Edit: Find/Change

Performing a variable search using the wildcard character

To search for variable spellings of a word, use the wildcard character as follows (for this example, let's search for all instances of "color" and "colour"):

1. Choose Edit: **Find/Change**.

2. In the Find What field, enter "col\?r". To insert the wildcard character, press (Command) [**Control**]-?, or simply type a backslash followed by a question mark.

3. Establish the remaining settings of your search. For example, if you enter "color" in the Change To field, all instances of "colour" are changed to "color." If you simply establish formatting settings, both occurrences of the word are affected without changing the spelling.

NOTE

This technique only has limited uses. For example, the "line" will not appear in multiple boxes, nor will it appear if it is longer than the box. You may be better off drawing a series of vertical lines, positioning them next to the desired text boxes, and grouping them together.

Edit: Style Sheets

Formatting run-in heads

When a paragraph contains a run-in head, the first few characters, words, or lines appear in a different typeface. Since multiple styles will exist in the same paragraph, you cannot apply a paragraph style sheet to generate this effect. Instead, you must define and apply a character style:

1. Choose Edit: **Style Sheets**.

2. Choose Character from the New button pop-up. The Edit Character Style Sheet dialog appears.

3. Name the style "Run-in head."

4. Using the available options, set the desired formatting of the style.

5. Click OK to return to the Style Sheets dialog.

6. Click Save to close the dialog.

7. Use the Content Tool to highlight a range of text you wish to format.

8. In the Style Sheets Palette, click the new character style.

9. Repeat as necessary throughout the document.

10. If you must change the characteristics of the run-in head, do not locally format the text—instead, choose Edit: **Style Sheets**, double-click the character style in the Style Sheets dialog, and make the necessary changes there.

Formatting a series of "Based On" styles

The Based On option is used when a series of style sheets share many characteristics, but the paragraph formatting differs slightly. For example, if a document (such as the text of this book) contains a style sheet for bulleted items, it typically shares the same font, point size, and leading as the style sheet for body text. However, the Space Before/Space After, indent, and alignment values are specific to each style. By basing the bulleted style sheets on the body text style, you accomplish two things:

• After creating the body text style, you can immediately adopt the character formatting without having to manually establish all the settings again.

• If necessary, you can edit all the shared formatting simply by editing the body text style sheet. Again, this prevents you from having to edit each style sheet individually.

To create a series of Based On styles, follow these steps (for this example, let's use paragraph styles for Body Text and Bullets):

1. Choose Edit: **Style Sheets**.

2. Choose Paragraph from the New button pop-up.

3. In the Edit Paragraph Style Sheet dialog, name the new style "Body Text."

4. Click the Edit button.

5. In the Character Attributes dialog, establish the desired settings for the Body Text style, and click OK.

6. Establish the desired Format, Tab, and Rule settings for the Body Text style.

7. Click OK to close the Edit Paragraph Style Sheet dialog.

8. To create the next style, choose Paragraph from the New button pop-up.

9. In the Edit Paragraph Style Sheet dialog, name the new style "Bulleted Text."

10. Set Body Text in the Based On pop-up. The Body Text character attributes appear in the Description field.

11. Establish the desired Format, Tab, and Rule settings for the Bulleted Text style.

12. Click OK to close the Edit Paragraph Style Sheet dialog.

13. Click Save to close the Style Sheets dialog and save the two new styles.

14. Apply the styles as needed throughout the document.

To change the character attributes of these styles, follow these steps:

1. Choose Edit: **Style Sheets**.

2. Select the Body Text style, and click Edit.

3. In the Edit Paragraph Style Sheet dialog, click Edit.

4. Establish the desired settings in the Character Attributes dialog, and click OK.

5. Click OK to close the Edit Paragraph Style Sheet dialog.

6. Click Save to save the changes. Since the Bulleted Text style is based on the Body Text style, there's no need to specifically edit it—the new character formatting is automatically applied.

Deleting an existing style sheet

1. Choose Edit: **Style Sheets**.

2. Select the desired style in the scrolling list.

3. Click the Delete button. If the style hasn't been applied anywhere in the document, it simply disappears from the list. If it has been applied, the Replacement dialog appears, asking you to select a style sheet to apply to the text currently formatted with the deleted style.

Replacing all occurrences of an existing style sheet

Depending on the length and complexity of your document, a single style sheet can be applied dozens, hundreds, even thousands of times. To replace all occurrences of one style sheet with another, you don't have to apply the changes manually.

If you want to discard the currently applied style sheet, do the following:

1. Choose Edit: **Style Sheets**.

2. If necessary, define the new style sheet you wish to apply universally.

3. Select the style you wish to discard in the scrolling list.

4. Click the Delete button. When the Replacement dialog appears, set the new style in the Replace With pop-up, and click OK.

5. Click Save to close the Style Sheets dialog and apply the changes.

If you want to retain the currently applied style sheet for future use, do the following:

1. Choose Edit: Style Sheets.

2. If necessary, define the new style sheet you wish to apply universally.

3. Select the style you wish to replace in the scrolling list.

4. Click the Duplicate button. The Edit Style Sheet dialog appears, and the new style's name is the same as the original, with "copy" tagged on the end. Click OK to close the dialog (if desired, you can enter a completely new name, but do *not* enter the original style name). The duplicate style appears in the scrolling list.

5. Select the original style you wish to replace again.

6. Click the Delete button. When the Replacement dialog appears, set the new style in the Replace With pop-up, and click OK.

7. Click Save to close the Style Sheets dialog and apply the changes. All occurrences of the original style sheet are replaced with the new style, but the settings of the original style are still available in the duplicate item in the Style Sheets Palette.

Appending style sheets from an existing XPress document

Before style sheets can be appended from another XPress document, that document must be saved after the styles are created. There are two ways to append the styles:

1. In the document that will contain the copied style sheets, choose File: **Append**.

2. Locate the document containing the desired styles, and click Open.

3. In the Append To dialog, select the Style Sheets panel.

4. In the Available window, select the styles you wish to append. Shift-click to select continuous items. (Command) [**Control**]-click to select noncontinuous items.

5. Click the right-pointing arrow to move the style listings to the Including window.

6. When complete, click OK. The selected style sheets are now available in the currently open document.

7. If necessary, choose Edit: **Style Sheets** to make any additional adjustments or additions.

If desired, you can append style sheets directly from the Style Sheets dialog:

1. Choose Edit: **Style Sheets**.

2. Click the Append button.

3. Locate the document containing the desired styles, and click Open.

4. Follow steps 4 through 7 of the previous technique.

NOTE

When you append a style sheet, you also append any colors, Next Style or Based On styles, custom H&Js, or dashes and stripes settings built into the style's definition. There is no need to append these items separately.

Appending style sheets from a Microsoft Word document

To add the style sheets built into an MS Word document to your document's Style Sheets Palette, follow these steps:

1. Choose File: **Get Text**.

2. Locate the desired Microsoft Word file.

3. Check the Include Style Sheets box.

4. Click OK.

NOTE

If any of the styles in the text file are named the same as any existing XPress styles, the Style Sheet Conflict dialog appears, allowing you to rename or re-place the conflicting styles. This dialog almost always appears—both pro-grams include a style sheet called Normal, which is used to specify the default font. When properly using styles sheets, however, these styles should be ignored. If this is the case, it doesn't matter if you rename or replace the conflicting Normal items.

Edit: Colors

Defining a spot color

1. Choose Edit: **Colors**.

2. Click the New button.

3. Choose the desired item from the Model pop-up. In virtually all cases, you'll be referring to a swatch book such as Pantone's Color Formula Guide for spot inks. For this example, set PANTONE Coated.

4. Enter the desired number in the PANTONE field, in the lower right of the dialog. The correlating swatch is automatically selected in the above color list.

5. Check the Spot Color box.

6. If necessary, set a new option in the Halftone pop-up to establish a new screen angle.

7. Click OK.

NOTE

It is important that you do not rename the spot color. This way, the appro-priate color name will appear in the upper left of each film plate when the file is separated.

Defining a color based on CMYK components

To define a color selected from a process swatch book, follow these steps:

1. Choose Edit: **Colors**.

2. Click the New button.

3. Choose the desired color library from the Model pop-up. For this example, choose TRUMATCH.

4. Enter the desired number in the TRUMATCH field in the lower right of the dialog. The correlating swatch is automatically selected in the above color list.

5. Uncheck the Spot Color box.

6. Click OK.

To define a color based on your own CMYK percentages, follow these steps:

1. Choose Edit: **Colors**.

2. Click the New button.

3. Set CMYK in the Model pop-up.

4. Enter the desired values in the CMYK fields in the lower right of the dialog.

5. Uncheck the Spot Color box.

6. Click OK.

NOTE

Unlike spot colors, process colors always separate onto cyan, magenta, yellow, and black film plates. Therefore, you can give each process color a descriptive name, instead of using the numbers of a swatch book.

Defining a multi-ink color

Multi-ink colors allow you to combine preexisting colors in a single color definition. There are three basic ways to approach this technique:

- **Combine spot inks.** Here, you force multiple spot inks to overprint. Since spot inks are opaque, it's difficult to predict the final color. For the best results, set the Halftone value of each spot color to a different option. By default, all new spot colors have a Halftone setting of Black. If overprinting colors have the same angle, the color quality suffers, and *moiré,* or dot patterning, may result. To avoid this, set the Halftone value of the darkest color to Black (which outputs at 45°), and set the Halftone value of the lighter color to Cyan (105°).

  One of the most useful applications of this model is to combine a spot color with a shade of black, resulting in a darker version of the second spot ink.

- **Combine spot and process inks.** Here, you combine spot inks with the CMYK inks of a process job. Only combine these colors when producing a five-, six-, or seven-color job. If you create such a combination in a spot color document, additional plates result when the file is separated.

- **Combine process inks.** Here, you combine either cyan, magenta, yellow, and black inks, or combine predefined swatchbook colors. Note that when you combine swatchbook colors, you are combining two percentages of each CMYK component. For example, if you combine C: 45, M: 15, Y: 75, K: 10

with C: 15, M: 60, Y: 25, K: 0 at 100% shades, the resulting color is C: 60, M: 75, Y: 100, K: 10. If you combine them at 50% shades, the resulting color is C: 30, M: 38, Y: 50, K: 5.

Before creating a multi-ink color you must define the individual colors that will be in it. Then follow these steps:

1. Choose Edit: **Colors**.

2. Click the New button.

3. Set Multi-Ink in the Model pop-up.

4. In the color list, select the first ink.

5. Choose a value from the Shade pop-up. If you don't, the color will not be included in the multi-ink definition.

6. Select the second ink, and choose a value from the Shade pop-up.

7. Repeat as necessary for any remaining inks.

8. Click OK (see Figure A-13).

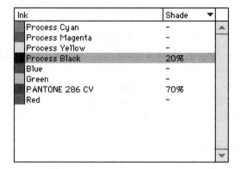

Figure A-13: When defining a multi-ink color you must establish a shade for each ink

---

NOTE

The Spot Ink box is not available when you define a multi-ink color. Instead, XPress uses the setting built into the color definitions of each component ink.

Globally replacing an applied color

Depending on the length and complexity of your document, a single color can be applied to dozens, hundreds, even thousands of items. To replace all occurrences of one color with another, you don't have to apply the changes manually.

If you want to discard the currently applied color do the following:

1. Choose Edit: **Colors**.

2. If necessary, define the new color you wish to universally apply.

3. Select the color you wish to discard in the scrolling list.

4. Click the Delete button. When the Replacement dialog appears, set the new color in the Replace With pop-up, and click OK.

5. Click Save to close the Style Sheets dialog and apply the changes.

If you want to retain the currently applied color for future use, do the following:

1. Choose Edit: **Colors**.

2. If necessary, define the new color you wish to universally apply.

3. Select the color you wish to replace in the scrolling list.

4. Click the Duplicate button. The Edit Colors dialog appears, and the new color's name is the same as the original, with "copy" tagged on the end. Click OK to close the dialog (if desired, you can enter a completely new name, but do *not* enter the original color name). The duplicate color appears in the scrolling list.

5. Select the original color you wish to replace again.

6. Click the Delete button. When the Replacement dialog appears, set the new color in the Replace With pop-up, and click OK.

7. Click Save to close the Colors dialog and apply the changes. All occurrences of the original color are replaced with the new color but the settings of the original color are still available in the duplicate item in the Colors Palette.

Defining a spot varnish

A spot varnish is a thin, transparent, protective coating, applied like an ink over certain page elements during on-press reproduction. Using a varnish is practically the same as adding a spot ink to the output and printing stages: it costs more, and it requires an additional film plate. To create the color that will represent the spot varnish in your document, follow these steps:

1. Choose Edit: **Colors**.

2. Set PANTONE in the Model pop-up.

3. Choose a bright, obviously colored swatch from the color list.

4. Enter Spot Varnish in the name field.

5. Check the Spot Color box.

6. Click OK.

For information on applying such a varnish in your document, see "The Colors Palette," later in this appendix.

Edit: Dashes & Stripes

Creating a dotted line style

Although XPress provides a single dotted line option by default—it's available in the Style (Line): **Line Style** pop-up—you can create dotted lines with different spacing values by doing the following:

1. Choose Edit: **Dashes & Stripes**.

2. Choose Dash from the New button pop-up.

3. Set the Endcap pop-up to Rounded.

4. In the ruler at the top of the dialog, click to place a single arrow at 0%. Do not click-drag to spread the arrows apart—if you do, you'll create an extended dash with rounded endcaps.

5. Click to place single arrows as desired across the ruler. Each arrow appears as a round dot in the dash preview below.

6. Establish the remaining settings as needed (see Figure A-14).

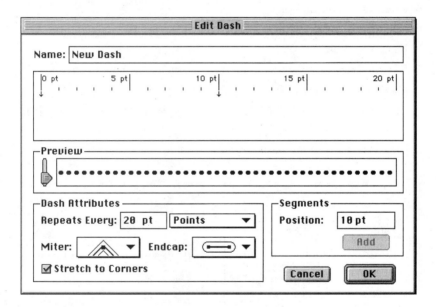

Figure A-14: The Edit Dash settings for a dotted line repeating every 10 pt.

Applying dashes and stripes to a curved line or text-path

To create a curved dash or stripe, define the desired item using Edit: **Dashes & Stripes,** or use the XPress presets. After creating the curve, choose the desired item from the Style (Line): **Line Style** submenu or the Line Style pop-up in the Measurements Palette.

Creating and applying two-color dashes

To apply a gap color to a line or frame specified with a dash, follow these steps:

1. Apply the desired dash using Item: **Frame** or Style (Line): **Line Style**.

2. Open the Item: Modify: **Line** panel.

3. In the Gap section, choose an item from the Color pop-up. If the color you want does not appear, you must first define it using Edit: **Colors**.

4. If desired, choose a tint value from the Shade pop-up.

To create separate dashes of alternating colors, follow these steps:

1. Choose Edit: **Dashes & Stripes**.

2. Choose Dash from the New button pop-up. Name this one "Dash 1."

3. In the Dash Attributes section, enter a number divisible by 4 in the Repeats Every field (for this example, let's enter 20), and choose Points from the associated pop-up.

4. Click-drag a dash that covers the first quarter of the ruler (0 pt. to 5 pt.).

5. Click OK to save the dash.

6. Select Dash 1 in the scrolling list, and click Duplicate.

7. Name the duplicate "Dash 2."

8. (Option) [**Alt**]-click the top of the ruler to remove the current arrows.

9. Click to place a single arrow at 0%.

10. Click-drag a dash that covers the third quarter of the ruler (10 pt. to 15 pt.).

11. Click OK to save the dash.

12. Click Save to close the Dashes & Stripes dialog (see Figure A-15).

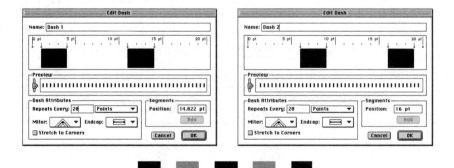

Figure A-15: The Edit Dash settings for separate dashes of alternating colors

---

NOTE

When defining these dashes, do not check the Stretch to Corners box.

To apply these two-color dashes to a frame, follow these steps:

1. Draw the desired box.

2. Choose Item: **Frame**, and apply Dash 1 at the desired weight and color. Click OK.

3. Leaving the box selected, choose Item: **Step and Repeat**. Enter 0 in both offset fields, and click OK.

4. Choose Item: **Frame**, and apply Dash 2. Set the desired color.

5. Select both boxes, and choose Item: **Group** to maintain their relative position.

To apply these dashes to a line or path, follow these steps:

1. Draw the desired line.

2. Choose Style (Line): **Line Style**, and apply Dash 1 at the desired weight and color. Click OK.

3. Leaving the line selected, choose Item: **Step and Repeat**. Enter 0 in both offset fields, and click OK.

4. Choose Style (Line): **Line Style**, and apply Dash 2. Set the desired color.

5. Select both lines, and choose Item: **Group** to maintain their relative position.

Creating a dash with alternating rounded and squared dashes

To create this effect, follow the steps described in the previous technique to create separate, overlapping dashes—only this time, set the Endcap pop-up in one of the dashes to Rounded (see Figure A-16).

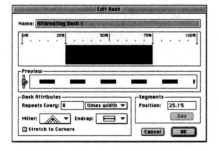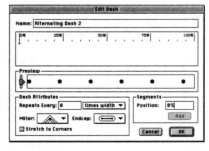

Figure A-16: The Edit Dash settings for alternating dots and dashes

---

Chapter 7, The Style Menu (Text)

Style: Text to Box

Creating and editing type based on Bézier curves

1. Draw a text box or text path.

2. Enter and format the text you wish to convert to Bézier curves. Edit as thoroughly as possible, including all tracking, kerning, and so forth.

3. Highlight the desired characters with the Content Tool.

4. Choose Style (Text): **Text to Box**. While the original characters remain untouched, their Bézier counterparts appear below. Delete the original text if you no longer need it.

5. Position the text as needed.

6. Activate the Item: Edit: **Shape** option.

7. Use the Item Tool and XPress' Bézier editing commands to further edit the character shapes.

8. When finished editing their shapes, uncheck the Item: Edit: **Shape** option.

9. To fill the shapes, apply a background color using the Colors Palette.

10. To stroke the shapes, choose Item: **Frame**, and set the desired weight and color (see Figure A-17).

Figure A-17: Editable text after converting to a box and turning on Item: Edit: Shape

---

NOTE

If you hold down the (Option) [**Alt**] key when choosing Style (Text): Text to Box, the converted shapes appear as an anchored picture box.

Creating and editing a character mask

1. Enter and format the desired text, as described previously.

2. Highlight the desired characters with the Content Tool.

3. Choose Style (Text): **Text to Box**. While the original characters remain untouched, their Bézier counterparts appear below. Delete the original text if you no longer need it.

4. Select the converted text, and choose File: **Get Picture**. Since the converted shapes are a merged picture box, the same imported graphic appears in every character.

5. Position the contents of the picture box by dragging with the Content Tool (see Figure A-18).

Figure A-18: A character mask containing a single graphic

To import a separate graphic into each character, follow these steps:

1. Enter and format text, then convert it to a box, as described previously.

2. Choose Item: Split: **Outside Paths**.

3. Select the individual shapes with the Item Tool, and choose Item: **Group** to maintain their relative positions.

4. Select the first character shape with the Content Tool, choose File: **Get Picture**, and import the desired graphic.

5. Repeat as necessary for the remaining characters.

6. To frame the characters, select them all, and choose Item: **Frame** (see Figure A-19).

Figure A-19: A character mask with a separate graphic in each shape

Creating character-shaped text boxes

To create a text box based on a single character, follow these steps:

1. Enter and format the desired character, then convert it to a box, as described previously.

2. Choose Item: Content: **Text** to convert the picture box to a text box.

3. Enter or import the desired text into the new text box (see Figure A-20).

To create a text box based on multiple characters, follow these steps:

1. Enter and format the desired characters, then convert them to a box, as described previously.

2. Choose Item: Content: **Text** to convert the picture box to a text box. At this point, the characters are still a single merged text box—text will not flow properly through the shapes.

3. Choose Item: Split: **All Outside Paths**.

4. Use the Linking Tool to create a text chain from the first character to the last.

5. Enter or import the desired text into the new text box (see Figure A-21).

Figure A-20: A character-shaped text box, after setting Style (Text): Alignment to Justified, and checking the Run Text Around All Sides box in the Item: Modify: Text panel

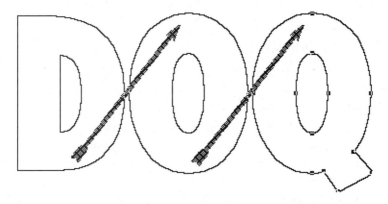

Figure A-21: The linking order of a character-based text chain

For the best results, use the following techniques after importing text into a character-shaped text box:

- Choose Style (Text): Alignment: **Justified** to make both indents follow the contours of the letter-shaped box.

- In the Item: Modify: **Text** panel, check the Run Text Around All Sides box. This way, the text flows consistently around the awkward loops, curves, and angles of the text box.

- If framing the box, apply a Text Inset value in the Item: Modify: **Text** panel. This way, the edges of the text won't be flush against the colored frame.

Style: Formats

Formatting hanging indents

When a paragraph has a *hanging indent,* its first line extends beyond the left indent. Creating this effect requires manipulating the First Line and Left Indent values in the Style: **Formats** dialog. This effect forms the basis for techniques such as bulleted and numbered lists. Follow these steps to create a simple hanging indent:

1. Determine the amount of the indent. Although you can easily change this value later on—and the actual amount will depend on the desired effect—it helps if you have a starting point. For this example, let's use a value of 14 pt.

2. Choose Style: **Format.**

3. Enter 14 pt. in the Left Indent field.

4. Enter –14 in the First Line field. (You must enter the values in this order; since the First Line value is based on the current position of the Left Indent, you cannot enter a value that would position the first line beyond the edge of the text box.)

5. If locally formatting a paragraph, click Apply to preview the effect. If defining a style sheet, save it, and apply it to the desired text.

The paragraph's first line appears to extend 14 pt. beyond the left indent of the paragraph. In actuality, the first line doesn't move, and the left indent is increased by 14 pt. (see Figure A-22).

Formatting bulleted lists

In a bulleted list, the bullets must extend beyond the left indent of the list text. Follow these steps:

1. Create a hanging indent, as described previously.

2. At the start of each first line, press (Option) [**Alt**]-8 to enter a bullet.

3. After the bullet, press the Tab key. The cursor jumps to the left indent. (When you create a hanging indent, XPress automatically places an invisible tab stop at the left indent.)

4. Continue entering the desired text.

5. Repeat steps 2 through 4 for each paragraph of the bulleted list (see Figure A-23).

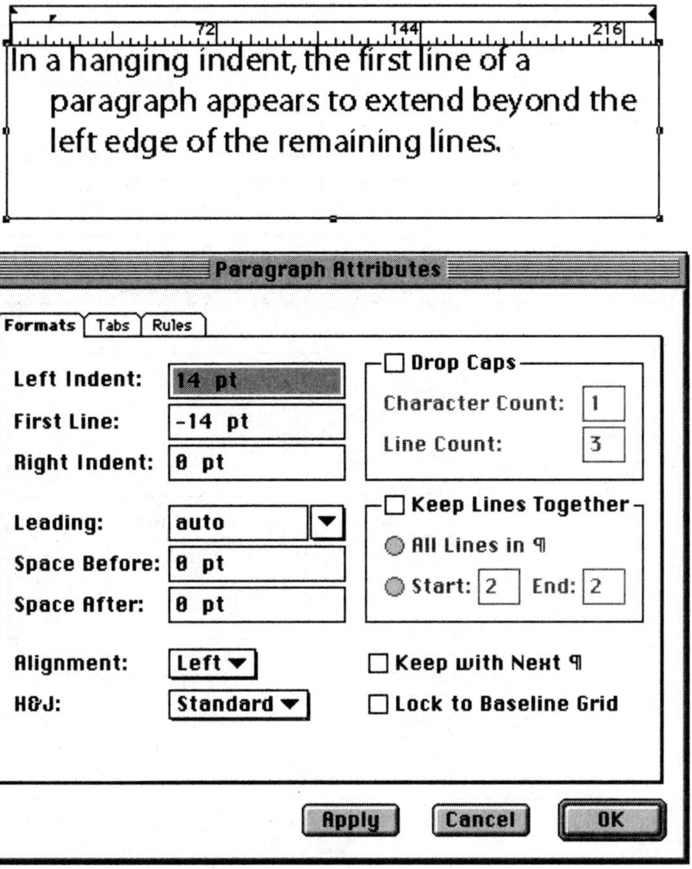

> In a hanging indent, the first line of a
> paragraph appears to extend beyond the
> left edge of the remaining lines.

Paragraph Attributes

| Formats | Tabs | Rules |

Left Indent: `14 pt`
First Line: `-14 pt`
Right Indent: `0 pt`

Leading: `auto` ▼
Space Before: `0 pt`
Space After: `0 pt`

Alignment: `Left ▼`
H&J: `Standard ▼`

☐ Drop Caps
Character Count: `1`
Line Count: `3`

☐ Keep Lines Together
◉ All Lines in ¶
◉ Start: `2` End: `2`

☐ Keep with Next ¶
☐ Lock to Baseline Grid

[Apply] [Cancel] [OK]

Common Techniques

Figure A-22: The Style (Text): Format settings for a 14 pt. hanging indent

---

NOTE

When editing the amount of a hanging indent, remember to match the First Line and Left Indent values. For example, if you want to change the above example to 18 pt., set the Left Indent value to 18 pt., then change the First Line value to –18 pt.

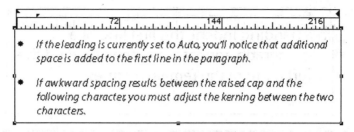

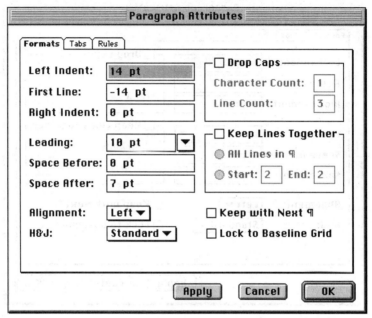

Figure A-23: The Style (Text): Formats settings for a bulleted list

Copying the attributes of one paragraph to another

When paragraphs in the same story have different Style (Text): **Format** settings, you can quickly copy the attributes of one paragraph to another, without opening the Paragraph Attributes dialog:

1. Insert the flashing cursor in the paragraph you want to change. If changing more than one paragraph, highlight them.

2. Hold down the (Option-Shift) [**Alt-Shift**] keys, and click the paragraph you want to mimic.

Defining a raised cap

When a paragraph starts with a raised cap, the very first letter is set to a larger point size. Follow these steps:

1. Highlight the first character of the top paragraph in a text box.

2. Increase the point size (see Figure A-24).

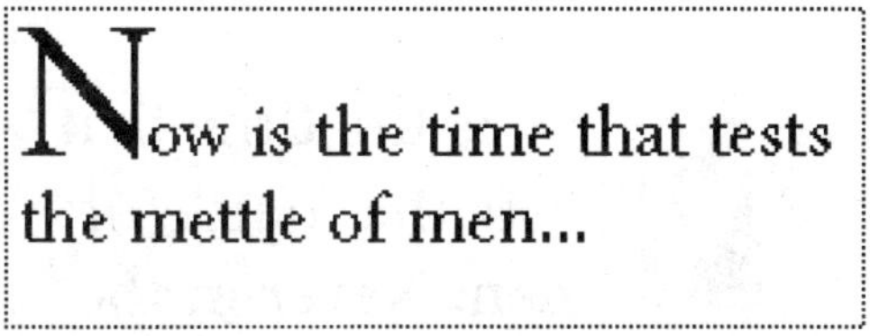

$$N\text{ow is the time that tests the mettle of men...}$$

Figure A-24: A 48 pt. raised cap

After creating the raised cap, the following may occur:

- If the leading is currently set to Auto, you'll notice that additional space is added to the first line in the paragraph. To remove this effect, set a numerical leading value.

- If awkward spacing results between the raised cap and the following character, you must adjust the kerning between the two characters. Insert the flashing cursor between them, and use the Kern arrows of the Measurements Palette.

Defining a raised cap with a hanging indent

1. Create and adjust a raised cap, as described previously.

2. Insert the flashing cursor between the raised cap and the following letter.

3. Press (Command) [**Control**]-\ to insert the Indent Here character (see Figure A-25).

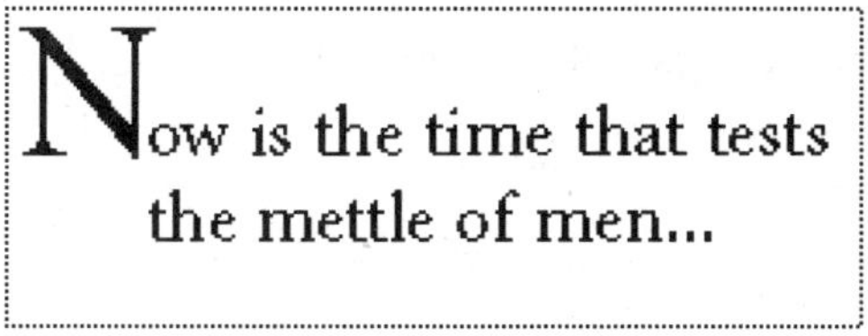

$$N\text{ow is the time that tests the mettle of men...}$$

Figure A-25: A 48 pt. raised cap after inserting the Indent Here character

Creating a graphical drop cap

1. Create an ornate character in another application.

2. Draw a picture box, and import the graphic.

3. Select the box with the Item Tool.

4. Choose Edit: **Cut**.

5. Select a text box with the Content Tool, and insert the flashing cursor at the start of the first paragraph.

6. Choose Edit: **Paste** to anchor the picture box.

7. Select the anchored box with the Item Tool.

8. In the Item: Modify: **Box** panel, click the Ascent option in the Align to Text section (see Figure A-26).

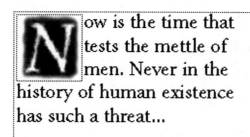

Figure A-26: A drop cap based on an anchored graphic

NOTE

To create a hanging graphical drop cap, place the flashing cursor between the anchored box and the following character, and press (Command) [**Control**]-\ to insert the Indent Here character.

Editing a drop cap

To change the font, size, or coloring of a standard drop, you must first highlight the character. Depending on its size and orientation, this can be a slightly confusing process. Use the following technique:

1. Insert the flashing cursor just before the second letter in the paragraph.

2. Hold down Shift, and press the left arrow key.

Style: Tabs

Creating tables

Although many XTensions are available that quickly generate tables (such as Tableworks' *Entable*), you can create basic tables with relative ease using XPress' tabs. In the following example, let's create a four-column table, using Left Aligned tab stops:

1. Enter the first line of text, pressing the Tab key after the first, second, and third items.

2. Choose Style (Text): **Tabs** to access the Tabs panel of the Paragraph Attributes dialog. The tab ruler appears along the top edge of the text box.

---

3. Set Left in the Align pop-up.

4. Click on the tab ruler to place tab stops in the desired position. These stops will align the second, third, and fourth items in the line.

5. Click Apply to preview the settings. Make any necessary changes, clicking Apply after each adjustment. Remember that the stops must be far enough apart to accommodate the longest range of text that will appear in each column.

6. When satisfied, click OK to close the dialog (see Figure A-27).

Pangaea	13.6%	Even	+4%
Siam	4%	Uneven	-23%
Sudetenland	23%	Solid	+12%

Figure A-27: Possible tab settings for a four-column table

After placing the desired stops, you can proceed in the following directions:

- If you're simply creating a basic, standalone table, insert the cursor at the end of the first line, press Return, and continue entering text. After typing the first, second, and third item in each line, press the Tab key to jump to the next tab stop.

- If you're going to use these settings in a larger document, create a paragraph style sheet. Do this quickly by leaving the cursor inserted in the formatted line and choosing Edit: **Style Sheets**. As you can see in the Description field, the tab stops are already included in the new style. If you've already created a body text style, set it in the Based On pop-up. When you apply the style in the future, the tab stops are applied to the paragraph—you must still enter the tab space characters.

- To add horizontal rules beneath each line of text, use Style (Text): **Rules**. Although the results depend on the font, size, and leading already applied to the text, try entering a Rule After with an Offset value of 20% to 35%.

- To add vertical lines between the columns, draw them with the Orthogonal Line Tool. When finished, select the lines, and choose Item: **Group**. If the table is in a standalone text box, include the box in the group. If the table is part of a larger body of text, note that the lines will not flow with the table if the text reflows.

Defining tabs with dot leaders

1. Insert the cursor in the appropriate line of text, and choose Style (Text): **Tabs**.

2. Click the tab ruler to place a stop in the desired location.

3. Enter a single period in the Fill Character field. To spread out the dots, enter a period followed by a space.

4. Click Apply to preview the effect.

5. Click OK to close the dialog (see Figure A-28).

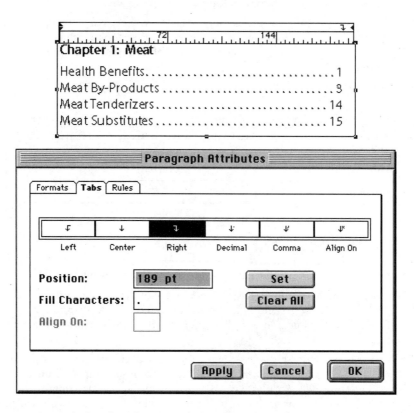

Figure A-28: Style (Text): Tab settings for a tab containing a dot leader

---

Chapter 8, The Style Menu (Picture)

Style: Contrast

In some instances it may be necessary to adjust the tonal values of a graphic file. Applications such as Photoshop and Painter offer a wide variety of powerful tools for making such changes. These applications alter the contents of the graphic files themselves. In some instances, however, it's desirable to edit the way a graphic *prints* but not the source graphic *itself*. Additionally, in many work environments, image editing applications are simply not available. In these cases, it will be necessary to rely upon XPress' Contrast command.

Applying simple contrast to an image

Contrast is added to an image by making the dark tones darker and the light tones lighter. However, be careful to avoid destroying image detail, which occurs when you make tones in the image too light to be seen, or so dark they become black.

To add contrast to an image, follow these steps:

1. Select the desired graphic with the Item or Content Tool.

2. Choose Style: **Contrast**.

3. Select the Spike Tool. Handles appear on the Contrast Curve at regular 10% intervals—these can only be moved up (greater ink output) and down (lighter ink output).

4. Position the handles so the four handles on the right side of the Contrast Curve (tones 60%–100%) increase incrementally in value. Position the four handles on the left of the contrast curve (tones 0%–40%) decrease incrementally in value.

5. The resulting Contrast Curve will appear as a flat "S" shape. Avoid harsh jumps in tone and flat curve segments.

6. Click Apply to preview the affect of the adjustment. When the results are satisfactory, click OK (see Figure A-29).

Converting a Grayscale image to black-and-white line art

To convert a continuous-tone Grayscale image to an image that prints as only 100% and 0% black (white), do the following:

1. Select the desired graphic with the Item or Content Tool.

2. Choose Style (Picture): **Contrast**.

3. Click the High Contrast Tool. The Contrast Curve flattens on the top (100% black) and bottom (0% black), connected by a vertical line. The position of the vertical line left to right determines the tones mapped to black or white.

4. Reposition the vertical portion of the Contrast Curve by dragging it to the left or right with the Hand Tool. Tones to the right of the vertical portion of the curve are mapped to black; tones to the left of the vertical portion are mapped to white.

5. Click Apply to preview the affect of the adjustment.

6. When the results are satisfactory, click OK (see Figure A-30).

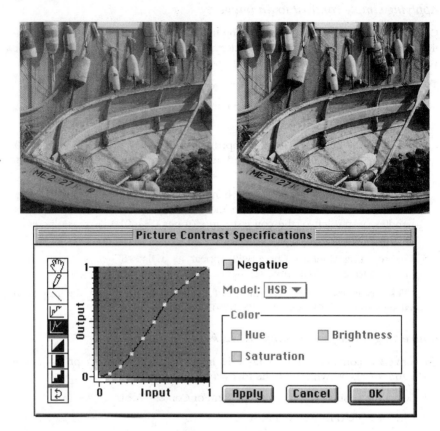

Figure A-29: A halftone before (l) and after applying simple contrast

---

NOTE

Once familiar with the shape of adjustment curves, it may be more efficient to rough out the shape of the Contrast Curve with the Pencil Tool first, then fine tune the position of handles on the curve with the Spike Tool.

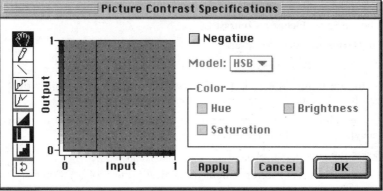

Figure A-30: A halftone image before (l) and after converting to black-and-white line art

Converting a CMYK image to black-and-white line art (single black plate only)

This method strips all colors except black from the image and adjusts the remaining values. Since in many color separations black is not present in lighter tones, this method may result in the complete loss of lighter areas.

1. Select the desired graphic with the Item or Content Tool.

2. Choose Style (Picture): **Contrast**.

3. Set CMYK in the Model pop-up.

4. Uncheck the Black box.

5. Using the Hand Tool, drag the Contrast Curve all the way to the right of the graph. Note that doing so forces the curve to lie flat along the bottom of the graph, setting the value for all cyan, yellow and magenta in the image to 0%.

6. Uncheck the Cyan, Magenta, and Yellow boxes, and check the Black box.

7. Click the High Contrast Tool.

8. Use the Hand Tool to reposition the vertical portion of the Contrast Curve as needed.

9. Click Apply to preview the affect of the adjustment.

10. When the results are satisfactory, click OK.

Converting a CMYK image to black-and-white line art (enriched black)

This method changes values to black or white based on their relative appearance, not their ink content. This provides a more accurate method of creating line art, but unlike the previous technique, it results in a file that prints on all four process color plates. You must determine which method is appropriate for your particular print job before either is applied:

1. Select the desired graphic with the Item or Content Tool.

2. Choose Style (Picture): **Contrast**.

3. Set HSB in the Model pop-up.

4. Uncheck the Brightness box.

5. Using the Hand Tool, drag the Contrast Curve all the way to the right of the graph. The result is a Grayscale version of the CMYK file.

6. Uncheck the Hue and Saturation checkboxes. Once these boxes are deselected, check the Brightness checkbox.

7. Select the High Contrast Tool.

8. Use the Hand Tool to reposition the vertical portion of the Contrast Curve as needed.

9. Click Apply to preview the effects of the adjustment.

10. When the results are satisfactory, click OK.

Desaturating a color image

1. Select the desired graphic with the Item or Content Tool.

2. Choose Style (Picture): **Contrast**.

3. Set HSB in the Model pop-up.

4. Uncheck Hue and Brightness, leaving Saturation active.

5. Select the Hand Tool, and drag the Contrast Curve to the right. For best results, drag a small adjustment, and click Apply to preview its effect. Continue adjusting the position of the curve until the results are satisfactory.

6. To fine tune the Curve, switch to the Pencil, Line or Spike Tools to make adjustments.

Ghosting a Grayscale image

Before ghosting an image, determine the tonal value that the darkest image pixels will reduce to. For example, 100% black may become 50% gray after ghosting.

1. Select the desired graphic with the Item or Content tool.
2. Choose Style (Picture): **Contrast**.
3. Select the Line Tool.
4. Position the Line Tool in the lower-left corner of the Contrast Curve graph (0 Input/0 Output). Click and drag to the right, so the right edge of the curve ends on the output value you determined the darkest pixel should become.
5. Click on the Apply button to preview the effects of the adjustment.
6. Redraw the curve with the Line Tool as needed. When the results are satisfactory, click the OK button to accept the adjustment (see Figure A-31).

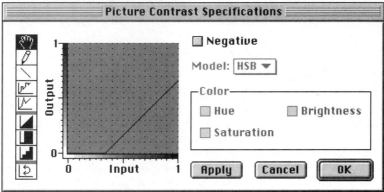

Figure A-31: A halftone image before (l) and after ghosting

Ghosting a color image

Before ghosting an image, determine the tonal value that the darkest image pixels will reduce to.

1. Select the desired graphic with the Item or Content Tool.

2. Choose Style (Picture): **Contrast**.

3. Set CMY in the Model pop-up.

4. Select the Line Tool.

5. Position the Line Tool in the lower-left corner of the Contrast Curve graph. Click and drag to the right, so the right edge of the curve ends on the output value that you determined the darkest pixel should become.

6. Click Apply to preview the effect of the adjustment.

7. Redraw the curve with the Line Tool as needed. When the results are satisfactory, click the OK button to accept the adjustment.

To create the effect of ghosting a specific part of an image, follow these steps:

1. Select the desired graphic with the Content Tool.

2. Choose Item: **Step and Repeat**, entering 0 in the Offset fields. A duplicate of the selected image appears directly on top of the original.

3. Ghost the duplicate image using the techniques described previously.

4. Use the Item or Content Tool to resize the picture box, cropping the ghosted image to the desired proportions (see Figure A-32).

Posterizing to a specific number of steps

When you *posterize* an image, you reduce the available colors to a specific number. The Contrast Curve in such an image would look like a staircase, with each tonal value in the image being a "step." Before posterizing an image to a specific number of flat tonal steps, you must determine the desired number of tones.

1. Select the graphic with the Item or Content Tool.

2. Choose Style (Picture): **Contrast**.

3. The graph portion of the Picture Contrast Specifications dialog box is marked into a 10 × 10 grid of dotted lines. Divide the number of steps in the grid (horizontal or vertical) by the number of tones you would like in the image. The quotient will be the number of grid squares (horizontal or vertical) each tonal step will occupy. For example, to posterize an image to 5 separate tones, divide 10 (the squares in the grid) by 5 (the tones in the resulting image). The result is 2. Each tonal step in the Contrast Curve will occupy 2 squares in the grid.

4. Select the Line Tool, and position the cursor in the lower-left corner of the graph (the 0 Input/0 Output position). Shift-drag to the right the number of squares you previously determined the step should occupy in step 3. The curve flattens across those tones.

Figure A-32: Ghosting part of an image by ghosting and cropping a duplicate of the original graphic

5. Release the mouse button, and move the cursor up the same number of squares you dragged across horizontally. Shift-drag to the right the number of squares you determined in step 3. Continue this process until the graph is completed (see Figure A-33).

6. To fine tune the curve, select the Posterizer Tool. Handles are added to the curve between each 10% marker. Drag the handles up or down to change the shape of the curve.

7. Click Apply to preview the effects of the adjustment.

8. When the results are satisfactory, click OK.

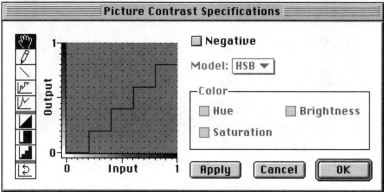

Figure A-33: A halftone before (l) and after posterizing to 5 steps

Chapter 10, The Item Menu

Item: Step and Repeat

Generating horizontal and vertical rules for a form

To evenly place a series of horizontal lines, follow these steps:

1. Use the Orthogonal Line Tool to draw the first line in the desired position. For the best results, draw the topmost line in the form.

2. Establish the line's thickness, length, and color.

3. Choose Item: **Step and Repeat**.

4. Enter the desired number of duplicates in the Repeat Count field. Remember that one line already exists—for example, if you want a total of 24 lines, enter 23 in the field.

5. Set the Horizontal Offset field to 0. In the Vertical Offset field, enter the desired space between the lines.

   If you must fit a certain number of lines in a specified space, you may have to manually determine the offset value. In this case, divide the height of the space by the desired number of duplicates. For example, if you must fit 18 lines in a space 5 inches high, the offset value is .294 inches, or 21.1 pt. (5 ÷ 17 = .294; .294 × 72 = 21.1 pt.). Therefore, after drawing the first line and choosing Item: **Step and Repeat**, enter 17 in the Repeat Count field, 0 in Horizontal Offset, and 21.1 pt. in Vertical Offset.

6. Click OK to generate the duplicates.

To evenly place a series of vertical lines, follow these steps:

1. Use the Orthogonal Line Tool to draw the first line in the desired position. For the best results, draw the leftmost line in the form.

2. Establish the line's thickness, length, and color.

3. Choose Item: **Step and Repeat**.

4. Enter the desired number of duplicates in the Repeat Count field. Remember that one line already exists—for example, if you want a total of 8 lines, enter 7 in the field.

5. Set the Vertical Offset field to 0. In the Horizontal Offset field, enter the desired space between the lines.

   If you are placing vertical lines in addition to a series of horizontal lines, you may have to manually determine the offset value. In this case, divide the length of a horizontal line by the desired number of duplicates. For example, if you must fit 8 vertical rules across a 6.5 inch line, the offset value is .928 inches, or 66.85 pt. (6.5 ÷ 7 = .928; .928 × 72 = 66.85 pt.). Therefore, after drawing the first line and choosing Item: **Step and Repeat**, enter 7 in the Repeat Count field, 66.85 pt. in Horizontal Offset, and 0 pt. in Vertical Offset.

6. Click OK to generate the duplicates.

After creating all the lines of the form, select them all with the Item or Content Tool, and choose Item: **Group**.

If you need to uniformly adjust the spacing between a series of rules—for example, if you need to change it from 18 pt. to 20 pt.—you don't have to delete them and start over. Instead, follow these steps:

1. Select all the horizontal or vertical lines, whichever ones you need to adjust. (If you've grouped the lines, you must first choose Item: **Ungroup**.)

2. Choose Item: **Space/Align**.

3. To adjust the vertical spacing of horizontal lines, check the Vertical box, set Items in the Between pop-up, and enter the new amount in the Space field. To adjust the horizontal spacing of vertical lines, check the Horizontal box, set Items in the Between pop-up, and enter the new amount in the Space field.

Common Techniques

4. Click Apply to preview the adjustment.

5. When satisfied, click OK.

Item: Constrain

Constraining items to a box

To manually constrain a series of items to a box, follow these steps:

1. Draw a box around the items you wish to constrain. This box should be the exact width and height of the desired constrained area.

2. Leaving the box selected, choose Item: **Send to Back**.

3. Make sure the items you want to constrain fit completely within the new box.

4. Use the Item Tool to select the constraining box, as well as the items above it.

5. Choose Item: **Group**.

6. Choose Item: **Constrain**.

NOTE

To create a constraining relationship, you don't necessarily have to create a new box. For example, if you want to constrain items to an imported graphic, or a series rules to a text box, just make sure that the largest box is positioned *behind* all the items you wish to constrain.

Item: Merge

Item: Merge: Intersection example

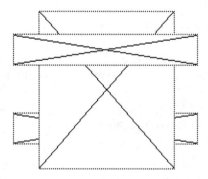

Figure A-34: Items merged using the Intersect option

Item: Merge: Union example

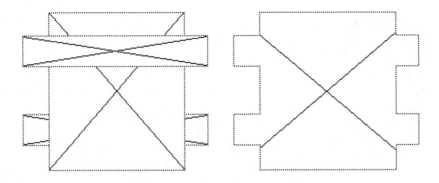

Figure A-35: Items merged using the Union option

Item: Merge: Difference example

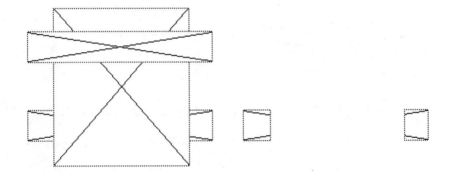

Figure A-36: Items merged using the Difference option

Item: Merge: Reverse Difference example

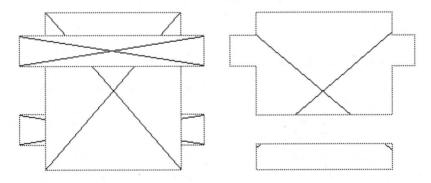

Figure A-37: Items merged using the Reverse Difference option

Item: Merge: Exclusive Or example

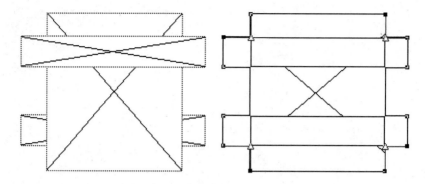

Figure A-38: Items merged using the Exclusive Or option

Item: Merge: Combine example

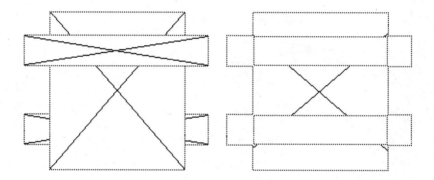

Figure A-39: Items merged using the Combine option

Chapter 11, The Page Menu

Page: Section

Renumbering an entire document

1. Navigate to the first document page using Page: **Go To** or the Document Layout palette.
2. Select Page: **Section**, or click in the Page Number field of the Document Layout Palette. The Section dialog box appears.
3. Click the Section Start option.
4. Enter the starting number for your document in the Number field.

> **NOTE**
>
> If you choose a numbering scheme other than Arabic numerals, the starting number you choose is translated to that numbering method. For example, when you set the numbering to uppercase Arabic letters, "5" becomes "E."

Partially renumbering a document

Partially renumber a document by inserting a Section start after the first page. Follow these steps:

1. Navigate to the desired document page using Page: **Go To** or the Document Layout Palette.
2. Select Page: **Section**, or click in the Page Number field of the Document Layout Palette. The Section dialog box appears.
3. Click the Section Start option.
4. Enter the starting number for your new section in the Number field.
5. Click OK.

Here, the page numbering starts at 1, but changes at the Section Start page. For example, if you set page 5 of an 8-page document to start numbering at 20, the numbering of the entire document is as follows: 1, 2, 3, 4, 20, 21, 22, 23.

Adding multiple sections to a document

You can create as many sections as you have pages in your document. A common technique is to start sectioning at page 1, then continue adding sections as needed throughout the document. Follow these steps:

1. Navigate to the first page of the document.
2. Select Page: **Section**, or click in the Page Number field of the Document Layout Palette. The Section dialog box will appear.
3. Click the Section Start option.
4. Set the starting number, prefix, and format for the new section.
5. Click OK.
6. Navigate to the page that will start the next section.
7. Repeat steps 2 through 5.

Removing a section designation

Follow these steps to remove a section start:

1. Navigate to the starting page of the section. It's identified by the asterisk under the page icon in the Document Layout Palette.
2. Select Page: **Section**, or click in the Page Number field of the Document Layout Palette. The Section dialog box appears.

3. Uncheck the Section Start box.

4. Click OK. Note that the pages numbered by the old section now adopt the page numbering of any section appearing before them. If no such section exists, the document page numbering reverts back to normal.

Including a prefix before page numbers

Sectioned page numbers can also contain a common prefix. This is often done to designate the pages of a particular chapter (for example, 2.11, 2.12, 2.13 . . .). You can specify up to four characters as a prefix for the actual page numbers. Follow these steps:

1. Navigate to the desired section start page.

2. Select Page: **Section**, or click the Page Number field of the Document Layout Palette. The Section dialog box will appear.

3. Click the Section Start option.

4. Set the starting number and format for the new section.

5. In the Prefix field, enter the characters that will precede each page number, including any hyphen, period, or space. For example, to add a chapter designation, add the chapter number and a period: "2."

6. Click OK.

Changing page numbers

If you change the location of a page within the document, the page numbering also changes:

- If you change the location of a page within a section, the Prefix and Format remains the same.

- If you move a page into a new section, the Prefix and Format change to match that section.

- If you move a section start page, you include or exclude pages from the section, depending on where the page is positioned.

Starting page numbering on a left-facing page

XPress does not allow you to position an odd-numbered page as a left-facing page, regardless of its section numbering. However, if you want the first page of the document to appear as a left-facing page, follow these steps:

1. Navigate to the *second* page of the document.

2. Choose Page: **Section**.

3. Check the Section Start box.

4. Enter an even number in the Page Number field. ("2" will suffice.)

5. Click OK.

6. Use Page: Delete or the Document Layout Palette to remove page 1.

> **NOTE**
>
> Since this document now starts at page 2, you should avoid using automatic page numbering. However, this technique allows you to treat *all* of your pages as two-page spreads, without having to work with a blank first page.

Chapter 12, The View Menu

View: Thumbnails

Using thumbnails to rearrange pages within a document

Use this technique instead of choosing Page: **Move** or dragging icons in the Document Layout Palette to rearrange pages in a document:

1. Choose View: **Thumbnails**.
2. Select the desired pages you wish to move. To select a single page, click it once. To select a continuous range of pages, hold down the Shift key, and click the first and last page of the desired range. To select noncontinuous pages, (Command) [**Control**]-click them.
3. Click-drag one of the selected pages. As you drag, the selected pages appear as outlines. Move the cursor to the desired position of the selected pages. The cursor will change to a right- or down-pointing arrow, indicating the new position.
4. Release the mouse button.

Using thumbnails to copy pages to another document

1. Open the document you wish to copy pages *from*.
2. Open the document you wish to copy pages *to*. For the best results, resize the document windows so they appear side by side.
3. Choose View: **Thumbnails** in *both* documents.
4. In the first document, select the thumbnails you wish to copy.
5. Drag them into the second document. As you drag, the cursor will change to a left- or down-pointing arrow, indicating the position of the new pages.
6. Release the mouse button.

> **NOTE**
>
> When copying thumbnails into another document, the width and height of second document must be *at least* the same as the first. For the best results, they should share identical dimensions.

Using thumbnails to copy master pages to another document

XPress doesn't allow you to drag master page thumbnails to another document—in fact, View: **Thumbnails** is not even available when a master page is active. Instead, follow these steps:

1. Open the document containing the desired master pages.

2. Open the document you wish to copy the master pages to. For the best results, resize the document windows so they appear side by side.

3. Set both documents to View: **Thumbnails**.

4. In the first document, select a page that has been formatted with the desired master page.

5. Drag the page into the second document.

6. In the second document, Use Page: **Delete** or the Document Layout Palette to remove the new page. The copied master page information still remains, ready to be further edited, or applied to the document's pages.

Using thumbnails to rescue a corrupted document

Occasionally, an XPress document becomes corrupt. When this occurs, you may not be able to save or print the document. This is often the result of a bad *file* and not necessarily bad page *elements*. You can attempt to rescue your work by dragging the page information of the corrupt file into a new document:

1. Create a new document with dimensions identical to the original (including width, height, and facing pages). There is no need to insert any new pages.

2. Set both documents to View: **Thumbnails**.

3. Shift-click the first and last page icon to select all the pages in the first document.

4. Drag them into the second document, positioning them beneath the first page.

5. In the second document, delete the first page.

6. Save the document and examine the page information.

7. Close the first document and continue editing the second.

Creating temporary thumbnail page numbers

The only way to determine the page number of a thumbnail is to select a page from the Go To Page pop-up or the Document Layout Palette and see which page jumps to the upper left of the document window—if you simply select a thumbnail, its page number is not displayed. Follow these steps to create temporary thumbnail page numbers, which will assist you in selecting the appropriate pages:

1. Navigate to the first master page of your document.

2. Drag a large text box on the pasteboard, beside the page. The box should overlap the page edge by just a fraction of an inch.

3. If the master page has facing pages, draw a text box beside the left and right page.

4. In each text box, enter the flashing cursor, and press (Command) [**Control**]-3 to insert the automatic page number character.

5. Select the character, and set it to a large size, such as 120–150 pt.

6. If the document has multiple master pages, repeat steps 2 through 5 as needed.

7. Return to the document pages, and choose View: **Thumbnails**.

8. There should be a box beside each thumbnail, displaying the current page number.

9. When finished moving or copying thumbnails, return to the master pages and delete the text boxes.

View: Show/Hide Baseline Grid

The Baseline grid is a tool for visualizing the leading grid of a document. A leading grid is an imaginary set of lines that run the entire width of the document, crossing columns and pages. The purpose of this grid is to ensure that the baselines of the text will align across those columns and pages all the way down the page. The grid is often applied only to the body copy or main text of the document; however, the rest of the text must be built so the grid can be maintained by the body copy. In a document with a well-developed grid, one could place a ruler on any line in the body copy, and its baseline would align to any body copy to the right or left.

NOTE

Consider the leading grid to be a paragraph-level formatting issue, much like leading itself. When you create or edit such a grid, you will affect an entire paragraph at a time.

Creating a leading grid

To create a leading grid, first choose the leading value for the body copy of the document. Then, base the leading grid on that value. In most cases the two will simply be the same. Once chosen, creating the leading grid is a matter of styling a paragraph so that the height of each line is always a multiple of the leading grid value. For example, if the body copy uses a leading value of 15 pt., then the document will be built on a 15 pt. leading grid, and the possible line heights are 15 pt., 30 pt., 45 pt., and so on. To create a style based on that grid, set the following style characteristics:

1. First, set the leading value of the paragraph, using either Style (Text): **Leading**, the Measurements Palette, or by building it into the style sheet for that para-

graph. Unless you are going to use Space Before/Space After values, the leading value needs to be a multiple of the leading grid value.

2. Set the Space Before and/or Space After values for the paragraph using Style (Text): **Formats** or by building it into the style sheet for the paragraph. Make sure the sum of the Space Before, Leading, and the Space After values for the paragraph is a multiple of the leading grid value.

3. Make sure that any Rule Above or Below the paragraph also fits within the paragraph's vertical spacing. Remember that a rule above will sit a specific distance above the baseline of the first line of text in the paragraph. That distance can be calculated by adding the absolute offset value to the width of the rule. For example, if the offset value is 20 pt. and the rule is 5 pt. wide, then the top of the rule will be 25 pt. from the baseline of the first line of text in the paragraph. The rule below will set the offset value plus the width of the rule below the baseline of the last line in the paragraph.

4. In the Edit: Preferences: Document: **Paragraph** panel, set the baseline grid increment to match the desired leading grid.

5. Set the **First Baseline** value in the **Item: Modify Text** panel for the text box(es) to contain the text. The value should be enough to allow the entire first paragraph to fit between the first baseline and the top of the text box—including any Space Before values.

NOTE

When setting the offset value for a rule above or below, use the absolute value by typing the unit code for the unit you wish to use. Do not use the default value (percentage) because it's difficult to set rules precisely with this unit of measurement.

Creating a leading grid with half-increment values

Creating a half-increment grid will give some flexibility in designing with a leading grid. This is especially true when adding picture elements to the page.

1. Divide the normal Leading grid by two.

2. Enter that value into the Baseline Grid: Increment to match the leading grid, using the Paragraph panel in Preferences: **Document**.

Assigning text to a leading grid

Once the grid has been established, it can be used to format the text. It is best to create the leading grid initially by building styles sheets instead of locally formatting a series of paragraphs:

1. Apply the various style sheets to the text in your document.

2. Use horizontal ruler guides to see if the baselines of the text align across columns and/or pages.

---

3. When using lists in a document, add all of the Space Before, Leading, and Space After values to see if the result is a multiple of the leading grid. If not, add extra space before the first list item and extra space after the last list item to increase the resulting sum to a multiple of the leading value.

Chapter 13, The Utilities Menu

Utilities: Usage: Fonts

Font Usage has a number of capabilities beyond listing those fonts currently in use by the document.

Pinpointing missing fonts

When XPress warns of a missing typeface, it is helpful to know where in the document that typeface is used:

1. Select the missing font from the list of fonts in the Utilities: Usage: **Fonts** panel.

2. Click Show First. XPress jumps to the first occurrence of that font. Often, a single paragraph, tab, or space character will be locally formatted with a font not used anywhere else in the document.

3. If it doesn't show up, it may not actually be used in text anywhere. In such cases, look for the font as part of a style sheet or default setting on a master page.

Substituting for fonts not supplied with a document

If the document refers to fonts that are not available to your system, you can substitute the missing font with an available one:

1. Select the missing font from the list in the Utilities: Usage: **Fonts** panel.

2. Click **Replace**.

3. In the Replace Font dialog, select the replacement from the pop-up list of available fonts.

NOTE

Although you can replace fonts easily with this tool, documents with large amounts of text will often experience reflow of the text as a result of doing this. Examine any document that uses substituted fonts very carefully.

Utilities: Usage: Pictures

Reviewing and reestablishing graphic links

Before submitting work to a printing service or before printing the work, check to determine that the links between the document and the graphic files are current.

1. Open the **Utilities: Usage: Picture** panel.

2. Examine the listed pictures. If the status is okay, then the link is current.

3. If the Status is Missing, the link is broken. Update it by clicking Update, and locating the file using the Find dialog.

4. To assist you in locating the missing picture, select More Information, and note the last known location of the picture.

Jumping to a particular graphic in a long document

When a picture's status is anything other than okay, you may want to see the picture to help you correct the potential problem:

1. Select the picture from the list in the Utilities: Usage: **Picture** panel.

2. Click Show.

3. When satisfied, press Done. The page containing the graphic remains on the screen.

Utilities: Build Index

Formatted nested index example

color modes
default colors for, 60
determining colors and, 384
gamut (see gamut)
inverting images and, 196
list of, 160–162
Magic Wand Tool and, 16
pasting and, 144
rasterizing and, 84
saving images in, 86

Figure A-40: A nested index consisting of multiple subentries

Formatted run-in index example

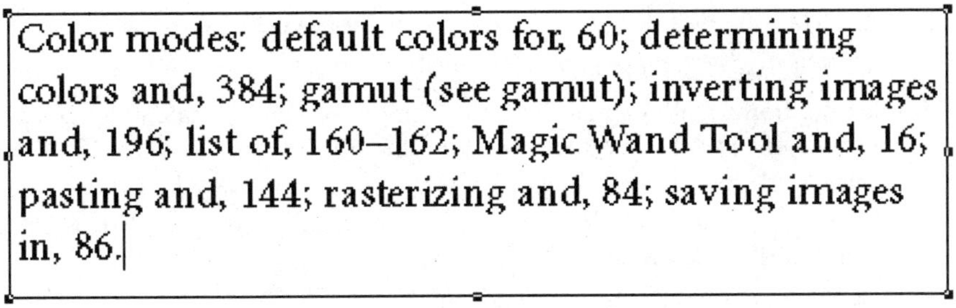

> Color modes: default colors for, 60; determining colors and, 384; gamut (see gamut); inverting images and, 196; list of, 160–162; Magic Wand Tool and, 16; pasting and, 144; rasterizing and, 84; saving images in, 86.

Figure A-41: A run-in index consisting of a single paragraph

Utilities: Tracking Edit

Applying a single-value tracking edit

Use this technique to apply the same tracking value to a font, regardless of its size:

1. Choose Utilities: **Tracking Edit**.
2. In the Tracking Edit dialog, select the specific font you wish to edit.
3. Click Edit to access the Edit Tracking dialog.
4. Click-drag the horizontal line that bisects the graph.
5. To tighten the overall tracking, drag the line down; to loosen the overall tracking, drag the line up. Keep an eye on the Track readout in the upper-right corner of the dialog—you can ignore the Size readout since you're applying the same value to all point sizes.
6. When the tracking is set to the desired value, release the mouse button.
7. If you need to adjust the value after releasing the mouse button, click-drag the single point that already exists—otherwise, you'll split the curve.
8. When satisfied, click OK to close the dialog.
9. If desired, choose another font from the Tracking Edit dialog, and repeat steps 2 through 8. If you're finished, click Save.

Tightening tracking as point size increases

Use this technique to incrementally decrease a font's tracking as its size increases. For this example, we'll establish the following settings:

- All sizes between 0 and 12 pt. will retain the font's default tracking.
- The tracking of sizes between 12 and 96 pt. will gradually decrease from 0 to −10 units.
- All sizes over 96 pt. will track at −10.

Follow these steps:

1. Choose Utilities: **Tracking Edit**.

2. In the Tracking Edit dialog, select the specific font you wish to edit.

3. Click Edit to access the Edit Tracking dialog.

4. Click the horizontal line that bisects the graph, placing a single point at 12 pt. To make this easier, drag the point until the Size readout displays 12 pt. and the Track readout displays 0 units.

5. Click to place another point, dragging it until the Size readout displays 96 pt. and the Track readout displays −10 units.

6. Click OK to close the Edit Tracking dialog.

7. Click Save to close the Tracking Edit dialog.

NOTE

If desired, you can drag the first point over the 0 line, which results in positive tracking values applied to smaller type sizes.

Loosening tracking as point size increases

Use this technique to incrementally tighten a font's tracking as its size increases. For this example, we'll establish the following settings:

• All sizes between 0 and 18 pt. will retain the font's default tracking.

• The tracking of sizes between 18 and 48 pt. will gradually increase from 0 to 10 units.

• All sizes over 48 pt. will track at 10 units.

Follow these steps:

1. Choose Utilities: **Tracking Edit**.

2. In the Tracking Edit dialog, select the specific font you wish to edit.

3. Click Edit to access the Edit Tracking dialog.

4. Click the horizontal line that bisects the graph, placing a single point at 18 pt. To make this easier, drag the point until the Size readout displays 18 pt. and the Track readout displays 0 units.

5. Click to place another point, dragging it until the Size readout displays 48 pt. and the Track readout displays 10 units.

6. Click OK to close the Edit Tracking dialog.

7. Click Save to close the Tracking Edit dialog.

Utilities: Kerning Table Edit

Adjusting an existing kern pair in a kerning table

Here, we'll adjust the spacing of one of the kern pairs built into a font:

1. Choose Utilities: **Kern Table Edit**.

2. In the Kerning Table Edit dialog, choose the font you wish to edit. Make sure you choose the version labeled "«Plain»."

3. Click Edit to access the Edit Kerning Table dialog.

4. Scroll through the Kerning Pairs list to locate and select the pair you wish to adjust. Or insert the cursor in the Pair field, and type the characters.

5. If you know the new kern amount you want to apply, enter it in the Value field. Otherwise, click the arrows beside the field. Simply click to increase or decrease the value in increments of 10; (Option) [**Alt**]-click to adjust in increments of 1. Scrutinize the effect of the new value in the Preview section.

6. When satisfied with the value, click Replace. The new value appears next to the kern pair in the Kern Pairs list.

7. Select another pair, if necessary. If finished, click OK to close the Edit Kerning Table dialog.

8. If desired, choose another font in the Kerning Table Edit dialog, and repeat steps 3 through 7. If you're finished, click Save.

Adding a new kern pair to a kerning table

Here, we'll add a value for a kern pair not built into a font:

1. Choose Utilities: **Kern Table Edit**.

2. In the Kerning Table Edit dialog, choose the font you wish to edit. Make sure you choose the version labeled "«Plain»."

3. Click Edit to access the Edit Kerning Table dialog.

4. Insert the cursor in the Pair field and type the desired kern pair.

5. If you know the new kern amount you want to apply, enter it in the Value field. Otherwise, click the arrows beside the field. Simply click to increase or decrease the value in increments of 10; (Option) [**Alt**]-click to adjust in increments of 1. Scrutinize the effect of the new value in the Preview section.

6. When satisfied with the value, click Add. The new pair and its value appear in the Kern Pairs list.

7. Select or add another pair, if necessary. If finished, click OK to close the Edit Kerning pairs dialog.

8. If desired, choose another font in the Kerning Table Edit dialog, and repeat steps 3 through 7. If you're finished, click Save.

Chapter 15, The Document Layout Palette

Creating a basic printer spread imposition

When you design a facing-page document, the pages are initially set up as a *reader spread*. Here, the side-by-side page arrangement mimics the order of appearance in the final printed and bound project. However, when these pages are imposed prior to running on-press, they must be arranged as *printer spreads*. Here, the document pages that actually appear on the same press page are placed side by side. After the project is printed, folded, and bound, the pages read in the proper order.

For example, examine an 8-page publication. As you flip through it, page 2 appears next to page 3, page 6 appears next to page 7. These are the reader spreads. Now examine the separate sheets of paper that make up the publication: page 1 is printed next to page 8, page 2 is next to page 7, page 3 is next to page 6, and page 4 is next to page 5. These are the printer spreads.

There are three ways to establish the necessary imposition:

- Let your print vendor impose the pages according to their own specifications. For many designers, this is the most desirable course of action. Most print shops have unique requirements—such as the space between pages, accommodating creep in a large document, and handling bleeds and crossovers—that the ordinary user simply cannot predict. In this case, you must output your document as individual page films, which are then handed over to the print shop.

- Use a dedicated imposition application, such as PressWise. Here, you print the document into a PostScript file, which is then brought into the desired program. This option allows you to establish much more specific page arrangements and output options, based on the requirements of a particular project or press.

- Establish a basic imposition in XPress. This is not a very powerful option, since XPress offers no specific imposition or spacing controls. However, if your document is fairly simple—it contains 8 pages or less and has no crossovers or bleeds—you can impose the pages yourself using the Document Layout Palette. After rearranging the pages, you must print the document with the Spreads box checked in the File: Print: **Document** panel. This way, the side-by-side pages are output on the same film plate, using one set of crop and registration marks.

To impose pages in XPress, you must rearrange them in the Document Layout Palette. Note that this technique has the following restrictions:

- The page numbers in the palette do not correspond to the actual numbers that will appear on each page. For example, if you move page 8 to appear next to page 1, the palette lists it as page 2. If the pages contain automatic page numbers, you must replace them with hard numbers. (Highlight the number on each page, and type the same character. This breaks the link to the master page, preventing the page from renumbering when you move it.)

- If the last page in the document is linked to a facing master page, you may not be able to successfully place it next to page 1. Since the pages at the top of the palette can only appear to the right of the vertical line, any page linked to a left-facing master page will be linked to a right-facing master page after moving it. If the master page contains no information—or if it's a single-sided master page—you can impose the last and first pages without risk.

To impose a four-page document in a single-sided document, follow these steps (note that the following page numbers used refer to the numbers that appear in the Document Layout Palette, not the numbering of the specific document pages—therefore, the same page numbers will be referenced more than once):

1. In the Document Layout Palette, click-drag page 4.
2. Place it to the left of page 1.
3. Click-drag page 4.
4. Place it to the right of page 3.

To impose a four-page document in a facing page document, follow these steps (see Figure A-42)

1. In the Document Layout Palette, click-drag page 4.
2. Place it to the right of page 1.
3. Click-drag page 2 (this is the page you just positioned).
4. Drag until the cursor is placed between the vertical line and page 1. When the cursor changes to a right-pointing arrow, release the mouse button.

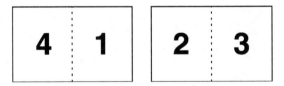

Figure A-42: The required arrangement of a four-page imposition

To impose an 8-page single-sided document, follow these steps (see Figure A-43):

1. In the Document Layout Palette, click-drag page 8.
2. Place it to the left of page 1.
3. Click-drag page 8.
4. Place it to the right of page 3.
5. Click-drag page 8.
6. Place it to the left of page 5.
7. Click-drag page 8.
8. Place it to the right of page 7.

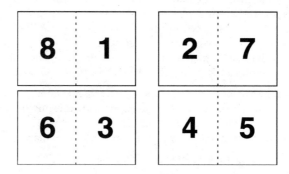

Figure A-43: The required arrangement of an eight-page imposition

To impose an 8-page facing page document, follow these steps:

1. In the Document Layout Palette, click-drag page 8.

2. Place it to the right of page 1.

3. Click-drag page 2 (this is the page you just positioned).

4. Drag until the cursor is placed between the vertical line and page 1. When the cursor changes to a right-pointing arrow, release the mouse button.

5. Click-drag page 8.

6. Place it between pages 3 and 4. When the cursor changes to a right-pointing arrow, release the mouse button.

7. Click-drag page 8.

8. Place it between pages 5 and 6. When the cursor changes to a right-pointing arrow, release the mouse button.

Establishing multipage spreads

Occasionally, you'll need to create a multipage spread within a document. This will allow you to output two or more pages on the same film plate. Common uses of this technique include designing a publication cover that contains an attached foldout unit. In the following example, let's create a three-page spread:

1. Create a document containing at least three pages. For the best results, create a single-sided document.

2. In the Document Layout Palette, click-drag page 2.

3. Place it to the left of page 1.

4. Click-drag page 3.

5. Place it to the left of page 2. When you view the document, the three pages appear side by side.

6. When outputting the document, make sure the Spreads box is checked in the File: Print: **Document** panel.

Preparing pages with bleeds for output

When you want a graphic or colored box to extend to the page edge of a printed piece, you must create a *bleed*. Here, you extend the item beyond the page boundary by at least an eighth of an inch. After the page is output and run on-press, the pages are trimmed to match the page dimensions. Any colors extending beyond the crop marks are trimmed as well, creating the effect of printing to the edge of the page.

If you want a colored item to extend all the way to the binding, you must still create a bleed. However, in a facing-page document, you cannot extend colors into the neighboring page. Instead—just before output—you must separate the pages in the Document Layout Palette, *then* create the necessary bleeds. The pages will be output as individual page films, and the print shop can impose the pages as required before reproduction.

To prepare a document for such bleeds, follow these steps (in this example, let's use an eight-page document):

1. In the Document Layout Palette, click-drag page 7.

2. Place it above page 8. When the cursor changes to a down-pointing arrow, release the mouse button. Pages 7 and 8 both appear to the left of the vertical line.

3. Drag page 7 to the right of the vertical line. This way, it resumes its original status as a right-facing page.

4. Click-drag page 5.

5. Place it above page 6. When the cursor changes to a down-pointing arrow, release the mouse button. Pages 5 and 6 both appear to the left of the vertical line.

6. Drag page 5 to the right of the vertical line.

7. Click-drag page 3.

8. Place it above page 4. When the cursor changes to a down-pointing arrow, release the mouse button. Pages 3 and 4 both appear to the left of the vertical line.

9. Drag page 3 to the right of the vertical line (see Figure A-44).

10. Navigate to each page containing the aforementioned bleed, and extend the appropriate colored items at least an eighth of an inch beyond the page boundary.

NOTE

When outputting bleeds of any sort, be sure to notify your output and print vendors. If you are outputting your own documents, be sure to add the desired bleed value in the Bleed field of the File: Print: **Document** panel.

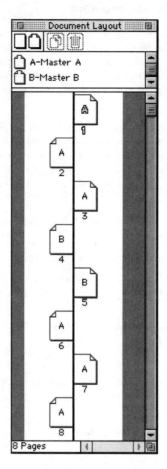

Figure A-44: The Document Layout Palette, displaying the arrangement of the separated pages

Preparing pages with crossovers for output

When a single graphic, rule, or colored box extends across two facing pages, it's known as a *crossover*. Unless it extends across the center spread of a document (the two pages in the center of the printed piece, which can be successfully output as a spread), these will cause problems during output. When you output individual page films that contain a crossover, it will only appear on the left-facing page—no information appears on the right-facing page. To ensure proper output, two things must occur:

- Copies of the image must appear on each page, in the correct position.

- The pages must be separated in the Document Layout Palette (as described in the previous technique), and each graphic must bleed beyond the inner page edge. This way, the professional responsible for imposing the films can properly align them before reproduction.

To duplicate the graphic, follow these steps (for this example, let's assume a single graphic crosses over from page 2 to page 3 of a document):

1. Select the graphic with the Item Tool.

2. Choose Item: **Step and Repeat**. Enter 0 in the Horizontal and Vertical Offset values, and click OK.

3. Leaving the duplicate item selected, drag the center handle on the left edge of the box to the right. Crop the image to the left edge of page 3.

4. Select the underlying graphic.

5. Drag the center handle of the right edge of the box to the left. Crop the image to the right edge of page 2. Although the graphic is now split into two components, it should appear the same as the original on-screen.

To prepare the crossover for output, follow these steps:

1. In the Document Layout Palette, click-drag page 3.

2. Place it above page 4. When the cursor changes to a down-pointing arrow, release the mouse button. Pages 3 and 4 both appear to the left of the vertical line.

3. Drag page 3 to the right of the vertical line. This way, it resumes its original status as a right-facing page.

4. Navigate to page 2.

5. Drag the center handle of the right edge of the picture box so it extends at least an eighth of an inch beyond the right page edge.

6. Navigate to page 3.

7. Drag the center handle of the left edge of the picture box so it extends at least an eighth of an inch beyond the left page edge (see Figure A-45).

Chapter 17, The Colors Palette

Recoloring text

1. Using the Content Tool, highlight the text you wish to color.

2. Select the Text Color icon from the top of the Colors Palette

3. Click the name of the color you wish to apply to the text. Shades can be applied by choosing a value from the pop-up menu at the top of the Colors Palette or by entering a value into the Shade field. Values from .1% to 100% are available.

Coloring a frame

The Colors Palette only affects the principal color of the frame—it does not affect Gap color.

1. Using either the Item or Content Tool, select the item you would like to color.

2. Select the Frame Color icon in the top of the Colors Palette.

Figure A-45: Two separated document pages, containing the duplicate graphics and bleeds required to reproduce a crossover

---

NOTE

Since these pages will be output as bleeds, you must notify your output and print vendors. If you are outputting your own documents, be sure to add the desired bleed value in the Bleed field of the File: Print: **Document** panel.

---

3. Click on the name of the color you wish to apply to the frame. Shades can be applied by choosing a value from the pop-up menu at the top of the Colors Palette or by entering a value into the Shade field.

Recoloring a box

1. Using either the Item or Content Tool, select the item you would like to color.

2. Select the Background Color icon from the top of the Colors Palette.

3. Click on the name of the color you wish to apply to the box. Shades can be applied by choosing a value from the pop-up menu at the top of the Colors Palette or by entering a value into the Shade field.

Coloring an Imported Image

Applying color to an imported graphic in XPress does not change the data in the imported graphic file—rather, it changes how that graphic will print in that specific document. As such, it can be a handy method of coloring imported objects while

---

keeping file sizes of graphics down. Be aware, however, that some post-processing applications may disregard the colorizing instructions generated by XPress. Talk to your service provider to ensure that colorizing graphics in XPress does not cause problems for their workflow.

1. Using either the Item or Content Tool, select the item you would like to color.
2. Select the Picture Color icon in the top of the Colors Palette.
3. Click on the name of the color you wish to apply to the box. Shades can be applied by choosing a value from the pop-up menu at the top of the Colors Palette or by entering a value into the Shade field.

Coloring a line

1. Using either the Item or Content Tool, select the item you would like to color.
2. Select the Line Color icon from the top of the Colors Palette.
3. Click on the name of the color you wish to apply to the line. Shades can be applied by choosing a value from the pop-up menu at the top of the Colors Palette or by entering a value into the Shade field.

Creating reversed type

1. Using the Content Tool, highlight the type to be reversed.
2. Select the Text Color icon from the top of the Colors Palette.
3. Click White in the Colors Palette.
4. Select the Background Color icon from the top of the Colors Palette. Click on the name of the color the text should be reversed out of.

Adding rich black to the default palette

Any color defined with no XPress documents active becomes a default color which loads every time a new document is created. To add a rich black to the default palette:

1. Determine the color composition of the rich black. Typically, a rich black is composed of 100% black and a tint of some other process color(s). A common mixture is 100% Black, 60% Cyan. Printers frequently have specific values they prefer for their rich blacks.
2. With no XPress documents open, select Edit: **Colors**. The Default Colors dialog is activated.
3. Click New to access the Edit Colors dialog box.
4. Name the color appropriately, set the Model to CMYK, and uncheck the Spot color checkbox. Next, set the CMYK color readouts to the values determined previously in step 1.
5. Click OK to close the Edit Colors dialog box. Click Save to add the color to the default palette.

Creating a linear one-color blend

1. Select the object to contain the blend with either the Item or the Content Tool. Only boxes may contain blends.

2. Select the Background Color icon from the top of the Colors Palette. When the Background Color icon is selected, the Blend pop-up menu is activated. Set the Fill-type pop-up menu to Linear Blend.

3. Click the Color #1 button. Next, click on the name of the color you wish to blend in the Colors Palette. If necessary, set a shade for the color as well.

4. Click the Color #2 button. Set this color to either White or to a 0% shade of Color #1.

5. Set the angle for the Blend in the Angle field of the Colors Palette. Values from −360° to 360° are permissible and may be set in .001° increments.

Creating a linear two-color blend

1. Select the object to contain the blend with either the Item or the Content Tool. Only boxes may contain blends.

2. Select the Background Color icon from the top of the Colors Palette. When the Background Color icon is selected, the Fill-type pop-up menu becomes activated. Set the Fill-type pop-up menu to Linear Blend.

3. Check the Color #1 radio button. Next, click on the name of the color you wish to blend in the Colors Palette. If necessary, set a shade for the color as well.

4. Once Color #1 is set, check the Color #2 radio button. Set this color as desired, including a shade if necessary.

5. Set the angle for the Blend in the Angle field of the Colors Palette. Values from −360° to 360° are permissible and may be set in .001° increments.

Creating a linear blend of more than two colors

Single XPress items can only blend between two colors. Blends between more than two colors must be created with multiple objects.

1. Create an object containing a linear blend between two colors as described previously.

2. Create a second object. Prepare a Blend for the object such that one of its two Blend colors is the same as one of the Blend colors from the first object.

3. Arrange the two objects together so that they abut along the sides which contain the common color.

4. Continue the process for as many objects as you wish to have in the final blend.

5. Select all the objects that make up the macro blend and choose Item: **Group** to prevent the objects from being nudged out of position accidentally (see Figure A-46).

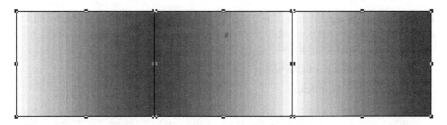

Figure A-46: Using multiple boxes to produce a linear blend containing more than two colors

Masking a blend with a line art image

This technique will allow you to fill a line art image with a color blend:

1. Create a Picture box. Set the Background color of the Picture box to a Blend as described previously.

2. Choose File: **Get Picture** to import a line art (1-bit) TIFF.

3. Resize the Picture box so it fits snugly around the imported graphic.

4. With either the Item or Content Tool selected, choose Style: **Negative**.

5. Select the Picture Color icon from the top of the Colors Palette, and click White (see Figure A-47).

Figure A-47: One-bit line art masking a linear blend

Masking multiple linear blends with a line art image

This technique is similar to the technique for creating a blend with more than two colors. Follow the steps in the preceding technique for masking a blend with a line art image, then do the following:

1. Select the line art image with either the Item or Content Tool.

2. Choose Item: **Duplicate**.

3. Using the Colors Palette, set Blend Color #1 of the newly duplicated second object to the same value as Color #2 of the original object. Set Blend Color #2 of the duplicate object to the third color in the final blend.

4. Select both objects, and choose Item: **Space/Align**. In the Space/Align dialog, choose both Horizontal and Vertical alignment between Centers. This will place one graphic exactly on top of the other.

5. Select the graphic on top (the duplicate). Using either the Item or Content tool, click-drag the left center picture box handle to the right. This will crop part of the top picture, allowing the picture behind it to be exposed.

6. To make the blend appear correct, select the bottom (original) graphic, and drag its right center picture box handle to the left. Resize the Picture box such that its left side and the duplicate graphic's right side abut precisely. Exact positioning is very important—check to make sure no gaps exist. Repeat this process for as many colors as are required in the blend.

7. Once the graphics are in the correct positions, select them all, and choose Item: **Group** (see Figure A-48).

Blending into enriched black

When blending from one color into 100% black, you'll have much better results when the black is enriched with the first color. Otherwise, the middle part of the blend may appear washed out and imprecise. When blending a spot color into black, follow these steps:

1. Determine the first color of the blend. For this example, let's use PMS 185.

2. Determine the shade of the first color of the blend. For this example, we'll use 70%.

3. Choose Edit: **Colors**, and click New.

4. Choose Multi-Ink from the Model pop-up. Specify that the color be made up of 70% PMS 185 and 100% black. Close the dialog, and save the color.

5. Select the box that will contain the blend.

6. In the Colors Palette, click the Background Color icon, and choose Linear Blend from the Blend pop-up.

7. Set the first blend color to 70% PMS 185. Set the second color to the multi-ink item you just defined.

Figure A-48: Duplicating and cropping line art to create the effect of masking blends containing multiple colors

When blending a process color into black, follow these steps:

1. Determine the first color of the blend. For this example, let's use TRUMATCH 6-a.

2. Choose Edit: **Colors**, and click New.

3. Choose CMYK from the Model pop-up. Specify that the new color contain 100% black, as well as percentages of dominant components from the other process color. For example, TRUMATCH 6-a is made up of M: 100 and Y: 100. In this case, you can add 50% magenta and yellow to the color to enrich the black. Close the dialog, and save the color.

4. Select the box that will contain the blend.

5. In the Colors Palette, click the Background Color icon, and choose Linear Blend from the Blend pop-up.

6. Set the first blend color to TRUMATCH 6-a. Set the second color to the new item you just defined.

Creating a spot varnish plate

After creating a spot varnish definition (as described in the "Edit: Colors" section, earlier in this appendix), you must apply it to the appropriate document items in order to generate the varnish plates when the file is separated. Follow these steps (in this example, let's apply a varnish to a single rectangular graphic):

1. Select the desired graphic with the Item Tool.

2. Choose Item: **Step and Repeat**. Enter 0 in the Horizontal and Vertical Offset fields. A copy of the picture box appears directly on top of the original.

3. Select the duplicate with the Content Tool.

4. Delete the contents of the picture box.

5. In the Colors Palette, click the Background Color icon, and click the Spot Varnish color.

6. Leaving the box selected, open the Trap Information Palette.

7. Set the background color of the box to Overprint. This will ensure that the underlying graphic outputs properly when the file is separated.

NOTE

When creating spot varnish plates, many designers prefer to duplicate the document and apply the varnishes there. Then they delete *all* other page information, so only the varnish-tagged boxes appear in the correct position on the appropriate pages. This way, there is no risk of the spot varnish color interfering with the output of the remaining colors. Remember to supply the varnish file with the original document, with a note that specifically explains which pages to print.

Chapter 18, The Trap Information Palette

Trapping with a process bridge

When working with spot colors, the issue of trapping is ever-present—if the colors touch, they must be trapped. In a process document, however, you can sidestep the need for applying additional trap values by planning to use colors that share percentages of component inks sufficient to create a *process bridge*.

A process bridge occurs when two adjacent items share at least 20% of one component color (cyan, magenta, yellow, or black). This generally eliminates the possibility of white gaps appearing as a result of on-press misregistration because the most that can be revealed are colors common to both items.

NOTE

Depending on the adjacent colors, additional trapping may still be necessary. When an adjoining item contains a significantly higher percentage of one component ink, misregistration may result in a visible third color.

Using enriched blacks

When applying large areas of black in a four-color job, two limitations of the transparent ink become evident:

- **Knockout blacks cover poorly.** Paper grain is visible through process black, and the color appears slightly faded or washed out. This is especially evident when compared to denser blacks.

- **Overprint blacks cover poorly.** In theory, overprinting black removes the need for trapping. But if you overprint too large an area—for example, if you place a large black box over a full-color image—you can see the underlying inks through the black.

To compensate for these problems, you must create *enriched blacks*, or colors that contain 100% black plus additional percentages of certain process inks. The extra ink increases the density of the black, making it appear fuller and darker.

NOTE

To differentiate between different types of enriched blacks, I refer to them as *rich black* (which contains one additional process component) and *super black* (which contains more than one). See the following two techniques for more information.

Creating a "rich" black

Rich blacks—which contain one additional process ink—are appropriate for the following occasions:

- When the edges of the black object are fully exposed.

- When a black box *straddles*, or partially covers other image information.

Traditionally, a rich black consists of 60% cyan (the *undercolor*) and 100% black. If all edges of a black item are fully exposed, these values are perfectly acceptable. When the black item is adjacent to other colors, however, cyan may not be the best option. Instead, choose an undercolor that creates a sufficient process bridge with the surrounding image area. Magenta or yellow may be a better choice.

Here, you add only one extra ink because of the exposed edges. XPress has a built-in function called *keepaway*, where the undercolor is drawn back from the edge of the black by the Auto Amount trapping value. This way, should misregistration occur, the undercolor is still covered by the black—extra colors just increase the likelihood of fringe, one or more of the components peeking out from the edge like a multicolored halo.

Follow these steps to create a rich black:

1. Choose Edit: **Colors**.

2. Click New to access the Edit Color dialog. Name the color "Rich Black" or "100K, 60C."

3. Set CMYK in the Model pop-up.

4. Enter 60% in the Cyan field and 100% in the Black field.

5. Make sure the Spot Color box is not checked.

6. Click OK, and save the color.

Creating a "super" black

A super black is comprised of three undercolors instead of simply one—50% cyan, 50% magenta, 50% yellow, and 100% black. This provides the deepest, most satisfying process black you can reproduce on-press.

Super blacks are not appropriate for all occasions. Keep the following in mind:

- Apply a super black when all the edges of an item are buried within a larger range of color (such as placing a black box within an imported color image), or if the edges bleed completely off the page. These circumstances remove the possibility of fringe, since there are no exposed edges.

- When planning to use a super black, consult with your printer first. The ink density of 250% may be too high for either the intended paper stock or the printing press used to reproduce the project.

Follow these steps to create a super black:

1. Choose Edit: **Colors**.

2. Click New to access the Edit Color dialog. Name the color "Super Black" or "100K, 50C, 50M, 50Y."

3. Set CMYK in the Model pop-up.

4. Enter 50% in the Cyan, Magenta, and Yellow fields, and 100% in the Black field.

5. Make sure the Spot Color box is not checked.

6. Click OK, and save the color.

Trapping EPS graphics before importing into a document

Vector-based graphics must be trapped in their original application before you import them into XPress. This is because XPress' trapping tools cannot affect the contents of any EPS file. Follow these steps to create a simple trap in both programs:

1. Create a foreground and background object. For this example, let's place a circle colored PMS 185 (bright red) over a square colored PMS 287 (dark blue).

2. Determine which color is lighter or darker. In this example, PMS 185 is lighter than PMS 287—therefore, the red shape will spread slightly into the blue.

3. Apply a red stroke to the circle. In both programs, a stroke value straddles the path—half the established width appears inside the shape, half the value appears outside. The half placed outside the shape will provide the trap.

4. Set the stroke width to *twice* the intended trap value. For example, if you want a .3 pt. trap, set the width to .6 pt.

5. Set the stroke to Overprint. This way, the stroke outside the shape will over-print the background color when the graphic is separated.

6. Save the file as an EPS, and import it into XPress.

NOTE

Both Illustrator and FreeHand have automatic trapping filters, which use a different technique to apply traps. Here, new thin shapes are added to the graphic, which provide the necessary overprint.

Creating XPress-based duotones

Halftones are reproduced using only one ink—usually, black. In a duotone, multiple inks are used to expand a halftone's rather limited tonal range. For the best results, create a duotone in a program like Adobe Photoshop. There, you have much greater control over the distribution of colors, because you can edit a separate tone curve for each ink. Also, Photoshop ships with bundle of preset duotone curves, already tested to produce optimal print results. If using Photoshop is out of the question, you can create rough-and-ready duotones in XPress— just be aware that your control over the final result is extremely limited.

The first technique combines a halftone with a solid color (in this example, let's use black and Pantone 264 CV):

1. Draw a picture box, and import a Grayscale image.

2. In the Colors Palette, set the box's background to Pantone 264 CV.

3. In the Trap Information Palette, make sure the Picture setting is set to Over-print. This way, when the file is output, the black halftone prints directly over the second color.

To reduce the color intensity of the duotone, reduce the Shade value of the background color. If the second color is particularly dark, reducing the shade is necessary.

NOTE

When overprinting two different spot colors, they must be set to different screen angles. In the previous example, Pantone 264 CV will output most successfully when the Halftone pop-up (in the Edit Color dialog) is set to Cyan. This way, the screen angle is set to 105°, which will not conflict with the default black angle of 45°.

The second technique involves duplicate halftone images (in this example, let's use cyan and black):

1. Draw a picture box, and import a Grayscale image.

2. In the Colors Palette, click the Picture Color icon, then click Cyan to color the image.

3. Leaving the image selected, choose Item: **Step and Repeat**. Enter 0 in the Horizontal and Vertical Offset fields.

4. Color the duplicate image Black.

5. In the Trap Information Palette, set the black image to Overprint.

6. Select both boxes, and choose Item: **Group**.

Creating a semitransparent drop shadow

For this technique, we'll add a semitransparent drop shadow beneath a single character. Follow these steps:

1. Draw a text box. Enter and format the desired character.

2. Highlight the character, and choose Style (Text): **Text to Box**. (Note that converting to a box is not required—it just makes handling the character and its shadow easier.) Discard the original text.

3. Select the character, and apply the desired color.

4. Leaving the character selected, choose Item: **Step and Repeat**. If you prefer, enter the desired offset value. Otherwise, simply create a duplicate, and drag it to the desired position.

5. Color the lower-level box 50% black.

6. Group the two boxes, and position them over an imported graphic or colored box.

7. Select the underlying shadow with the Content Tool.

8. In the Trap Information Palette, set the background color to Overprint. Although the box doesn't appear to overprint the underlying information on-screen, it will when the file is separated and run on-press.

Chapter 20, The Index Palette

Adding an index entry

1. Highlight the desired word or phrase in your XPress document.
2. In the Index Palette, establish the desired settings in the Level, Style, and Scope pop-ups.
3. Click Add.

To change an existing entry, follow these steps:

1. In the Index Palette, click to select the desired entry.
2. Click the Edit button, or double-click the entry.
3. Highlight the contents of the Text field, and type a new entry. The selected entry automatically changes.

Resorting a new index entry

1. Highlight the desired word or phrase.
2. In the Index Palette, click to place the cursor in the Sort field.
3. Enter the desired listing. For example, if you've highlighted "23-Skiddoo" and you want it to appear in the "T" section of the index, enter "Twenty-three skiddoo" in the Sort field.
4. Click Add.

To resort an existing entry, follow these steps:

1. In the Index Palette, click to select the desired entry.
2. Click the Edit button, or double-click the entry.
3. Enter a new listing in the Sort field. The selected entry automatically resorts.

Adding second-, third-, and fourth-level subentries

1. In the Index Palette, click to place the right-pointing arrow next to the entry that will receive the subentry. (You cannot add a subentry without selecting an existing entry.)
2. Choose the desired entry level from the Level pop-up.
3. Click Add.

APPENDIX B

XPress Shortcuts

Tool Palette Shortcuts

Action	Macintosh Shortcut	Windows Shortcut
Show/Hide Tool Palette	F8	F8
Toggle between Item and Content Tool	Shift-F8	Shift F8
Activate tools in downward sequence	Option-F8, or Command-Tab	Alt-F8, or Alt-Control-Tab
Activate tools in upward sequence	Option-Shift-F8, or Command-Shift-Tab	Alt-Shift F8, or Alt-Control-Shift-Tab
Keep a tool selected	Option-click tool	Alt-click tool
Open Tool tab of Document Preferences	Double-click item Creation tool or zoom tool	Double-click item Creation tool or zoom tool

The Item Tool

Action	Macintosh Shortcut	Windows Shortcut
Select multiple items or points	Shift-click	Shift-click
Select hidden item	Option-Command-Shift-click where items overlap	Alt-Control-Shift-click where items overlap
Deselect all items	Tab (Item Tool selected)	Tab (Item Tool)
Moving with no constraints	Command-drag	Control-drag

Action	Macintosh Shortcut	Windows Shortcut
Moving with horizontal/vertical constraints	Command-Shift-drag	Control-Shift-drag
Constrain rectangle to square or oval to circle	Shift while creating or resizing	Shift while creating or resizing
Constrain straight line angle to 0°/45°/90°	Shift while creating, resizing, or rotating	Shift while creating, resizing, or rotating
Open Modify dialog box	Double-click item with Item Tool	Double-click item with Item Tool
Nudge left 1 pt.	←	←
Nudge left $\frac{1}{10}$ pt.	Option- ←	Alt- ←
Nudge right 1 pt.	→	→
Nudge right $\frac{1}{10}$ pt.	Option- →	Alt- →
Nudge up 1 pt.	↑	↑
Nudge up $\frac{1}{10}$ pt.	Option- ↑	Alt- ↑
Nudge down 1 pt.	↓	↓
Nudge down $\frac{1}{10}$ pt.	Option- ↓	Alt- ↓

The Content Tool

Action	Macintosh Shortcut	Windows Shortcut
Nudge picture left 1 pt.	←	←
Nudge picture left $\frac{1}{10}$ pt.	Option- ←	Alt- ←
Nudge picture right 1 pt.	→	→
Nudge picture right $\frac{1}{10}$ pt.	Option- →	Alt- →
Nudge picture up 1 pt.	↑	↑
Nudge picture nudge picture up $\frac{1}{10}$ pt.	Option- ↑	Alt- ↑
Nudge picture down 1 pt.	↓	↓
Nudge picture down $\frac{1}{10}$ pt.	Option- ↓	Alt- ↓
Change font by selecting font field in Measurements Palette	Option-Command-Shift-M	Alt-Control-Shift-M
Apply previous font	Option-Shift-F9	Control-Shift-F9
Apply next font	Option-F9	Control-F9
Enter single Symbol font character	Command-Shift-Q	Control-Shift-Q
Enter single Zapf Dingbats font character	Command-Shift-Z	Control-Shift-Z
Copy formats to selected paragraphs in text chain	Option-Shift-click	Alt-Shift-click

Action	Macintosh Shortcut	Windows Shortcut
Drag-copy text (Interactive Preference on)	Shift-drag	Shift-drag
Drag text (Interactive Preference off)	Command-Control-drag	Does not apply
Drag-copy text (Interactive Preference off)	Command-Control-Shift-drag	Does not apply
Moving the Text Insertion Point		
Position text insertion point	One click	One click
Move cursor to previous character	←	←
Move cursor to next character	→	→
Move cursor to previous line	↑	↑
Move cursor to next line	↓	↓
Move cursor to previous word	Command- ←	Control- ←
Move cursor to next word	Command- →	Control- →
Move cursor to previous paragraph	Command- ↑	Control- ↑
Move cursor to next paragraph	Command- ↓	Control- ↓
Move cursor to start of line	Option-Command- ←	Alt-Control- ← or Home
Move cursor to end of line	Option-Command- →	Alt-Control- → or End
Move cursor to start of story	Option-Command- ↑	Alt-Control- ↑ or Control-Home
Move cursor to end of story	Option-Command- ↓	Alt-Control- ↓ or Control-End
Highlighting Characters		
Highlight word	Two clicks in the word	Two clicks in the word
Highlight word and its period, comma, etc.	Two clicks between word and punctuation	Two clicks between word and punctuation
Highlight line	Three clicks	Three clicks
Highlight paragraph	Four clicks	Four clicks
Highlight story	Five clicks	Five clicks
Highlight previous character	←	←
Highlight next character	→	→
Highlight previous line	↑	↑
Highlight next line	↓	↓

Action	Macintosh Shortcut	Windows Shortcut
Highlight previous word	Command- ←	Control- ←
Highlight next word	Command- →	Control- →
Highlight to previous paragraph	Command- ↑	Control- ↑
Highlight to next paragraph	Command- ↓	Control- ↓
Highlight to start of line	Option-Command- ←	Alt-Control- ← or Home
Highlight to end of line	Option-Command- →	Alt-Control- → or End
Highlight to start of story	Option-Command- ↑	Alt-Control- ↑ or Control-Home
Highlight to end of story	Option-Command- ↓	Alt-Control- ↓ or Control-End
Deleting Characters		
Delete previous character	Delete	Backspace
Delete next character	Shift-Delete	Delete or Shift-Backspace
Delete previous word	Command-Delete	Control-Backspace
Delete next word	Command-Shift-Delete	Control-Delete or Control-Shift-Backspace
Delete highlighted character	Delete	Delete or Backspace
The Rotation Tool		
Constrain item rotation to 0°/45°/90°	Shift while rotating	Shift while rotating
The Zoom Tool		
Zoom in	Control-click or drag	Control-space-click/drag
Zoom out	Control-Option-click/drag	Alt-Control-space-click/drag
The Text Box Tools		
Resize box (proportional)	Option-Command-Shift-drag handle	Alt-Control-Shift-drag handle
Resize box (constrained)	Command-Shift-drag handle	Control-Shift-drag handle
Resize box (nonproportional)	Command-drag handle	Control-drag handle
The Picture Box Tools		
Center picture to box	Command-Shift-M	Control-Shift-M
Fit picture to box	Command-Shift-F	Control-Shift-F
Fit to box maintaining proportions	Option-Command-Shift-F	Alt-Control-Shift-F
Resizing Boxes		
Resize box constraining box shape	Shift-drag	Shift-drag

Action	Macintosh Shortcut	Windows Shortcut
Resize box maintaining aspect ratio	Option-Shift-drag	Alt-Shift-drag
Resize box and scale picture	Command-drag	Control-drag
Resize box and scale picture constraining box	Command-Shift-drag	Control-Shift-drag
Resize box and scale picture maintaining proportions	Option-Command-Shift-drag	Alt-Control-Shift-drag
Resize box (proportional)	Option-Command-Shift-drag handle	Alt-Control-Shift-drag handle
Resize box (constrained)	Command-Shift-drag handle	Control-Shift-drag handle
Resize box (nonproportional)	Command-drag handle	Control-drag handle

Scaling Pictures

Increase scale 5%	Option-Command-Shift->	Alt-Control-Shift- >
Decrease scale 5%	Option-Command-Shift-<	Alt-Control-Shift- <

The Line Tools

Constrain straight line angle to 0°/45°/90°	Shift-while creating, resizing, or rotating	Shift-while creating, resizing, or rotating
Increase line width by preset range	Command-Shift->	Control-Shift->
Increase line width by 1 pt.	Option-Command-Shift->	Alt-Control-Shift->
Decrease line width by preset range	Command-Shift-<	Control-Shift-<
Decrease line width by 1 pt.	Option-Command-Shift-<	Alt-Control-Shift-<

Editing Bézier Lines

Delete Bézier point	Option-click point	Alt-click point or Back-space (Item Tool)
Delete active Bézier point while creating item	Delete (Item Tool)	Backspace
Add Bézier point	Option-click segment	Alt-click segment
Corner to smooth point	Control-drag curve handle	Control-Shift-drag curve handle
Smooth to corner point	Control-drag curve handle	Control-Shift-drag curve handle
Smooth to corner point while creating item	Command- Control-drag curve handle	Control-click point, then press Control-F1

Action	Macintosh Shortcut	Windows Shortcut
Edit Bézier while creating item	Command while creating item	Control
Retract curve handles	Control-click point	Control-Shift-click point
Expose curve handles	Control-drag point	Control-Shift-drag point
Select all Bézier points in active item	Command-Shift A or triple-click point	Control-Shift A or triple-click point
Select all Bézier points in active path	Double-click point	Double-click point
Constrain active point to 45° movement	Shift-drag point	Shift-drag point
Constrain active curve handle to 45° movement	Shift-drag curve handle	Shift-drag curve handle
Convert Bézier line to filled-center Bézier box	Option-Item: Shape	Alt-Item: Shape

Dialog Controls

Action	Macintosh Shortcut	Windows Shortcut
Dialog Panels		
Display next tab	Command-Tab	Control-Tab
Display previous tab	Command-Shift-Tab	Control-Shift-Tab
Value Fields		
Highlight next field	Tab	Tab
Highlight previous field	Shift-Tab	Shift-Tab
Highlight field with text insertion bar	Double-click	Double-click
Cut	Command-X	Control-X
Copy	Command-C	Control-C
Paste	Command-V	Control-V
Revert fields/dialog to original values	Command-Z	Control-Shift-Z
Undo	Does not apply	Control-Z
Perform math by combining operators	+ (addition) − (subtraction) * (multiplication) / (division)	+ (addition) − (subtraction) * (multiplication) / (division)
Buttons		
OK (or bordered button)	Return or Enter	Enter
Cancel	Command- . (period)	Escape
Yes	Command-Y	Y
No	Command-N	N
Apply	Command-A	Alt-A

Action	Macintosh Shortcut	Windows Shortcut
Keep Apply button selected (except in Space/Align)	Option-Command-A or Option-click Apply button	Control-click Apply button
Set button in Tabs (in Paragraph Attributes)	Command-S	Control-S
Scrolling Lists		
Select continuous components in list	Shift-click	Shift-click
Select noncontinuous components in list	Command-click	Control-click

The File Menu

Action	Macintosh Shortcut	Windows Shortcut
New Document	Command-N	Control-N
New Library	Option-Command-N	Alt-Control-N
Open	Command-O	Control-O
Reflow text as current version of QuarkXPress	Option-Open (in Open dialog)	Alt-Open (in Open dialog)
Close	Command-W	Control-F4
Close all document windows	Option-click close box or Option-Command-W	Does not apply
Save	Command-S	Control-S
Save As	Option-Command-S	Alt-Control-S
Revert to last Auto Save document	Option-File: Revert to Saved	Alt-File: Revert to Saved
Get Picture	Command-E	Control-E
Import picture at 36 dpi	Shift-click Open in Get Picture	Shift-click Open in Get Picture
Import color TIFF, JPEG, or Scitex CT as Grayscale	Command-click Open in Get Picture	Control-click Open in Get Picture
Import Grayscale TIFF, JPEG, or Scitex CT as B&W	Command-click Open in Get Picture dialog	Control-click Open in Get Picture dialog
Import EPS without adding spot colors	Command-click Open in Get Picture dialog	Control-click Open in Get Picture dialog
Reimport all pictures in document	Command-click Open in Open dialog	Control-click Open in Open dialog
Get Text	Command-E	Control-E
Save Text	Option-Command-E	Alt-Control-E
Append	Option-Command-A	Alt-Control-A
Save Page as EPS	Option-Command-Shift-S	Alt-Control-Shift-S

Action	Macintosh Shortcut	Windows Shortcut
Document Setup	Option-Command-Shift-P	Alt-Control-Shift-P
Page Setup Panel	Option-Command-P	Alt-Control-P
Print	Command-P	Control-P
Quit	Command-Q	Control-Q

Edit Menu

Action	Macintosh Shortcut	Windows Shortcut
Undo	Command-Z or F1	Control-Z
Cut	Command-X or F2	Control- X
Copy	Command-C or F3	Control-C
Paste	Command-V or F4	Control-V
Select All	Command-A	Control-A
Find/Change	Command-F	Control-F
Change Find Next button to Find First	Option-Find Next	Alt-Find Next
Wildcard character (Find only)	Command-?	Control-?
Tab character	Command-Tab	Control-Tab
New Paragraph character	Command-Return	Control-Enter
New Line character	Command-Shift-Return	Control-Shift-Enter
New Column character	Command-Enter	\c
New Box character	Command-Shift-Enter	\b
Previous box page number character	Command-2	Control-2
Current box page number character	Command-3	Control-3
Next box page number character	Command-4	Control-4
Punctuation space character	Command-. (period)	Control-. (period)
Flex space character	Command-Shift-F	Control-Shift-F
Backslash character	Command- \	Control- \
Close Find/Change	Option-Command-F	Alt-Control-F
Application Preferences	Option-Command-Shift-Y	Alt-Control-Shift-Y
Document Preferences	Command-Y	Control-Y
Open Paragraph panel	Option-Command-Y	Alt-Control-Y
Open Trapping panel	Option-Shift-F12	Control-Shift-F12
Open Tool panel	Double-click item creation or zoom tool	Double-click item creation or zoom tool

Action	Macintosh Shortcut	Windows Shortcut
Style Sheets	Shift-F11	Shift-F11
Colors	Shift-F12	Shift-F12
H&Js	Option-Command-H or Option-Shift-F11	Control-Shift-F11

Style Menu (Text)

Action	Macintosh Shortcut	Windows Shortcut
Size: Other	Command-Shift- \	Control-Shift- \
Increase font size by preset range	Command-Shift->	Control-Shift->
Increase font size by 1 pt.	Option-Command-Shift->	Alt-Control-Shift->
Decrease font size by reset range	Command-Shift-<	Control-Shift-<
Decrease font size by 1 pt.	Option-Command-Shift-<	Alt-Control-Shift-<
Type Styles		
Plain	Command-Shift-P	Control-Shift-P
Bold	Command-Shift-B	Control-Shift-B
Italic	Command-Shift-I	Control-Shift-I
Underline	Command-Shift-U	Control-Shift-U
Word underline	Command-Shift-W	Control-Shift-W
Strike through	Command-Shift- /	Control-Shift- /
Outline	Command-Shift-O	Control-Shift-O
Shadow	Command-Shift-S	Control-Shift-S
All Caps	Command-Shift-K	Control-Shift-K
Small Caps	Command-Shift-H	Control-Shift-H
Superscript	Command-Shift- + (plus)	Control-Shift-0 (zero)
Subscript	Command-Shift- - (hyphen)	Control-Shift-9
Superior	Command-Shift-V	Control-Shift-V
Increase horizontal/ vertical scale by 5%	Command-]	Control-]
Increase horizontal/ vertical scale by 1%	Option-Command-]	Alt-Control-]
Decrease horizontal/ vertical scale by 5%	Command-[	Control-[
Decrease horizontal/ vertical scale by 5%	Option-Command-[	Alt-Control-[
Increase Kern/Track by $\frac{1}{20}$ em	Command-Shift-}	Control-Shift-}
Increase Kern/Track by $\frac{1}{200}$ em	Option-Command-Shift-}	Alt-Control-Shift-}

Action	Macintosh Shortcut	Windows Shortcut
Decrease Kern/Track by $\frac{1}{20}$ em	Command-Shift- {	Control-Shift- {
Decrease Kern/Track by $\frac{1}{200}$ em	Option-Command-Shift- {	Alt-Control-Shift- {
Baseline Shift up 1 pt.	Option-Command-Shift- + (plus)	Alt-Control-Shift-)
Baseline Shift down 1 pt.	Option-Command-Shift- - (hyphen)	Alt-Control-Shift- (
Character	Command-Shift-D	Control-Shift-D
Alignment		
Left	Command-Shift-L	Control-Shift-L
Center	Command-Shift-C	Control-Shift-C
Right	Command-Shift-R	Control-Shift-R
Justified	Command-Shift-J	Control-Shift-J
Forced	Option-Command-Shift-J	Alt-Control-Shift-J
Leading	Command-Shift-E	Control-Shift-E
Increase leading by 1 pt.	Command-Shift-"	Control-Shift-"
Increase leading by $\frac{1}{10}$ pt.	Option-Command-Shift-"	Alt-Control-Shift-"
Decrease leading by 1 pt.	Command-Shift-:	Control-Shift-:
Decrease leading by $\frac{1}{10}$ pt.	Option-Command-Shift-:	Alt-Control-Shift-:
Formats	Command-Shift-F	Control-Shift-F
Tabs	Command-Shift-T	Control-Shift-T
Rules	Command-Shift-N	Control-Shift-N
Text to Box (anchor boxes and delete text)	Option-Text to Box	Alt-Text to Box

Style Menu (Picture)

Action	Macintosh Shortcut	Windows Shortcut
Negative	Command-Shift- - (hyphen)	Control-Shift- - (hyphen)
Contrast	Command-Shift-C	Control-Shift-O
Halftone	Command-Shift-H	Control-Shift-H

Style Menu (Line)

Action	Macintosh Shortcut	Windows Shortcut
Width: Other	Command-Shift- \	Control-Shift- \

Item Menu

Action	Macintosh Shortcut	Windows Shortcut
Modify	Command-M	Control-M
Frame	Command-B	Control-B
Clipping	Option-Command-T	Alt-Control-T
Runaround	Command-T	Control-T
Duplicate	Command-D	Control-D
Step and Repeat	Option-Command-D	Alt-Control-D
Delete	Command-K	Control-K
Group	Command-G	Control-G
Ungroup	Command-U	Control-U
Lock/Unlock	F6	F6
Bring to Front	F5	F5
Bring Forward	Option-Bring to Front or Option-F5	Control-F5
Send to Back	Shift-F5	Shift-F5
Send Backward	Option-Send to Back or Option-Shift-F5	Control-Shift-F5
Space/Align	Command- , (comma)	Control- , (comma)
Shape (convert Bézier line to filled-center Bézier box)	Option-Item: Shape	Alt-Item: Shape
Edit		
Shape	Shift-F4	F10
Runaround	Option-F4	Control-F10
Clipping Path	Option-Shift-F4	Control-Shift-F10
Point/Segment Type		
Corner Point	Option-F1	Control-F1
Smooth Point	Option-F2	Control-F2
Symmetrical Point	Option-F3	Control-F3
Straight Segment	Option-Shift-F1	Control-Shift-F1
Curved Segment	Option-Shift-F2	Control-Shift-F2

Page Menu

Action	Macintosh Shortcut	Windows Shortcut
Go to Page	Command-J	Control-J
Display (master pages)	Shift-F10	Shift-F4
Display (next master page)	Option-F10	Control-Shift-F4
Display (previous master page)	Option-Shift-F10	Control-Shift-F3
Display document (master page displayed)	Shift-F10	Shift-F4

View Menu

Action	Macintosh Shortcut	Windows Shortcut
Scrolling		
With Page Grabber Hand	Option-drag	Alt-drag
Enable Live Scroll (Inter-active Preference off)	Option-drag scroll box	Does not apply
Disable Live Scroll (Interactive Preference on)	Option-drag scroll box	Does not apply
To start of document	Control-A	Control-Home
To end of document	Control-D	Control-End
Up one screen	Control-K	Page up
Down one screen	Control-L	Page down
To first page	Control-Shift-A	Control-Page up
To last page	Control-Shift-D	Control-Page down
To previous page	Control-Shift-K	Shift-Page up
To next page	Control-Shift-L	Shift-Page down
To previous spread	Does not apply	Alt-Page up
To next spread	Does not apply	Alt-Page down
Extended keyboard		
Start of document	Home	Does not apply
End of document	End	Does not apply
Up one screen	Page up	Does not apply
Down one screen	Page down	Does not apply
To first page	Shift-Home	Does not apply
To last page	Shift-End	Does not apply
To previous page	Shift-Page up	Does not apply
To next page	Shift-Page down	Does not apply
Changing Zoom Percentage		
Any view to Actual Size (Caps Lock on)	Option-click	Control-1 (one)
Actual Size to Fit in Window (Caps Lock on)	Option-click	Control-0 (zero)
Any view to 200%	Option-Command-click	Alt-Control-click
200% to Actual Size	Option-Command-click	Alt-Control-click
Access view percent field	Control-V	Alt-Control-V
Fit in Window	Command-0 (zero)	Control-0 (zero)
Fit largest spread in window	Option-Fit in Window or Option-Command-0 (zero)	Alt-Fit in Window or Alt-Control-0 (zero)
Actual Size	Command-1	Control-1

XPress Shortcuts

Action	Macintosh Shortcut	Windows Shortcut
Thumbnails	Shift-F6	Shift-F6
Show/Hide Guides	F7	F7
Show/Hide Baseline Grid	Option-F7	Control-F7

Tiling and Stacking Documents

Action	Macintosh Shortcut	Windows Shortcut
Windows submenu	Control-Tile/Stack	Does not apply
Tile or Stack at Actual Size	Command-Tile/Stack	Does not apply
Tile or Stack at Fit in Window	Option-Tile/Stack	Does not apply
Tile or Stack at Thumbnails	Shift-click title bar	Does not apply
Shortcut to Window submenu	Control-Shift-Tile/Stack	Does not apply
Tile or Stack at Actual Size from title bar	Command-Shift-Tile/Stack	Does not apply
Tile or Stack at Fit in Window from title bar	Option-Shift-Tile/Stack	Does not apply
Tile or Stack at Thumbnails from title bar	Option-Shift-Tile/Stack	Does not apply
Snap to Guides	Shift-F7	Shift-F7
Show/Hide Rulers	Command-R	Control-R
Delete horizontal ruler guides	Option-click horizontal ruler	Alt-click horizontal ruler
Delete vertical ruler guides	Option-click vertical ruler	Alt-click vertical ruler
Show/Hide Invisibles	Command-I	Control-I
Preview	Option-Shift-F7	Control-Shift-F7
Show/Hide Tools	F8	F8
Show/Hide Measurements	F9	F9
Show/Hide Document Layout	F10	F4
Show/Hide Style Sheets	F11	F11
Show/Hide Colors	F12	F12
Show/Hide Trap Information	Option-F12	Control-F12
Show/Hide Lists	Option-F11	Control-F11

Redrawing the Screen

Action	Macintosh Shortcut	Windows Shortcut
Halt redraw	Command- . (period)	Escape
Force redraw	Option-Command- . (period)	Shift-Escape

Utilities Menu

Action	Macintosh Shortcut	Windows Shortcut
Check Spelling (word)	Command-L	Control-W
Check Spelling (story)	Option-Command-L	Alt-Control-W
Check Spelling (document)	Option-Command-Shift-L	Alt-Control-Shift-W
Lookup (Check Spelling)	Command-L	Alt-L
Skip (Check Spelling)	Command-S	Alt-S
Add (Check Spelling)	Command-A	Alt-A
Add all suspect words to auxiliary dictionary	Option-Shift-Done	Alt-Shift-Close
Suggested Hyphenation	Command-H	Control-H
Open Usage: Fonts panel	F13	Does not apply
Open Usage: Pictures panel	Option-F13	Does not apply

Measurements Palette

Action	Macintosh Shortcut	Windows Shortcut
Display palette	F9	F9
Highlight first field (or display palette)	Option-Command-M	Alt-Control-M
Highlight font field (or display palette)	Option-Command-Shift-M	Alt-Control-Shift-M
Highlight next field	Tab	Tab
Highlight previous field	Shift-Tab	Shift-Tab
Exit/Apply	Return or Enter	Enter
Exit/Cancel	Command- . (period)	Escape

Document Layout Palette

Action	Macintosh Shortcut	Windows Shortcut
Display palette	F10	F4
Open Section dialog box for selected page	Click lower-left corner of palette	Click lower-left corner of palette
Open Insert Pages dialog box	Option-drag master page into document area	Alt-drag master page into document area

Style Sheets Palette

Action	Macintosh Shortcut	Windows Shortcut
Display palette	F11	F11
Display edit style sheet pop-up menu	Control-click style sheet	Right-click style sheet name
Open Edit Style Sheet dialog box	Command-click style sheet	Control-click style sheet
Apply No Style, then style sheet	Option-click style sheet	Alt-click style sheet name

Colors Palette

Action	Macintosh Shortcut	Windows Shortcut
Display palette	F12	F12
Open Colors dialog box	Command-click color name	Control-click color name

Trap Information Palette

Action	Macintosh Shortcut	Windows Shortcut
Display palette	Option-F12	Control-F12
Lists Palette		
Display palette	Option-F11	Control-F11
Index Palette		
Display palette	Option-Command-I	Alt-Control-I
Highlight text field	Option Command-I	Alt-Control-I
Click Add button	Option-Command-Shift-I	Alt-Control-Shift-I
Edit highlighted index entry	Double-click	Double-click

Entering Special Characters

Action	Macintosh Shortcut	Windows Shortcut
Indent here	Command-\	Control-\
Discretionary new line	Command-Return	Control-Enter
New paragraph	Return	Enter
New line	Shift-Return	Shift-Enter
New column	Enter	Enter (keypad)
New box	Shift-Enter	Shift-Enter (keypad)
Right-indent tab	Option-Tab	Shift-Tab
Hyphens and Dashes		
Breaking standard hyphen	- (hyphen)	- (hyphen)

Action	Macintosh Shortcut	Windows Shortcut
Nonbreaking standard hyphen	Command- =	Control- =
Discretionary (soft) hyphen	Command- - (hyphen)	Control- - (hyphen)
Break at discretionary hyphens only	Command- - (hyphen) immediately before word	Does not apply
Nonbreaking en dash	Option- - (hyphen)	Alt-Control-Shift- - (hyphen)
Breaking em dash	Option-Shift- - (hyphen)	Control-Shift- =
Nonbreaking em dash	Option-Command- =	Alt-Control-Shift- =
Spaces		
Breaking standard space	Space	Space
Nonbreaking standard space	Command-Space or Command-5	Control-5
Breaking en space	Option-Space	Control-Shift-6
Nonbreaking en space	Option-Command-Space or Option-Command-5	Alt-Control-Shift-6
System 7 with World-Script	Option-Control-Space	Does not apply
Breaking flexible space	Option-Shift-Space	Control-Shift-5
Nonbreaking flexible space	Option-Command-Shift-Space	Alt-Control-Shift-5
Breaking punctuation space	Shift-Space	Shift-Space or Control-6
Nonbreaking punctuation space	Command-Shift-Space	Control-Shift-Space or Alt-Control-6
Automatic Page Numbers Characters		
Previous text box	Command-2	Control-2
Current text box	Command-3	Control-3
Next text box	Command-4	Control-4

XPress
Shortcuts

Index

P

Page Menu, 259–274, 508
  techniques for using, 468–471
Page Select field, 276
page size, 45–47
page tools, 3–12
PageMaker files, opening in XPress, 422
pages
  adding, 49, 262–265, 350
  copying to another document, 471
  deleting, 265–266, 351
  dimensions of, changing, 80–81
  displayed (Document Layout Palette),
      347–348
  facing, 49, 262
    blank, 349
    copying, 279
  imposing, 345
  master (see master pages)
  moving, 266–268, 347
  numbering, 263, 269–272, 385
    of chapters, 271
    techniques for, 468–471
  saving as EPS files, 74–79
  selecting, 5, 347
  single-sided, 261–262, 279
    blank, 349
  with bleeds, preparing, 483
Pages field (Print dialog), 86
PANTONE
  Coated color model, 148
  Process color model, 149
  ProSim color model, 149
  Uncoated color model, 149
paper size, 45
paragraph styles, 358
  applying, 200, 354–355
  copying, 452
  editing, 137–140
paragraphs
  adding rules above/below, 198–200
  formatting, 189–193
Paste command (Edit Menu), 101–102
pasteboard, preferences, 115
pasting, 6
  color, 361
  graphics, 9
  Measurements Palette and, 326
  styles, from another document, 353

techniques for, 429–431
text, 9
paths, 29–33
  moving, 6
  scaling, 404
  trapping, 380–381
  types of, 31
Photoshop
  color modes and, 66
  converting brightness values to
      XPress percentages, 147
  using to crop graphics, 20
Photoshop, opening XPress files in, 422
picture box tools, 22–24, 501
picture boxes, 19–24, 201–210
  coloring, 369–370
  converting to Bézier curves, 20
  editing contents of, 219–221
  flipping, 210
  Measurements Palette and, 325,
      332–334
  preferences, 21
  scaling, 21
  trapping, 379
  (see also boxes)
points, 30–33
  converting, 341
  moving, 340, 342
  types of, 30–31
posterizing, 207
  technique for, 462–463
PostScript
  errors, 94
  files, creating, 426–428
PPD files, 83, 308–310
PPD Manager dialog (Utilities Menu),
    309–310
preferences
  Auto Save, 116
  display, 112–113
  document, 118–131
  guides, 281
  indexes, 131–133
  leading, 123
  pasteboard, 115
  picture boxes, 21
  quotation marks, 115
  rulers, 119, 120
  scrolling, 114

tools, 127–129
trapping, 120, 129–131
unit of measurement, 119
Preferences (Edit Menu), 112–133
preformatting (see formatting)
Preview panel (Print dialog), 97
Preview pop-up (Save Page as EPS File
  dialog), 77–78
previewing
  dashes, 166
  hyphenation, 293
  stripes, 169
Print Book button (Book Palette), 54
Print dialog (File Menu), 85–97
print styles, 169–172
printer spread impositions, techniques
  for creating, 480–482
printing
  books, 54
  composites, 424
  documents, 82–97
  graphics, 302
  separations, 424–425
  thumbnails, 279
Publish and Subscribe (Edit Menu),
  103–105

Q
quitting, XPress, 97
quotation marks, 65, 115, 398

R
raised caps, formatting, 453
Redo command (Edit Menu), 98–99
registration marks, adding to printouts,
  88
repositioning (see moving)
resizing (see size)
reversed type, technique for creating,
  487
RGB color model, 143, 147
  as Colors Palette default, 365
  editing, 208
rotating
  Bézier items, 340
  boxes (picture and text), 217

graphics, 334
graphics in boxes, 220
lines, 336–339
picture boxes, 332
techniques for, 397
text, 222
text boxes, 328
text columns, 222
Rotation Tool, 10–11, 397–398
RTF files, 71
ruler guides, 510
rulers, 119
  guides, 120
  showing and hiding, 284–285
rules (see lines)
Runaround command (Item Menu),
  232–236
runarounds, editing, 256
run-in heads, formatting, 435

S
Save As dialog (File Menu), 61
Save Page as EPS dialog (File Menu),
  76–79
Save Text dialog (File Menu), 71
scaling
  characters, 180
  graphics, 333, 502
  paths, 404
  picture boxes, 21
  text, 175
screen values, defining, 209–210
scrolling, 276–277, 509
  preferences, 114
searching (see Find/Change)
Section dialog (Page Menu), 271–272
segments, 30, 31
  converting, 341
  moving, 340
Select All command (Edit Menu), 103
selecting, 3–5, 7–8, 103
  pages, 347
  points, 31
  segments, 31
  text, 500
    in linked boxes, 41
  thumbnails, 279

U

Undo command (Edit Menu), 98–99
Ungroup command (Item Menu), 244
units of measurement, preferences, 119
Unlinking Tool, 41–42
Utilities Menu, 286–322, 511
   techniques for using, 475–479

V

versions (of XPress), opening, 56
View Menu, 275–285, 509–510
   techniques for using, 471–475
viewing, thumbnails, 280

W

wildcards, using with Find/Change, 435
Word Count dialog (Utilities Menu), 286
wrapping, text, 232–236

X

XPress Dictionary file, 286
XPress files, opening in other programs,
   422–423
XTensions, 117–118, 304–305
   Cool Blends, 366–368
   Index, 388
XTensions Manager (Utilities Menu),
   305–308

Z

zero origin, 284, 344
zooming, 277–278, 509
   Zoom field, 275–276
   zoom tools, 11–12, 275–276, 501
      magnification range of, 128

About the Author

Donnie O'Quinn is a graphic arts consultant, on-site trainer, and author based in Portland, Maine. Classroom-based programs under his direction were described as "hands down, the best prepress training in the Northeast," by Printing Industries of New England. His past clients include Apple Computer, MetaCreations, and *MacUser* magazine, as well as service bureaus, designers, and printers from New York to Nova Scotia. When not working or writing, he readies his overpowered '74 Chevy for a top-down, high-speed pursuit of the American dream.

Colophon

The animal featured on the cover of *Quark XPress in a Nutshell* is a hare. A small grazing mammal, the hare is generally larger than a rabbit, has longer ears, softer fur, and longer, more powerful hind legs. When chased, hares rely on speed and sudden changes in direction (called "jinking") to elude pursuers. Wide-set eyes give them a wide angle of vision. Primarily nocturnal, they can scent enemies, thump the ground with a hind leg when alarmed, and, in turn, sense the nearby thumping of other startled hares.

Hares occupy open country, and are mainly solitary except during breeding season. The pre-mating antics of the males include bucking, bounding, kicking, and standing on hind legs to box with one another; thus the saying, "Mad as a March hare." These boisterous exercises can sometimes include a dozen or more participants. The hare's acknowledged reproductive prowess helps compensate for its high rate of predation.

Edie Freedman designed the cover of this book, using a 19th-century engraving from the Dover Pictorial Archive. The cover layout was produced by Kathleen Wilson with Quark XPress 3.32 using the ITC Garamond font.

The inside layout was designed by Nancy Priest and implemented in Frame by Mike Sierra. The text and heading fonts are ITC Garamond Light and Garamond Book. The screen shots that appear in the book were created in Adobe Photoshop 4 and the illustrations were created in Macromedia Freehand 7.0 by Robert Romano. This colophon was written by Michael Kalantarian.

Whenever possible, our books use RepKover™, a durable and flexible lay-flat binding. If the page count exceeds RepKover's limit, perfect binding is used.

More Titles from O'Reilly

Graphics/Multimedia

Encyclopedia of Graphics File Formats, 2nd Edition

By James D. Murray &
William vanRyper
2nd Edition May 1996
1154 pages, Includes CD-ROM
ISBN 1-56592-161-5

The second edition of the *Encyclopedia of Graphics File Formats* provides the convenience of quick look-up on CD-ROM, up-to-date information through links to the World Wide Web, as well as a printed book—all in one package. Includes technical details on more than 100 file formats. The CD-ROM includes vendor file format specs, graphics test images, coding examples, and graphics conversion and manipulation software. An indispensable online resource for graphics programmers, service bureaus, and graphic artists.

Director in a Nutshell

By Bruce A. Epstein
1st Edition August 1998 (est.)
450 pages (est.), ISBN 1-56592-382-0

Director in a Nutshell is the most concise and complete guide available for Director®. The reader gets both the nitty-gritty details and the bigger context in which to use the multiple facets of Director. It is a high-end handbook, at a low-end price—an indispensable desktop reference for every Director user.

Photoshop in a Nutshell

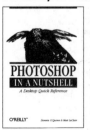

By Donnie O'Quinn & Matt LeClair
1st Edition October 1997
610 pages, ISBN 1-56592-313-8

Photoshop 4's powerful features make it the software standard for desktop image design and production. But they also make it an extremely complex product. This detailed reference defines and describes every tool, command, palette, and sub-menu of Photoshop 4 to help users understand design options, make informed choices, and reduce time spent learning by trial-and-error.

QuarkXPress in a Nutshell

By Donnie O'Quinn
1st Edition June 1998 (est.)
552 pages (est.), ISBN 1-56592-399-5

This quick reference describes every tool, command, palette, and sub-menu in QuarkXPress 4, providing users with a detailed understanding of the software so they can make informed choices and reduce time spent learning by trial-and-error.

Developing Web Content

Frontier: The Definitive Guide

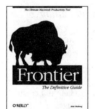

By Matt Neuburg
1st Edition February 1998
618 pages, 1-56592-383-9

This definitive guide is the first book devoted exclusively to teaching and documenting Userland Frontier, a powerful scripting environment for web site management and system level scripting. Packed with examples, advice, tricks, and tips, *Frontier: The Definitive Guide* teaches you Frontier from the ground up. Learn how to automate repetitive processes, control remote computers across a network, beef up your web site by generating hundreds of related web pages automatically, and more. Covers Frontier 4.2.3 for the Macintosh.

WebMaster in a Nutshell

By Stephen Spainhour &
Valerie Quercia
1st Edition October 1996
374 pages, ISBN 1-56592-229-8

Web content providers and administrators have many sources for information, both in print and online. WebMaster in a Nutshell puts it all together in one slim volume for easy desktop access. This quick reference covers HTML, CGI, JavaScript, Perl, HTTP, and server configuration.

O'REILLY™

TO ORDER: **800-998-9938** • *order@oreilly.com* • *http://www.oreilly.com/*
OUR PRODUCTS ARE AVAILABLE AT A BOOKSTORE OR SOFTWARE STORE NEAR YOU.
FOR INFORMATION: **800-998-9938** • **707-829-0515** • *info@oreilly.com*

Developing Web Content

WebMaster in a Nutshell, Deluxe Edition

By O'Reilly & Associates, Inc.
1st Edition September 1997
374 pages, includes CD-ROM & book
ISBN 1-56592-305-7

The Deluxe Edition of WebMaster in a Nutshell is a complete library for web programmers. It features the Web Developer's Library, a CD-ROM containing the electronic text of five popular O'Reilly titles: HTML: The Definitive Guide, 2nd Edition; JavaScript: The Definitive Guide, 2nd Edition; CGI Programming on the World Wide Web; Programming Perl, 2nd Edition—the classic "camel book"; and WebMaster in a Nutshell, which is also included in a companion desktop edition.

HTML: The Definitive Guide, 2nd Edition

By Chuck Musciano & Bill Kennedy
2nd Edition May 1997
552 pages, ISBN 1-56592-235-2

This complete guide is chock full of examples, sample code, and practical, hands-on advice to help you create truly effective web pages and master advanced features. Learn how to insert images and other multimedia elements, create useful links and searchable documents, use Netscape extensions, design great forms, and lots more. The second edition covers the most up-to-date version of the HTML standard (HTML version 3.2), Netscape 4.0 and Internet Explorer 3.0, plus all the common extensions.

Dynamic HTML: The Definitive Reference

By Danny Goodman
1st Edition July 1998 (est.)
1128 pages (est.), ISBN 1-56592-494-0

Dynamic HTML: The Definitive Reference is an indispensable compendium for Web content developers. It contains complete reference material for all of the HTML tags, CSS style attributes, browser document objects, and JavaScript objects supported by the various standards and the latest versions of Netscape Navigator and Microsoft Internet Explorer.

Web Client Programming with Perl

By Clinton Wong
1st Edition March 1997
228 pages, ISBN 1-56592-214-X

Web Client Programming with Perl shows you how to extend scripting skills to the Web. This book teaches you the basics of how browsers communicate with servers and how to write your own customized web clients to automate common tasks. t is intended for those who are motivated to develop software that offers a more flexible and dynamic response than a standard web browser.

Designing for the Web: Getting Started in a New Medium

By Jennifer Niederst
with Edie Freedman
1st Edition April 1996
180 pages, ISBN 1-56592-165-8

Designing for the Web gives you the basics you need to hit the ground running. Although geared toward designers, it covers information and techniques useful to anyone who wants to put graphics online. It explains how to work with HTML documents from a designer's point of view, outlines special problems with presenting information online, and walks through incorporating images into web pages, with emphasis on resolution and improving efficiency.

Information Architecture for the World Wide Web

By Louis Rosenfeld & Peter Morville
1st Edition January 1998
226 pages, ISBN 1-56592-282-4

Learn how to merge aesthetics and echanics to design web sites that "work." This book shows how to apply principles of architecture and library science to design cohesive web sites and intranets that are easy to use, manage, and expand. Covers building complex sites, hierarchy design and organization, and techniques to make your site easier to search. For webmasters, designers, and administrators.

Developing Web Content

CGI Programming on the World Wide Web

By Shishir Gundavaram
1st Edition March 1996
450 pages, ISBN 1-56592-168-2

This book offers a comprehensive explanation of CGI and related techniques for people who hold on to the dream of providing their own information servers on the Web. It starts at the beginning, explaining the value of CGI and how it works, then moves swiftly into the subtle details of programming.

JavaScript: The Definitive Guide, 3rd Edition

By David Flanagan & Dan Shafer
3rd Edition June 1998 (est.)
800 pages (est.), ISBN 1-56592-392-8

This third edition of the definitive reference to JavaScript covers the latest version of the language, JavaScript 1.2, as supported by Netscape Navigator 4.0. JavaScript, which is being standardized under the name ECMAScript, is a scripting language that can be embedded directly in HTML to give web pages programming-language capabilities.

Learning VBScript

By Paul Lomax
1st Edition July 1997
616 pages, includes CD-ROM
ISBN 1-56592-247-6

This definitive guide shows web developers how to take full advantage of client-side scripting with the VBScript language. In addition to basic language features, it covers the Internet Explorer object model and discusses techniques for client-side scripting, like adding ActiveX controls to a web page or validating data before sending it to the server. Includes CD-ROM with over 170 code samples.

Designing Web Content

Photoshop for the Web

By Mikkel Aaland
1st Edition April 1998
238 pages, ISBN 1-56592-350-2

Photoshop for the Web shows you how to use the world's most popular imaging software to create Web graphics and images that look great and download blazingly fast. The book is crammed full of step-by-step examples and real-world solutions from some of the country's hottest Web producers, including *HotWired*, c|net, *Discovery Online*, *Second Story*, *SFGate*, and more than 20 others.

Web Navigation: Designing the User Experience

By Jennifer Fleming
1st Edition October 1998 (est.)
250 pages (est.), Includes CD-ROM
ISBN 1-56592-351-0

Web Navigation: Designing the User Experience offers the first in-depth look at designing web site navigation. Through case studies and designer interviews, a variety of approaches to navigation issues are explored. The book focuses on designing by purpose, with chapters on entertainment, shopping, identity, learning, information, and community sites. The accompanying CD-ROM includes a tour of selected sites, a "netography," and trial versions of popular software tools.

Designing with Animation

By J. Scott Hamlin
1st Edition September 1998 (est.)
250 pages (est.), ISBN 1-56592-441-X

Designing with Animation treats the subject of Web animation with a level of sophistication that both meets the needs of today's demanding professionals and pushes the envelope for amateur animators. Topics include GIF animation, advanced animation techniques, seamless integration of animation, creative interactive animation with Java, JavaScript, and Macromedia Flash, vector-based and 3D animation, adding sound to animation, and animation techniques with Photoshop.

O'REILLY™

TO ORDER: **800-998-9938** • **order@oreilly.com** • **http://www.oreilly.com/**
OUR PRODUCTS ARE AVAILABLE AT A BOOKSTORE OR SOFTWARE STORE NEAR YOU.
FOR INFORMATION: **800-998-9938** • **707-829-0515** • **info@oreilly.com**

Designing Web Content

Designing with JavaScript

By Nick Heinle
1st Edition September 1997
256 pages, Includes CD-ROM
ISBN 1-56592-300-6

Written by the author of the
"JavaScript Tip of the Week" web site,
this new Web Review Studio book
focuses on the most useful and
applicable scripts for making truly interactive, engaging web
sites. You'll not only have quick access to the scripts you
need, you'll finally understand why the scripts work, how to
alter the scripts to get the effects you want, and, ultimately,
how to write your own groundbreaking scripts from scratch.

GIF Animation Studio

By Richard Koman
1st Edition October 1996
184 pages, Includes CD-ROM
ISBN 1-56592-230-1

GIF animation is bringing the Web
to life—without plug-ins, Java programming, or expensive authoring
tools. This book details the major
GIF animation programs, profiles work by leading designers
(including John Hersey, Razorfish, Henrik Drescher, and Erik
Josowitz), and documents advanced animation techniques. A
CD-ROM includes freeware and shareware authoring programs, demo versions of commercial software, and the actual
animation files described in the book. *GIF Animation Studio*
is the first release in the new Web Review Studio series.

Shockwave Studio

By Bob Schmitt
1st Edition March 1997
200 pages, Includes CD-ROM
ISBN 1-56592-231-X

This book, the second title in the
new Web Review Studio series, shows
how to create compelling and functional Shockwave movies for web
sites. The author focuses on actual Shockwave movies, showing how the movies were created. The book takes users from
creating simple time-based Shockwave animations through
writing complex logical operations that take full advantage of
Director's power. The CD-ROM includes a demo version of
Director and other software sample files.

How to stay in touch with O'Reilly

1. Visit Our Award-Winning Site

http://www.oreilly.com/

★ "Top 100 Sites on the Web" —*PC Magazine*
★ "Top 5% Web sites" —*Point Communications*
★ "3-Star site" —*The McKinley Group*

Our web site contains a library of comprehensive
product information (including book excerpts and
tables of contents), downloadable software, background articles, interviews with technology leaders,
links to relevant sites, book cover art, and more.
File us in your Bookmarks or Hotlist!

2. Join Our Email Mailing Lists

New Product Releases
To receive automatic email with brief descriptions
of all new O'Reilly products as they are released,
send email to:
listproc@online.oreilly.com
Put the following information in the first line of
your message (*not* in the Subject field):
subscribe oreilly-news

O'Reilly Events
If you'd also like us to send information about
trade show events, special promotions, and other
O'Reilly events, send email to:
listproc@online.oreilly.com
Put the following information in the first line of
your message (*not* in the Subject field):
subscribe oreilly-events

3. Get Examples from Our Books via FTP

There are two ways to access an archive of example
files from our books:

Regular FTP
• ftp to:
  ftp.oreilly.com
  (login: anonymous
  password: your email address)
• Point your web browser to:
  ftp://ftp.oreilly.com/

FTPMAIL
• Send an email message to:
  ftpmail@online.oreilly.com
  (Write "help" in the message body)

4. Contact Us via Email

order@oreilly.com
To place a book or software order online. Good for
North American and international customers.

subscriptions@oreilly.com
To place an order for any of our newsletters or
periodicals.

books@oreilly.com
General questions about any of our books.

software@oreilly.com
For general questions and product information
about our software. Check out O'Reilly Software
Online at **http://software.oreilly.com/** for software and technical support information. Registered
O'Reilly software users send your questions to:
website-support@oreilly.com

cs@oreilly.com
For answers to problems regarding your order
or our products.

booktech@oreilly.com
For book content technical questions or
corrections.

proposals@oreilly.com
To submit new book or software proposals to our
editors and product managers.

international@oreilly.com
For information about our international distributors
or translation queries. For a list of our distributors
outside of North America check out:
http://www.oreilly.com/www/order/country.html

O'Reilly & Associates, Inc.
101 Morris Street, Sebastopol, CA 95472 USA
TEL   707-829-0515 or 800-998-9938
       (6am to 5pm PST)
FAX   707-829-0104

International Distributors

UK, Europe, Middle East and Northern Africa (except France, Germany, Switzerland, & Austria)

INQUIRIES
International Thomson Publishing Europe
Berkshire House
168-173 High Holborn
London WC1V 7AA, UK
Telephone: 44-171-497-1422
Fax: 44-171-497-1426
Email: itpint@itps.co.uk

ORDERS
International Thomson Publishing Services, Ltd.
Cheriton House, North Way
Andover, Hampshire SP10 5BE,
United Kingdom
Telephone: 44-264-342-832 (UK)
Telephone: 44-264-342-806 (outside UK)
Fax: 44-264-364418 (UK)
Fax: 44-264-342761 (outside UK)
UK & Eire orders: itpuk@itps.co.uk
International orders: itpint@itps.co.uk

France

Editions Eyrolles
61 bd Saint-Germain
75240 Paris Cedex 05
France
Fax: 33-01-44-41-11-44

FRENCH LANGUAGE BOOKS
All countries except Canada
Telephone: 33-01-44-41-46-16
Email: geodif@eyrolles.com

ENGLISH LANGUAGE BOOKS
Telephone: 33-01-44-41-11-87
Email: distribution@eyrolles.com

Germany, Switzerland, and Austria

INQUIRIES
O'Reilly Verlag
Balthasarstr. 81
D-50670 Köln
Germany
Telephone: 49-221-97-31-60-0
Fax: 49-221-97-31-60-8
Email: anfragen@oreilly.de

ORDERS
International Thomson Publishing
Königswinterer Straße 418
53227 Bonn, Germany
Telephone: 49-228-97024 0
Fax: 49-228-441342
Email: order@oreilly.de

Japan

O'Reilly Japan, Inc.
Kiyoshige Building 2F
12-Banchi, Sanei-cho
Shinjuku-ku
Tokyo 160 Japan
Tel: 81-3-3356-5227
Fax: 81-3-3356-5261
Email: kenji@oreilly.com

India

Computer Bookshop (India) PVT. Ltd.
190 Dr. D.N. Road, Fort
Bombay 400 001 India
Tel: 91-22-207-0989
Fax: 91-22-262-3551
Email: cbsbom@giasbm01.vsnl.net.in

Hong Kong

City Discount Subscription Service Ltd.
Unit D, 3rd Floor, Yan's Tower
27 Wong Chuk Hang Road
Aberdeen, Hong Kong
Telephone: 852-2580-3539
Fax: 852-2580-6463
Email: citydis@ppn.com.hk

Korea

Hanbit Publishing, Inc.
Sonyoung Bldg. 202
Yeksam-dong 736-36
Kangnam-ku
Seoul, Korea
Telephone: 822-554-9610
Fax: 822-556-0363
Email: hant93@chollian.dacom.co.kr

Taiwan

ImageArt Publishing, Inc.
4/fl. No. 65 Shinyi Road Sec. 4
Taipei, Taiwan, R.O.C.
Telephone: 886-2708-5770
Fax: 886-2705-6690
Email: marie@ms1.hinet.net

Singapore, Malaysia, and Thailand

Longman Singapore
25 First Lok Yan Road
Singapore 2262
Telephone: 65-268-2666
Fax: 65-268-7023
Email: daniel@longman.com.sg

Philippines

Mutual Books, Inc.
429-D Shaw Boulevard
Mandaluyong City, Metro
Manila, Philippines
Telephone: 632-725-7538
Fax: 632-721-3056
Email: mbikikog@mnl.sequel.net

China

Ron's DataCom Co., Ltd.
79 Dongwu Avenue
Dongxihu District
Wuhan 430040
China
Telephone: 86-27-3892568
Fax: 86-27-3222108
Email: hongfeng@public.wh.hb.cn

Australia

WoodsLane Pty. Ltd.
7/5 Vuko Place, Warriewood NSW 2102
P.O. Box 935,
Mona Vale NSW 2103
Australia
Telephone: 61-2-9970-5111
Fax: 61-2-9970-5002
Email: info@woodslane.com.au

All Other Asia Countries

O'Reilly & Associates, Inc.
101 Morris Street
Sebastopol, CA 95472 USA
Telephone: 707-829-0515
Fax: 707-829-0104
Email: order@oreilly.com

The Americas

McGraw-Hill Interamericana Editores,
S.A. de C.V.
Cedro No. 512
Col. Atlampa 06450
Mexico, D.F.
Telephone: 52-5-541-3155
Fax: 52-5-541-4913
Email: mcgraw-hill@infosel.net.mx

Southern Africa

International Thomson Publishing Southern Africa
Building 18, Constantia Park
138 Sixteenth Road
P.O. Box 2459
Halfway House, 1685 South Africa
Tel: 27-11-805-4819
Fax: 27-11-805-3648

O'REILLY™

TO ORDER: **800-998-9938** • order@oreilly.com • http://www.oreilly.com/
OUR PRODUCTS ARE AVAILABLE AT A BOOKSTORE OR SOFTWARE STORE NEAR YOU.
FOR INFORMATION: **800-998-9938** • **707-829-0515** • info@oreilly.com

O'REILLY™

O'Reilly & Associates, Inc.
101 Morris Street
Sebastopol, CA 95472-9902
1-800-998-9938

Visit us online at:
http://www.ora.com/
orders@ora.com

O'REILLY WOULD LIKE TO HEAR FROM YOU

Which book did this card come from?

_____

Where did you buy this book?
- ❏ Bookstore
- ❏ Direct from O'Reilly
- ❏ Bundled with hardware/software
- ❏ Other _____

- ❏ Computer Store
- ❏ Class/seminar

What operating system do you use?
- ❏ UNIX
- ❏ Windows NT
- ❏ Other _____

- ❏ Macintosh
- ❏ PC(Windows/DOS)

What is your job description?
- ❏ System Administrator
- ❏ Network Administrator
- ❏ Web Developer
- ❏ Other _____

- ❏ Programmer
- ❏ Educator/Teacher

❏ Please send me O'Reilly's catalog, containing a complete listing of O'Reilly books and software.

Name _____

Company/Organization

Nineteenth century wood engraving
of a bear from the O'Reilly &
Associates Nutshell Handbook®
Using & Managing UUCP.

POST CARD

BUSINESS REPLY MAIL

FIRST CLASS MAIL   PERMIT NO. 80   SEBASTOPOL, CA

Postage will be paid by addressee

O'Reilly & Associates, Inc.
101 Morris Street
Sebastopol, CA 95472-9902